CONCISE COLLEGE TEXTS

LABOUR LAW

OTHER BOOKS IN THIS SERIES:

Tort, by C. D. Baker
Public Law, by Professor G. Borrie
The Making of Business Contracts, by A. Harding Boulton
Public International Law, by D. J. Latham Brown
Criminal Law and Procedure, by I. G. Carvell and E. Swinfen Green
Administrative Law for Surveying Students, by H. W. Clarke
Constitutional and Administrative Law, by H. W. Clarke
Contract, by F. R. Davies
The English Legal System, by K. J. Eddey
Hotel and Catering Law, by David Field
Family Law, by Judge H. B. Grant
Land Law, by E. Swinfen Green and N. Henderson
Advanced Level Law, by B. Jones
British Government Today, by B. Jones
Estate Duty in England and Wales, by A. Douglas Lawton
(Adapted from *An Outline of Estate Duty in Scotland*, by G. Herbert Brown and John M. Halliday)
Civil and Criminal Procedure, by J. R. Lewis
Landlord and Tenant, by J. R. Lewis and J. A. Holland
General Principles of Law, by C. R. Newton
Banking Law, by S. Twum
Patents, Trade Marks, Copyright and Industrial Designs, by T. A. Blanco White and Robin Jacob

AUSTRALIA
The Law Book Company Ltd.
Sydney: Melbourne: Brisbane

CANADA AND U.S.A.
The Carswell Company Ltd.
Agincourt, Ontario

INDIA
N. M. Tripathi Private Ltd.
Bombay

ISRAEL
Steimatzky's Agency Ltd.
Jerusalem: Tel Aviv: Haifa

MALAYSIA: SINGAPORE: BRUNEI
Malayan Law Journal (Pte.) Ltd.
Singapore

NEW ZEALAND
Sweet & Maxwell (N.Z.) Ltd.
Wellington

PAKISTAN
Pakistan Law House
Karachi

CONCISE COLLEGE TEXTS

LABOUR LAW

BY

CHARLES D. DRAKE, M.A., LL.B.

of the Middle Temple, Barrister-at-Law
Professor of Law, University of Leeds

SECOND EDITION

LONDON

SWEET & MAXWELL LIMITED

1973

First edition 1969
Second edition 1973

Published in 1973 by
Sweet & Maxwell Limited of
11 New Fetter Lane, London,
and printed in Great Britain
by Richard Clay (The Chaucer
Press) Ltd., Bungay, Suffolk

SBN Hardback 421 16380 1
Paperback 421 16390 9

PREFACE TO THE SECOND EDITION

In this edition, I have endeavoured to accommodate the main changes in labour law since 1969. Those changes have not been hard to find. Ever since *Rookes* v. *Barnard* in 1964 we seem to have been living in the frenetic atmosphere of reformist activity. If days lost through strikes and industrial *anomie* are guides, the last state seems to be worse than the first. Some would have us believe that the Industrial Relations Act 1971, or governments intent on plunging us into the nemesis of the corporative state, are the reasons for our present condition. The real reasons are likely to lie deeper. The rising expectations of working people, the attitudes engendered by the Welfare State, the uncertainty caused by profound structural changes in industry (not excluding automation), fears of Europe and the multi-national corporation, the decline of "authority," the waning attraction of the work ethic and political activism on the industrial front, would all seem to have played some part. Attention has largely shifted from the political to the economic arena. Confronted on the one hand with inflation, poor investment and slow economic growth, governments are finding it increasingly difficult to meet the claims of those, including the lower-paid, who demand a share in the "good life." Once again, the problem of reconciling the tradition of autonomous collective bargaining with some sane prices and incomes policy has come to the fore and once again the law backed by criminal sanctions has been pressed into service. Against such a background, and the shrieks of the ideologues, it is difficult to write objectively of the law as it is. This I have attempted to do without nailing any colours to any particular mast. There are already too many people with total solutions.

In its first incarnation, this book received not unkindly treatment at the hands of the critics, several of whom had constructive suggestions from which I have now been able to profit. Thus, collective bargaining has been accorded separate treatment in a chapter on its own, although the impact of the collective agreement on individual contracts of employment has been treated along with the latter. At the risk of appearing rather churlish, I have to confess that I do not feel that the time has yet come when the collective relations of management and labour can take precedence over the individual employer–employee relationship. Some 4,500 complaints of unfair dismissal during the first seven months during which that remedy became available testify to the continuing importance of the individual relationship. The complaints also demonstrate that detestation of the 1971 Act is selective in nature. Resisting all exhortations, I have eschewed the use of footnotes or the relegation of footnotes to the end of chapters or the end of the book; to have succumbed on this would have given the book pretensions to being a reference book, which clearly it is not.

I have endeavoured to state the law as at February 1973 in the hope that the inexorable process of legislation, judicial decisions, etc. will not have rendered too much damage to the text of this work by the date of publication. One future pitfall of which readers of this book can be warned now is the Social Security Bill which, when the text of this book was being written, was passing through Parliament. When the bill becomes law it will affect the portions of this book dealing with national insurance, but, as the date when it will come into force is not at the moment known, I decided to state the law in this book as at the time of writing. A note on more recent developments follows the tables and immediately precedes the text.

It is a pleasure, at least on this occasion, to acknowledge debts. Too numerous to mention individually by name, I record my indebtedness to former students in the University of Durham who made pertinent comments which I now "pass-off" as my own. Among my present colleagues in the Faculty of Law, University of Leeds, I am particularly indebted to Mr. Patrick A. Lovell, LL.B., B.C.L., a professing neophyte in the field of labour law, who generously agreed to paragraph the book and prepare the tables of cases and statutes, an ordeal from which, presumably, he has emerged as something less of a neophyte. Professor Brian Hogan set me right on those passages which touched on the criminal law. Another of my colleagues, Miss Catherine Todd, LL.B., submitted to the thankless task of reading some of the chapters and saved me from solecisms which, but for her, would have been inflicted on the hapless reader. It would be a poor thing if those who have generously come to my aid were to be implicated in such errors as may remain; for these I must bear responsibility. Finally, I might add that I had deferred the writing of the second edition until such time as labour law would settle down. It became apparent to me that this was unlikely to occur. Because of this and the waning longanimity of the Publishers (who have shown remarkable patience) Miss Christine Henderson, who had undertaken to type out the manuscript, received, successively, nothing, and, later, a veritable avalanche with which to cope. That she coped accurately and without complaint is a testimony to her resilience.

February 1973

CHARLES D. DRAKE

CONTENTS

PART TWO
PROTECTIVE LEGISLATION

TABLE OF CASES

TABLE OF STATUTES

NOTE OF RECENT DEVELOPMENTS

THE following recent cases and statutes have occurred since the manuscript was received by the publishers. Space does not permit the printing of anything more than a reference by name and report to the cases, and the barest outline of the statutes so that readers are put on reference to that existence. These recent developments are not noted in the Tables of Cases or Statutes or the Index, but sources for the cases and year and chapter numbers for the statutes are given so as to enable readers to find them elsewhere.

The "organisation test" (para. 26)
See *Beloff* v. *Pressdram Ltd.* [1973] 1 All E.R. 241.

Statutory particulars of employment (paras. 62–66)
See *Parkes Classic Confectionery Ltd.* v. *Ashcroft* [1973] I.T.R. 43.

Control of Employment Agencies (para. 79)
The Employment Agencies Act 1973 will come into force when the Secretary of State for Employment makes regulations laying down standards for private employment agencies.

Industrial training (para. 91 *et seq.*)
The Employment and Training Act 1973 received the Royal Assent on July 25, 1973 and makes provision for (i) an independent Manpower Services Commission which will be responsible for the public employment and training services and for the co-ordination of industrial training as a whole; (ii) the provision of a careers service by local authorities; and (iii) modifications to the Industrial Training Act 1964.

Vocational training
The Education (Work Experience) Act 1973 permits children who now stay on at school for an extra year to gain work experience as part of their education. The part-time employment of children will be controlled by regulations to be made by the Secretary of State when the Employment of Children Act 1973 comes into force. Such regulations will replace the patchwork quilt of local authority byelaws which at present regulate the employment of children out of school hours.

Subrogation (paras. 139–140)
See *Morris* v. *Ford Motor Co.* [1973] 2 W.L.R. 843, C.A.

Rights under s. 5 (para. 147)
As to the distinction between discrimination against employees and discrimination against an unregistered trade union of which those employees are members, see *King* v. *Post Office* [1973] I.C.R. 120 and *Central Electricity Board* v. *Coleman* [1973] I.C.R. 230, and for criticism of this distinction, see *Post Office* v. *Crouch* [1973] I.C.R. 366.

Vicarious liability (para. 156)
See *Iqbal* v. *London Transport Board, The Times*, June 7, 1973.

Trucking (paras. 195, 197)
See *Daley* v. *Radnor* (1973) 117 S.J. 321.

Counter-Inflation Act 1973 (paras. 219–223)
This Act (which succeeded the temporary Act described in the text at paras. 220–222), establishes two corporate agencies to administer controls over prices and incomes—the Price Commission and the Pay Board.

Dismissal (paras. 238, 281, 299)
See *Penrose* v. *Fairey Surveys Ltd.* [1973] I.C.R. 26; *Lees* v. *Arthur Graves* (*Lees*) *Ltd.* [1973] I.C.R. 90; *McAlwane* v. *Boughton Estates* [1973] 2 All E.R. 299; also *Dixon* v. *Stenor Ltd.* [1973] I.C.R. 157 and *Hare* v. *Murphy Brothers Ltd.* [1973] I.C.R. 331.

Unfair dismissal (paras. 279 *et seq.*)
Unfairness (para. 282 *et seq.*): see *Clarkson International Tools* v. *Short* [1973] I.C.R. 191; *Lewis Shops Group* v. *Wiggins* [1973] I.C.R. 335; *Winterhalter Gastronom Ltd.* v. *Webb* [1973] I.C.R. 245; *Rigby* v. *British Steel Corporation* [1973] I.C.R. 160; *James* v. *Waltham Holy Cross U.D.C.*, *The Times*, June 12, 1973; and *Axe* v. *British Domestic Appliances Ltd.* [1973] I.C.R. 133.

Burden of proof (paras. 282–283): see *Green* v. *Southampton Corporation* [1973] I.C.R. 153; *Midland Foot Comfort Centre* v. *Moppett* [1973] I.C.R. 219.

Compensation (paras. 292–294): see *Penrase* v. *Mander Bros.* [1973] I.R.L.R. 167.

Redundancy
Re-organisation of work (paras. 304–305): see *Chapman* v. *Goonvean and Rostowrack China Clay Co. Ltd.* [1973] I.C.R. 310.

Work of a particular kind (para. 310): see *Amos* v. *Max-Arc Ltd.* [1973] I.C.R. 46; and *Runnals* v. *Richards & Osborne Ltd.* [1973] I.C.R. 225.

Offer of new employment (paras. 311–314): see *Harris* v. *E. Turner & Sons* (*Joinery*) *Ltd.* [1973] I.C.R. 31.

Transfer of business (para. 315): see *Ubsell* v. *Paterson* [1973] I.C.R. 86; *Cartin* v. *Botley Garages Ltd.* [1973] I.C.T. 144; *Deaway Trading Ltd.* v. *Calverley*, *The Times*, July 24, 1973.

Employer's liability (para. 374)
See *Westwood* v. *Post Office* [1973] 2 W.L.R. 135.

Organisation of workers (paras. 445–475)

Natural justice (para. 458): see *Santer* v. *National Graphical Association* [1973] I.C.R. 60.

Refusal to admit (para. 460): see *Hey* v. *Yorkshire Society of Textile Craftsmen* [1973] I.T.R. 185; and *Phillips* v. *N.A.L.G.O.* [1973] I.T.R. 865.

Resignation of member (para. 461): see *Ashford* v. *A.S.T.M.S.* [1973] I.C.R. 296.

Membership rights (para. 462): see *Carling* v. *N.U.G.M.W.* [1973] I.C.R. 267, and for the *sequelae* to the *Goad* Case see *Goad* v. *A.U.E.W.* (No. 2) [1973] I.C.R. 42; *Goad* v. *A.U.E.W.* (No. 3) [1973] I.C.R. 108 and *Eckman* v. *Midland Bank Ltd.* [1973] I.C.R. 71.

Rules (paras. 473–474): see *Sherard* v. *A.U.E.W. The Times*, April 26, 1973.

Agency shop agreement—conscientious objection (para. 514). See *Drury* v. *Bakers' Union* (*Southern District*) [1973] I.R.L.R. 171.

Recognition (para. 517). See *T.S.A.* v. *Post Office* [1973] I.C.R. 173, and *T.U.B.E.* v. *William Hill* (*Park Lane*) *Ltd.* [1973] I.C.R. 252; also *N.U.B.E.* v. *Barclays Bank Ltd.* [1973] I.C.R. 167.

Industrial dispute (para. 567). *Cory Lighterage* v. *T.G.W.U.* [1973] I.C.R. 339; and *Cater* v. *Law Society* [1973] I.C.R. 113.

Picketing (para. 607). See *Hunt* v. *Broome* [1973] I.C.R. 281.

Unfair industrial practice (para. 611), s. 96: see *Stewart* v. *A.U.E.W.* [1973] I.C.R. 129, and *Howitt Transport Ltd.* v. *T.G.W.U.* [1973] I.C.R. 1.

S. 33 (3) (a) (para. 632): see *Langston* v. *A.U.E.W.* [1973] I.C.R. 211.

PART ONE

INDIVIDUAL ASPECTS OF LABOUR LAW

INTRODUCTION

What is labour law?

Labour law is that branch of law which treats of persons in their 1
capacity as workers, using that term without its proletarian undertones, just as the economist deals with labour as one of the factors of production. "Labour Law" is preferable to "Industrial Law" as a title for two main reasons. First, it has been pointed out that the latter title is a misnomer in that books bearing that title do not deal with the law relating to industry in its entirety, as, for example, topics like company law, industrial property and taxation, but in fact concentrate on the legal aspects of employment. Secondly, the title "Labour Law" has now become consecrated by usage in the United States, in Europe and elsewhere, so that, without denying that the content and emphasis in each system must inevitably reflect national differences, the adoption of such a title here would demonstrate that we are not lacking in international comity.

Labour law cuts across the conceptual boundaries of contract, 2
tort, crime and the like. Contract is invoked (some would say, mistakenly invoked) to elucidate the nature of the employer–employee relationship. The law of tort determines the civil liability of the individual and, more importantly from the sociological point of view, the group. Central to the economic torts is the notion of interference in contract. That opaque body of law—the law of associations—seeks to identify the status of the group, whether corporate or unincorporate. There is considerable vagueness as to the precise nature of the legal régime which governs that new recruit to the corporate species—the registered trade union, a phenomenon which the T.U.C. policy of non-registration has rendered more academic than real.

Without impugning Durkheim's thesis that evolving, industrial societies tend to abjure punitive sanctions in favour of restitutive sanctions, the criminal law still plays a limited, residual role in the law of labour relations. Adjectival law, including the esoteric rules surrounding equitable remedies, can play a part in the tense atmosphere of labour relations and have given rise to the fear that we shall share the unhappy experience of the Americans with their "labour injunction." The dockers' contempt cases of 1972 revealed the far-reaching effects which the committal of workers for contempt of court can produce. Labour law is no exception to the shifting balance of our law towards statutory law. Important matters such as industrial health and safety, social insurance and equal pay are now regulated in varying degrees by Act of Parliament.

3 Historically, the relationship between master and man was generally a personal nexus. The master often worked alongside his journeyman or apprentice, the latter not infrequently residing with his master to whose *dominica potestas* he was subject—Maine's "tyrant enthroned by each hearthstone," a tyrant not averse to administering a sharp cuff on the ear when the occasion demanded it. Except for industries such as the wool trade, the market was small in the sense that the producer could identify the consumer of his product.

4 All of this was rudely disturbed by the Industrial Revolution. The new productive techniques utilising the new machinery and a division of labour, the improvements in transport and communications and the vastly increased capital market facilitated by the emergence of the registered company with limited liability capital, resulted in a scale of production which isolated the worker from his employer (often a registered company), the product and the consumer. The worker became an "exchangist" whose labour was treated as a prime cost of production in much the same manner as raw materials were, and are, treated. But as section 6 of the Clayton Act in the United States reminds us, "the labor of a human being is not a commodity or article of commerce."

5 Nor have we yet reached "post-industrial society." Technological change and the decline of traditional industries such as coal-mining or shipbuilding have thrown up the human problems of redundancy and have caused attention to be turned to greater job security for workers. The State commits large sums of money under the Industry Act 1972 in order to correct the decline in the regions and to assist industry outside those areas which require special assistance. The labour force is changing slowly in character to meet the new conditions. Distinctions between blue- and white-collar workers are being eroded at the same time as the numbers of the former tend to diminish. Service industries have grown despite the selective employment tax, now abandoned.

6 Above all, the growing interdependence of industry has taken place against the background of an increasingly secularised and acquisitive society in which industrial trials of strength become more and more disruptive to society as a whole. The dialectical materialist points to the increased cartelisation of labour and capital, and the destructive effects of the conflict of each, as evidence of the inevitable death throes of capitalism. The liberal democracies, with their mixed economies, seek by legislation, both at national and international level, to achieve a balance between a size suitable for

economical production and a size which will not give monopoly or oligopoly power.

Labour law in this country exhibits certain features which marks it off from foreign systems. 7

First and foremost there was, until 1971, the tradition of "abstentionism" on the part of the State and the Law in labour relations. The voluntarist thesis was based on the principle that management and labour should be left to work out their own salvation, free of state interference or legal regulation. The system was, and indeed still is, based on a tradition of autonomous collective bargaining in which the economic strength of the employer is met by the "countervailing force" of the trade union. Furthermore, such bargaining is invariably non-contractual in nature resting, as it does, on the goodwill of the parties rather than legal sanctions, although often backed by the ultimate sanction of industrial action. The famous Whitley Report of 1917 was founded on the premise that industry ought to make its own agreements and patch up its own disagreements. Newer common law countries, like Australia and New Zealand, have been forced to rely upon a statutory system of conciliation and arbitration, although this system tends to conceal the existence of much autonomous bargaining. 8

Various reasons have been proffered for the unique antipathy of the British towards legal regulation of their industrial relations. Some point to the early industrialisation of Britain and the emergence of a strong labour movement prior to the granting of universal suffrage. Those later in the field, such as Germany and France, required legal support for trade unions which were, and still are, weaker than in this country. Others, who believe in class warfare, see the law as the protector of property and the judges as the apologists of the ruling classes. Some liberals decry any interference with labour relations as the beginning of a slide into the corporative state as in pre-war Germany where the unions became the agents of the State in preserving the "National Front." Certainly, relationships between labour and the judiciary have not always been of the happiest. Unpopular decisions such as *Taff Vale*, *Osborne* and, more recently, *Rookes*, have produced such a clamour that remedial legislation has been passed to neutralise them. This gave the law of industrial relations rather a piece-meal character. 9

Despite their insistence on the importance of collective bargaining, unions in the nineteenth century, and since, have recognised that their objectives can sometimes be met only by what the Webbs termed "The Method of Legal Enactment." The shortening of the working day, or the establishment of tolerable conditions in factories, require uniform solutions by Act of Parliament. Because of 10 the difficulty of unionising the "sweated trades," legislation was required to lay down minimum pay and holidays in those trades and those later brought within the ambit of minimum pay legislation. Agricultural workers also required similar treatment. By reason of its pre-occupation with pay and hours of work, organised labour was conspicuously deficient in securing proper severance payments for workers rendered redundant by technological advance or structural decline in industry. The problem of redundancy was, therefore, largely left to the Redundancy Payments Act 1965, which imposed a statutory obligation upon employers to make payments to redundant employees. Again, notwithstanding long-standing T.U.C. pressure for equal pay, it was not until 1970 that provision was made for equal pay as between men and women. The problem of racial discrimination as regards employment and trade union membership required legislative intervention in 1968. The Contracts of Employment Act 1963 (now the Contract of Employment Act 1972) gave employees, with the requisite period of qualifying service, rights to minimum periods of notice, in addition to help concretise the terms of employment contracts by requiring employers to give certain particulars thereof. Legislative interventions of the kinds described are justified on the ground that they provide a "floor of rights" above which free and voluntary collective bargaining can take place.

11 The view that lack of reliance upon legal sanctions is an index to the maturity of an industrial relations system has not commanded universal assent. Critics see in the pursuit of sectional ends, evils such as inflation, restrictive practices, harm to the economy and inconvenience to the public, evils which are more pronounced in an interdependent society with large-scale units of production. A further complication is the emergence of "shop-floor power" seen by some as industrial democracy at its best and by others as industrial anarchy and the negation of true trade union leadership. The unions object that altruism in a selfish society is impossible.

12 Those who looked for a fundamental change to the Donovan Commission were disappointed. Despite its numerous recommendations, that Commission was essentially gradualistic in tone and rejected the idea that the law might play a more interventionist role in labour relations.

13 The same could not be said of *Fair Deal at Work* which, by the vicissitudes of politics, was the *fons et origo* of the Industrial Relations Act 1971, an Act which was brought in to provide "a more positive framework of law" for labour relations in this country. That Act rests on four principles, namely—(a) the principle of collective bargaining freely conducted on behalf of workers and employers and with due regard to the general interests of the community; (b) the principle of developing and maintaining orderly procedures in industry for the peaceful and expeditious settlement of disputes by negotiation, conciliation or arbitration, with due regard to the general interests of the community; (c) the principle of free association of workers in independent trade unions, and of employers in employers' associations, so organised as to be representative, responsible and effective bodies for regulating relations between employers and workers; and (d) the principle of freedom and security for workers, protected by adequate safeguards against unfair practices, whether on the part of employers or others. Even the most perfervid supporters of this Act did not claim that it would usher in a new industrial millennium in which inflation (with its adverse effect on low-paid workers), and stagnating industrial production would disappear. Within its avowed objective of providing a more orderly system responding to the national weal, the Act has had little effect to date. The voluntarists explain the failure by pointing to the impossibility of regulating by law a system based upon voluntary agreement. The jurists have put this another way, pointing to the inutility of "made law" superimposed upon customary or "implicit law" arising from the interactions of management and labour in their daily adjustments to one another. Be this as it may, it would seem that a "Kill the Bill" campaign played no little part.

It can now be seen that the facultative nature of registration (which plays such an important part in the Act) offered a hostage to fortune which the unions were not slow to seize. Unions which defied the T.U.C.'s direction not to register found themselves "excommunicated" from the ranks of the faithful. The policy of non-registration was accompanied by a policy of non-cooperation. Trade unionists declined to serve on the Industrial Court (thereby depriving the court of the tripartite structure—labour, management and "neutral"—so common in British institutions in the field of industrial relations). They also withdrew from the C.I.R. and the industrial tribunals, and refused to appear in proceedings before the Industrial Court, although, later, "self-defence" before that court was permitted. If some unions availed themselves of this limited right, other unions and groups of workers maintained their intransigent hostility to the court and all its works. The "neutral" intervention of the Official Solicitor in the dockers' contempt cases of 1972 was particularly odious to those who saw the crown of secular martyrdom plucked from them.

The Act also contains some muddy jurisdictional divisions which 14
have given rise to differences between the "ordinary" courts administering "ordinary" law, and the new "industrial" courts or

tribunals dispensing the new, policy-orientated law of industrial relations. The declining prestige of the Industrial Court induced one applicant to seek an injunction in the High Court at a time when an injunction of the Industrial Court was still extant. The Act also raised the spectre of governmental interference in the judicial process. In its studious avoidance of criminal sanctions, the Act had the unfortunate effect of placing enforcement willy-nilly in private hands, sometimes with embarrassing consequences for the government.

With the gift of hindsight, one can now see that the Act has had little general effect on industrial behaviour. A few unions have registered under the Act (and paid the price for their apostasy) and a few employers have made use of the right to complain of unfair industrial practices. The great majority of unions and their members have, however, carried on as before as though the Act did not exist. If the Act has had any effect, it may have "educated" some workers to the extent that it draws attention to the rights of individuals and the rights of the community as relevant considerations to be borne in mind in the pursuit of self-interest. Unions still exist to advance the working terms and conditions of their members, and still refuse to act as the agents of the state or the law. Even at T.U.C. level the last few years have witnessed a serious estrangement between government, employers and trade unions; an estrangement which has prevented all three coming together to set the right tone for a working and expansionist community.

15 This preference for industrial autonomy has left its mark on labour law, quite apart from the struggles over the Industrial Relations Act. Until recently, the books relied upon cases far removed from modern society; cases concerning paupers' settlements under the Re-Settlement Act and cases stressing the servant's subjection to the control or *imperium* of the master. At a time when the general or yearly hiring was the rule, the waggoner who refused to take his horses to the marshes because his dinner was ready, or the harvester who refused to work late because strong beer was not brought to him, might lose his year's pay because of his disobedience. The law has only slowly accommodated itself to the social changes wrought by full employment, social insurance and a changed attitude to authority and to what is sometimes termed the "work ethic." That the law can manage the accommodation is shown by cases such as *Richardson* v. *Koefod* (1969), where the embarrassing presumption of the yearly hiring, which had survived in emasculated form from our pre-industrial society, was quietly laid to rest.

The realisation that the personal nature of the relationship between master and servant of past times has now largely given way to a depersonalised relationship between the enterprise and the worker has, notwithstanding trade union dubiety, caused attention to be turned to methods of articulating the worker into the concept of the enterprise as a whole. The increasing flow of reports from bodies such as the Industrial Court, the industrial tribunals and the C.I.R. provides a rich vein of materials for the scholar and the practitioner.

Another feature of British labour law is the manner in which it **16** elevates the individual contract of employment into a position of peculiar importance. Described as "the corner-stone of the edifice" in our labour law (O. Kahn-Freund in *The System of Industrial Relations in Great Britain*, 1954, p. 47), the primacy of the contract of employment is shown by the rule that the express terms of such a contract take effect to the exclusion of implied terms inconsistent therewith, *e.g.* terms implied from collective bargains. Even as individualistic a society as the United States denies effect to such express terms of an individual contract of employment as conflict with the terms negotiated by the bargaining agent in the appropriate unit. Recognising the importance of the individual contractual link between employer and employee, legislation occasionally operates "through" the contract, as in the case of wages regulation orders laying down minimum rates of pay under the Wages Councils Act 1959, or, more recently, the right to equality of treatment as regards terms and conditions of employment between men and women workers, for which provision is made by the Equal Pay Act 1970.

This legal emphasis upon the individual nexus between the **17** employee and his employer, set against the industrial fact that the vast majority of employees have their terms and conditions of employment settled by collective bargaining, has not escaped criticism. Rejecting the individual contract as "a core of rubble" some would find a solution in the notion of a status relationship between employer and employee, whereas others consider that the reality of collective negotiation should find reflection in the law. Of the two aspects of the collective bargain, *viz.* the consensual and the normative, the former has only rarely, and this notwithstanding the Industrial Relations Act 1971, achieved contractual effect, whilst the latter is only effective to settle terms and conditions in individual contracts in those circumstances where the latter expressly or impliedly incorporate the collectively agreed terms and conditions, or where incorporation takes place statutorily as described above. Section 8 of the Terms and Conditions of Employment Act 1959, as amended, is yet another example of statutory terms operating via the contract of employment. A collective bargain may not be enforceable between the parties thereto, but, may be enforceable in the context of an individual employment contract into which it has been imported.

18 The common law may in the past have flirted with the Prerogative, and since 1688, with Parliament, but its true love is the Individual. It is not surprising that our Labour Law bears this individualistic imprint to this day.

Chapter 1

THE EMPLOYER–EMPLOYEE RELATIONSHIP; APPRENTICESHIP

The evolution of the modern employee from medieval serfdom confirms the truth of Sir Henry Maine's observation that progressive societies show a movement from status to contract. The exchange of feudal services for money payments marked the beginning of a change in which the cash nexus replaced customary rights. In the centuries which followed this "commutation of services," the freedom of the worker was apparent rather than real. On the one hand he was subject to rigorous statutory control, *e.g.* the Statute of Labourers and, later, the Elizabethan Poor Law, whilst on the other hand crafts or "mysteries" were strictly controlled by the guilds. The individualistic common law sometimes had brushes with the latter as is shown by the *Tailors of Ipswich Case* (1614) in which the individual's "right to work" was vindicated. In *Nagle* v. *Fielden* (1966), the court declined to strike out a cause of action on the ground that the refusal by the stewards of the Jockey Club to issue a trainer's licence to a woman disclosed no cause of action. **19**

It was not until the Industrial Revolution had liberated the economic forces of labour, capital, land and enterprise that anything recognisable as the modern employee emerges. "Freedom of contract," the legal counterpart of the economic doctrine of laissez-faire, replaced the old statutory controls with the freedom of the individual to contract with whom he will and upon what terms he can best secure. It swiftly became apparent however that what was good for some was not good for all, as Engels showed in his *Condition of the Working Class in 1844*. Labour organised itself in order to meet on roughly equal terms employers who, in the second half of the nineteenth century, were often joint stock companies, whilst conditions of employment were gradually improved by protective legislation passed as the result of the efforts of "humanitarians" such as Shaftesbury. The increasing specialisation of labour widened the gap between the employer and the employee since the former was no longer necessarily the superior in skill. The individual tended to become submerged in the group, whether a trade union or an employers' association. Some writers, finding contract to be an unsatisfactory "corner-stone," perceive a movement from contract to status. But it is too early to say that contract has disappeared as the basis of British labour law. **20**

I. Definition of "Employee"

Tests to determine whether or not the employee–employer relationship exists

21 Prominent amongst the problems surrounding the applicability of a particular rule is the problem of ascertaining the precise nature of the clientèle affected by that rule. Labour law is no exception. An answer to the question—"employee or non-employee?" may prove to be decisive in several legal contexts, both common law and statutory. Examples are vicarious liability, the rights and duties of employer and employee *inter se*, employers' liability and its insurance, social insurance benefits, compensation for redundancy or unfair dismissal, personal tax liability and the exigibility of taxes such as industrial training levy or selective employment tax (recently abolished). The legal category subsumed in the term "employee" is not necessarily a constant referent in all of these, or other, circumstances, each of which may demand different shades of emphasis in the selection of and, the weight to be attributed to, the various criteria. A taxi-cab driver may be the bailee of a cab belonging to another person whom he may render vicariously liable in tort under certain Acts (London Hackney Cab Act 1843; Town Police Clauses Act 1847), whilst, at the same time, ranking as a self-employed person under an "off the clock" agreement for the purposes of the Redundancy Payments Act 1965 (*Challinor* v. *Taylor* (1972)).

A useful reminder of the inconstancy of definition according to context is provided by Vaisey J. in *London General Cab Co. Ltd.* v. *I.R.C.* (1950), a case in which drivers, who had paid part of their receipts to the owners of the cab, were held for tax purposes not to be employed under contracts of service:

> "It may well be that in one case the driver is the agent of the owner, in another case he may be the servant of the owner, and a third case may be one of simple bailment. I also think that it may be two or more of those classes of association when viewed from different angles, that is to say, the driver may be, for the purposes of the National Insurance Act 1946, a servant of the owner, and for the purposes of the return of income tax he may be regarded as an independent contractor": (see also National Insurance (Industrial Injuries) Act 1965, Sched. 1, para. 12).

The definition of the "employee" has posed a conundrum for the common law. Despite Thesiger L.J.'s warning in *Yewens* v. *Noakes* (1880) at p. 538 of the report, that "definitions" are proverbially dangerous and repeated judicial asseverations as to the hopelessness of finding any "magical formula," various "tests" have been employed.

(a) *The "control" test*

Yewens v. *Noakes* itself contains the much-cited definition by Bramwell B.—"A servant is a person subject to the command of his master as to the manner in which he shall do his work." The right of the master to prescribe not only the end (the "what") but also the means (the "how"), the time (the "when") and the place (the "where") has been seized on as the essence of the "control test." Faced with situations where control cannot be exercised, such as the train driver driving his train, or the professional worker, such as the hospital doctor, exercising his skill, the control test has been transmuted into a residual "right of control" exerciseable by disciplinary sanctions, including dismissal. But control, or right of control, as the sole determinant of the employer–employee relationship became increasingly unreliable as a test, although it still plays an important part. The growing complexity of modern industrial society with its attendant specialisation, the often impersonal nature of the employee's relationship with his employer, usually a corporate employer more interested in results than modalities, full employment and the growth of "shop-floor" power, are amongst the factors which have contributed to the decline of control as an exclusive criterion. 22

(b) *The "multiple" test*

In the post-war years the courts have utilised a range of criteria 23 of which control, which is still important, is only one. Lord Thankerton referred to four indicia in *Short* v. *Henderson* (1946) *viz.*, (1) the power of selection, (2) the payment of wages or other remuneration, (3) the right of suspension or dismissal, and (4) the right of control, itself often "critical and decisive." Since then, the list of relevant indicia has been widened into a multiple test in which the totality of the circumstances is looked at and which may involve the balancing of those circumstances against each other. No exhaustive list of indicia can be framed and the weight to be attached to each varies with the circumstances.

A multiple test was applied in *Morren* v. *Swinton and Pendlebury Borough Council* (1965) where the argument that, because a resident engineer appointed by a local authority worked under the instructions of a firm of consultant engineers he was therefore not an employee for the purposes of local government superannuation, was rejected. Although the American Restatement emphasises the control or right to control the "physical conduct" of the servant in the performance of his service, the American cases have ranged over numerous factors other than that of control. The hours of work, the regularity of work, the geographical limitation to a place of work, the possession of skill, the attitude of the community (the so-called "sociological test"), manner of appointment and dismissal, type of remuneration, ownership of instrumentalities, the chance of profit or loss, the intention of the parties, and the individual's insurance and tax status, have all been taken into account without attributing conclusive effect to any one factor. Indeed a person subject to control may turn out not to be a servant at all, whereas someone not subject to control may nevertheless be adjudged to be a servant.

24 The three conditions necessary for a contract of service were adumbrated by MacKenna J. in *Ready Mixed Concrete Ltd.* v. *Minister of Pensions and National Insurance* (1968):

1. Agreement by the servant in consideration of a wage or other remuneration to provide his own work and skill in the performance of some service for his master. In the vast majority of cases the service will be both personal and contractual. That this is not always so is shown by *Market Investigations* v. *Minister of Social Security* (1969) where a part-time interviewer for market research purposes was held to be employed under a contract of employment, even though she could work for other employers, and notwithstanding that she earned a fixed fee without any arrangement as to time off, sick pay, or holidays. Sometimes it may be possible that the employee is contractually entitled to send a reasonably qualified substitute as in *Global Plant Hire* v. *Secretary of State for Health and Social Security* (1972), where the Divisional Court, clearly influenced by the degree of control present, declined to interfere with the Minister's determination that two drivers of earth-moving equipment, hired out with the equipment by their employers, were employed under contracts of service, notwithstanding that there was a clear intention that they should be regarded as self-employed persons who stamped their own insurance cards and paid tax under Schedule D.
2. Subjection to control, which is "a necessary, though not always a sufficient, condition of a contract of service." It is submitted, with respect, that control is not invariably a necessary condition as the *Morren* case (see para. 23) indicates.
3. The negative condition that the other provisions of the contract are not inconsistent with it being a contract of service. Doubt has rightly been cast on the utility of this negative condition as a workable rule. Several cases in the past few years have involved the delicate balancing of factors both for and against the existence of a contract of service. Not surprisingly, a part-time teacher in a drama school, who had been accorded considerable latitude in matters such as syllabus, mode of teaching and leave of absence, to enable him to

appear in plays, was held in *Argent* v. *Minister of Social Security* (1968), not to be employed under a contract of service. Conversely, but also not surprisingly, seven clerical employees in a firm of solicitors, who had entered into a written partnership agreement in respect of their earnings from that firm, were held to have continued under their original contracts of service which were varied only as to the mode of payment. Although the point was left open, it is submitted that a contract of service with a partnership as employee is, as such, impossible, although there is nothing to prevent a joint hiring, as where a cook and a chauffeur, both married, are employed together. Whether or not a corporation can be an employee remains undecided in private (although not public) law. Acts which refer to an "individual" clearly exclude the corporation. Apart from these, it is dangerous to say that a corporation can never be an employee, but it is hard to think of an example where this would be possible.

Because of the difficulty involved in balancing one set of factors **25**
against another, and because of the uncertainty thereby caused, it is sometimes necessary to provide arbitrary, statutory clarification for certain purposes. For example, regulations categorise market research and public opinion interviewers, employed for not more than twenty-eight hours in any contribution week, as self-employed persons for the purposes of social security (S.I. 1971 No. 1728). A bigger problem has been posed by the growth of "labour-only" contractors in the building and construction industry, which led to the appointment of a Committee of Inquiry under the chairmanship of Professor Phelps-Brown. Amongst the Committee's proposals was a system of registration for such contractors. *Construction Industry Training Board* v. *Labour Force Ltd.* (1970), in which the respondents had sent out workers to contractors who needed their services, but had retained responsibility for tax and social security contributions, typifies the difficulty in making a proper classification. There, the court concluded that the workers in question were neither the employees of the respondents nor of the contractors to whom they had been sent, being either self-employed or belonging to a category *sui generis*. Clarification of the status of such workers is provided in relation to liability to the industrial training levy and tax by statutory intervention (respectively S.I. 1970 No. 471, and Finance Act 1971, ss. 29, 30, and S.I. 1971 No. 1688, made thereunder).

(c) *The "organisation" test*

Denning L.J. (as he then was) made the radical observation that **26** "the test of being a servant does not rest nowadays on submission to orders. It depends on whether the person is part and parcel of the organisation" (*Bank voor Handel en Scheepvaart N.V.* v. *Slatford* (1953) at p. 295 of the report). The "organisation" test takes into account the degree of integration into the organisation whether it be a ship, a factory, or a hospital. Those who are sufficiently "integrated" into the enterprise are employees unlike those who merely perform adjunctive work. A window-cleaner who comes to clean the office windows once a month in return for an agreed charge, who provides his own equipment and hires his own helpers, would not be considered to be an integral part of the organisation. It is likely that he would be considered to be an independent entrepreneur taking his own chance of profit or loss.

The test was referred to in *Whittaker* v. *Ministry of Pensions and National Insurance* (1967), where Mocatta J. held that a trapeze artiste (who had suffered a broken wrist as the result of a fall during her "act") was entitled to industrial injuries benefit as an employed person, the other circumstances specified in her written contract, such as helping to unload and load chairs when the circus moved and undertaking to perform duties as an usherette when not engaged in her "act," showing that she "had no real independence and had to carry out her contractual duties as an integral part of the business of the company during her engagement."

Regrettably, the test has not received the support which it deserves. Admittedly, it does raise difficulty in connection with professional workers in an organisation (on which, see below at para. 35), but the non-acceptance of the test may be partially attributable to two considerations. First, organised labour has tended to stress the conflictive aspect of industrial relations and to put forward the interests of the worker as an exchangist or contractualist. Secondly, legal thinking in this country, unlike that in Germany, has not evolved any coherent, structural concept of the enterprise as a "community of interests." There would seem to be no insuperable objection to utilising a composite test in conjunction with the organisation test, so that a consideration of the relevant factors will lead one to deciding whether or not a particular person is part and parcel of the organisation.

27 The construction of a written contract of employment is a matter of law. Although there are dicta which assert that it is a question of fact whether or not a particular, unwritten contract is a contract of service, cases over the past few years treat this question as one of mixed fact and law, or, more accurately, as one involving the drawing of legal inferences from primary facts. *Global Plant Hire Ltd.* (above, para. 24) shows that an appellate court may be reluctant to interfere with a decision which does not contain a proposition of law *ex facie* false.

Special categories of servants

28 Employees as a legal category are not a homogenous group, in that particular sub-categories may require special treatment. Domestic servants, whose work involves the running of a residential establishment (not necessarily a private home), are entitled to (and must give) one month's notice or to notice given at or before the end of the first fortnight to expire at the end of the first month. It has been held that the old action for loss of services (*actio per quod servitium amisit*) is limited to the services of domestic or menial servants (*I.R.C.* v. *Hambrook*, below, para. 174). Such servants are specifically excluded from certain statutory provisions, *e.g.* truck legislation and the provision for the summary settlement of disputes between employer and workman (as to which see below, paras. 194 *et seq.*, 270). The manual worker is protected by the Truck Acts in so far as the form and the manner in which he receives his wages is regulated, including permissible deductions from such wages. Teachers in state schools who are employed by local education authorities have their terms of employment settled in practice by a statutory Burnham Committee.

29 Employment in the public service tends to reflect the particular needs of governmental organs. Civil servants have in law, though not in practice, precarious tenure of office in that they are dismissible during Her Majesty's pleasure. When the Industrial Relations Bill was going through Parliament, attention was drawn to the possibility that civil servants might be held not to be "employees" and thereby unprotected against unfair dismissal. The Bill was therefore amended to include in the provenance of the Act those in Crown employment and workers who are Crown employees although it contains adaptations reflecting the constitutional position of the Crown with regard to enforcement of legal process and other matters (Industrial Relations Act 1971, s. 162). The curious legal status of the civil servant is based on the principle of governmental effectiveness—a principle which does not govern employees in the nationalised industries who are not civil servants.

30 With regard to local government officers, the Local Government Act 1972 permits a local authority to appoint such officers as it thinks necessary for the proper discharge of its functions (s. 112 (1)). This provision rids local authorities of the statutory obligation contained in the Local Government Act 1933 to appoint certain officers, *e.g.* clerk, treasurer, and medical officer of health, although other enactments requiring or authorising the appointment of particular

officers, *e.g.* chief education officers, fire brigade officers, and chief constables, are unaffected (s. 112 (4)). The requirement of ministerial consent to the dismissal of certain officers is also missing, a reform which, by denying sanctuary in Whitehall to the dismissed officer, will meet the criticisms of those who did not like the Janus-like faces of the chief officer—one of which pointed to the local authority whilst the other pointed to the Minister. The Act also provides for the placing of local authority staff at the disposal of other authorities (s. 113 (1)), for the disqualification of members in connection with paid offices in the authority (s. 116), and, by section 117, for disclosure by officers of interests in contracts.

31 A category which requires separate treatment is the indeterminate category of "office-holders" deriving their status from common law and statute. The office-holder cannot be dismissed without first being told what is alleged against him and being given the opportunity to present his defence or explanation. It was on these grounds that the dismissal of the chief constable in *Ridge* v. *Baldwin* (1964), was held to be void. Also entitled to "natural justice" are the clergyman in the Established Church, the teacher employed by a Scottish education authority (*Malloch* v. *Aberdeen Corporation* (1971)) and, possibly, the vice-chancellor of a university (*Vidyodaya University* v. *Silva* (1965)). The contrast between the office-holder and the ordinary employee is revealed in *Taylor* v. *National Union of Seamen* (1967), a case which concerned the allegedly wrongful dismissal of a trade union officer. It was held that the rules of natural justice (broadly connoting absence of bias and a chance to refute the charge) were inapplicable to the dismissal *qua* employee of the union but applied to the extent that his dismissal might prejudice his eligibility for office in the union.

32 The conferment of a remedy for unfair dismissal by the Industrial Relations Act and the formulation of a form of industrial "due process" for employees subject to disciplinary sanctions, including dismissal, goes some of the way towards reducing the contrast between office-holder and employee. Nevertheless, dismissal of an office-holder in breach of natural justice is *ultra vires* and void, whereas the employee who has been unfairly dismissed has, at most (and apart from any claim to compensation), the chance of obtaining from the tribunal a *recommendation* that he be re-engaged, *i.e.* the dismissal is otherwise effective.

Statutory definitions

33 Statutory definitions need to be construed within their own particular contexts. Both the Redundancy Payments Act 1965 and the

Contracts of Employment Act 1972 use substantially the same definition of the "employee" despite the different purpose which each Act subserves. The employee connotes an individual who has entered into, or works under, a contract with an employer, whether the contract be for manual labour, clerical work or otherwise, be expressed or implied, oral or in writing, and whether it be a contract of service or of apprenticeship. Both Acts include an employee whose employment has ceased. With the limitation that in either case the employment must be contractual, the scope of the definition is wide, the words "or otherwise" not signifying work *ejusdem generis* with manual or clerical work.

Section 167 (1) of the Industrial Relations Act 1971 is simpler, defining an employee for the purposes of that Act as "an individual who has entered into or works under (or, where the employment has ceased, worked under) a contract of employment." In all of these Acts, including the 1971 Act which uses synonymity rather than definition (" 'contract of employment' means a contract of service or of apprenticeship . . ."), the ineluctable problem of finding the attributes of a contract of service forces us to resort to the cases and the "tests" which they provide (see above, paras. 21 *et seq.*).

Other statutory definitions similar to but not necessarily the **34**
same as "employee" are those of "workman" (section 8 of the Industrial Courts Act 1919, which includes a person who contracts "personally to execute any work or labour," *i.e.* an independent contractor. However, truck legislation applies to workmen as defined by section 10 of the Employers and Workmen Act 1875, from which are excluded domestic servants.)

Certain portions of the Industrial Relations Act 1971, such as **35**
those dealing with unfair dismissal, affect only the "employee." Much of the Act, however, deals with the "worker." That this term has extremely wide application will be appreciated when it is seen that it includes any individual who works, or normally works, or seeks to work, (a) under a contract of employment, or (b) under any other contract to perform personal work or services for another party to the contract who is not a professional client of his, or (c) in employment under, or for the purposes of, a government department, excluding the armed forces, to the extent that such employment is not covered by either of the preceding categories. Not only is the definition wide for the persons whom it includes, *e.g.* the professional man who renders services other than to a professional client, but also for the absence of a contractual link, *e.g.* the trade unionist *refused* employment because of his trade union membership who may have a claim under section 5 (2) (*c*). Police officers are neither employees nor workers for the purposes of the 1971 Act.

The term "worker" in section 24 of the Wages Councils Act 1959 draws upon the now common form definition of employee given in the Redundancy Payments Act 1965 and the Contracts of Employment Act 1972, except that a person under contract personally to execute any work or labour is included, whereas casual employment is excluded (but see the surprising decision in *Westall Richardson Ltd.* v. *Roulson* (1954)). As for "employed persons" under social security legislation, employment in Great Britain under any contract of service or apprenticeship is the most important category of insurable employment in the National Insurance (Industrial Injuries) Act 1965. We have seen that the classification of insured persons for the purposes of the National Insurance Act 1965 has given us a fair quota of leading cases.

36 A further point concerning statutes is their sphere of operation. Thus, protective legislation needs to be approached with care, in that duties may be imposed upon a person who need not necessarily be an employer, *e.g.* the statutory duties contained in the Factories Act 1961 are cast upon the "occupier" (a term nowhere defined in the Act). In *Blakely* v. *C. & H. Clothing Co.* (1958) the plaintiff worked for a firm which occupied part of a building in which a lift was installed and operated by the owners. B. was injured when the lift moved as he was putting his hand through the outer gate to close the inner gate of the lift. *Held* that the employers had not broken their common law duty, but that the *owners* were in breach of section 22 of the Factories Act 1937 (since repealed). Conversely, the statutory duties may be owed to persons who are not necessarily employees of the defendant (see *Massey-Harris-Ferguson (Manufacturing) Ltd.* v. *Piper* (1956), in which Lord Goddard C.J., construing the phrase "persons employed" as used in statutory regulations, said: "The test is whether a person is employed in the factory, not whether he is employed by the occupier"; *cf. Stanton Ironworks Co. Ltd.* v. *Skipper* (1956)). A few statutory provisions apply to that survivor of the domestic system, the outworker, still used in those trades in which manual skill plays a part, *e.g.* section 133 of the Factories Act 1961, which requires lists of outworkers to be kept. The broad ambit of an Act may be narrowed in particular cases. For example, neither a person employed by his or her spouse nor certain relatives employed as domestic servants in a private household are entitled to statutory redundancy payments.

37 Dock workers do not fall readily into any recognisable legal category. Unlike ordinary employees, they work under highly regulated statutory schemes applicable to certain ports. Under these schemes, provision is made for National and Local Dock Labour Boards, for the registration of dock workers, their terms and conditions of employment and their dismissal. Cases such as *Barnard* v. *National Dock Labour Board* (1953), and *Vine* v. *National Dock Labour Board* (1957), indicate that the dismissal of dock workers can raise issues more germane to administrative law than to labour law. A series of decisions serving to limit the geographical ambit of "dock work" and the growth of unregulated "container traffic" outside the docks at a time when dock work proper was declining, were the chief factors which led to the dock strike of 1972 and the imprisonment of the five dockers for contempt of court during that strike.

Non-employees who render service

A person may render service without reward and without, there- **38**
fore, a contract of employment, yet affix his principal with liability for wrongs committed in the course of performing that service. Most of the litigation however has turned not on the question of pay versus no pay but upon the more important question of employee versus independent contractor.

The common law (perhaps influenced by Roman Law) tended in the past to hold that the exercise of professional skill was incompatible with the existence of a contract of service. The "hospital cases," decided since the introduction of the National Health Service, show that doctors, nurses and radiographers are capable of being employees, whilst the mystique of professionalism is further eroded by the Industrial Relations Act 1971, which manages to accommodate professionals, other than those performing service for a professional client, under the pragmatic rubric of "worker" (see above, para 35).

As we have seen, the distinction may be vital in questions such as vicarious liability, rights and duties of the parties, and the application of legislation. Prior to 1971, trade disputes legislation gave immunity against tortious liability for inducing breach of the contract of employment (but not for breach of any other type of contract, *e.g.* a commercial contract). Cases such as *Emerald* v. *Lowthian* (1966), and *Ready Mixed Concrete* v. *Cox* (1970), showed that the immunity would not obtain if the contract in question were not a contract of employment. The Industrial Relations Act 1971 implements the recommendation by the Donovan Commission that the distinction between the two types of contract should be abolished in connection with industrial disputes legislation.

In *Re C. W. & A. L. Hughes Ltd.* (1966), a gang of "labour-only" sub-contractors was held not to be in the employment of a company within the meaning of section 319 (4) of the Companies Act 1948, so that neither the members of the gang nor those who had advanced money for the payment of their wages ranked as preferential creditors in a liquidation, as employees would, to a limited extent, have done. The heavy burdens cast upon employers over the last decade or so, such as selective employment tax, industrial training levy, increased social security contribution, compulsory insurance (see para 120, below) and compensation for redundancy and unfair dismissal have caused some employers to seek ways of escaping from these burdens by purporting to employ persons as independent contractors. The building industry is, as we have seen (above, para. 25), the chief example of this tendency, but others have sought to emulate the example so provided.

39 Service may be provided by an agent, *i.e.* a person with legal authority to act on behalf of a principal so as to affect the latter's legal relations with third persons. For certain purposes, such as vicarious liability or the duty of good faith, the relevant rules may apply indifferently to employee and agent. The liability of the master or principal for his employee or agent involves the application of the same test, *viz.* was the servant or agent acting on behalf of and within the scope of the authority conferred by the master or principal. That the servant usually has more permanent employment and a wider range of duties and discretions than the agent does not mean that different tests are applied to each but rather that the same test is producing different results. Sometimes the agent will possess a "general authority" to affix his principal with liability, as in the case of *Heatons Transport Ltd.* v. *T.G.W.U.* (1973), where an unregistered union was held liable for blacking operations conducted by its shop stewards whose authority to continue such operations had not been effectively withdrawn. The House of Lords rejected the notion of duality in the shop steward's role, namely, to borrow Edmund Burke's language, as the representative of his inferiors and the delegate of his superiors.

40 A partner is a legal creature distinct from the employee in that he is engaged in carrying on a business with another or others in common, with a view of profit; the payment of a salary to a partner does not make him an employee of the firm, whilst the employee does not become a partner merely because he is paid at a rate which varies with the profits. "Co-partnership" is an imprecise term, used to signify worker participation in profits, and rarely, if ever, involves a partnership in the legal sense of that term.

41 The director of a registered company is a versatile creature, combining in one person the roles of "officer," agent, fiduciary and "primary organ." The versatility of the director does not, however, include that of "employee," unless he has a service contract with the company, as in *Lee* v. *Lee's Air Farming Ltd.* (1961), where the

governing director, who held all the shares in the company save one, was killed whilst piloting an aircraft during aerial topdressing. His widow was held entitled to workers' compensation under a New Zealand Act. This case was followed in *Road Transport Industry Board* v. *Readers Garage Ltd.* (1969), in which the Divisional Court rejected the decision of an industrial tribunal which had refused to accord the status of an employee to a managing director who held $99\frac{1}{2}$ per cent. of the shares in a company, remitting the case back to the tribunal in order to ascertain whether or not there was a contract of service between the company and the managing director. That was a case concerning the industrial training levy (a form of payroll tax).

Perhaps more questionably, one finds that redundancy payments have been awarded to directors with service contracts, notwithstanding that they have been classified as self-employed persons for tax and social security purposes. Accepting fully the proposition that definitions need to be applied eclectically, one wonders if the tribunals have not, perhaps, been a shade too deferential to the principle of corporate personality and consequently too reticent to lift the corporate veil to ascertain the director's position in the company. In one case (*Robinson* v. *George Sorby Ltd.* (1966)), the tribunal had no such inhibitions, finding that the managing director was in truth the company and "controlled himself," but refusing a redundancy payment because he did not have a service contract.

It is submitted that the presence of a service contract should not preclude the tribunal from piercing the veil to find out the director's shareholding interest and the origin of any decision to close down the company or its business. It is doubtful if those who framed the Act envisaged that a director, albeit with a service contract, who uses his controlling interest to force a decision, perhaps quite arbitrarily, to close down the business, would be eligible to hold out his hand for a redundancy payment, some of which comes from public money.

II. The Contract of Employment

Reference has already been made to the distinctive primacy which British labour accords to the individual contract of employment. An employee who agreed to accept, say, £30 per week, is prima facie not entitled to invoke a term fixed by a National Joint Council which lays down a wage of, say, £40 per week (*Hulland* v. *William Sanders & Son* (1945): but see the impact of collective bargaining, discussed below at para. 49). The contract of employment is subject to the general principles of the law of contract concerning 42 agreement, consideration (separately discussed at para. 182, below), intention to create legal relations, compliance with formal requirements and illegality.

Terms of the contract

43 The terms of the contract may be *express*, *i.e.* formulated by the parties, or incorporated into the contract from some external source, such as a collective bargain (the impact of which is discussed separately below), or a book of works rules. There is little doubt that the statutory notice of particulars of employment required by section 4 of the Contracts of Employment Act 1963 (now 1972) (see below, para. 62) has done much to concretise certain terms of employment. Mackinnon L.J.'s statement in *O'Grady* v. *M. Saper Ltd.* (1940), that the contract of employment is "usually concluded orally by people who rarely think out and still more rarely express, any terms" (at p. 473 of the report) is echoed in similar judicial utterances.

44 Two reasons are proffered for the vagueness which commonly surrounds contracts of employment. In the first place, employees do not normally think of their employment as a contractually regulated relationship at all but rather as a code of rules to which they subscribe. This code is something which is normally settled between the employer and the union. If things go wrong, the employee is more likely to turn to the shop steward than a solicitor, except where statutory rights to redundancy payment or compensation for unfair dismissal are involved. Three million dismissals per year succeed in producing only a tiny crop of cases on wrongful dismissal at common law. This would appear to reveal either stoicism in the face of defeat or a preference for extra-legal remedies. Secondly, there is the reason given by Lon L. Fuller that relationships of authority, *i.e.* between superior and inferior, tend to be afflicted by a chronic reciprocity of silence on all matters touching the existence and exercise of the authority itself (*Anatomy of the Law*, p. 113). Explicit contract requires an optimum social distance between parties on roughly equal terms—a state of affairs which does not characterise the typical employer–employee relationship.

45 It is sometimes a nice question whether a particular statement is contractual or merely evidential of a contract. The statutory notice required by section 4 of the Contracts of Employment Act 1972 is an example of a statement having evidential value only. A further possibility is that a statement may be informative and not contractual, as in *Gallagher* v. *Post Office* (1970), where an assurance by a Post Office instructress to two telephonists that they would be entitled to join either a guild or a union was adjudged to be informative and non-contractual in nature. By withdrawing recognition from the guild, the Post Office was held to have broken neither an implied term in the contracts of employment of the two plaintiffs that the guild would continue to receive recognition, nor an express term to the same effect, thereby rejecting the second limb of the plaintiffs' claim that a written term, referring to the discussion and negotiation of variations of conditions of service with "appropriate staff associations," expressly precluded the Post Office from withdrawing recognition from the guild.

The vacuum left by the scanty express contract may be partially **46**
filled by terms implied *in fact*, *i.e.* terms which rest on the presumed intent of the parties and which are implied to give their agreement business efficacy. A term of this description cannot be added "because the court thinks it would have been reasonable to have inserted it into the contract" (*per* Scrutton L.J. in *Reigate* v. *Union Manufacturing Co.* (1918), at p. 605 of the report); this may only be done where the implication is required to give the contract business efficacy so that, had the attention of the parties been drawn to the gap, they would have answered, "Of course, so and so will happen; we did not trouble to say so; it is too clear."

If, however, a party has no knowledge, actual or constructive, of a particular matter, it is impossible to reply to the "officious bystander" in the terms just described, as in *Spring* v. *National Amalgamated Stevedores and Dockers Society* (1956), where the union's argument that Spring's expulsion from membership of the union complied with the "no-poaching rule" in the "Bridlington Agreement" between unions was held not to justify the union's action for the reason that Spring knew nothing of that Agreement. The conduct of an employee or of his co-employees may furnish evidence as to the terms of the contract, so that, for example, an employee who has, in the past, agreed to work outside the normal place of work may find that he cannot lawfully refuse a direction to do so on a later occasion. Evidence based on conduct is nonetheless a dubious guide in that the employee's past conduct may equally be consistent with a non-contractual variation in a normal method of working.

An employee may be deemed to contract with his employer against the background of a custom which is certain, notorious and reasonable, whether prevailing in the employer's undertaking, in the trade, or in the locality. A weaver was held to be bound by a practice providing for reduced wages in respect of faulty work in the leading case of *Sagar* v. *Ridehalgh* (1931). "I think it is clear," said Lawrence L.J., "that the plaintiff accepted employment in the defendant's mill on the same terms as the other weavers employed at the mill." Custom, however reasonable, certain and notorious, cannot be invoked to nullify or vary an express term in the contract, so that, for example, an express term that wages are to be payable during sickness will not yield to a contrary trade practice. If there is no express term covering a particular matter, the courts have considerable latitude. The words of Pilcher J. in *Orman* v. *Saville Sportswear Ltd.* (1960), at p. 1065 of the report—"If the employer seeks to establish an implied condition that no wages are payable, it is for him to make it out, and the court, in construing the written contract will not accept any implied term which will not pass the test laid down . . . in *Reigate* v. *Union Manufacturing Co.* . . ."—show that the court's premise or presumption can play an important part.

47 Terms *implied by law* are, in truth, legal duties masquerading in legal guise. Such terms may be implied at common law or under statute. Many of the implied duties of employer and employee which, with us, are contractually implied, are, in foreign countries, set out in labour codes. Thus, the implied term that contracts of employment permit a strike after notice not less than that required to terminate those contracts (*Morgan* v. *Fry* (1968), at p. 728 of the report: *cf.* Industrial Relations Act 1971, s. 147, below, at para. 578), or the implied term that a party to a contract must not set out wilfully to frustrate the whole commercial purpose of the contract by "working to rule" (*Secretary of State for Employment* v. *ASLEF* (*No. 2*) (1970)) can only be rested on presumed intent by a stretch of the imagination. In *O'Brien* v. *Associated Fire Alarms Ltd.* (1968), the Court of Appeal once more dipped into the thesaurus of the implied term and came up with an implication that men who lived in Liverpool, and had worked in that area, could not be sent by their employer to work in Barrow-in-Furness, Lord Denning M.R. propounding a term as to "commutability," *viz.* that the men could not be sent beyond normal travelling distance of their homes. Salmon L.J. (as he then was) preferred to arrive at the same conclusion by looking at the past conduct of the parties. The parturition of implied terms by that fecund mistress, the common law, certainly permits the law to be adapted to changed conditions.

48 Terms implied by law include those *implied by statute.* The statutorily-implied term has been used piece-meal in labour law which also uses other methods, such as the sanction of crime, or of tort or, sometimes, conciliation, to achieve its ends. Thus, protective industrial legislation operates by means of the sanctions of inspection, crime and tort. Refusing a claim for damages based on breach of contract for failing to comply with statutory duties affecting mines Greer J. in *Browning* v. *Crumlin Valley Collieries Ltd.* (1926) said: "I do not think it would have occurred to any one that it was necessary to make the statutory provisions in question part of the contract" (at p. 527 of the report—the same judge finding the implied term of "no work, no pay" and, in any case, tracing the loss to the stoppage of the mine on discovery of the unsafe state of the mineshaft and not to the breach of statutory duty).

Even so, the statutorily-implied term is sometimes used. Examples are to be found in minimum wage legislation (below, paras. 201 *et seq.*), the Equal Pay Act 1970, awards of the Industrial Arbitration Board concerning recognised terms and conditions of employment under the Terms and Conditions of Employment Act 1959, as amended (below, para. 57), and under section 127 of the Industrial Relations Act 1971 (awards concerning failure to carry on collective bargaining with a trade union recognised as sole bargaining agent and failure to disclose information to employees). Not dissimilar to the French notion of "extension," is the statutory extension of collective bargaining achieved by the Terms and Conditions of Employment Act 1959, s. 8, which, as amended, is discussed below in connection with collective bargaining.

The impact of the collective bargain

The collective bargain subserves two main functions, *viz.* (i) a consensual function, and (ii) a normative function. The former represents the collective bargain as an agreement between the parties—employer or employers' association on the one side and organisation of workers or federation of workers' organisation on the other. Under the so-called "corporate theory," the parties to the bargain act as principals in their own right. This carries with it the corollaries that members of the organisations privy to the agreement cannot assert rights or be subjected to duties under the collective agreement either by reason of treating the organisation as their "agents" (although in rare cases this is possible), or as their "trustees" (so as to enforce a "third-party beneficiary right"). The consensual function of the collective agreement is discussed in Chapter 8, below. **49**

Even in those countries which recognise the enforceability of the collective agreement by the parties *inter se*, it is admitted that the normative effect of the bargain, *i.e.* the manner in which it settles terms and conditions of employment, is more important in practice. Despite one or two judicial utterances *per incuriam*, and the fateful concession of counsel in *Rookes* v. *Barnard* (in which he conceded that a collectively-agreed no-strike clause had become part of the individual contracts of employees), it is clear both that the doctrine of privity of contract remains the basis of contract law in this country and that it applies to the collective agreement. *Holland* v. *London Society of Compositors* (1924) is an illustration. There, **50**

P, who had come to London, was refused admission to Union A, despite the latter's agreement with Union B that admission would be granted. It was held that P could not sue for breach of contract as a stranger to that agreement.

51 But that part of the collective agreement—the "substantive" part, as it is called—which deals with terms and conditions of employment may become part of an individual contract of employment in the following ways:

(a) *Express incorporation*

52 The contract of employment may expressly incorporate apt terms in the collective agreement. In *National Coal Board* v. *Galley* (1958), the plaintiff succeeded in establishing breach of contract against colliery deputies who had refused to work on Saturdays. Apart from its unique character as a case in which an employer had the temerity to sue his own employees, *National Coal Board* v. *Galley* showed that colliery deputies, who had refused to work on Saturdays, could be sued successfully for a breach of a term in their contracts that they would work "such days or part days in each weeks as may reasonably be required by the employer." This latter term had been agreed between the deputies' union and the employer, but had become incorporated into the deputies' contracts of employment, probably because it was expressly referred to in the contracts, although the judgment does take account of the fact that the deputies had worked on the terms of the agreement. Even an oral reference to "union rates" has been held to import the terms of a collective bargain, irrespective of whether or not the employee is a member of the union: *Hooker* v. *Lange, Bell & Co.* (1937).

Recent cases show that the statutory notice required by section 4 of the Contracts of Employment Act 1963 (now the Contracts of Employment Act 1972) can serve to demonstrate that the parties intended to import collectively agreed terms into their contracts of employment. It is not essential that the term to be imported should be specifically set out in the collective agreement. One of the factors which influenced the court in *Stevenson* v. *Tees-side Bridge and Engineering Ltd.* (1971) (a case in which a steel erector had contested his employer's right to send him to different parts of the country) was the clear implication of the national agreement (imported into the steel erector's contract by virtue of the statutory notice alluded to above) that travelling was an essential feature of the job, although nowhere expressly stated in that agreement. By agreeing to mobility, and subsequently working away from home, the employee showed that he was attempting to approbate and reprobate at the same time.

Because a particular collective agreement happens to be unenforceable, it does not follow that terms in that agreement cannot be enforceable in the individual context. Indeed, a term may be incorporated into individual contracts of employment from a collective agreement which is no longer extant, as appears from *Morris* v. *C. H. Bailey Ltd.* (1969), where working rules, agreed between an employers' association and a confederation of trade unions, continued to regulate contracts of employment into which they had been expressly imported, notwithstanding the termination of the agreement and, thereby, the rules. The same case, incidentally, underlines the importance of distinguishing between the collective agreement and the individual contract of employment, holding that termination of the former did not suffice to terminate the latter. On occasions, it has been clear that contracts of employment have been regulated by collective bargaining but difficult to say which collective bargain applied. 53

The emergence of local or plant bargaining within the framework of what the Industrial Relations Act 1971 terms "more extensive bargaining arrangements," *e.g.* national bargaining, has posed difficult questions for the courts and tribunals whose decisions have not escaped criticism (see K. W. Wedderburn, *The Legal Force of Plant Bargaining* (1969) 32 M.L.R. 99). Although the courts do not seem reluctant to incorporate "no-strike" agreements from collective bargains, there are certain parts of a collective agreement, especially that laying down a "procedure agreement," which are inapt for incorporation into an individual relationship for the simple reason that they envisage the regulation of *collective* relations. The late Lord Donovan expressed the view that the nebulous drafting of many collective agreements would render them unenforceable by reason of vagueness or uncertainty; if this is the case, such agreements could not be enforced via individual contracts.

(b) *Implied incorporation*

Secondly, collectively agreed terms may be impliedly incorporated into the contract of employment. A much-cited (and much-distinguished) case hostile to implied incorporation is *Young* v. *Canadian Northern Railways Co.* (1931). Y, who had been orally appointed as an employee of C at "the going rate," claimed that his dismissal, with its attendant loss of seniority, violated the terms of a collective wage agreement. The Judicial Committee of the Privy Council, however, declined to imply the terms of the wage agreement into Y's contract of employment. The parties had admittedly acted on the terms of the wage agreement, but their conduct did not 54 necessarily point unequivocally to contractual agreement, since it was equally consistent with employers applying the wage agreement "as a matter of policy." Nor did the Judicial Committee feel that the agreement was "adapted for conversion into or incorporation with a service agreement." The decision is probably best confined to its facts, *viz.* that the terms of that particular agreement did not lend themselves to transplantation into service contracts, and it cannot be treated as deciding against implied incorporation as such. In several cases resort has been had to the conduct of the parties.

The *Young* case did not prevent the tribunal in *Joel* v. *Cammell Laird* (*Ship-repairers*) *Ltd.* (1968), from finding that employees were not entitled to refuse a transfer from ship-repairing work to shipbuilding work as agreed in a collective agreement. The employees (1) had specific knowledge of the agreement, and (2) showed by their conduct that they accepted the agreement. In any case, the agreement had become part of their personal contracts of service by virtue of the statutory notice given to them under section 4 of the Contracts of Employment Act 1963 (although why the tribunal should have considered this last of all is unclear). It was also noted that some one thousand men had been transferred in the past. Even so, the conduct of a particular person or persons is not, as has already been indicated, an infallible guide to contractual intent. A person may agree to certain measures, such as a temporary change of working methods, or a change in the place of work, as a purely voluntary accommodation to the employer's interests. On the other hand, there is little which is equivocal in the conduct of an employee who asks to be paid the extra 14 shillings per day payable to "travelling men" under the terms of a collective agreement, but who, after receiving that payment for a period, refuses to perform work in another part of the country.

55 Just as the weaver in *Sagar* v. *Ridehalgh* (above, para. 46) was deemed to contract against the background of custom, it is possible that the employee will be deemed to contract against the background of collective agreements which have become metamorphosed into trade practice or "crystallised custom," as it has been termed. What started off as agreement may, like the Coventry Toolroom Agreement, become a custom applicable to a particular trade. It is curious that the definition of collective agreement in section 166 (1) of the Industrial Relations Act 1971 includes not only an "agreement," but also an "arrangement" prescribing, *inter alia*, terms and conditions of employment, the latter denoting trade usage and custom. Thus, in *Maclea* v. *Essex Lines Ltd.* (1933), it was found, as a question of fact, that the conduct of the parties, and, in particular, the payment of five shillings per day, as prescribed by a certain rule, showed that the latter had been incorporated into the contract.

A caution must be given here against attempting to treat trade **56**
practices as matters susceptible to regulation by means of contract. Britain's early industrialisation and its preference for pragmatism has bequeathed a skein of usages which are "understood" rather than "expressed." Matters such as working conditions, the tea-break, compassionate leave-of-absence, the holiday rota and even the organisation of the work itself may be left in the limbo of trade usage. Although the Irish case of *Brendan Dunne* v. *Fitzpatrick* (1958) distinguishes between express or implied *terms* having contractual effect, and non-contractual *conditions* concerning the physical environment in which work is performed, the expression "terms and conditions of employment," as used in this country, normally denotes contractually enforceable terms and conditions. Thus, an "industrial dispute" may concern either the "terms and conditions of employment," or "the physical conditions in which any workers are required to work" (Industrial Relations Act 1971, s. 167 (1): *cf.* the Industrial Courts Act 1919 in which a "trade dispute" may concern "the terms of the employment or . . . the conditions of labour of any person"). "Recognised terms and conditions of employment" may become enforceable in the context of individual contracts of employment by an award of the Industrial Arbitration Board under section 8 (1) of the Terms and Conditions of Employment Act 1959; presumably conditions of the amorphous nature under discussion cannot be enforced in this way. Statutory recognition of custom is to be found in the Restoration of Pre-War Trade Practices Acts 1944 and 1950 which guaranteed to the trade unions the restoration of "trade practices," such as those aimed at the prevention of dilution, which had been surrendered by the unions in order to further the war effort during the Second World War. Those who drafted the 1944 Act made no attempt to catalogue the trade practices which they had in mind.

(c) *Incorporation by statute*

We have nothing in this country comparable to the statutory **57**
procedure for settling terms and conditions of employment which is employed in Australia and New Zealand. An award under the New Zealand Conciliation and Arbitration Act 1954 takes the form of a judicial decree but is, in substance, a legislative code setting out terms and conditions of employment within an industry. Again, we have nothing comparable to the general device whereby collectively agreed terms may be "extended" to employees in some particular way, as in France, Eire and Canada.

Even so, there are some ways in which effect may be given to collective bargains by statute. Prominent amongst these is section 8 (1) of the Terms and Conditions of Employment Act 1959, as amended by the Industrial Relations Act 1971. Where a trade union or employer's association (*i.e.* a *registered* organisation) reports a claim in writing to the Secretary of State concerning the non-observance of recognised terms and conditions of employment, *i.e.* terms and conditions established in any trade or business or industry, or section thereof, either generally or in any district, which have been settled by an agreement or award, the Secretary of State may refer such claim to the Industrial Arbitration Board after satisfying himself that the claim cannot be settled by appropriate machinery. The Industrial Arbitration Board, if satisfied that the claim is well founded and the terms and conditions are not less favourable than the recognised terms and conditions, must make an award requiring the employer to observe the recognised terms and conditions as respects all workers of the relevant description employed by him. This award takes effect "as an implied term of the contract of employment."

Writers have expressed the view, and it is supported here, that contrary to the general rule, the "implied term" resulting from the award does not, in this case, give way to an express term inconsistent therewith where the latter has been agreed *before* the award or, more doubtfully, *after* the award. A county court decision (*Fox* v. *Pianoforte Supplies* (1963)) interprets the provision in the section that an award "shall cease to have effect on the coming into operation of an agreement or award varying or abrogating the recognised terms or conditions" as applying to an agreement in a contract of service which varies or abrogates the award. The juxtaposition of "agreement or award" indicates, however, that it is a collective agreement which is intended and not an individual agreement.

58 Other examples of statutory incorporation into contracts of employment are discussed in Chapter 3, which deals with remuneration. Section 3 of the Equal Pay Act 1970, for example, provides for the adaptation of collective bargains containing provisions which are discriminatory within the terms of that Act. The results of such adaptation enable those whose contracts of employment are affected by a collective agreement, whether by express or implied incorporation, or by statutory incorporation under section 8 of the Terms and Conditions of Employment Act 1959 (in the manner just described), to enforce the so-called "equal pay" requirement as a matter of personal contract. Section 127 of the Industrial Relations Act 1971 uses the device of statutory implication into individual contracts in connection with awards of the Industrial Arbitration

Board consequent upon claims concerning failure to carry on collective bargaining with a sole bargaining agent or failure to disclose information to employees.

On a somewhat different footing, because they confer statutory 59 rather than statutorily-implied contractual rights, are the provisions in social security legislation giving statutory force to supplementary schemes, including those agreed collectively, and the provisions in the Redundancy Payments Act 1965 enabling an employee to enforce severance of employment terms in a collective agreement if the Secretary of State has made an order substituting the collectively-agreed terms for the statutory right to a redundancy payment (*ibid.* s. 11). The Industrial Arbitration Board is not prevented from making an award concerning the observance of collectively agreed terms and conditions of employment because an order under section 11 of the 1965 Act has been made covering some or all of those terms, but to the extent that the award covers these latter terms it operates subject to section 11, *i.e.* statutorily.

Formalities

From 1954, when the Statue of Frauds 1677, was partially 60 repealed, the general rule has been that a contract of employment may arise from agreement, whether expressed in a deed, a written memorandum or even orally, or from conduct. Apprentices and seamen are the exceptions.

A parol contract cannot create the relationship of master and 61 apprentice, for which an indenture, deed, or agreement in writing is required by section 2 of the Apprentices Act 1814, although it is possible that such a contract may rank as a contract of service. The Pearson Court of Inquiry recommended simplification of the "surprisingly bulky" articles required by merchant shipping legislation. Section 1 of the Merchant Shipping Act 1970, which followed the Pearson Report (Cmnd. 3211), requires "an agreement in writing" between each person employed as a seaman in a ship registered in the United Kingdom and the persons employing him, all of whom must sign. The agreement must be on the terms of a "crew agreement" the form and content of which require the approval of the Department of Trade and Industry.

To remedy a situation in which employees were frequently 62 ignorant of the precise terms of their contract, section 4 of the Contracts of Employment Act 1963 required employers to give a written statement of certain particulars of employment. Under what is now section 4 of the Contracts of Employment Act 1972, an employer is obliged, not later than thirteen weeks after the beginning of an employee's period of employment, to give to the employee a written statement identifying the parties, specifying the date when the employment began, and giving certain particulars (as at a certain date not more than one week before the statement is given), *viz.*—

(a) the scale or rate of remuneration, or the method of calculating remuneration,
(b) the intervals at which remuneration is paid,
(c) terms and conditions relating to hours of work,
(d) terms and conditions relating to—
  (i) entitlement to holidays and holiday pay,
  (ii) incapacity for work due to sickness or injury, including any provision for sick pay, and
  (iii) pension arrangements (other than those statutory schemes in which there is a statutory requirement that employees must be apprised of their rights), and finally
(e) the length of notice which the employee is obliged to give and entitled to receive.

Furthermore, the statement must include a note—

(i) indicating the nature of the employee's rights under section 5 of the Industrial Relations Act 1971 (rights in connection with membership of a trade union), and
(ii) specifying grievance procedure, and
(iii) explaining the steps involving such procedure, or referring to a document which is reasonably accessible to the employee and which explains those steps.

63 If there are no particulars to be entered that fact must be stated. Presumably an employer can give a nil return under items (ii) and (iii) in the note referred to in the last paragraph if he has no grievance procedure. Equally it seems clear that a note concerning trade union rights under (i) above *must* be given. Unlike the note, the statement may refer the employee to some document which he has reasonable opportunities of reading in the course of his employment, or which is made reasonably accessible to him in some other way (a provision which has been said to permit reference to some readily accessible collective agreement). It will be seen, therefore, that the way has been opened to allow of the incorporation of terms from collective bargains into contracts of employment (see *Camden Exhibition and Display* v. *Lynott* (1966), where the statutory statement had this effect). The statement need not be given to an employee whose contract has been reduced to writing, provided that he has received a copy of the contract (or has reasonable opportunities of reading a copy in the course of his employment, or a copy is made reasonably accessible to him in some other way), and provided the express terms of the contract afford the particulars required in the statutory statement; but such an employee must receive the note normally included in a statement (see above), or have reasonable opportunities of reading such a note in the course of his employment, or the note is made reasonably accessible to him in some other way. The 1972 Act also provides for notification of changes in the terms of employment.

Certain employees are not entitled to particulars of any sort **64**
under the Act, *e.g.* those whose hours of employment are less than twenty-one hours per week (subject to variation by order), registered dock workers engaged in dock work, employees in the mercantile marine or in fishing boats, those having certain familial relationships, either of consanguinity or affinity, with their employer, Crown servants and employees engaged in work wholly or mainly outside Great Britain (but not those temporarily sent on a short cruise outside the territorial waters so that they might be summarily dismissed!).

The written statement is not the contract and is not even con- **65**
clusive evidence of the terms of the contract (*per* Lord Parker C.J. in *Turriff Construction Ltd.* v. *Bryant* (1967)). How are disputes (which may involve an ex-employee within three months of ceasing to be employed) concerning either the failure to give a statement, or the giving of a statement containing particulars which are controverted by the employee, resolved? Abandoning the criminal sanctions used in its original incarnation, the Act enables the Industrial Tribunal (set up in 1964) to settle certain questions. Should the employer fail to give a written statement as required, the tribunal has power, upon a reference by the employee, to determine the particulars which ought to have been included or referred to in the statement. If the tribunal exercises this power the particulars so determined are deemed to have been given by the employer. Should a question arise as to the sufficiency or adequacy of the particulars, the tribunal may, on a reference by either employer or employee, confirm or amend the particulars or substitute other particulars for them.

The line between settling particulars (a matter for the tribunal) **66**
and settling disputes arising out of those particulars (a matter for the "ordinary" courts) is a fine one, not always and understandably appreciated by the layman. For example, the tribunals have been prepared to determine whether accommodation was provided free by an employer or should have been deducted from wages, but have been unprepared to institute proceedings for failure to supply a statement, or to award a sum in respect of holiday pay or pay in lieu of notice. No doubt, when, in due course, the industrial tribunal is given jurisdiction to award damages for breach of the contract of

employment (see Industrial Relations Act 1971, s. 113) the now-chagrined claimant who is shunted from pillar to post will then be mollified. Despite recent emphasis upon job evaluation and job definition, the latter much improved by CODOT (the new method of classifying jobs published by the Department of Employment, and used in some firms), it still remains true that important areas of the employment relationship, particularly those concerning the nature of the job and the place of work, remain as clouded as ever.

Illegal contracts of employment

67 A contract of employment, like any other contract, may be impugned for illegality, whether statutory or common law. Sometimes a statute may expressly attach contractual invalidity to certain agreements, *e.g.* sections 1, 2 and 3 of the Truck Act 1831, avoiding certain "trucking" agreements (as to "trucking," see below, para. 194). It may be, however, that the statute in making certain agreements criminal says nothing concerning the *civil* effect of such agreements. In that event, the common law may step in and add the sanction of contractual invalidity to the criminal sanction, for example, agreements exacting premiums from apprentices covered by wages regulation orders (Wages Councils Act 1959, s. 16).

Common law "illegality" attaches to agreements to commit a legal wrong, *e.g.* a tort or crime, or to agreements against public policy. The latter involve some purpose or activity of which the law disapproves, such as immorality, even though such purpose or activity is not itself a nominate legal wrong. "Illegality" therefore, in this extended sense, comprises "gradations of turpitude" (as it has been somewhat heavily termed) with agreements such as a conspiracy to murder at one end of the scale and agreements in restraint of marriage or of trade at the other, the latter not being necessarily totally void

Effect of illegality

68 Two cases illustrate the differing effects of illegality upon a contract of service:

1. *The contract may be entirely vitiated.* In *Napier* v. *National Business Agency* (1951), N was employed by the N.B.A. as secretary and accountant at a fixed weekly salary with an additional fixed sum per week for "expenses" which both knew was considerably in excess of N's actual expenses. N was summarily dismissed and claimed, in default of notice, his salary for the period of notice to which he claimed he was entitled but no sum in lieu of "expenses." It was held that the inclusion of a sum for fictitious expenses, the

purpose of which was to defraud the Revenue, rendered the entire contract illegal.

2. *The contract may be vitiated only in part.* In *Kearney* v. *Whitehaven Colliery Co.* (1893), K, a collier employed by W, agreed that he was to receive nothing for a tub containing a certain proportion of dirt. It was held: (i) such a contract was illegal under section 12 of the Coal Mines Regulation Act 1887, which allowed the employer either to pay for the whole tub, or to deduct for extraneous materials, but (ii) this illegality did not dispense K from observing the contractual requirement of fourteen days' notice when leaving his employment. *Note* the dictum of A. L. Smith L.J. at p. 714 of the report: "The rule is, that if the consideration is tainted with illegality, either in whole or in part, all the promises depending upon that consideration must fail; but if the consideration be not tainted with illegality, either in whole or in part, then if one of the several promises depending upon it be illegal in itself and the others legal, the legal promises stand, and may be enforced against the person who has made them."

Restraint of trade

For our purposes, the restraint of trade imposed upon the employee is important. A distinction is drawn between the inevitable restraint imposed upon an employee during the currency of his employment and the restraint which becomes operative when he leaves his employment. In *Esso Petroleum Co.* v. *Harper's Garage (Stourport)* (1968), Lord Pearce justified the former type of restraint, because it aims at procuring the worker's "absorption," whereas the latter type of restraint seeks to achieve the "sterilisation" of his working capacity. In *Young* v. *Timmins* (1831), a covenant not to work for others during the currency of the contract was held to be unlawful as a partial restraint of trade not supported by consideration in that there was no obligation to furnish work. This case was not overruled by the *Esso* case and demonstrates that, exceptionally, such a restraint may be held invalid "if during the contract one of the parties is too unilaterally fettered" (*per* Lord Pearce at pp. 328–329 of the report). **69**

Since the decision in *Mason* v. *Provident Clothing & Supply Co. Ltd.* (1913) (which put beyond doubt that there is no distinction between general and partial covenants) all covenants in restraint of trade are prima facie void unless they can be justified as reasonable (a) in the interests of the parties, and (b) in the public interest. The canons of reasonableness are not fixed like the laws of the Medes and the Persians, so that in endeavouring to reflect changing social and economic conditions a balance has to be struck between freedom of contract and freedom to work. An employer cannot protect himself from competition from his former employee, nor from the latter's exercise of the skill and experience acquired during his employment, but he may, by a properly drawn covenant, protect his trade secrets and his business connection. Paradoxically, the more the employer strives to protect himself the greater the likelihood that the covenant will be struck down as excessive in scope, area or time. Thus, in *Commercial Plastics Ltd.* v. *Vincent* (1965), a covenant was struck down because (a) it was world-wide in effect when such wide protection was unnecessary and (b) it purported to restrain the former employee in a field of work other than that upon which he had been engaged.

70 An example of the employer who did not overreach himself is provided by *Home Counties Dairies Ltd.* v. *Skilton* (1970), where the Court of Appeal upheld a covenant in a milkman's service contract under which the milkman agreed that for one year after leaving his employer's service he would not sell or serve milk or dairy produce to, or solicit orders for milk or dairy produce from, any person who had been a customer of the employer during the last six months of his service to the latter. Upholding an appeal against the refusal of an injunction to restrain the employee, who had left his employment, from working on the same round for a rival milkman, the court found that this was not a covenant against competition by an ex-employee (which would have been void), but legitimate protection of the employer's trade connection. Although the covenant did not say so, construction of the contract as a whole showed that it was not intended to prevent employment in some other trade, *e.g.* in a grocery business which sold butter and cheese. The argument that the covenant was unreasonably wide to the extent that it purported to prevent the ex-employee from serving a customer of his late employer who had, for example, moved from Surrey to Leeds was rejected because such a possibility was "far-fetched" and outside the contemplation of the parties. Reality, and not semantics or metaphysics, was the concern of the court. Similarly, short shrift was bestowed on the argument that the covenant, if applied, would apply in relation to persons who were not customers of the first employer at the time when his employee left his service. As had been pointed out in *G. W. Plowman & Son Ltd.* v. *Ash* (1964) at p. 572 of the report, the first employer may reasonably hope that his customers will return and may protect himself against the frustration of that hope by his ex-employee.

71 It must not be assumed that an employer who omits to secure an express covenant from his employee is completely at the mercy of the latter's right to compete. An employee is under a duty of fidelity to his employer (see para. 134, below), which duty may be enforced even after the employee has left his employer's service, *e.g.* where he makes use of a list of customers or of some confidential information belonging to his late-employer which he was perspicacious or fortunate enough to acquire as an employee. It has been suggested that the reason why employers insist on an express covenant rather than rely on the implied contractual duty of the employee is to be found in the deterrent effect of the former (R. W. Rideout, *Principles of Labour Law*, p. 91). Another reason may lie in the employer's psychological need to have in "black and white" the protection of his vital business interests.

Severance

It is possible for the court, without writing a new covenant, to **72**
strike out words from an unduly wide covenant or to construe a covenant as containing two or more provisions some of which are struck out. This is termed *severance*. An example of severance is provided by *Scorer* v. *Seymour-Jones* (1966), in which the plaintiff, employed as a negotiator-clerk in the defendant's Kingsbridge office (they also had an office in Dartmouth), set up business as an auctioneer-estate agent within five miles of Kingsbridge after his dismissal by the defendants, despite a covenant that he would not engage in any capacity in the business of auctioneer, surveyor or estate agent within a five-mile radius of the defendant's Kingsbridge or Dartmouth offices. It was held that the defendants were entitled to protection as regards their Kingsbridge clientèle, since the plaintiff had acquired "contacts and information" of the recurring clientèle and also concerning properties in that area, but that the covenant must be struck out in relation to Dartmouth.

Surprisingly, the public interest criterion has only been raised in two cases. In *Wyatt* v. *Kreglinger & Fernau* (1933), the plaintiff, a former employee, sued the defendants for breach of contract in discontinuing his pension. The action failed for reasons which are hard to elicit, but it was agreed in the Court of Appeal that if there was a contract it was contrary to public policy in that the plaintiff's agreement not to re-enter the wool trade would, if enforced, have the effect, according to Scrutton L.J., of depriving the country of the services of a man of sixty years of age who was quite competent to enter into business. The promise to pay the pension and the promise not to compete were interdependent promises so that the plaintiff could not enforce the former. Despite criticisms, this case was followed in *Bull* v. *Pitney-Bowes Ltd.* (1967), where it was said that the criticisms were based upon economic conditions which no longer prevailed.

Employee not a party to restrictive agreement

73 The doctrine of restraint of trade may operate to the benefit of a worker not a party to the restrictive agreement, as is shown by *Kores Manufacturing Co. Ltd.* v. *Kolok Manufacturing Co. Ltd.* (1959), where mutual covenants entered into between two companies, whereby each undertook not to employ the other's former employees for five years after they had left the other's employment, were held to be excessive in that they affected all employees, irrespective of whether they possessed secret or confidential information or not, and also because of the unreasonable duration of the restriction. This was an action between employers. May an *employee* claim that such a restriction is invalid? *Eastham* v. *Newcastle United Football Club* (1964), shows that at least a declaration may be obtained. In that case, the plaintiff, a professional footballer employed by the defendants, obtained a declaration that the "retain and transfer" system was in restraint of trade.

Other vitiating elements

74 The contract of employment may be affected by some element rendering it either voidable, such as misrepresentation, duress or undue influence, or rendering it void, such as mistake. The contract of employment is not one of the utmost good faith (*uberrimae fidei*) so that there is no obligation to volunteer adverse information, *e.g.* in *Fletcher* v. *Krell* (1872), where the summary dismissal of a governess, discovered to be a divorcée, was held to be wrongful in that concealment of a fact (not amounting to fraud) did not enable the contract to be avoided (nor does the suppression of a criminal conviction necessarily justify summary dismissal—*Hands* v. *Simpson, Fawcett & Co. Ltd.* (1928)). In *Bell* v. *Lever Bros. Ltd.* (1932), the House of Lords refused to set aside what would now be termed a "golden handshake" upon the discovery of facts which would have justified immediate dismissal. "If he," asked Lord Atkin, referring to the employer, "gives his cook a month's wages in lieu of notice can he, on discovering that the cook has been pilfering the tea and sugar, claim the return of the month's wages?" Lord Atkin thought not.

Freedom of Contract

75 Freedom of contract remains the shaky pedestal upon which British labour law rests. The right to select the person with whom one hopes to enter a contract, and the autonomous right of the parties to a contract to settle terms mutually acceptable to each, are seen as the legal postulates of a free society. Apart from war, when the direction of labour and capital are necessary to mobilise a nation's resources, the State is expected to use the carrot rather than the stick to achieve objectives such as the modernisation of industry or the elimination of regional distortions. The Industry Act 1972 contains an impressive array of financial carrots.

Besides this, the use of forced labour is now proscribed by the international community. Conventions and Recommendations of the International Labour Organisation, and the European Convention for the Protection of Human Rights and Fundamental Freedoms (ratified by the United Kingdom) provide their own method of enforcement. With a view to promoting the free movement of workers, Articles 3 and 48 of the Treaty of Rome, and Regulations made thereunder, provide for the abolition of obstacles to the free movement of persons and services and for the abolition of any discrimination based on nationality between workers of the member states as regards employment, remuneration and other working conditions. The term "workers" includes not only manual workers, but all those employed under a contract of service, and "discrimination" has been interpreted to include "social factors," such as housing, ownership and family rights. The social insurance position of the migrant worker has also been protected. 76

Although it has long been the rule that anyone setting foot on English soil is automatically a free man (*Somersett's* case (1772)) it was settled in *Nokes* v. *Doncaster Amalgamated Collieries Ltd.* (1940), that the "contractualist" employee cannot be transferred like a chattel. If labour is an "input" to the economist and a "prime cost" to the cost accountant, the contract of employment is, to the lawyer, an unassignable "chose in action." In the *Nokes* case, Lord Atkin affirmed the fundamental common law freedom of the citizen to choose his employer, a freedom carrying with it the corollary that his services, once secured, cannot be transferred without his assent, adding that this freedom is "the main difference between a servant and a serf." It has been pointed out that a person who has, or acquires, a controlling interest in the share capital of a company may effect far-reaching changes in that company without the consent of its employees. Lord Atkin's remark that "The identity of the company is preserved," is countered by the exclamation "But how tenuous and unreal this identity is!" (L. C. B. Gower, *Modern Company Law*, 3rd ed., p. 201). 77

It may be interposed here that for the purposes of vicarious liability, it is sometimes necessary to determine who the employer is at a particular moment of time. An excavator with driver may be hired out by Employer A to B and cause tortious harm in the course of his employment whilst performing work for B. Although it is possible that A might remain as the "general employer," he may be 78 able to discharge the onus of proof that the driver has come under a degree of control from B sufficient to render the latter vicariously liable for the driver's tort *e.g.* where the driver negligently injures a person whilst working under B's directions and control. The presumption is that the employee remains in the employment of his "general employer" and only rarely has the employer been able to show that a transfer of liability has taken place. Even where he succeeds in doing this and the employee is treated as the temporary employer's servant "*pro hac vice*," the use of this latter phrase ought not to conceal that what has taken place is an artificial transfer of liability and not the transfer of the employee's contract of service. It is noticeable that the decision whether or not such an artificial transfer of liability has taken place revolves largely on the question of control, in contrast to the wider-ranging inquiry which is used to determine the existence of a contract of employment (see para. 21, above).

The distinction between the vicarious liability of the "temporary" employer and the assignment of a contract of service was referred to by Lord Parker C.J. in *Smith* v. *Blandford Gee Cementation Co. Ltd.* (1970), at p. 163 of the report, his lordship stressing that a contract of service cannot be assigned unilaterally; there must be a discharge of the old agreement of service and a novation, a new contract formed." In that case the Divisional Court was confronted with the dilemma of a man who had indubitably entered into a contract of service with the National Coal Board but who, for all practical purposes, had entered into the employment of a company which performed work for the N.C.B. The court was able to escape from its dilemma by finding an estoppel against the company, based on its conduct and the issuance of a statutory notice under the Contracts of Employment Act 1963 showing itself as employer, which prevented it from denying that it was the man's employer, a finding which dispensed the court from the task of determining whether or not a true novation had occurred.

79 If then, freedom of contract remains the rule, it is a rule which, if applied as a juridical concept in a situation of social or economic inequality, can produce undesirable results; indeed, some would say that freedom of contract between unequals is meaningless. The growth of trade unionism is explicable only as a means of opposing the economic strength of the employer with "countervailing force." Freedom of contract may produce evils such as bad industrial conditions or "trucking," which need ameliorative statutes—factory legislation or truck legislation. Such legislation is more effective to prescribe standards than collective bargaining which is necessarily fragmented in scope.

We live, as Lord Wright reminded us, in a selfish society. Special groups may require special protection. Women and young persons are protected as regards hours of work and conditions by legislation, such as the Factories Act 1961, and the Mines and Quarries Act 1954. Minimum wage legislation (see Chapter 3) protects those for whom there is either no collective bargaining machinery or machinery which is inadequate to secure minimum pay. The Equal Pay Act 1970 (see Chapter 3) seeks to redress the inequality between men and women as regards terms and conditions of employment, including but not, despite the title to the Act, limited to terms concerning pay. The problems of the disabled with regard to vocational training and employment are dealt with by the Disabled Persons (Employment) Acts 1944 and 1958. Section 9 (1) of the 1944 Act requires those employing a substantial number of employees to give employment to a specified quota of persons registered as being handicapped by disablement. In a selfish society, ritual deprecation of the plight of the disabled is not enough—freedom of contract must be limited, although it is noteworthy that the Acts do not confer any actionable rights upon individuals.

The Race Relations Act 1968 makes it unlawful to discriminate **80**
on grounds of colour, race or ethnic or national origins against any person (a) who is seeking employment, (b) during employment, or (c) who is dismissed from employment. The Act is much narrower in scope than the American Civil Rights Act 1964 and does not strike at discrimination based on class, politics or religion. It has been argued that discrimination on religious grounds might be caught by the Act where religion is linked in a unique way with race or ethnic origins as seems to be the case with persons of the Jewish faith. That "national origins" is not synonymous with nationality is demonstrated by *London Borough of Ealing* v. *Race Relations Board* (1972), where the House of Lords held that the exclusion of a Pole from a housing list because he was not a British subject within the British Nationality Act 1948 was upheld on the basis that this was not discrimination by reference to "national origins," but discrimination by reference to nationality, and therefore outside the ambit of the Act (but see Art. 48 of Treaty of Rome, referred to above). Discrimination signifies treatment less favourable than that accorded to other persons, subject to the reservation that "separate but equal" treatment is equiparated with less favourable treatment. Discrimination in employment by an employee in the course of his employment (by, for example, a personnel officer) is attributed independently of knowledge to the employer whose liability is then additional to that of the employee: it is, however, a defence to legal proceedings if the employer can prove that he took such steps as were

reasonably practicable to prevent the employee from doing discriminatory acts of the same description as the act in question.

81 The emphasis upon conciliation rather than legal enforcement explains the elaborate procedure under which complaints of discrimination are processed. Although a complaint of discrimination can be made to the Secretary of State for Employment, the Race Relations Board or a conciliation committee, it is for the Secretary of State to decide whether he will refer the complaint to a body of persons suitable to consider the complaint (in practice this will mean existing joint industrial grievance machinery and the like), or, if he is not satisfied that there is such a body, to the Race Relations Board for investigation by it or a conciliation committee. The civil sanctions of injunction, damages, or revision of contracts, are sought by the Board and not by the complainant. In the case of injunctive relief, the court must be satisfied that in addition to the unlawful act in question the defendant has in the past engaged in like discriminatory acts and also that he is likely to engage in such conduct in the future. In the case of damages, the Board is accountable for damages received to the person on whose behalf they were obtained.

82 The rather complex procedures for conciliation are given in Schedule 2, dealing with complaints relating to employment; Schedule 3, Part II, concerns investigations relating to employment where no complaint has been made. Although civil proceedings under the Act can only be brought before certain nominated county courts sitting with assessors "and not otherwise" (s. 19 (1), (2), (7)), the House of Lords held in the *Ealing* case (discussed above) that the High Court still had jurisdiction to make a declaration at the suit of the borough council against whom a complaint of discriminatory treatment had been made to the Race Relations Board. "Section 19 and sections 20 to 24 all deal with the enforcement of the Act by the Race Relations Board. I can find nothing in the Act which ousts the jurisdiction of the courts to grant a declaration" said Viscount Dilhorne ((1972), at p. 375 of the report). This decision can be explained as necessary on the facts of the particular case to enable a local authority to know how its housing policy stood. If it were extended to confer a direct right of recourse for a declaration in all circumstances, the whole purpose of the 1968 Act, which was to obtain conciliation rather than enforcement, would be subverted. It would be of little practical consequence to say that because a declaration affords no coercive relief it does not rank as "enforcement"; a declaration of the High Court has a persuasive effect amounting almost to "enforcement."

83 Discrimination in connection with employment which would otherwise be unlawful is permitted in certain exceptional cases.

Although the initial exemption of employers with small numbers of employees ended on November 25, 1972, other exemptions remain. The first concerns those who in good faith discriminate in the engagement of employees, or in the selection of employees for work within the undertaking or part thereof, for the purpose of preserving a reasonable balance amongst persons of different racial groups. Other exceptions relate to employment in a private household, employment outside Great Britain or on a ship or aircraft outside Great Britain, the provision of separate sleeping rooms, mess rooms or sanitary accommodation in respect of employment on a ship and, finally, employment which requires the attributes of a particular nationality or descent.

Discrimination on the prohibited grounds (above) in the admission, treatment and expulsion of members of organisations or employer or workers or other organisations concerned with the carrying on of trade, businesses, professions or occupations is unlawful.

III. Apprenticeship

The contract of apprenticeship has as its "substantial object" the **84**
vocational training of the aspirant to a trade or profession. Learning, rather than serving, differentiates apprenticeship from employment proper and this carries with it a correlative duty upon the master to instruct. The apprentice who has served his time acquires a status which "gets him off to a good start in the labour market" (*per* Widgery L.J. in *Dunk* v. *George Waller* (1970), at p. 169 of the report). Whilst it may formerly have been the case, as the moral philosopher, Paley, put it, that "Instruction is their hire," the modern apprentice expects and receives payment for his services, albeit at a rate less than that payable to a "time-served" man. Because of his inexperience, the employer is under a higher duty of care than would be the case with experienced employees (*Kerry* v. *Carter* (1969)).

It is remarkable that the legal definition of apprenticeship has survived the vicissitudes of medieval guild apprenticeship, of what has been termed the period of "statutory apprenticeship" (from the Statute of Artificers 1563 to the Apprentices Act 1814, during which a seven-year apprenticeship was required by law) to the modern system of "voluntary apprenticeship" to the employer. The individualistic, contractual basis of modern apprenticeship is in practice qualified by trade union control of entrants and their skills. More than 100 national agreements concerning apprenticeship are registered with the Department of Employment.

Features of apprenticeship

85 As a contractual relationship apprenticeship exhibits certain peculiar features which mark it off not only from contracts in general but from contracts of service in particular. Although an adult may be an apprentice (*R.* v. *Inhabitants of Edingale* (1830)), most apprentices are, or begin their apprenticeship as, minors. The age of majority was reduced from twenty-one to eighteen years by the Family Law Reform Act 1969, s. 1 (1). Contracts of employment or apprenticeship, *if* beneficial to a minor, are exceptions to the general contractual incapacity of minors. Individually disadvantageous terms do not render the contract voidable if, taken as a whole, the contract is for the minor's benefit (*cf. Corn* v. *Matthews* (1893), in which a contract containing a term that the apprentice should not be entitled to wages in the event of a lock-out was held to be voidable).

We have already seen that the apprenticeship contract may be concluded in writing or by deed. Since, as we shall see, it would appear that the apprentice cannot generally be sued upon the covenants in the agreement, it is common for the parent or guardian to sign the agreement as well with a view to the due performance of the agreement, possibly with liability as surety for a stated amount. The advantage is that, in the event of non-performance by the apprentice, the master may sue the parent or guardian in damages or enforce the security. If the agreement sets forth the particulars of employment required by section 4 of the Contracts of Employment Act 1972, including the date when the contract expires and a copy thereof is made available as required by that section, no separate written statement of particulars need be given. The statutory periods of notice specified in section 1 (1) of the Act do not apply in the case of apprentices holding fixed-term contracts, other than contracts for a term certain of four weeks or less (which are treated as contracts of indefinite duration and therefore subject to the periods of statutory notice—s. 1 (4)).

The master's remedies for breach

86 Whilst the apprentice may sue the master for damages for breach of contract, the master's remedies against the defaulting apprentice are more circumscribed. In the absence of local custom, the apprentice, unlike the employee, cannot be sued in damages for wrongful departure or neglect of his duties, a rule which is historically ascribable to the master's right to chastise the apprentice or to bring him before the justices (*Gylbert* v. *Fletcher* (1630)).

Yet another historical common law appanage was the rule that the master could not, in the absence of express contractual provision, treat the contract as ended by reason of the apprentice's fundamental breach, *e.g.* for persistent absence or grave disobedience.

However, although it would appear (and this view is controverted) that the master cannot take the active step of dismissing the apprentice for misconduct in the absence of an express or customary term, he may, and this amounts in practice to a form of rescission, fall back on the passive measure of refusing to perform *his* obligations so that, when sued by the apprentice, he can plead the apprentice's default as a defence. In *Learoyd* v. *Brook* (1891), the master, when he discovered that his apprentice was an habitual thief, declined to continue the apprenticeship. A. L. Smith J. agreed that in an ordinary apprenticeship deed the master's covenants are independent, *i.e.* not dependent upon performance by the apprentice of his covenants, but added that, "Where an apprentice by his own wilful act prevents a master from teaching him, the master can set this up as a defence when sued upon his covenant to keep, teach, and maintain the apprentice, irrespective of the question whether the apprentice has performed his obligations under the deed or not."

In similarly archaic vein are the remedies conferred upon the **87**
master by the Employers and Workmen Act 1875, section 6 of which gives courts of summary jurisdiction the same powers as in employer and workman cases. This Act applies to apprentices to the business of a workman where either no premium is charged, or, if charged, does not exceed £25. The exaction of a premium is now extremely rare, even in the professions. Disputes between an apprentice to whom the Act applies and his master, arising out of or incidental to their relation as such, may be heard by a court of summary jurisdiction. In addition to their powers to adjust and set off the claims of the parties as in the case of workmen (subject, however, to a jurisdictional limit of £10 per claim), the justices may rescind the instrument of apprenticeship with such order for the repayment of any premium, in whole or in part, as they think just. Section 7 enables the justices to make an order against a surety in damages for breach of the apprenticeship contract, not exceeding in amount the limit (if any) to which he is liable under the instrument. The Draconian and apparently ignored powers of justices to order the apprentice to perform his duties, and to order his imprisonment for non-compliance with the same, were swept away by section 11 (*b*) of the Family Law Reform Act 1969.

In general, breach of the contract of employment ceased to be a crime in 1875. One of the exceptions which remains is the anachronistic crime of wilfully and without lawful excuse failing to provide food, clothing and medical aid to apprentices (Conspiracy and

Protection of Property Act 1875, s. 6), a crime which survives in theory despite the virtual disappearance of the apprentice who "lives in" and the advent of socialised medicine.

Termination of the relationship

88 Apart from the completion of apprenticeship, the relationship may end by reason of the death or serious illness of either master or apprentice, the dissolution of partnership, the winding up of a company and the bankruptcy of the master (the adjudication in bankruptcy of the master operates as a complete discharge of the indentures if either the bankrupt or the apprentice gives notice—Bankruptcy Act 1914, s. 34; the trustee in bankruptcy has certain powers, *e.g.* to repay a fee or to transfer indentures). Diminution of the master's business need not, *per se*, terminate the apprenticeship, in that it may still be possible to give instruction (*Batty* v. *Monks* (1865)).

What is the position where the cessation or diminution of business, or its removal elsewhere, renders the apprentice redundant? If an implied term to keep the business going can be found, the premature determination of a fixed-term contract excuses the apprentice from his obligation to perform the contract and confers upon him a right to damages. That there may, in certain circumstances, be such an implied term is shown in *Turner* v. *Goldsmith* (1891), a case concerning ordinary employment, but nevertheless applicable to apprenticeship. The wrongful dismissal of an apprentice, including a "constructive dismissal" in the form of wrongful termination of the contract by closing down the business, entitles the apprentice to claim damages on a scale more liberal than that used in connection with employees (on which see para. 260, below). This is borne out by *Dunk* v. *George Waller* (above) in which an apprentice, who had been wrongfully dismissed at a time when fifteen months of his four years' apprenticeship remained, was awarded damages which included not only loss of earnings and training during the fifteen months, but also loss of future prospects. Unlike an ordinary employee who merely loses his job on dismissal, an apprentice additionally loses the status which he would have attained as a "time-served" man, and for this he must, notwithstanding the difficulty of assessment, receive recompense.

89 On the other hand, the contract of apprenticeship, like other contracts, is subject to the possibility that it may be frustrated by some external event. Apart from remedies as to return of premium under the Employers and Workmen Act 1875 (below), the common law provides that an apprentice who has received no benefit will be entitled to a return of the whole of his premium on grounds of failure of consideration (but see *Steinberg* v. *Scala* (*Leeds*) *Ltd.* (1923), for a useful reminder of the danger of assuming too readily a "failure of consideration" in connection with contracts by minors).

Additionally, the apprentice, since he is included in the category **90**
"employee," is prima facie entitled to a redundancy payment if he is otherwise eligible, *viz.* has a minimum of 104 weeks of continuous employment, excluding employment under the age of eighteen years. By virtue of section 15 of the Redundancy Payments Act 1965, an apprentice engaged under a fixed-term contract for two years or more is not entitled to a payment in respect of non-renewal if, before the expiry of his contract, he has agreed in writing to forgo his claim (without prejudice, however, to his claim for premature determination of the contract).

Industrial training

Industrial training in this country has been traditionally carried **91**
out by individual employers. This resulted in considerable unevenness in the standards of training from firm to firm and the emergence of a chronic shortage of suitably qualified skilled labour. To cure these defects, the Industrial Training Act 1964 imposed new responsibilities upon industry in the matter of training by establishing a Central Training Council and separate Industrial Training Boards for industry (of which there were, in 1972, twenty-seven statutory Boards covering some 15 million persons, *i.e.* 80 per cent. of those within the Act, apart from non-statutory Boards for local government and the merchant navy). The mainspring of the new scheme was a levy/grant system under which the levies on employers in the different industries were used to enable the Boards to make grants or loans to those employers who provided courses or facilities approved by the appropriate Board. Employers who neglected their training responsibilities paid the levy but got back little or nothing in the form of grants.

There is little doubt that the scheme with its financial carrots and financial sticks has done much to improve the quality of industrial training. At the same time, it came to be recognised that the scheme had its defects. It failed to deal with training problems across different industries and found the small firm an intractable problem. It still left a considerable number of persons without proper industrial training despite the fact that they were within the scope of the Act. The levy/grant system was unpopular chiefly because of the large number of "paper transactions" in which no money changed hands.

Improvements in the 1964 scheme were announced in the consultative document, *Training for the Future*, issued in 1972 by the

Department of Employment. Amongst these are (1) a new Training Opportunities Scheme (now in operation) which aims to train 100,000 men and women a year (60–70,000 by 1975); (2) the establishment of a National Training Agency as a departmental agency to co-ordinate the work of the Industrial Training Boards (which will continue in existence); and (3) the phasing out of the levy/grants system after 1973 accompanied by greater use of public funds through the National Training Agency.

92 Concurrently with the establishment of Training Boards, the work of the Government Training Centres has been expanded to provide training and re-training for those who need skills. At the same time, it is generally recognised that the G.T.C.s are only scratching the surface of the potentially large demand for re-training facilities, although plans for another 3,000 places, additional to the 11,000 places already provided, are now being put into effect. The proposed figure of 100,000 mentioned in the preceding paragraph includes facilities to be provided in colleges of further education. From a recent survey carried out on behalf of the Department of Employment, it appears that trainees in G.T.C.s are much younger on the average than the male working population and that most of them are successful in obtaining jobs at the conclusion of their training except for a substantial minority of nearly 17 per cent. which experiences difficulty in obtaining employment. Union acceptance of the re-trained worker is not generally a serious problem, bearing in mind that 36 per cent. of trainees go to employments in which there is no union organisation, although it is noteworthy that trainees entering the engineering industry experience some setbacks in this respect (O.P.C.S., Social Survey Division, *Post-Training Careers of Government Training Centre Trainees*, 1972).

93 Complementary to the industrial training given in such centres, or under arrangements controlled by a Training Board, is the vocational training given in establishments of further education, either on a full or part-time basis. The raising of the school-leaving age from fifteen to sixteen from September 1, 1972, puts off for a further year the time when the child enters industrial or vocational training as described above. There are those who foresee the time when post-school training will be put upon a compulsory, full-time basis using special training centres and trained instructors rather than a system which still retains the philosophy of "exposure to the job" or "sitting by Nellie."

CHAPTER 2

THE RELATIONSHIP
(A) AS BETWEEN THE PARTIES
(B) AS REGARDS THIRD PARTIES

(A) *The Relationship Between the Parties*

IT will be convenient to examine in this chapter the employment **94**
relationship, first, as regards the complex right-duty relationships between the parties and, secondly, as regards the rights and liabilities of third persons. Naturally the parties to the contract are primarily interested in their rights and duties, *e.g.* the employee who is injured at work, or who is refused a "reference" on leaving it, will wish to know if he has any redress against his employer should the latter refuse any assistance. But other persons may find that they have rights and liabilities in certain circumstances. Thus the lorry driver who negligently knocks down a pedestrian commits a tort, but the pedestrian will be more interested in learning that an action may also lie against the lorry driver's employer, who will normally command greater resources. Conversely, a third person who induces a party to a contract to commit a breach of that contract may be guilty of a tort, since the law preserves the right of parties "to have their contractual relations preserved inviolate without unlawful interference by others" (Lord Denning M.R. in *Emerald* v. *Lowthian* (1966)). Again, a third person may carelessly injure an employee, so that his employer is deprived of valuable services and may further be obliged to pay wages during the employee's absence from work.

The internal relations between the parties are primarily fixed by **95**
the express terms of the contract. Because contracts of employment are infrequently comprehensive in scope, the courts have managed in their necessarily casuistic manner to evolve principles regulating the reciprocal rights and duties of the parties, principles which, in many foreign countries, are explicitly set forth in a Labour Code. Although many matters are regulated by statute, it is true, as Professor O. Kahn-Freund reminds us, that "statutes are not the primary factor in filling the blank of the empty 'contract of employment.' The primary factor is of course the collective agreement," which often deals with matters left untouched by the contract of employment, such as the effect of interruptions caused by bad weather, power cuts, transport difficulties, and so forth (*Labour and the Law*, pp. 23–24). We have already seen that the "substantive

part" of the collective agreement may become part of the individual contracts by incorporation into the latter (see above, para. 49). The Code of Practice made under the Industrial Relations Act 1971 provides a guide, cynics would say a "Sermon on the Mount," to good relations between management and labour. The rules set out in the Code, *e.g.* those relating to disciplinary procedures, are not laws, for the breach of which proceedings can be taken. Breach of the rules in the Code, however, is admissible in proceedings before the Industrial Court or an industrial tribunal. The T.U.C., also not to be outdone, has produced its own *Guide to Good Industrial Relations*.

It is proposed to deal with the common law fixing the duties of the employer and the employee and, on grounds of convenience if not conceptual clarity, with the individual rights conferred by the Industrial Relations Act 1971. The employer's duty with regard to remuneration, including equal pay, is discussed in Chapter 3.

I. The Employer's Duties

96 The most important of the employer's duties is to take reasonable precautions to secure the physical safety of his employees (a duty which sounds in contract as well as in tort), but we will first briefly discuss the extent of the employer's duty in regard to the provision of work, in indemnifying his employee, in giving him a "character" and so forth.

1. The provision of work

97 Although it may seem strange on first impression, there is prima facie no duty upon the employer to provide his employee with work.

"It is true that a contract of employment does not necessarily, or perhaps normally, oblige the master to provide the servant with work. Provided I pay my cook her wages regularly she cannot complain if I choose to take any or all of my meals out": *Collier* v. *Sunday Referee Publishing Co. Ltd.* (1940), *per* Asquith J. at p. 650 of the report. The rule is reasonable since it may be impossible for certain employers to ensure that work is always available, as in building or shipbuilding. To the general rule there are exceptions:

(1) Failure to provide work may involve not only loss of remuneration (where this depends on the work done) but also loss of publicity. Damages taking into account the latter factor were awarded in *Herbert Clayton & Jack Waller Ltd.* v. *Oliver* (1930), in which an American actor, who had been given one of the leading parts in a musical comedy, was held to have rightly refused an

inferior part. The *Clayton* case (and earlier cases, *e.g. Clayton-Greene* v. *De Couville* (1920)) might be better treated under breach of contract since they raise not only the question of providing work, but also the question of providing work of a type suitable for the employee according to his contract. Thus in *Yetton* v. *Eastwoods Froy Ltd.* (1967), in which a joint managing director was held entitled to refuse the offer of continued employment as assistant managing director, Blain J. adverted to the harm done to the plaintiff's reputation by the publication of his "demotion" in the *Financial Times* as one of the factors justifying the plaintiff in refusing the offer. The breach may take the form of selling the business so that an employee appointed to a "specific office" for a fixed period, *e.g.* as editor, finds that his "office" has vanished (*Collier* case, above).

(2) If the employee's remuneration depends upon his performing **98**
work, as in the case of payment by commission or by piece, failure to provide work would "sterilise" the worker rather than "absorb" him. In *Bauman* v. *Hulton Press Ltd.* (1952), it was held that the defendants "were bound to give the plaintiff a reasonable amount of work to enable him to earn that which the parties must be taken to have contemplated." Likewise, and the inference again is one of fact rather than law, it was held that a workman employed on piece-work who had been given one month's notice but no work was entitled to a reasonable sum (*Devonald* v. *Rosser & Sons* (1906)). A stimulant towards the efficient use of labour is provided by section 6 of the Redundancy Payments Act 1965, which permits of claims for redundancy payments in the event of lay-off or short-time working for certain periods (see *Puttick* v. *John Wright & Sons Ltd.* (1972), discussed below, paras. 191, 302).

2. Indemnity against liabilities and losses

The employee is entitled to be indemnified against all liabilities **99**
and losses which he properly incurs in the performance of his work, as where he is exposed to claims for libel and slander unwittingly committed in the discharge of his work (*Re Famatina Development Corporation Ltd.* (1914)) and similarly where he is entrusted with an unlawful mission on which he embarks without knowing of the illegality, as in *Burrows* v. *Rhodes* (1899), where the plaintiff was induced to take part in the Jameson Raid, or *Gregory* v. *Ford* (1951), where a lorry driver was sent on to the highway in an uninsured lorry (which would not now be an offence by the lorry driver if he neither knew nor had reason to believe that the vehicle was not insured).

3. References

100 The duty to provide a testimonial or "reference" to the departing employee is social rather than legal. If the employer gives a reference, the following main considerations are relevant. First, if the statements made concerning the employee are true, the employer cannot be made civilly liable either for (1) defamation (defined as the publication of a statement which lowers a person's standing in society or which causes him to be shunned or avoided), the reason being that the truth, however harmful, lowers a person's standing to its proper level, or for (2) deceit, for this presupposes a "false statement," and here there is none. Secondly, assuming that a reference does contain defamatory material, the employer may still escape liability if he can show that the statement was made in pursuance of a social duty (as it would be if made to a prospective employer) and without improper motives. In other words the employer must prove that he had, when making the statement, qualified privilege and also the absence of malice. Thirdly, where an unwarrantably eulogistic reference is given (perhaps to speed the employee's departure!), the employer, if he gave the reference knowing it to be false, or recklessly indifferent to its truth or falsehood, may find himself liable, at the suit of the new employer, for deceit. In 1964 the House of Lords decided that liability for negligent misstatement could arise quite apart from any contractual relationship and it would appear that this principle applies in the present context (*Hedley Byrne & Co. Ltd.* v. *Heller & Partners Ltd.* (1964)).

4. Provision of board and lodging

101 The decline in the master's obligation to provide board, lodging and medical attention where necessary typifies the evolution of labour law out of family law. Nowadays it is exceptional for the apprentice or the employee to live with his employer. Unless there is contractual provision to this end, the employer is no longer expected to board and feed his employee, whilst the advent of the welfare state has rendered the duty to provide medical aid otiose. The employer might be liable in negligence for failing to notify the appropriate medical authority should his employee fall sick or meet with an accident. Protective legislation may impose a duty to provide medical facilities, *e.g.* first-aid boxes or medical supervision.

5. Provision of safe system of work

102 The increasing industrialisation of the nineteenth century (and the acceptance of mobility as a thing good in itself) have brought the

problem of the injured worker to the fore. The first half of the nineteenth century revealed judicial uncertainty as to the apportionment of the risks inseparable from the increased scale and tempo of industrial production; it was not until the second half of the century that the law gradually accepted that the worker could not possibly be a self-insurer in relation to the industrial risks which he had to run. The common law evolved rules for employers' liability which drew a distinction between the personal duty of the master and his vicarious liability for the acts and omissions of his servants which caused injury to fellow servants. A master was (and still is) liable for his own personal acts and omissions together with breaches of his "primary duties" to supply a safe system of work, proper appliances and efficient personnel; in these respects there could be fault (*culpa*) since he had a measure of responsibility.

The common law, however, was reluctant to saddle the master with responsibility for the acts or omissions of servants which might cause injury to fellow servants, and developed a doctrine of common employment (or of *collaborateur*) by virtue of which the worker, in the words of Lord Cranworth, must be taken to know "that want of care on the part of a fellow-workman may be injurious or fatal to him, and that against such want of care his employer cannot by possibility protect him" (*Bartonshill Coal Co.* v. *Reid* (1858)). The doctrine of common employment was abolished by section 1 (1) of the Law Reform (Personal Injuries) Act 1948, although the theoretical distinction between personal and vicarious liability remains.

In *Wilson's & Clyde Coal Co.* v. *English* (1938) the employer was **103**
liable for an unsafe system of work in his mine although he had entrusted his responsibility (as he was required to do) to a colliery agent. The triple classification of the employer's duty in that case into duties concerning safe system, plant and appliances, and efficient personnel has been criticised on the grounds that there is only a single duty and, more recently, the tendency has been to consider the employer's duty as one aspect of that general duty in the law of negligence, which "one man owes to another" and which transcends "particular legal categories." Certainly the concept of "safe system of work" had become extremely wide, covering as it did the layout of the work (both for repetitive operations, *e.g.* a car assembly line, or a single operation, *e.g.* loading or unloading a vehicle), activities incidental to the work, *e.g.* washing up a tea-cup, and work outside the employer's immediate control. An example of the latter is provided by *Bradford* v. *Robinson Rentals Ltd.* (1967), in which an employer who had sent a fifty-seven-year old employee on a long journey in an unheated van in very wintry conditions, was held liable for the frostbite suffered as a result of the journey.

The duty to maintain reasonable precautions in addition to installing or specifying them at the outset must be read subject to the test of practicability. In *Wilson* v. *Tyneside Window Cleaning Co.* (1958) the plaintiff, an experienced window-cleaner, was injured when a handle by which he was supporting himself came adrift, causing him to fall. Dismissing the plaintiff's action, the court held that "it would be too heavy a burden to lay on the employers to say that they must inspect all the premises where their men work. If the men are properly taught their job, are provided with proper equipment, warned of dangers and told not to clean defective windows but report the matter, it seems unnecessary to me to lay down that the employer must inspect every window beforehand."

Duty cannot be delegated

104 The "personal" nature of the employer's common law duty implies that the duty is non-delegable, *i.e.* as in *Wilson's & Clyde's* case, above; it is no defence to show that the employer has deputed a servant, agent or independent contractor to install and maintain proper precautions. To admit such a defence would effectively deprive the worker of redress in modern conditions of large-scale enterprise. Of the three duties referred to in *Wilson's & Clyde's* case (above) that relating to plant and appliances has had a chequered history. In *Davie* v. *New Merton Board Mills Ltd.* (1938), the House of Lords resolved a conflict in the cases by holding that an employer incurs no liability in negligence to an employee who has suffered injury by reason of using a defective tool which has been negligently manufactured by a third party, provided such tool has been obtained from a reputable source and the employer has made such inspection of the tool as is reasonable in the circumstances. In its turn the House of Lords decision evoked considerable criticism for the way in which it imposed upon the employee the incubus of proving negligence against someone who might be untraceable, difficult to sue (such as a foreign manufacturer), or even bankrupt. It was pointed out that *Biddle* v. *Truvox Engineering Co. Ltd.* (1952), had already made an inroad on the worker's protection by holding that the vendor or hirer of machines in breach of section 17 (2) of the Factories Act 1937 (now section 17 (2) of the Factories Act 1961), whilst subject to a penalty, incurs no civil liability to employees who might be injured as a result of the breach.

105 To meet these criticisms, the Employer's Liability (Defective Equipment) Act 1969 was passed, after starting as a private member's Bill. This Act provides that an employee who suffers personal injury in the course of his employment in consequence of a defect in equipment provided by his employer for the purposes of the employer's

business may recover damages against his employer if the defect in the equipment is attributed wholly or partly to the fault of a third party, whether identified or not. Once the "fault" of the third party is demonstrated, the injury is deemed to be also attributable to negligence on the part of the employer whose liability is, therefore, in effect, strict, although subject to the defences of contributory negligence, contribution and contract. "Equipment" includes any plant and machinery, vehicle, aircraft and clothing, and it is immaterial if the employer acquired it by purchase, hire or even loan. By erecting some special rules for one of the "triple duties" mentioned in *Wilson's & Clyde's* case, the Act seems to run counter to the judicial trend towards treating negligence as a unity rather than as a "wilderness of single instances."

Reasonable care

The duty is to take reasonable care to protect the safety of the **106**
employee: employers "do not warrant the adequacy of plant, or the competence of fellow-employees, or the propriety of the system of work" (*Wilson's & Clyde's* case, above). "Reasonable foreseeability" serves to demarcate both the scope of the duty of care and liability for harm resulting from breach of that duty. Thus, where a worker, instructed to clean up some viscous liquid which had escaped on to the factory floor and provided with the necessary wherewithal, injured himself by slipping in the execution of this "simple task," he was held disentitled to damages (*Vinnyey* v. *Star Paper Mills* (1965)). Such a decision is in line with Viscount Simonds' deprecation of "any tendency to treat the relation of employer and skilled workman as equivalent to that of nurse and imbecile child." The student will doubtless echo the feeling that we have a "surfeit of authorities" on this subject; in the last few years the courts have treated the application of the broad "reasonable care" formula in individual cases as one of fact and not law.

The vagueness of the formula is its chief merit since it permits of variability; thus the known susceptibilities of particular employees, the nature of the work, industrial practice, the size of the risk, the skill of the worker and the state of scientific knowledge are amongst the factors which have been taken into account. The liability of the employer in *Paris* v. *Stepney Borough Council* (1951), and the non-liability of the employer in *James* v. *Hepworth & Grandage* (1968), can be explained, at least partially, on the basis that, in the former case, the employer knew that a fitter with one eye ran a greater risk of blindness than a person with sight in both eyes, whereas in the latter case the employer did not know that the Jamaican could not read the notices enjoining the wearing of protective clothing. Again, the supplier of a carcinogenic substance may be under a higher duty of care than the manufacturer who uses that substance for manufacturing purposes (*Wright* v. *Dunlop Rubber Co. Ltd.* (1971)).

107 Although there may be a statutory duty to safeguard an employee's property (Factories Act 1961, s. 59: *McCarthy* v. *Daily Mirror Newspapers Ltd.* (1949)), the employer is under no duty of care with regard to the property of employees, in the absence of any assumed liability by reason of contract or otherwise (*Deyong* v. *Sherburn* (1946)).

Vicarious liability for tort of employee

108 The rule that an employer is liable for the torts of his employee committed in the course of his employment (an exception to the legal postulate that liability is personal rather than vicarious) will be dealt with below. Nevertheless, it may briefly be noted here that, with the disappearance of the unloved doctrine of common employment, the employer may be liable to employee A in respect of a tort (not merely the tort of negligence) committed by fellow-employee B in the course of the latter's employment. For legal purposes it matters nothing that the victim happens to be a fellow-employee rather than a third party. As will be seen the "course of employment" test provides difficulties in marginal cases, although perhaps *O'Reilly* v. *National Rail and Tramway Appliances Ltd.* (1966) is scarcely marginal.

109 There the employers were held free of liability to one of their employees who had responded, with predictable results, to an invitation, meant as a practical joke, from a workmate to hit a live shell with a sledgehammer. Although horseplay and practical joking are part of human nature and an employer must take reasonable care to protect workers from the same, the invitation by the workmate was a single act of misbehaviour completely outside the scope of his employment (*cf. Hudson* v. *Ridge Manufacturing Co. Ltd.* (1957), where an employee's propensity to horseplay was known to the employers, and *Chapman* v. *Oakleigh Animal Products Ltd.* (1970), where the employers were held liable to a boy of sixteen and a half years who was injured while complying with a request from a senior employee to put his hand up the spout of a grinding machine to clear a blockage (meant as a practical joke) when the machine was accidentally started)).

Contributory negligence and volenti non fit injuria

110 Assuming prima facie liability (whether personal or vicarious) on the employer's part, two questions arise.

First, does the negligence of the plaintiff worker debar him from recovering? However complicated the answer to this question might have been before 1945, since the Law Reform (Contributory Negligence) Act, in that year, the answer is clear. Section 1 (1) enacts that a claim "shall not be defeated by reason of the fault of the person suffering the damage," with the rider that the damages recoverable against the other party who is partly at fault "shall be reduced to such extent as the court thinks just and equitable having regard to the claimant's share in the responsibility for the damage." The two requirements are:

(1) The plaintiff should himself have been negligent. As regards this, Lord Wright's warning given in 1939 is still relevant:

> "What is all-important is to adapt the standard of what is negligence to the facts, and to give due regard to the actual conditions under which men work in a factory or mine, to the long hours and the fatigue, to the slackening of attention which naturally comes from constant repetition of the same operation, to the noise and confusion in which the man works, to his preoccupation in what he is actually doing at the cost perhaps of some inattention to his own safety" (*Caswell* v. *Powell Duffryn* (1940) at p. 178 of the report).

(2) His negligence must have contributed to his injuries. Nor- **111**
mally, this will mean that the plaintiff will have contributed in the causal sense to the accident, but that this is not always the case is shown in *O'Connell* v. *Jackson* (1972), where a motor-cyclist's failure to wear a crash helmet was held to be contributory negligence notwithstanding that such failure played no causal part in the accident itself. The more normal situation is typified by *Williams* v. *Port of Liverpool Stevedoring Co. Ltd.* (1956). In this case, the plaintiff, one of a gang of six men directed to unload bags from a barge, starting at the top, was injured when a bag fell on him, owing to his (and his colleagues') disregard of instructions, given before the commencement of the work and subsequently renewed. It was held that (1) the employers were vicariously liable for the negligence of the other members of the gang, but (2) the damages would be reduced by half because of the plaintiff's contributory negligence. Two unusual features of this case were (1) the plaintiff himself had been personally instructed to level off the bags and (2) the bold argument that since all six men were equally to blame the plaintiff should receive five-sixths of the damages; an equitable rather than an arithmetical solution was however reached.

Secondly, does consent on the part of the plaintiff affect the **112**
employer's liability? At the outset it should be noted that there is ambiguity in the word "consent," since it may mean (1) consent to

what would otherwise be a tort, *e.g.* a person employed as a sparring partner cannot complain if he is struck a normal blow whilst boxing, and (2) consent to the risk of injury. In either sense there are grounds for saying that consent negatives liability in the first place so that, strictly speaking, it is not a "defence" at all. Towards the end of the nineteenth century, the House of Lords, displaying greater empathy than it had formerly shown with industrial realities, drew a distinction between knowledge of a risk and consent to that risk; a distinction which recognised that workers often prefer to continue working despite risks of which they are aware and possibly fear. Thus in *Bowater* v. *Rowley Regis Corporation* (1944), a carter, injured when the horse bolted, was held to be entitled to damages in respect of the negligence of his employers, who, knowing of the horse's vicious disposition, had overruled his protests; in the pungent words of Goddard L.J., "He was a horsekeeper, not a horsebreaker"! It is submitted that the "defence" of consent (*volenti non fit injuria*) has no application where the employer obtains the employee's agreement to the waiver of the former's primary duties as set out in *Wilson's & Clyde's* case (above, para. 103). This is not the same as saying that an employee cannot agree to run risks, for in certain avocations, such as that of the film stuntman, the nature of the work (reflected in the high rate of remuneration) necessarily entails risk; even then the criteria of *Wilson's & Clyde's* case operate, so that the employer must provide a "safe" system appropriate to the relativities of risk involved.

Assessment of damages

113 In some torts, such as trespass, the plaintiff can sue without proof of damage, but in practice the injured employee will usually be concerned with those torts, almost invariably negligence, in which proof of damage is a necessary ingredient. In this latter connection, to establish a breach of duty is insufficient; the plaintiff must generally go on to show (a) that the damage resulted from such breach (remoteness of damage), and (b) that the damage entitles him to pecuniary compensation (measure of damages; the measure may have been predetermined by the parties as a genuine attempt to pre-estimate the loss (*liquidated damages*) or, as is usual, left for the court to assess (*unliquidated damages*)). Thus, under (a) an employer will not be held liable to an employee who exacerbates a damaged foot (for which the employer is liable) by walking on it too soon in defiance of doctor's orders.

Damages are of two sorts: *general damages*, being compensation which the law presumes to have resulted from the defendant's tort, and *special damages*, which must be claimed and proved with exactitude, *e.g.* claims for medical expenses, travelling expenses and loss of wages already incurred.

General damages include loss of future earning capacity, loss of expectation of life (by which is meant not loss of years on an actuarial basis, but loss of prospective happiness), pain and suffering subjectively experienced, and medical expenses (ignoring private benevolence or public benevolence in the form of a "free" health service: *Daish* v. *Wauton* (1972)). Although it is convenient to itemise claims under the foregoing heads, the items are not separate heads of compensation but only a fair and reasonable way of arriving at what is composite figure made up of several parts (*Fletcher* v. *Autocar & Transporters* (1968), a reminder against the danger of overlapping if the separate items are merely added up). The removal of the task of assessing such items in monetary terms from juries has done much to clarify the necessarily pragmatic principles upon which the assessment rests as well as producing greater uniformity (amounting, in a sense, almost to a "tariff") in the amount of awards for particular forms of loss. **114**

Loss of earnings, or rather loss of earning capacity, is easier to quantify than loss of happiness. In assessing the former, the courts capitalise the damages by the traditional method of multiplier and multiplicand; the multiplier being the number of years which the plaintiff might otherwise have been expected to work, the multiplicand being the annual amount of the loss which he is expected to suffer. In determining each of these a wide range of factors is taken into account; some of which, such as the likelihood of promotion or the expectation of increments, go to increase the damages, whilst others, such as war, accident, ill-health and the possibility of alternative employment, are discounting factors. In not using an actuarial basis for the estimation of damages, and in ignoring the likely effect of inflation on lump sum awards, the courts have been the butt of some criticism. Notwithstanding this, they have declined to substitute the actuarial method for the traditional method, although they accept that the former may sometimes furnish a useful cross-check on the latter (*Mitchell* v. *Mullholland* (1971)). On inflation, their attitude is ambivalent, some judges taking the view that to exclude the likely effect of inflation is unrealistic, whilst others consider that money should be treated as retaining its value at the date of judgment. **115**

The present confused state of the law is due to the lack of any consistent principle. By asking the question "What should the plaintiff receive?" the courts have evolved the principle that the defendant ought to pay for the loss which he has caused, ignoring "collateral benefits," which is really a question-begging formulation. In answering the separate question "What should the defendant pay?" the courts make judgments on public policy and on what is "just and fair." The present casuistry needs urgent reform and has led to an examination of the problem by the Law Commission for England and Wales.

116 An action for damages for personal injury (including death) caused by negligence, nuisance or breach of duties must be brought within three years (as opposed to six years, which is the normal period of limitation for actions in tort) by virtue of section 2 (1) of the Law Reform (Limitation of Actions, etc.) Act 1954. Because of the danger that the victim might not know that his injury was attributable to negligence, nuisance, or breach of duty, within the three-year period, the Limitation Act 1963 (an Act which, according to Lord Reid, has a "strong claim to being the worst drafted Act on the statute book": *Smith* v. *Central Asbestos Co. Ltd.* (1972)), permitted the court to increase the period by twelve months, a period which has now been further increased to three years by the Law Reform (Miscellaneous Provisions) Act 1971, s. 1. In the *Smith* case (above), the House of Lords held that the employee did not know that the material facts of his case were "facts of a decisive character" until such time as he had reasonably obtained advice on his legal rights.

117 The hopeful litigant will learn that the damages so assessed represent a theoretical *maximum* from which further reductions may be made, as follows. Section 2 (1) of the Law Reform (Personal Injuries) Act 1948 requires that in assessing damages for personal injury there shall be taken into account against any loss of earnings or profits which has accrued or probably will accrue to the injured person from the injuries one-half of the value of any rights which have accrued or probably will accrue to him in respect of industrial injuries benefit, industrial disablement benefit or sickness benefit for the five years beginning with the time when the cause of action accrued, and regard shall be had to the total damages without taking into account questions of contributory negligence or reductions by virtue of agreement. Section 2 is an exception to the new system of industrial injuries insurance introduced in 1946 under which the benefits were to be payable without regard to legal entitlements at common law (including statutory claims), unlike the repealed workmen's compensation statutes which provided redress that was *alternative* to common law claims.

The courts experienced some difficulty with disablement benefit which, since it involves loss of faculty which may be permanent, is difficult to relate to the five-year period mentioned in the section, but the matter was settled by the Court of Appeal in *Hultquist* v. *Universal Pattern and Precision Engineering Co. Ltd.* (1960), which held that only such proportion of the gratuity as is apportionable (using the injured person's expected life) to the remainder of the five years was affected by the section. In *Eley* v. *Bedford* (1972), MacKenna J. refused to reduce damages by taking time-barred claims into account, holding that such claims were valueless and also that section 2 was exhaustive and did not admit of a duty to mitigate loss —in this case prompt prosecution of statutory rights. Even if the duty to mitigate loss had existed, his lordship considered that it merely raised a duty to act reasonably and that someone who does not know that he has a right does not act unreasonably in refusing to exercise it.

The second important factor concerns the application of the **118**
Gourley principle (*British Transport Commission* v. *Gourley* (1956)) whereby damages for personal injury or breach of contract must so far as loss of earnings is concerned reflect the tax element if the damages are not taxable in the recipient's hands—a principle which has been extended from personal injury awards to, *inter alia*, awards for wrongful termination of contract. The application of the *Gourley* principle has raised a host of problems. Amongst these is the problem of relating an employee's damages to other income. One aspect of this fell for decision in *Lyndale Fashion Manufacturers* v. *Rich* (1973) where it was held that, as between the employee's damages for breach of contract (£495) and his other income (£1,343), the former must be treated as the top part of his income (taking into account earned income relief), thereby attracting a higher rate of tax in the assumed assessment.

Another problem arises as a consequence of the Finance Act 1960 (now the Income and Corporation Taxes Act 1970, ss. 187–188) which charges to tax payments exceeding £5,000 by way of compensation for loss of office, including damages for wrongful dismissal. Clearly the *Gourley* principle applies to awards up to £5,000. To deal with awards exceeding that amount, four possible solutions have been suggested (see *Whiteman and Wheatcroft on Income Tax and Surtax*, paras. 15–13 *et seq.*). In *Bold* v. *Brough, Nicholson & Hall* (1964), it was held, that in such a situation, the first £5,000 should be treated as the whole award and not as the top and most heavily taxed slice.

The Rule in *Gourley's* case has withstood the criticisms made of **119**
it, *e.g.* that it reduces the liability of defendants without enriching the Inland Revenue; and also that it estimates liability to a future, variable and (theoretically!) temporary tax liability against the background of the plaintiff's present liability to tax, subject to the likelihood that he will, at least so far as unearned income is concerned, take reasonable measures to minimise his tax liability. The principle

of *restitutio in integrum* upon which *Gourley's* case rests has also been used to justify the deduction of social security benefits, other than the deduction specifically provided for in section 2 of the Law Reform (Personal Injuries) Act 1948, and which was formerly thought to be the sole exception to the rule that social security benefits were to be disregarded. In their desire to ensure that the injured employee does not enjoy what one judge has termed a "fortuitous windfall," the courts have deducted from damages national insurance unemployment benefit and national insurance contributions but have declined to deduct gifts, the proceeds of private insurance, a disablement pension payable up to retiring age from a contributory pension scheme, and state retirement pension. It would appear that it is no longer valid to distinguish between benefits claimable as of right and discretionary benefits, *e.g.* supplementary benefit.

Compulsory insurance

120 Most responsible employers insure themselves under employers' liability policies. To deal with those who do not effect such policies and whose lack of resources makes legal redress illusory in any practical sense, the Employers' Liability (Compulsory Insurance) Act 1969, requires every employer (other than one excepted by the Act) carrying on business in Great Britain, to insure against liability for bodily injury or disease sustained by his employees and arising out of, and in the course of, their employment in Great Britain in that business. The insurance must be contained in one or more approved policies with an authorised insurer and regulations made under the Act have required that the sum of at least £2 million must be insured in respect of claims from one or more employees arising out of any one occurrence. The regulations also prohibit the insertion of certain restrictive conditions in policies under the Act (although the insurer may reserve a right of subrogation), and provide for the issue, display, production and inspection of certificates of insurance.

Insurance of liability, whether voluntary or compulsory, therefore spreads a liability which has fallen on the insured amongst the policyholders generally, a consideration which has prompted some to question the "loss-shifting" role of the law of tort, and others to question whether "loss-spreading" by insurance undermines any "deterrent effect" inherent in awards of damages to the extent that the loss is ultimately borne by policyholders and consumers (who bear the ultimate cost of premiums).

121 A deeper criticism relates to the requirement that liability in a negligence action is based on fault (*culpa*) determined by litigation.

Whilst some are lucky in the "forensic lottery," as it has been termed, others receive nothing for meritorious claims, perhaps because they are scared of the law, fearful of incurring hostility from their employer or unable to discharge the intimidating incubus of proof incumbent upon anyone who alleges negligence and, as will be seen, breach of statutory duty (see Chapter 5). There has been widespread pressure in recent years to review the operation of the common law system of damages for personal injuries. Amongst the stimuli towards such a review must be counted Professor P. S. Atiyah's book on *Accidents, Compensation and the Law*, the example of the Woodhouse Report in New Zealand (which recommended the replacement of compensation according to fault by compensation from social insurance), the criticisms of the Robens Committee on Safety and Health at Work (see below, para. 394) and the tragic Thalidomide Affair. On December 19, 1972, the Government announced that a Royal Commission on Civil Liability for Death and Injury would be set up under the chairmanship of Lord Pearson to consider to what extent, in what circumstances, and by what means, compensation should be payable in respect of death or personal injury (including ante-natal injury) suffered by a person—

(a) in the course of employment,
(b) through the use of a motor vehicle or other means of transport,
(c) through the manufacture, supply or use of goods or services,
(d) on premises belonging to or occupied by another, or
(e) otherwise through the act or omission of another where compensation under the present law is recoverable only on proof of fault or under the rules of strict liability.

The effect of the death of the employer or employee

So far we have discussed the employer's liability and its quantification in terms of money on the assumption that the employee has suffered a non-fatal injury. Does the death of the employee from the injury, either immediately or after the lapse of time, make any difference, and what effect does the death of the employer make if he dies before an action can be begun? **122**

Two questions must be clearly separated. (a) What is the effect of death on *subsisting* causes of action? (b) Does death itself *create* a right of action, and if so, in favour of whom?

(a) *On subsisting causes of action*

Prior to the Law Reform (Miscellaneous Provisions) Act 1934, the common law, with some minor exceptions, treated death as **123** extinctive of both liability and the right to sue. It was felt that some redress ought to be afforded to the victims of road accidents regardless of whether they or the tortfeasors died. Accordingly, section 1 (1) of the 1934 Act provides that all causes of action subsisting or vested in any person on his death shall survive against or, as the case may be, for the benefit of his estate. Certain "personal" actions were excluded of which defamation remains excluded. The action on behalf of the deceased must be brought within the period of limitation (see above, para. 116). If it is the tortfeasor who dies, the action cannot be brought unless proceedings were pending at the death of the tortfeasor or are begun not later than six months after his personal representative has taken out representation to his estate.

It will be seen therefore that should an employee die as the result of the employer's tort (almost invariably negligence), the damages will go to swell the estate of the deceased (apart from other claims, since the 1934 Act is of general application). It may surprise the layman to learn that the damages available to the injured worker, *e.g.* for pain and suffering, loss of earnings and loss of expectation of life, are still claimable even though the victim has died. Thus if he survived the accident for a short period and was not unconscious, damages could be given for pain and suffering; conversely, even though his death was instantaneous, damages for loss of expectation of life could be claimed, although the House of Lords has indicated that in the event of death very moderate figures will be chosen. In *Yorkshire Electricity Board* v. *Naylor* (1968), the House of Lords reinstated an award of £500 which the trial judge had given to the administratrix of the estate of a deceased employee who had died instantaneously from an electric shock. In setting aside an increase to £1,000, which the Court of Appeal had awarded, their lordships disapproved of the distinction which had been drawn from an erroneous interpretation of the case of *Benham* v. *Gambling* (1941), namely, between adults and young children, whereby awards to the latter had been smaller.

(b) *As a cause of action*

124 Prior to the Fatal Accidents Act 1846, the common law held that the death of a person was not, as such, a tort actionable either on behalf of the deceased or by third persons. The Act, as amended by the Fatal Accidents Act 1959, makes an inroad upon this principle which otherwise remains valid. Section 1 of the 1846 Act provides that whenever the death of a person is caused by the wrongful act, neglect or default of another, such as would (if death had not ensued) have entitled the injured person to sue and recover damages in respect thereof, then the person who would have been liable if death had not ensued shall be liable to an action for damages, notwithstanding the death of the person injured.

The action lies for the benefit of the deceased's dependants, a class which was widened by the Act of 1959 to include the spouse, parent, child, grandparent, grandchild, together with the brother, sister, uncle or aunt (or their issue) of the deceased. Illegitimate and adopted children are now included. Since *dependancy* is the crux of the claim, the dependants, as defined above, receive a sum representing their loss of expected pecuniary benefit.

The nineteenth-century judges, several of whom were good **125**
judges of horseflesh, were not averse to passing judgment upon what in the current argot is termed the "remarriageability factor." Typical of the reluctance of modern judges to pass judgment upon a widow's chance of remarriage is Phillimore J.'s rhetorical question "Am I to ask her to put on a bathing dress?", when the witness box would conceal her natural endowments (*Buckley* v. *John Allen & Ford* (*Oxford*) *Ltd.* (1967), at p. 644 of the report). The question is answered by section 4 of the Law Reform (Miscellaneous Provisions) Act 1971, which now requires the court to ignore either the widow's remarriage or her prospects of remarriage. In awarding damages under the Acts to a widow for loss of dependency, the House of Lords awarded loss of interest on the savings which her husband would have made, in addition to an increase to off-set liability to tax on part of the award—the Rule in *Gourley's* case in reverse, as it were (*Taylor* v. *O'Connor* (1971)). If the facts disclose a loss of potential support, this may be allowed as where a son aged seventeen years is killed leaving a mother and a father who has returned to work after a stroke. The court will not clutch at possibilities, *e.g.* that, despite an estrangement, a reconciliation between husband and wife *might* at some future date occur.

The action is a completely new one bestowed on the dependants; **126**
the reference in section 1 to the deceased having "if death had not ensued" the right to sue merely alludes to a necessary prerequisite to an action by the dependants. If the deceased had surrendered his claim, *e.g.* by accepting a settlement, the dependants have no claim, whereas if he had merely *limited* the liability of the defendants, the dependants have a claim free from the limitation. The curious manner in which the dependants' rights are intertwined with those of the deceased is shown in the provision that contributory negligence by the latter will reduce the damages claimable by or on behalf of the dependants. The action must be brought within three years (two years for fatalities at sea) of the death; normally the deceased's personal representative will take the action on behalf of the dependants, but should there be no personal representative or a personal

representative who takes no action within six months of the death, any beneficiary may sue.

Although damages under the Fatal Accidents Acts are normally recovered by the personal representatives on behalf of the dependants, such damages form no part of the deceased's estate and are therefore outside the predatory grasp of the deceased's creditors and the Estate Duty Office. Damages under the 1934 Act go, as we have seen, to swell the deceased's estate so that as part of his estate they are available for creditors (including the Estate Duty Office) whose claims have priority over the claims of beneficiaries; these claims may have to "abate" if there is a surplus after the payment of debts which is insufficient to meet the claims of the beneficiaries in full.

127 The sums received by the dependants under the 1934 Act, net of administration expenses and estate duty, reduce *pro rata* their claims under the Fatal Accidents Acts; this causes little trouble in practice since it is usual to join the two actions. If, for some reason, separate actions are brought, that brought under the 1934 Act proceeds without taking into account the possibility of an award under the Fatal Accidents Acts; an action under the latter Acts must take into account any damages which have been or may be awarded under the 1934 Act. But the separate nature of the claims is underlined in the event of the deceased's estate not passing to his dependants, who would then obtain their damages in full under the 1846–1959 Acts.

II. The Employee's Duties

128 The duties of the employee are, as in contract generally, primarily left to the "autonomy of the contract," the parties being left free to settle the norms of their own particular relationship within the substantive and procedural requirements of the law. If the court has before it an express term regulating the rights and duties of the parties, it is freed from the voyage of discovery on the seas of "duties implied by law." An example is *Swain* v. *West* (*Butchers*) *Ltd.* (1936), where a general manager contractually agreed to "do all in his power to promote, extend and develop the interests of the company." He confessed acts of dishonesty by the managing director and himself to the chairman of the company who gave him, if not absolution, an assurance that he could stay on. It was held that the general manager, who had nevertheless been dismissed, could not succeed in a claim for breach of contract since the chairman's promise was not supported by consideration; the manager had done something which he was contractually obliged to do.

The law imports certain terms into the agreement. Such terms fall into two categories: (i) "imperative norms" imposed by the law which preclude any "contracting out," *e.g.* the employer's duty at common law to provide a system of work (we have seen that statutory protective provisions do not usually operate as contractual terms, see *Browning* v. *Crumlin Valley Collieries*, above, para. 48); (ii) norms which apply in the absence of contractual agreement. It may occasionally be a nice question to decide into which category a particular implied duty falls.

Before summarising the employee's duties, two important con- **129**
siderations should be borne in mind. First, the various duties about to be examined are rules of indeterminate application in the infinitely variable facts of individual cases. For example, misconduct by an employee constitutes a breach of duty but the determination of what amounts to misconduct in a given situation is a question of fact, as judicial warnings have testified; what is misconduct in one situation may well be perfectly innocuous in another. However frustrating to the seeker after certainty, the element of generality inherent in these common law rules permits of a continuing balancing of social criteria. An example is *Initial Services Ltd.* v. *Putterill* (1968), in which the Court of Appeal had to weigh the employee's duty of confidence against the wider public interest. The employee in that case had, before tendering his resignation, disclosed confidential information relating to his employer's affairs to a national newspaper showing a secret agreement which might have violated the Restrictive Trade Practices Act 1956. The Court of Appeal was not prepared to rule that the employee had no right to disclose the information.

Secondly, breach of implied duty gives rise to certain remedies **130**
at the suit of the party not in default. In the first place, breach of an implied duty or term will, if "seriously incompatible" with the continuance of the relationship, constitute a "fundamental breach" entitling the party not in default to treat the contract as rescinded. A breach of this nature by the employer justifies the employee in treating his own obligations as discharged, *e.g.* he may depart without giving the requisite contractual notice, or disregard other terms, such as a covenant restricting him from competing with his employer after the termination of the employment: conversely, in the event of a breach of this gravity by an employee, the employer may treat his own obligations as discharged so that, for example, he may give the employee an immediate *Nunc Dimittis* notwithstanding a requirement of notice. Another consideration is the relevance of the reason for dismissal in claims for unfair dismissal under the Industrial Relations Act, both in connection with the employer's onus of proof (*ibid.* s. 24 (1)), and as regards determination of the reasonableness of the employer's action in the circumstances (*ibid.* s. 24 (6)).

Finally, the employee's conduct may, at the discretion of the industrial tribunal, put his entitlement to a redundancy payment in jeopardy (Redundancy Payments Act 1965, ss. 2 (2), 10 (3)). The employee's duties may conveniently be grouped under the following heads.

The Code of Practice recognises that the legal relationship between employer and employee derives from the individual contract of employment (*ibid.* para. 18) but the same Code also contains precepts as to good industrial relations which may be taken into account in proceedings before the Industrial Court or the industrial tribunal. These precepts must, therefore, be borne in mind when considering the duties of the employee (and the employer).

1. Obedience

131 The employee must obey an order which is within the terms of the contract, express or implied, and which is not unlawful under the general law: "the general rule is obedience" said Alderson B. in *Turner* v. *Mason* (1845). The employee cannot be required to do something beyond the scope of his employment. Unless the contract permits it, he may lawfully refuse to obey an order which requires him to run the risk of physical injury or serious infection. That the contract sets a limit on managerial discretion is shown by *Price* v. *Mouat* (1862), where the jury found that the summary dismissal of a lace-dealer, paid annually, for refusing to "card" lace was wrongful. This case and that of *Yetton* (above, para. 97) show that an employee is entitled to hold the office to which he was appointed and to work appropriate to that office. The employer cannot unilaterally alter the terms of employment under a current contract, *e.g.* by sending the employee a letter demoting him and reducing his wages (*Marriott* v. *Oxford & District Co-operative Society Ltd.* (*No. 2*) (1970), where the employee's continuance under protest was not taken to indicate consent), or by sending a letter informing him that the restrictive practices enshrined in working rules are to be swept away at a future date (*Morris* v. *C. H. Bailey Ltd.* (1969), an instructive case). Similarly, in *Cowey* v. *Liberian Operations Ltd.* (1966), the circulation of a memorandum was held to be ineffective to alter terms despite the fact that the employee had initialled the memorandum.

132 We have already seen that questions of labour mobility, industrial, occupational or geographical are increasingly coming to the fore as one might expect in a time of rapid technological change. Confronted with an order outside the terms of the contract, an employee may (1) ignore it, or (2) treat it as a "constructive dismissal" if the order involves a fundamental breach of contract.

There is no lack of cases to show that there are more ways of killing a cat than drowning it; employers who order employees to perform radically different work have been held to have dismissed them, thereby incurring liability for wrongful dismissal and exposing them to liability in respect of unfair dismissal and redundancy (where the order to perform different work shows that the requirements of a business for work of a particular kind have ceased or diminished). Of course, there may be a consensual variation of contract, or a non-contractual variation of working arrangements (*Dorman Long & Co. Ltd.* v. *Carroll* (1945)).

The Christian's "slavery of love" was exploited by the Victorians (and, with different objectives, the dialectical materialists). The waggoner who refused to take his horses to the marshes because his dinner awaited him, and the domestic servant who disobeyed orders and visited her ailing mother, paid the price for their frowardness—a price which was particularly heavy where a general hiring existed in that the servant forfeited his wages to the end of the year, whether earned or not.

Laws v. *London Chronicle* (1959), shows that a single and isolated **133**
act of disobedience need not amount to a total repudiation of the contract of service. There, the plaintiff left a room despite an order (or possibly a request?) from the chairman of the company to remain after an altercation between the chairman and her immediate superior had been concluded by the latter's act in walking out of the room. "She was in a difficult position" said the judge at first instance, a remark which typifies the plight of the modern employee whose superiors, proximate and remote, are in law as likely as not to be fellow-employees. The test is not whether the disobedience takes place on one or several occasions but whether or not the disobedience manifests an intention to repudiate the whole contract. The underwriter who writes a risk, despite a specific order not to do so from his board of governors, commits a single act of disobedience justifying immediate dismissal. Karminski L.J. considered that the head gardener in *Pepper* v. *Webb* (1969), who had responded to his employer's order to plant some fuschias and geraniums with the remark—"I couldn't care less about your bloody greenhouse and sodding garden"—had, by disobeying a lawful and reasonable order, repudiated his contract. His lordship's brethren, however, whilst agreeing that the head gardener had repudiated his contract, took into account past episodes of insolence and insubordination of which the present episode was only the "last straw." Taking account of the gardener's conduct as a whole, and the "personal" nature of the relationship, the decision seems defensible despite the criticism which it has incurred.

2. Fidelity

134 The duty to serve faithfully is a portmanteau duty which rests on the principle that the employee should co-operate with his employer in order to further the latter's interests. "The practical difficulty in any given case is", as Lord Greene M.R. reminded us, "to find exactly how far that rather vague duty of fidelity extends" (*Hivac* v. *Park Royal Scientific Instruments Ltd.* (1946), at p. 175 of the report). A graphic and important example of the correlative duty not to frustrate the commercial purpose of the employer's business is provided by *Secretary of State for Employment* v. *ASLEF* (*No. 2*) (1972), where by meticulous observance of railway rules in response to union directions to "work-to-rule" the railways were brought, in some cases, to a standstill. Without going so far as to agree with the Industrial Court's view that what had happened constituted "a breach of the fundamental obligation of every employee to behave fairly to his employer and to do a fair day's work," and without denying that an employee might withdraw his goodwill and refuse to do more than his contract required, the Court of Appeal rejected the view that the employee could still wilfully obstruct the employer's business in order to bring it to a standstill. Such conduct would, in the court's view, break an implied term in the employee's contract of service.

135 The duty is protean in character. Sometimes it is rested on the right of the employer to protect his business interests. The service director who steers business to a rival company in which he has an interest or from which he receives a commission, the milkman who canvasses his masters' customers shortly before leaving to set up his own milk round, the solicitor who succumbs to the suggestion of one of his employer's wealthy clients that he should leave and undertake the client's business himself, the departing employee who compiles details of engines or lists of customers, and the director who learns of a patent for swimming pools, but suppresses his knowledge until he has had time to set up his own company to exploit the patent, are all examples of persons who have wrongfully furthered their own, as opposed to their employers', interests. *A fortiori*, the employee must account for property received on behalf of his employer, for bribes and for secret profits derived from the position which he holds. An Army sergeant who used his position to obtain a large sum of money for his services in connection with smuggling operations in Cairo was unable to recover the money which had been impounded by the military authorities. His argument that the Crown ought not to become *particeps criminis*, by sharing in the loot, was dismissed (*Reading* v. *Att.-Gen.* (1951)). An employee breaks

his duty of fidelity if he shows that he is unworthy of the trust reposed in him. That he may break this duty without "dishonesty" in its narrow sense is shown by *Sinclair* v. *Neighbour* (1967), where it was held that an employee, who had "borrowed" money from the till meaning to, and in fact replacing it, had been validly dismissed.

The imparting of confidential information to a third person may **136**
involve breach of the implied term concerning faithful service. The central feature of *Hivac* v. *Park Royal Scientific Instruments Ltd.* (above), a case to which the employees were not parties, was the risk that the employer, who had given the plaintiff's employees part-time work, would acquire confidential information belonging to the latter and relating to the manufacture of midget valves for deaf-aids. By inducing the plaintiff's employees to break their implied obligation not to disclose the plaintiff's "know-how," the defendants were committing a tort. It may be interpolated here that a third person who uses another's confidential information may be liable in damages even although he acquired that information in good faith. The *Hivac* case ought not, however, to be pressed too far, in view of the peculiar facts of that case and the peculiar time when those facts occurred. "It would be most unfortunate if anything we said should place an undue restriction on the right of a workman, particularly a manual workman, to make use of his leisure for his profit" warned Lord Greene M.R.

Nevertheless, the duty is not limited to "know-how" in the sense of technical information. A trade union official who, in order to enable the union to engage in collective bargaining, asks managers of licensed houses to complete a questionnaire giving details of expenses, takings, and wages was held to be restrainable on the grounds that the disclosure of such information would involve the managers in breach of their duty of confidentiality towards their employers (*Bent's Brewery Co. Ltd.* v. *Hogan* (1945)). In this connection it may be noted here that section 56 of the Industrial Relations Act 1971 requires employers to disclose information in their possession to trade union representatives for the purposes of collective bargaining, without which the representatives would be impeded to a material extent, if the disclosure of such information would be in accordance with good industrial relations practice. In this latter context, guidance is provided by the Code of Practice which, in due course, will include some or all of the recommendations of the recently-published Report of the C.I.R. on Disclosure of Information (Report No. 31). Section 158 of the same Act relieves the employer of the duty to give information on certain grounds, including disclosure which "would be seriously prejudicial to the interests of the employer's undertaking."

137 The duty of fidelity is prayed in aid to restrain the employee from wrongfully exploiting his own inventions whether they be patents, copyrights or plant and seed varieties. Normally the right to exploit will be regulated by contract; if this is not so, the employer has this right when the invention arose out of the employee's work, *e.g.* a research chemist, or as the result of opportunities or facilities available to him, even though not directly related to the employer's business (see *Sterling Engineering Co.* v. *Patchett*, below). As to patents in particular see *British Syphon Co. Ltd.* v. *Homewood* (1956), the Patents Act 1949, section 56 (2), and *Sterling Engineering Co.* v. *Patchett* (1955); in this last case it was held that there is in a contract of service an implied term that the benefit of inventions accrues solely to the employer and that section 56 (2) of the Patents Act 1949 (which allows for the benefit of an invention to be apportioned between employer and employee) could not apply since the "benefit" referred to by the Act meant "legally entitled benefit" which did not arise in this case.

3. Misconduct

138 Misconduct is another broad rubric which covers a multitude of sins. It is submitted that some nineteenth-century cases should be treated with reserve; the virtual disappearance of domestic service (at least from private homes), the secularisation of modern society and full employment have, *inter alia*, shifted the emphasis from moral disapproval of the employee's conduct to a more pragmatic inquiry whether the employee's misconduct interferes with the performance of his duties. Isolated outbursts of petulance, insolence and horseplay are, in the absence of special circumstances, scarcely likely to justify immediate dismissal (see *Laws*' case, above, para. 133). The pregnant maidservant is more likely to be dismissed because of her incapacity than by reason of her amorous proclivities. Drunkenness or excessive dancing which disables an employee from giving of his best may justify instant dismissal. In *Baster* v. *London & County Printing Works* (1899), a case of forgetfulness by an employee, the court held that, in deciding the propriety of instant dismissal, the misconduct must be related to the degree of damage likely to ensue to the employer, his property and his fellow-servants; the signalman who forgets to set his signal at danger patently commits a grave breach of his implied duty.

4. Employee's duty to indemnify: indemnity contrasted with contribution

139 If negligence by the employee, which is a form of misconduct, constitutes a breach of his implied duty possibly justifying summary

dismissal, will it impose upon the employee an obligation to indemnify his employer for loss suffered by the latter?

Until 1956, whilst it was clear that an employee who knowingly or recklessly inflicted damage upon his employer was liable to indemnify the latter, *e.g.* where he broke a machine in Luddite fashion or indulged in horseplay near delicate machinery, the position remained uncertain in relation to negligence on the employee's part. The question was authoritatively determined in that year in a manner which received a mixed reception.

In *Lister* v. *Romford Ice and Cold Storage Co. Ltd.* (1957), a lorry driver, whilst carelessly backing his lorry in a slaughterhouse yard, injured a fellow-employee, who happened to be his father, and who recovered damages of £1,600 from the employers. The employers now sought to be indemnified in respect of the damages and costs awarded to the father, claiming that it was an implied term that the lorry driver would perform his duties with proper care. It was held that the driver was liable to indemnify his employer in full; *per* Viscount Simonds it was

> "clear that it was an implied term of the contract that the appellant would perform his duties with proper care. The proposition of law stated by Willes J. in *Harmer* v. *Cornelius* has never been questioned: 'When a skilled labourer,' he said, 'artisan, or artist is employed, there is on his part an implied warranty that he is of skill reasonably competent to the task he undertakes,—*Spondes peritam artis.* . . . An express promise or express representation in the particular case is not necessary.' I see no ground for excluding from, and every ground for including in, this category a servant who is employed to drive a lorry which, driven without care, may become an engine of destruction and involve his master in very grave liability. Nor can I see any valid reason for saying that a distinction is to be made between possessing skill and exercising it. . . . Of what advantage to the employer is his servant's undertaking that he possesses skill unless he undertakes also to use it?"

His lordship was not prepared to admit an implied duty on the master's part to insure, at least for accidents on private premises in regard to which there is no statutory third-party insurance requirement.

The decision in *Lister's* case, in assimilating the possession of 140
skill and its exercise, throws upon labour a risk which some think should be borne by capital. An Interdepartmental Committee set up in 1957 to consider the implications of the decision rejected the idea of compulsory insurance but instead recommended (i) an extension of the "gentleman's agreement" on the part of certain

insurers whereby forbearance on their part would be shown; (ii) that trade unions should seek to include insurance cover for their members in collective bargains. As Lord Denning has said, "The cases show that we are approaching a time when servants will have to insure their masters." Certainly, the present position is somewhat unsatisfactory.

The employee's liability to indemnify, as illustrated by *Lister*, must now be contrasted with "contribution" among joint tortfeasors. If A and B jointly commit a tort against C, *e.g.* by assaulting him, they are jointly and severally liable to C for the tort of trespass to the person. C may sue A, or B, or A and B jointly. Further, if "the servant commits a tort in the course of his employment, then the master is a tortfeasor as well as the servant. The master is never treated as an innocent party" (*per* Denning L.J. in *Jones* v. *Manchester Corporation* (1952), at p. 870 of the report); the layman might share the surprise shown by Finnemore J. in *Semtex* v. *Gladstone* (1954), at p. 949 of the report: "I could never see why an employer, whose only liability is the vicarious liability of being responsible for what his servant does, should be called a joint tortfeasor, which should mean a person who took some part in the tort which is the subject of the action." The victim of a tort generally prefers to sue the employer rather than win a Pyrrhic victory over the employee who is likely to have little in the way of resources; if damages are recovered from the employer the latter may call upon the employee to "contribute" by virtue of section 6 of the Law Reform (Married Women and Joint Tortfeasors) Act 1935, which provides that any tortfeasor liable in respect of damage suffered as a result of a tort may recover contribution from any other tortfeasor who is, or would if sued have been, liable in respect of the same damage whether as a joint tortfeasor or otherwise, except that no person may thus recover contribution from any person entitled to be indemnified by him in respect of the liability in relation to which the contribution is sought. The same section confers upon the court a wide discretion to award such contribution as it finds to be "just and equitable"; it may exempt a person from contribution or order complete indemnity.

141 In the *Lister* case, above, Viscount Simonds and Lord Morton did not exclude the possibility that an employer might have claimed contribution up to 100 per cent. from the employee. But indemnity and contribution need not necessarily be concurrently available. In *Harvey* v. *O'Dell* (1958), H and G were employed by O'D. G, who was employed as a storekeeper, sometimes used his motor-cycle combination in his employer's business with the latter's consent. H and G, who had been engaged upon repair work at Hurley, went

in G's motor-cyle combination to Maidenhead for some tools and refreshment. On the return journey, G was killed and H was injured in an accident partly attributable to G's negligence. H sued O'D who claimed contribution from G's estate. *Held:* (1) O'D was vicariously liable to H for G's negligence; (2) O'D could not claim indemnity from G's estate for breach of the implied contractual duty to take care because G had been employed as a storekeeper and not as a driver; (3) O'D could, however, claim 100 per cent. *contribution* from G's estate.

The distinction drawn in the *Harvey* case has been criticised on the grounds that "any negligent act committed by the servant in the course of his employment constitutes a breach of his contract of service" (*Winfield on Tort*, 9th ed., at p. 544). To accept this would, with respect, place intolerable burdens upon employees outside the scope of their duties (*cf. Semtex* v. *Gladstone*, above, para. 140, in which driving was part of the employee's duties).

Negligence on the part of the employer precludes a claim for **142** indemnity and may reduce a claim for contribution. Thus, in *Jones* v. *Manchester Corporation* (1952), a hospital patient died in circumstances showing negligence on the part of the hospital board in selecting an inexperienced doctor and carelessness by the latter. It was held (rejecting indemnity from the doctor) that damages would be apportioned as to the hospital four-fifths and as to the doctor one-fifth.

III. The Closed Shop

Few issues have caused more controversy than that of the "closed **143** shop," evoking as it does a conflict between libertarianism and social solidarity. The Industrial Relations Act attempts to regulate by law the whole question of trade union rights as between employer and employee, although it must be emphasised at the outset that the rights so conferred are statutory and not contractual. It is however convenient to discuss them here.

It was estimated in 1964 that two out of every five workers worked in a "closed shop." A closed shop might exist by reason of formal agreement between the employer and a union or unions, or, as the result of an informal "understanding" and could take different forms. A person might be required to be a member of a union *before* obtaining employment (the "pre-entry" closed shop, *e.g.* where a craft requirement was a pre-condition of employment) or *after* obtaining employment (the "post-entry" closed shop). Union membership (like, its opposite, non-membership) might be a term of employment. The Donovan Commission rejected the possibility of prohibiting the closed shop, but advocated certain safeguards for individuals. The Industrial Relations Act 1971, however, represents an uneasy compromise between doctrinal abhorrence of the closed shop and acceptance of the part which properly defined rights to union membership can play in furthering good industrial relations.

144 The doctrinal abhorrence is revealed in section 6 which, subject to one exception, renders void any agreement purporting to (a) preclude an employer or employers from engaging workers who are not members of a union, registered or unregistered, or (b) preclude an employer or employers from engaging workers who have not been recommended or approved for engagement by a union or unions (the typical "union hiring hall" of the nineteenth century, and not unknown in this century). A worker who has been refused engagement by an employer because of a closed shop may apply to have the closed shop agreement declared void by the Industrial Court. An exception is provided whereby those in a vulnerable position, such as merchant seamen and actors, may seek protection in the form of an "approved closed shop agreement." Lord Pearce recognised the difficulty facing actors when he acknowledged in *Faramus* v. *Film Artistes Association* (1964), at p. 946 of the report, that "if all who wished were admitted, there would not be an adequate living for all." Some unions, such as the National Union of Seamen, which have applied for protection in this way have been suspended from affiliation with the T.U.C. The strict conditions under which the Industrial Court will approve an approved closed shop agreement are set out in sections 17, 18 and Schedule 1, and include provision for those who claim exemption from union membership on grounds of conscience and who may be allowed to pay the amount of the appropriate contribution to charity.

145 Most important of all is section 5 which, deriving its justification from international statements on human rights, confers upon every worker (on which see para. 35), *vis-à-vis* his employer, the right to join the trade union of his choice and, conversely, the right not to join a trade union. If he is a member of a trade union, he has the right to take part in the activities of the trade union, including union office, at an appropriate time. An employer, or person acting on his behalf, who (a) prevents or deters a worker from exercising these rights, or (b) dismisses, penalises or otherwise discriminates against a worker by reason of his exercising any such right, or (c) refuses to engage a worker either because he is not a member of a trade union, commits an unfair industrial practice which may be the subject of complaint to the industrial tribunal by the person affected. If the tribunal finds that the complaint is well-founded and considers that it would be just and equitable to do so, it may make an order declaratory of the complainant's right, and additionally, or alternatively, award compensation to the complainant (s. 106). If the complainant has been dismissed, the tribunal may also recommend reinstatement (s. 106 (4)). Section 118 limits the amount of compensation payable to a maximum of £4,160, or 104 weeks' pay, whichever is the less. If an employer offers a benefit in kind as a carrot to induce workers to refrain from exercising their rights under section 5, he will be regarded as having discriminated against those from whom he has withheld that benefit, provided he has conferred that benefit on one or more workers who have agreed to forego their rights (s. 5 (4)).

It is significant that the rights given under section 5 appertain **146**
only in relation to a "trade union" *i.e.* a registered organisation of workers. Whilst a worker cannot assert a right under section 5 to join, or take part in the activities of, an unregistered union, as in *Kenyon* v. *Miller* (1972) (where the dismissal of an employee for taking part in the activities of an unregistered union was held not to constitute an unfair industrial practice, notwithstanding that the activities in question had taken place outside both the employer's premises and working hours), he is at liberty to assert his rights under that section without indicating the particular union, registered or unregistered, which he proposes to join. The Industrial Court rejected the argument in *Cotter* v. *Lynch Bros.* (1972), that a worker who had announced his intention to join a union but who had not yet indicated which particular union he proposed to join was asserting a right outside the ambit of section 5, Sir John Brightman saying —"If a man says, 'I shall go either to Rome or to Paris' it is idle to contend that he has not indicated an intention to go to Rome. He does intend, conditionally upon his not going to Paris" (at p. 266 of the report).

So far as the worker with two years of qualifying service, who **147**
has been dismissed for asserting his trade union rights, is concerned, there is overlap between the unfair industrial practice in section 5 and unfair dismissal under section 22. Each falls within the jurisdiction of the industrial tribunal and attracts the same remedies. Whereas section 5 deals with trade union rights section 22 is concerned with a wide spectrum of reasons for dismissal. We have seen that section 5 provides no assistance to the member of the unregistered union. It does not follow that a member dismissed by reason of his membership of such a union would have no remedy under section 22, provided he had two years' service. "One need only instance by way of illustration the case of an unregistered trade union which is fully recognised by the employer for all negotiating purposes. It would be absurd to suppose that an employer, having

so recognised the unregistered union for negotiating purposes, might not be guilty of an unfair industrial practice (*unfair dismissal*) if he dismissed an employee for the reason only that he was a member of, or desired to join, that unregistered union which the employer recognised" (Sir John Brightman in *Cotter* v. *Lynch Brothers*, above: italics supplied).

Post Office v. *Ravyts* (1972) reminds us that judges are not oblivious of the virtues of stable bargaining arrangements arrived at in the traditional way. It was there said that discrimination against a registered trade union was not unlawful. Because such a union was a corporation distinct from its members, a refusal to recognise it for collective bargaining purposes did not constitute discrimination against its members who worked for the Post Office. But by placing these members at a disadvantage in the matters of grievances, and delivery of correspondence to the place of work, discrimination *contra* section 5 was held to have occurred.

148 It will be perceived that by making it an unfair industrial practice to *refuse* employment to a worker because he is or is not a member of a trade union, section 5 confers rights which are *statutory* and *not contractual*: if a person is refused employment there can be no contract of employment! The definition of "worker" in section 167 (1) includes not only someone who "works" but someone who "normally works or seeks to work."

In its provisions dealing with the "approved closed shop agreement" (above) and the "agency shop agreement," the Act resiles somewhat from the principle of free association enshrined in section 5. The "agency shop agreement" is discussed below in Chapter 8, where it will be seen that the individual may well be sacrificed upon the altar of industrial democracy in statutory form.

(B) *The Relationship as Regards Third Parties*

149 Although the employer–employee relationship is primarily concerned with the regulation of the rights and duties of the parties *inter se*, the relationship may be relevant in regard to third parties. First, the employee may commit torts and crimes or may enter into contracts in circumstances involving his employer in liability, civil or criminal. Secondly, third parties may deliberately or unknowingly interfere with the relationship, *e.g.* by inducing the employee to break his contract of employment or by injuring him so that the employer is deprived of his services. The liability of the employer to third persons arising from the acts or omissions of the employee will be treated first; this liability will usually concern the torts of the employee, but the employee's contracts and crimes will also be mentioned.

I. The Employer's Liability to Third Persons

In a broad sense, liability on the part of A for the acts or omissions 150 of B, is said to be "vicarious" as opposed to A's "personal" liability for his own acts or omissions.

The concept of vicarious liability is an exception to the broad principle in human, positive law, that ideally responsibility should be personal; the children ought not to suffer for the sins of the father. In classical Roman law, the *dominus* could, by handing over the slave or animal causing damage, be free of liability—seemingly even if the slave died during the action. In English law, the personal chattel causing death was claimable under the law of the deodand: a right which became inconvenient with the advent of the steam locomotive. No progressive society, however, can continue long with "personal" liability alone and still less with the attribution of personality to inanimate objects.

1. Vicarious liability in tort

In English law, the employer is vicariously liable for the torts of 151 his employee committed in the course of employment; such liability is *in addition* to, and not *instead of*, the tortious liability of the employee. The two limbs of this rule are, therefore, that (1) the tortfeasor must be a servant (see para. 21); (2) the tort must have been committed in the "course of employment." The second limb, the course of employment, will be examined here.

"*In the course of employment*"

The requirement that the tort must be committed in the course 152 of employment gives little difficulty in practice; it is in the marginal situations that the cases are baffling. The following passage from *Salmond on Torts*, has attracted repeated judicial blessings: "A master is not responsible for a wrongful act done by his servant unless it is done in the course of his employment. It is deemed to be so done if it is either (1) a wrongful act authorised by the master, or (2) a wrongful and unauthorised *mode* of doing some act authorised by the master" (16th ed., 1973, p. 474).

The employer is liable in tort, first, where he has authorised the commission of the tort, secondly, where he has assisted its commission and thirdly, where he has procured its commission (Atiyah, *Vicarious Liability in the Law of Torts*, p. 4); such liability, as the learned author points out, is personal rather than vicarious in the strict sense. Thus authorisation includes both an order to commit a tort (*e.g.* to dig a ditch in A's land, thereby constituting trespass) and an order which necessarily involves the commission of a tort (*e.g.* requiring the employee to dump rubbish near A's wall when it is inevitable that some of the rubbish will touch A's wall). The employer is also liable where he ratifies his employee's tort provided that (and the analogy with agency is close) the acts were done on behalf of the employer, who must have knowledge of the relevant facts.

The definition of a "wrongful and unauthorised mode" of doing an authorised act is more difficult. In *Hilton* v. *Thomas Burton* (1961), Diplock J. put it as follows:

> "I think that the true test can best be expressed in these words: Was the second defendant (*the employee*) doing something that he was employed to do? If so, however improper the manner in which he was doing it, whether negligent as in *Century Insurance Co. Ltd.* v. *Northern Ireland Road Transport Board* (1942), or even fraudulent as in *Lloyd* v. *Grace, Smith & Co.* (1912), or contrary to express orders as in *Canadian Pacific Railway* v. *Lockhart* (1942), the master is liable" (Italics mine).

153 As Professor Atiyah points out in his valuable work (*op. cit.*) there are two stages in the inquiry, *viz.* (i) determining the *authority* of the employee, and (ii) determining the connection between the servant's act and his authority, to see if the act is a mode of discharging that authority. The courts have not always consciously acted on this distinction.

Thus it has been held that the employer is not liable when the employee acts on a "frolic of his own." According to this test, the servant who dumps rubbish at a place other than that indicated by his employer so that more wages might be earned, the servant who takes his employer's vehicle on a new and unauthorised journey and the lorry driver, who, in crossing the road to seek refreshment after parking his lorry, causes an accident, all have in common the characteristic that they are acting for their own purposes. In the *Hilton* case, above, the employer was held not to be liable in respect of an accident caused by the negligence of his employee, who was returning from a separate journey to a public house after "fortifying the inner man." These cases can be resolved on the footing that the employee did not, at the relevant time, possess the authority to engage in these activities, which is not the same thing as saying that an employee may employ an unauthorised method of fulfilling his duty, *e.g.* where he makes a detour with his employer's vehicle, if such a detour can be reconciled with his duty: *A. & W. Hemphill Ltd.* v. *Williams* (1966).

154 Lord Denning M.R. posed (and answered) the following conundrum in *Morris* v. *C. W. Martin & Sons Ltd.* (1966) (in which cleaners were held liable for the theft of a coat by a servant responsible for cleaning it). Suppose the owner of a car leaves it at a garage for, say, repair and one of the garage-hands takes it out for a joy-ride and injures a motor-cyclist and the car. How is it, Lord Denning asked, that the motor-cyclist cannot recover from the employer since the employee was acting outside the course of his employment, whereas the owner can so recover? The difference lies in the nature of the two duties owed by the employer, *viz.* he is under a duty of care to the owner which he cannot escape by delegating to a servant, "whether the servant be negligent, fraudulent, or dishonest"; but there is no such duty to the motor-cyclist. Theft by a servant to whom was deputed the task of cleaning the coat rendered the master liable since he could not delegate his duty to the customer. It is otherwise where the servant obtains by virtue of his employment the opportunity to inflict a loss, *e.g.* in *Leesh River Tea* v. *British India Steam Navigation Co. Ltd.* (1967), in which shipowners were held not liable for the theft of a brass plate by a servant of the stevedores who were employed to discharge and load the ship: "The fact that the thief was a stevedore was quite fortuitous, as the theft had nothing to do with the work upon which he was engaged. The fact that his employment on board presented him with the opportunity to steal does not, in my judgment, suffice to make the shipowners liable" (*per* Salmon L.J. at p. 276 of the report). The two last-named cases reaffirm the principles laid down in the leading case of *Lloyd* v. *Grace, Smith and Co.* (above, para. 152), in which solicitors were held liable for the fraud of their managing clerk who had dishonestly procured a client to execute conveyances in his favour so that he might dispose of the properties. The deliberate nature of the clerk's act, its criminal nature, that it was done for his own benefit, did not prevent the employer from being liable; having granted to his employee authority as to a class of acts, he must remain liable if the employee exercises that authority for his own ends.

The conductor who drives the bus in the driver's absence, like **155**
the lorry driver who gives lifts to hitch-hikers, is doing a class of acts *dehors* the authority conferred upon him; *per contra*, the bus driver who sits beside the conductor who is driving and the lorry driver who permits a stranger to drive the lorry are performing, in a negligent fashion, something which as a question of fact may be said to lie within *their* duty, *viz.* to control the vehicle. This is not to say that the line between an unauthorised activity and an unauthorised mode of performing an authorised task is always crystal clear. In the *Century* case, above, the smoking of a cigarette whilst drawing petrol from a lorry was held to be an unauthorised mode of performing a task for which the employer was held liable just as the over-enthusiastic railway porter who uses physical violence in his

anxiety to see that passengers board the correct train was doing in dramatic style that which he was authorised to do. In *Warren* v. *Henley's Ltd.* (1948), a garage attendant threw a customer on the ground out of pique because the latter had reported him to the police for using violent language (the attendant had, erroneously, thought that the customer was leaving without paying the bill). Hilbery J. found that there was no evidence on which the jury could affix the employer with vicarious liability. Distinguishing cases in which violence might be considered to be incidental to the performance of a permitted act, as in the case of hire-purchase repossession agents, his lordship found that this "was an act entirely of personal vengeance. . . . It had no connection whatever with the discharge of any duty for the defendants." Such a connection was held to exist in *Poland* v. *John Parr & Sons* (1927), where a carter struck a boy whom he mistakenly believed to be pilfering objects from the cart. *Daniels* v. *Whetstone Entertainments Ltd.* (1962), falls neatly between the two last-named cases. In the course of an altercation in a dance-hall, the steward struck the plaintiff and later assaulted him severely outside the dance-hall. It was held that the employers were liable for the assault inside the hall since the steward was authorised to evict disorderly persons and forcibly to prevent their return; having done so, he was *functus officio* so that an element of "personal vengeance" was present in the second assault.

Effect of express prohibitions by employer

156 It is sometimes said that express prohibitions by the employer cannot affect the employer's liability, but this is too wide and a distinction must be drawn between prohibitions which delimit authority and those which relate to the manner in which the employee discharges his duty. Into the latter category falls the case of the bus driver who causes an accident by carelessly striving to overtake the bus belonging to a rival firm, even though expressly forbidden to do this (*Limpus* v. *London General Omnibus Co.* (1862)). The *Limpus* case (in which the employers were held liable) has sometimes been cited to support the proposition that a servant who acts in his master's interests is acting within the scope of employment. Without excluding the motives of the servant entirely, this is too wide since much will depend on the amount of discretion bestowed on the employee, *e.g.* a servant might act justifiably in rescuing his master's property in an emergency, but a filing clerk who took his master's large lorry onto the road because he wished to benefit his master might be seen to have taken an unduly enlarged view of his own discretion.

Crown servants

Until 1947 the principle of vicarious liability (*respondent superior*) had no application to the Crown; as "The King can do no wrong," any liability must necessarily lie upon the actual wrongdoer. The vast extension in central government in this century pointed the need for reform, and this was effected by the Crown Proceedings Act 1947, which, subject to important limitations, provided that "the Crown shall be subject to all those liabilities, in tort to which, if it were a private person of full age and capacity, it would be subject: (*a*) in respect of torts committed by its servants or agents . . ." (s. 2 (1)). Persons employed by public corporations may not be servants of the Crown, *e.g.* in those industrial or commercial corporations with (so called) legal and financial autonomy, which are themselves vicariously liable. **157**

Corporations

After some initial diffidence, the common law held that corporations could be held liable in tort, including those requiring a mental element, *e.g.* malice. The acts of the directors and governing officers of the corporation (who were treated as the *alter ego* of the corporation) were imputed to the corporation itself, so that it was personally liable. Humbler servants of the corporation who acted tortiously might render the corporation vicariously liable. Some difficulty has been experienced with what has been termed the "*ultra vires* tort," *i.e.* a tort committed by a servant of the corporation connected with some activity outside the statutory powers of the corporation (chartered corporations are subject to special rules). Since an act outside the statutory powers or the memorandum of association does not bind a corporation it would appear, as has been suggested, that "a corporation cannot be liable for a tort (whether personally or vicariously) which is committed in the course of a wholly *ultra vires* undertaking" (Atiyah, *Vicarious Liability in the Law of Torts*, p. 387). But a corporation acting with permissive powers may commit a tort, or be liable for its servant's tort, when the tort arose from the unauthorised performance of a power which might have been exercised in a non-tortious manner, *e.g.* an authority with power to build a small-pox hospital may be liable for nuisance if it builds it in a residential area so as to interfere with the health and comfort of the residents. Unincorporated bodies, *e.g.* clubs, societies, etc., often "employ" persons but a difficulty arises should the latter commit a tort in the course of employment in view of the fact that the association does not have the attribute of legal personality. This difficulty may be circumvented by (1) suing those **158** members who are the real employers, *e.g.* the committee-members, if such be the facts, or (2) bringing a representative action against a few members when the persons are employed by all the members.

159 The immunity in tort which trade unions had enjoyed since 1906 was swept away by the Industrial Relations Act 1971 which, broadly speaking, created a new wrong—the "unfair industrial practice"—cognisable by the Industrial Court and the industrial tribunals. That Act also distinguished between the registered and unregistered union, the former becoming a corporate body, the latter remaining an unincorporated association. The corporate trade union is, accordingly, liable, both personally and vicariously, in tort, to the extent that such liability survives the 1971 Act, and for the new unfair industrial practices in relation to which it (and its officials) are given special immunities. The unregistered (and therefore unincorporated) union can, however, bring and defend civil proceedings (including proceedings under the Act) in its own name (s. 154 (2)). The quasi-corporate attribute conferred on the unregistered union by that section influenced the House of Lords, in *Heatons Transport Ltd.* v. *T.G.W.U.* (1973), in concluding that the defendants could be made liable for the acts of its shop stewards which were unfair industrial practices. The liability of an unregistered union for the tortious acts of its agents or servants lay outside the scope of the *Heatons* case, but such liability is so closely connected that it is likely that similar considerations would apply to tort as were applied in that case.

Juridical basis of employer's liability

160 There has been much academic controversy on the question of whether the employer's liability is vicarious or personal. According to the latter theory, termed "the master's tort theory," the servant is merely the instrument whereby the master breaks his duty towards the third person. Whether this, or the traditional theory that the master is liable for his servant's tort is accepted (and the latter seems preferable), would appear to make little difference according to Atiyah (*op. cit.*) who rightly points out that the courts are more influenced by "pragmatic considerations" than "doctrinaire theories." In either event, the servant has a duty but, as Uthwatt J. pointed out in *Twine* v. *Bean's Express Ltd.* (1946) (cited to support the master's tort theory), "that is a coincidence, not a rule of law."

161 What is the position where the servant commits a tort in the course of his employment but for some reason his master is not liable, *e.g.* he has protected himself by an exemption clause or is exempted by law (as was formerly the case with trade unions)? Although it has been suggested that the employee can shelter under

the immunity of his employer (referred to as "vicarious immunity"), the tenor of the cases is the other way. Thus, where an employer contracts with a third person in terms which exempt the employer from liability for negligence, it seems clear that the servant is exposed to personal liability, assuming him to have been negligent, and cannot, in view of the doctrine of privity of contract (recently given a fresh lease of life by the House of Lords decision in *Beswick* v. *Beswick* (1968)), claim any benefit under the contract to which he is a stranger. Where the employer purports to extend to his employees the benefit of any exemption clause in his contract, the employee is unlikely to obtain vicarious immunity despite the argument that the master acted as agent or trustee for the servant in entering the contract. In *Genys* v. *Matthews* (1966), a bus driver was held liable in damages for personal injuries to a passenger without being able to shelter behind a term in the free pass (whether viewed as a contract or a licence) which purported to exclude the liability for both the corporation and its servants or agents "responsible for the driving, management, control or working of their bus system."

Various hypotheses have been put forward to explain the rationale of vicarious liability, ranging from Blackstone's emphasis upon the master's property in the servant, carrying with it liability for acts expressly or impliedly commanded, to the notion that the master should be liable for setting "the whole thing in motion" by employing the servant in the first place (*Duncan* v. *Findlater* (1839), *per* Lord Brougham at p. 910 of the report).

The modern justification for vicarious liability would, however, appear to be based to a large extent upon a rule of policy whereby risks are deliberately allocated; such allocation inclines towards what has been called "enterprise liability" on the grounds that employers are better able to withstand claims and can, if made liable, pass on their liability to consumers in the form of slightly higher prices reflecting the liability or the cost of insuring against it.

Independent contractor

Before leaving tort, it will be recollected that one of the main 162
reasons for distinguishing between the servant and the independent contractor was that the employer was vicariously liable for the torts of the former in the course of employment whilst the general rule is that he is not liable for the torts of his independent contractor. But there are certain exceptions to this latter rule. Thus the employer of an independent contractor will be liable where he has authorised or ratified the tort or where the independent contractor performs a duty which lies squarely upon the employer, *i.e.* is non-delegable. A

more difficult exception is the employer's liability for the non-collateral negligence of the independent contractor, *i.e.* negligence which is sufficiently connected with the task entrusted to the contractor. Thus, in *Holliday* v. *National Telephone Co.* (1899), the defendants, who were laying telephone wires under a street, contracted out the work of making connections. A plumber employed by the contractors caused an explosion, which injured a passer-by, by dipping a blowlamp into molten solder. The defendants were held liable since the negligence was sufficiently connected with the work which the contractors were charged to execute.

2. Liability for the employee's contracts

The employee as agent

163 An employee, as such, has no power to enter into contracts with third persons so as to bind his employer; it must be shown that the employee has been clothed with the power of an agent if the employer is to be bound. Clearly the employer is bound by his employee's contracts where he has conferred upon the employee agency powers, *e.g.* the purchasing officer, salesman and the bus conductor. The employee may be a "general agent" authorised to represent his principal in all matters or in all matters affecting a certain trade or business or matters of a particular kind. Such an agent may not only bind his principal when acting within the scope of his "express authority" but also when acting within the scope of his "apparent authority"; in exercising the latter type of authority, even in defiance of his principal's instructions, the agent may bind his principal. Such "apparent" or "ostensible authority" may be derived from law (*e.g.* the power of a partner to bind his co-partners under section 5 of the Partnership Act 1890) or from the normal incidents of the agent's or his employer's business. In *Watteau* v. *Fenwick* (1893), Wills J. said: "The principal is liable for the acts of the agent which are within the authority usually confided to an agent of that character, notwithstanding limitations, as between the principal and the agent, put upon that authority." A "special agent" is employed for a particular act or transaction "not being in the ordinary course of his trade, profession or business" (*Bowstead on Agency*, 13th ed., p. 7); such an *ad hoc* agent has, although the proposition has been criticised, no power to bind his principal beyond the sphere of express authority, *e.g.* a clerk, given time off to sell his employer's piano, would not bind his principal if he gave a warranty concerning the piano in breach of his instructions.

164 The employee may also possess agency powers (i) where his employer ratifies his act, provided that the employee acted *qua* agent, that the act is capable of ratification and that the employer when he ratified had knowledge of the act in relevant aspects; (ii) where the employer is "estopped" from denying a limitation on his agent's powers, *e.g.* where he habitually pays for unauthorised purchases by the employee; (iii) where the employee acted from "necessity" in his employer's interest provided that the necessity was real and communication with his employer was, in the circumstances, impossible.

The general rule, to the effect that the agent acquires neither rights nor liabilities on transactions entered into so as to bind his principal, is subject to some exceptions of which the most important is the doctrine of the "undisclosed principal," under which the agent is entitled to sue and may be sued by the third party (like the principal if he is "disclosed"). Naturally the agent who acts outside his express authority and, where appropriate, his apparent authority, does not bind his principal; but in this case the third party has redress against the "agent" for loss suffered in an action for "breach of warranty of authority"—an action to which the agent may be subject even though he was unaware that he had no authority or was exceeding his authority.

3. Liability for the employee's crimes

"In general," said Lord Morris, "criminal liability only results **165**
from personal fault. We do not punish in criminal courts for the misdeeds of others" (*Tesco Supermarkets Ltd.* v. *Nattrass* (1973), at p. 179 of the report). The individualised nature of criminal liability arises partly from the requirement of a mental state (*mens rea*) additional to that of the result which the law seeks to avoid (*actus reus*), and partly from the sanctions, retributive, deterrent and reformative, which are associated with criminal liability. The principle of individual responsibility is not so pronounced in the civil law since this is largely concerned with the adjustment of economic loss. The employer who was held liable in tort for the misdeeds of his managing clerk in the case of *Lloyd* v. *Grace & Co.* (para. 154, above) would not, had he been prosecuted, have been made criminally liable for those same misdeeds. As in the case of tort, it is easier to define the distinction between personal and vicarious liability than to apply the distinction to the facts of particular cases.

(a) *Personal liability*

An employer may be personally liable in crime, either as a **166**
"principal" who commits a crime, or as a "secondary party" who assists, whether present or not, in the commission of a crime. In *R.* v. *I.C.R. Haulage* (1944), a company was held guilty of conspiring to defraud with its managing director and others, showing that the

company itself was a principal since a person cannot be vicariously liable for common law conspiracy.

(b) *Vicarious liability*

167 Turning to vicarious liability, there are two groups of exceptions in which the employer may be held liable, one common law, the other statutory.

(i) *At common law.* An employer is liable for his employee's acts where these constitute (1) a public nuisance, (2) a criminal libel (a liability which, for those publishing newspapers or periodicals is much eroded by the Libel Act 1843), and probably (3) contempt of court.

(ii) *By statute.* But these common law exceptions have been dwarfed by a new genus of regulatory offence, usually punishable on summary conviction. In the last century, and more so in this, it has become common for Parliament to enact offences to ensure compliance with standards. A common feature of such legislation (which covers matters such as food and drugs, milk, agricultural produce, fertilisers, pharmacy, medicines, insurance and road traffic and a host of other matters) is that Parliament is deemed to be more concerned with seeing that the required standards are complied with than with the mental processes of grocers or dairymen. It is dangerous to generalise about these new so-called regulatory offences, as Lord Morris of Borth-y-Gest indicates in *Vane* v. *Yiannopoullos* (1965), at p. 506 of the report:

> "In general our criminal law requires that there should be mens rea in order to establish guilt. Parliament may, however, enact that mens rea is not necessary. There may be strict liability. So also it might be enacted that a person is guilty of an offence if his servant or agent does some act and does it with mens rea. It might be enacted that a person is guilty of an offence if some other person not his servant or agent does some act and does it with mens rea. It might be enacted that a person is guilty of an offence if there is mens rea either in him or in the person doing the act. It might be enacted that a person is guilty of an offence if an act is done by some other person even though there is no mens rea in anyone."

168 Confronted with a statutory offence which is silent on the question of *mens rea*, the court may, as a matter of judicial inference, have to draw two conclusions. The first might be that the offence is one of "strict liability," *i.e.* that the absence of *mens rea* is no defence. The presumption of statutory interpretation that a penal Act of Parliament prima facie requires *mens rea*, would, if applied to this type of offence ("quasi-criminal" as one judge put it), "stultify what, upon its fair construction, was the purpose of the legislation" (*per* Lord Evershed in *Vane's* case, above). An important reminder of the reluctance of the courts to extend this reasoning to acts "of a truly criminal character" is contained in *Sweet* v. *Parsley* (1969), a case which concerned the criminal liability of a person who, as occupier, permits the smoking of cannabis on his premises, or who is otherwise concerned in the management of premises used for such a purpose. The second inference which might have to be drawn, as a corollary of the first, is that the employer is liable for the acts and omissions of his employees. Thus, statutes which make it an offence for a person to "sell," "keep," "use" or "permit" certain things or activities, raise the question whether the physical actor, or his employer, or both, have committed the offence in question. Considerable difficulty has been encountered in construing what Professor Glanville Williams has termed the new "judicial dictionary." A shop assistant "sells" an article in the popular sense but it is the assistant's employer who is party to the contract of sale. Fortunately, some recent Acts are stating explicitly who is to be liable—the employer, the employee, or both.

Sometimes a mental element is an ingredient in this type of **169**
offence, as in *Allen* v. *Whitehead* (1930), in which the occupier of a café was held liable for "knowingly" permitting prostitutes to foregather in his cafe when he had left his manager with strict instruction in this matter. The rationale of the decision lay in the principle that a person cannot elude his statutory responsibilities by delegating the management and control of operations to a subordinate; to permit of such a defence would allow the occupier, in common parlance, to "pass the buck" so as to defeat the policy of the Act. If there is no such "delegation" the defendant may escape liability as in *Vane* v. *Yiannopoullos* (above, para. 167). In that case the holder of a restaurant licence was held (on appeal to the House of Lords) not to have "knowingly" sold liquor to persons not ordering meals, which a waitress had done while he was downstairs. Despite the doubts cast upon the delegation principle by some of the remarks of their lordships in the *Vane* case, the principle has been since applied in some licensing cases. Even so, those doubts must still remain, pending an authoritative decision by the House of Lords.

(c) *Corporate criminal liability*

Criminal liability, whether personal or vicarious, and whether **170**
"strict" or involving *mens rea*, is not affected by the circumstance that the employer is a corporation. Such a body may, of course, only act through physical persons. The latter may be either "the directing

will of the company" or within its "brain area", to use the words of Lord Morris of Borth-y-Gest in the *Tesco* case (above), or those who are subject to direction and control, being, so to speak, mere cogs in a machine devised by others. In the first group we have the notion of identification, namely, that the acts of such persons are, in truth the acts of the corporation and not merely its *alter ego*. In the *Tesco* case itself, the appellants who had been convicted of an offence under the Trade Descriptions Act 1968 committed by an oversight of a manager in one of their supermarkets were held entitled by the House of Lords to shelter under the statutory defence that the offence was due to the act or default of another person (*i.e.* their manager) and that they had exercised due diligence to prevent the occurrence in question. Because of his position in the organisation, the oversight of the manager was not attributed to the company itself which was therefore not personally liable. Because, to use Lord Diplock's words in that case, the rule "*Qui peccat per alium peccat per se* is not a maxim of the criminal law," there could be no question of vicarious liability, in the absence of any indications in the Act to that effect.

171 Now that the registered trade union has become a corporate body, it becomes liable in crime like any other corporation. The criminal liability of the unregistered union is less clear. The tendency to attribute quasi-corporate status to such a union in civil matters does not make it inconceivable that criminal liability might similarly attach. Trade unions, whether registered or not under the old law, could be convicted of crime under the Prices and Incomes Act 1966, and a similar provision is contained in section 5 (2) of the Counter-Inflation (Temporary Provisions) Act 1972, perhaps showing thereby that there is no doctrinal objection to the criminal liability of an unregistered union.

II. Liability of Third Persons

172 We must now turn to examine the extent to which third persons may incur liabilities to either the employer or the employee. Such liabilities chiefly arise because the third person has interfered in the contract relationship between the employer and employee, or because he has done something which has deprived the employer of the employee's services, *e.g.* by negligently injuring him or by seducing a female servant.

1. Interference with contract

173 In modern law, the parties to a contract (whether a contract of service or otherwise) are entitled to have their contractual relationship preserved inviolate from the intermeddling or wrongful acts of third persons. The dilemma of our law is that contract is a personal relationship between two parties carrying with it personal liability in the event of breach by either of the parties (the privity of contract idea) whilst, on a different plane, there is a prohibition so far as third persons are concerned that they should not procure or assist one of the parties to break his contract—the effect of the latter approach is that breach of contract, if procured or assisted by a third person, may become a tort by such third person. Because tortious interference with contract raises issues which, for present purposes, are more germane to industrial conflict, treatment of such interference is reserved for Chapter 9, below.

2. Loss of services *per quod servitium amisit*

Tortious interference with contract presupposes *some* knowledge **174**
of the contract in question; but what is the position where the employer loses his employee's services by reason of some wrongful act by a third person whether committed intentionally, *e.g.* assault and battery, or negligently, *e.g.* carelessly running him down with a motor-vehicle?

Apart from torts such as intimidation or interference with business relations the common law has been traditionally reluctant to concede any general principle that where A has contractual relations with B a tortious act committed by C in relation to A may also be tortious in relation to B. Widgery J., in *Weller* v. *Foot and Mouth Disease Research Institute* (1966) agreed that it was foreseeable that the escape of a virus likely to affect cattle in the vicinity was also likely to affect persons other than the owners of the cattle, *e.g.* cattle auctioneers, transport contractors, dairymen and so forth, but held that the duty of care in negligence could not be extended *ad infinitum* and cited the principle enunciated by Lord Simonds in *Att.-Gen. for New South Wales* v. *Perpetual Trustee Co.* (1955), "it is fundamental . . . that the mere fact that an injury to A prevents a third party from getting from A a benefit which he would otherwise have obtained does not invest the third party with a right of action against wrongdoer." Whilst it would be wrong to say that a rigid distinction exists between physical and economic loss as is shown in *Hedley Byrne Co.* v. *Heller & Partners* (1964), the common law is reluctant in cases involving proprietary loss to extend the ambit of the duty to take care so as to include loss arising from contractual relations, *e.g.* the transport contractor in the *Weller* case who had been commissioned to take the cattle to market.

Loss of services, however, has been historically treated not so much as an interference with contractual relations as an interference with a person's proprietary rights. (Blackstone said "The Master hath a Property in the Service of his Servant," just as a father had a "property" in his daughter's services.) Therefore, if a third person inflicted mayhem on a servant, or locked him up, or carelessly injured him, whereby the master was deprived of his services, the latter had a right of action (difficult to classify and therefore darkly named "innominate") because he had lost the services of his servant (*per quod servitium amisit*), although no action lay where the servant was killed. The scope of the action was, however, drastically restricted by *I.R.C.* v. *Hambrook* (1956), in which the Court of Appeal held that the action was limited to menial servants, *i.e.* those who could be regarded as members of a household, and not, for example, Inland Revenue Officers. The restriction imposed by this case, and the rule that in any case the instant death of the servant cannot found an action, have left little scope for the action.

175 If the action does lie it may be further restricted by the measure of damages which is based on the wages or other payments which the employer has paid the disabled servant, other than purely voluntary payments. An alternative approach, through quasi-contract, was adopted in *Receiver for the Metropolitan Police District Receiver* v. *Croydon Corporation* (1957), without success: the court held that where the plaintiffs' servant had been injured while in the course of duty by the defendants and while ill had been paid his wages by the plaintiffs (as they were statutorily required to do), the plaintiffs could not recover the sum paid to the servant as wages from the defendants in quasi-contract. Although the defendants' liability had been reduced in that the servant in an independent action against the defendants had made no claim for loss of wages (obviously not, since he had lost none!) they had not been unjustly enriched so that no claim in quasi-contract could lie. Lord Goddard C.J. agreed that the defendants had received a benefit "in one sense" but this stemmed from the plaintiff's pre-existing obligation to pay wages: "Their financial position has not been altered by a sixpence. Their duty is to pay wages whether the policeman is on duty or not, so long as his absence from duty is caused by an injury received in the course of his duty." The cumulative effect of these two cases (and others) was considered by the Law Reform Committee, which in its Report (Cmnd. 2017), which was not unanimous, recommended that (i) the action for loss of services should be abolished (together with actions for loss of consortium and for seduction), and (ii) an employer who has incurred loss in consequence of a tortious injury to his employee should be entitled to reimbursement from the tortfeasor to the extent that the tortfeasor's liability to the employee has been reduced in consequence of the action of the employer. These

recommendations have not so far been implemented, with the exceptions of actions in tort based on inducing a spouse to leave or remain apart from the other spouse, depriving a parent or person *in loco parentis* of the services of his or her child by raping, seducing or enticing that child, and harbouring a wife or child; these actions, which were cognate with the action *per quod servitium amisit*, were abolished by the Law Reform (Miscellaneous Provisions) Act 1970.

Of course, the employee who is tortiously injured by a third **176** party may himself sue the tortfeasor and recover damages in accordance with the principle of *restitutio in integrum*. If, therefore, the injured employee is covered by a sick-pay scheme and receives sick pay whilst away from work because of the injury, he must bring such sick pay into account. If damages were assessed solely by reference to what the plaintiff has lost, the assessment of damages would take into account all sorts of adventitious circumstances serving to reduce the loss. The *restitutio* principle is, however, modified by the rule requiring the exclusion of "collateral benefits" from the amount of damages payable by the tortfeasor. The courts have declined to take account of sums received by way of private benevolence (whether by the employer, or others), and of sums representing the fruits of insurance (see also the Fatal Accidents Act 1959 which excludes insurance moneys received as a result of the death). In *Parry* v. *Cleaver* (1970), the House of Lords, clearly influenced by the Fatal Accidents Act paradigm, held that a police constable, who, as the result of the respondent's negligence had been discharged from the police force and given a disability pension (treated on a contributory basis), did not have to account for that pension in claiming damages from the respondent on the ground that the pension scheme was in essence a form of insurance and intrinsically different from wages, although his earnings in alternative employment were taken into account, as was the disability pension in connection with his claim for loss of the full retirement pension to which he would otherwise have become entitled at normal retiring age.

Notwithstanding that *Parsons* v. *B.N.M. Laboratories Ltd.* **177** (1964) had taken unemployment benefit into account, Park J. refused in *Hewson* v. *Downs* (1970) to take account of state retirement pension when assessing the damages payable to a plaintiff who had been forced to retire because of injuries sustained at the hands of a negligent motorist, his lordship preferring to follow the "insurance principle" enunciated in the *Parry* case, where the pension had not been treated as a substitute for the capacity to earn, but as a "personal benefit." The exclusion of "collateral benefits" may, as in the *Parry* case itself, mean that a plaintiff is better off as the result of a tort than he would have been had no tort been committed against him. Professor Atiyah has criticised the differing consequences which ensue from the application of the *Gourley* (above, para. 118) and *Parry* (above, para. 176) principles (32 M.L.R. 397–407). His hope that the whole subject of damages for personal injury will be looked at afresh is now realised in the appointment of a Royal Commission to examine that very question (see para. 119, above).

Curiously, there has been little discussion of the employee who devotes a lifetime to his employer, thereby building up what has been described in extra-legal terms as "a property in the job," only to find that the "property" disappears when a third party injures or kills his employer so that the latter's business is closed down. Presumably, the employee must console himself with the thought that risks of this sort are so common that everyone accepts them as part of life.

CHAPTER 3

REMUNERATION

MOST of us need to work for money. Freedom of contract, based **178** on the individual contract of employment (*i.e. laissez-faire* in legal form), permits each of us in theory to sell our labour at its highest price on the market, but this is a development of the last 150 years or so. However, the doctrine has been eroded by a number of factors. Of these, the most important is the emergence of a trade union movement to which the individual contract was anathema because it encouraged underbidding by workmen who were reluctant to join the "general reserve of labour" and because, in any case, the individual bargain, as we have seen, could not be used to improve working conditions such as hours and sanitation and the like. To use the language of Sydney Webb, the unions were able to enforce the common rule by The Method of Collective Bargaining (*Industrial Democracy*, Chap. 2). The rules agreed between the trade union and the employer (or his association) constituted a code of minimum standards both in regard to wages and conditions to which, for example, "the wealthiest contractor and the builder on the brink of bankruptcy" were expected to conform (Webb, *op. cit.*, p. 175). It is interesting to note that both employers and unions were *ad idem* in their dislike of the long-term hiring, the "yearly bond," which was quite common in the first half of the nineteenth century; the employers disliked it because it proved too inflexible in the face of business fluctuations which might require men to be laid off at short notice; the unions disliked it because it put the men at the mercy of the employer who could interpret the contract as he wished. Perhaps the outstanding feature of our labour law was the voluntary principle, whereby management and labour were left to work out their own salvations with the minimum of state interference or legal intervention, but this principle was subject, in the late 1960s, to considerable attack and has now been very much eroded by the legislation of the 1970s.

After 1867, when the urban proletariat was enfranchised, the **179** unions showed greater interest in what the Webbs called The Method of Legal Enactment. Collective bargaining cannot always procure desired changes, either because of the need for some comprehensive regulation on a national scale, or because of trade union weakness. As a result we have a formidable code of industrial legislation governing the manner and form of wage payments (truck legislation), the establishment and observance of minimum standards, whether of wages (wages councils legislation), or of wages and conditions (Terms and Conditions of Employment Act 1959), or working conditions in particular places (factory, mines and quarries, shops and offices legislation). These legislative terms operate in different ways; sometimes they impose plain statutory duties, breach of which involves criminal and possibly tortious liability, *e.g.* the safety provisions of the Factories Act 1961; sometimes they operate through the individual contract of employment, *e.g.* wages councils orders; sometimes they operate in a devious way, *e.g.* the terms of a collective bargain may, as a result of a certain procedure, be given compulsory, normative effect in relation to individual contracts of employment, *e.g.* section 8 of the Terms and Conditions of Employment Act 1959, as amended. It might be added that the pressure for statutory control of employment may emanate from employers who wish to be protected against a rival prepared to save on labour costs: the Industrial Training Act 1964 (now subject to review: see para. 91, above) introduced a fair system which mitigated the unfairness whereby one firm "poached" the men trained by another firm more conscious of its training obligations. International commitments, such as those to the International Labour Organisation, the Council of Europe and, most important of all, the European Communities, will continue to affect our domestic legislation.

Our labour law is, as Professor O. Kahn-Freund points out, based on two features, namely, "the contractual foundation of the obligation to work and of the obligation to pay wages, and it is at the same time permeated by a tendency to formulate and to enforce an ever-growing number of imperative norms for the protection of the worker, norms which the parties to the contract cannot validly set aside" (30 M.L.R. 635).

180 From a formal, legal standpoint, the rules regulating remuneration in this country are part of a patchwork quilt made of the following:

1. The individual contract of employment, including terms implied therein.
2. Most important of all, the collective agreement.
3. Statutes controlling—
   (1) The mode of payment and deductions, *viz.* truck legislation and its variants.
   (2) the amount of remuneration, *viz.*
   Wages Councils Act 1959,
   Agricultural Wages Act 1948,
   Terms and Conditions of Employment Act 1959,

Fair Wages Resolution (1946),
Equal Pay Act 1970, and
Counter-Inflation (Temporary Provisions) Act 1972.

The simplest solution, at least from a lawyer's point of view, 181 would be a National Wages Act. This, however, presupposes a national wages policy and this has never been adopted here because of deep opposition from industry. The prospect of a twentieth-century "Just Wages Act" drafted by some latter-day Aquinas, like that of a comprehensive, national job-evaluation exercise, seems extremely remote given the conditions under which our labour market operates. Some foreign countries have enunciated a national minimum wage like that laid down in the Fair Labor Standards Act of the United States (where the coverage is by no means comprehensive). There has been some pressure for a national minimum wage in this country, but a departmental inquiry carried out by the Department of Employment showed that such a device might create more problems than it solved. There is in existence, of course, minimum wage regulation on a selective basis in this country, but the notion of a national minimum wage seems to have been rejected in favour of "negative income tax" on the lines set out in the recent Green Paper on a tax credit system (Cmnd. 5116) which would provide a minimum level of income by means of tax and social security rather than by interference with the mechanism of the labour market itself (see para. 402, below). There is not the same reluctance to interfere with the labour market at times of national emergency when statutory controls on increases in income have to be imposed.

I. The Individual Contract of Employment (including Common Law Terms)

Consideration must be present

An agreement to provide gratuitous services, unless under seal 182 (and the validity of a gratuitous contract of employment under seal has yet to be decided), is not binding. Typically, the employer provides "consideration" in the form of wages (or the promise thereof), whilst the employee provides consideration in the form of work (or the promise thereof); a contract which rests in promise is said to be executory, whereas one performed is said to be executed. In both events the contract is fully valid.

Valuable consideration

The consideration must be something which the law recognises 183 as having "value." Thus, a worker's promise to do something which he is already contractually bound to do is worthless in the eyes of the law and cannot support a promise of extra remuneration from the employer; labels such as "overtime" and "standby duty" are not conclusive since they may be contractually claimable by the employer without extra reward.

Once the law has accorded validity to the consideration, it remains, with minor exceptions, utterly indifferent to the "adequacy" of the value provided; such indifference is well shown, since otherwise the courts would have found themselves drawn willy-nilly into the role of price- and wage-fixing agencies. An English court cannot strike down an agreement whereby an adult worker agrees to work sixty hours a week for five shillings, at least as far as the common law is concerned. Nor is the form of consideration a matter for concern. Remuneration by lump sum, by gratuities from customers, by payments in kind, *e.g.* food and lodging (subject to truck legislation), by wages whether by time or by piece and, in the case of apprentices, by instruction, are all equally valid.

Position where no remuneration fixed

184 The cases fall into two groups. In the first group, it will be found that the party claiming remuneration has conferred upon the other party discretion to pay something or nothing as he chooses or, alternatively, has left the question of remuneration to be agreed in the future. In *Roberts* v. *Smith* (1859), the imprudent employee had accepted his employer's term, *viz.* "it is entirely left to me to give unto you such sum of money as I may deem right."

More recently, a joint managing director, appointed at "such remuneration . . . as the directors may determine," never received any remuneration during the short life of the company. Plowman J., upholding the liquidator's rejection of a claim of £400, said "the managing director is at the mercy of the board, he gets what they determine to pay him, and, if they do not determine to pay him anything, he does not get anything. That is his contract with the company, and those are the terms on which he accepts office" (*Re Richmond Gate Property Co. Ltd.* (1965), at p. 337 of the report). *Craven-Ellis* v. *Canons Ltd.* (1936) (in which an invalidly appointed director was awarded a sum for services rendered to the company) was distinguished on two grounds, *viz.* (a) the services in that case had not been rendered *qua* director; (b) there was no contract. In the *Richmond* case the existence of the contractual term concerning remuneration precluded the award of a *quantum meruit.*

185 In the second group of cases the courts have concluded from the facts that *some* remuneration was envisaged, the quantum of which the employer might decide. In these cases a reasonable sum (*quantum meruit*) has been awarded as in *Bryant* v. *Flight* (1839) ("the *amount* of payment I am to receive I leave entirely to you") (italics mine). No doubt it is true to say that the mere rendering of service, or, as was held in one case, the continuation over of paid service, does not *per se* raise an implication of payment, but nowadays the courts are more likely to garner from the circumstances a tacit agreement that some remuneration was intended, *e.g.* between parties dealing "at arm's length" in commercial matters, as opposed to a daughter helping in her father's business.

Payment pro rata

Consideration may be entire or divisible. A relevant example is **186**
the case of *Cutter* v. *Powell* (1795), in which the widow of a second mate who had died when two-thirds of the voyage was accomplished was held to be entitled to nothing, since the agreed sum of 30 guineas was payable on completion of the voyage. The rule in *Cutter* v. *Powell* that *pro rata* payment is not recoverable for partial performance of an entire contract survives and has produced harsh results. In *Lilley* v. *Elwin* (1848), an agricultural labourer on a general hiring was held to have been properly dismissed for leaving the harvest field, which he had done in chagrin at not being supplied with strong beer which, in his (mistaken) opinion, was his customary due. Coleridge J. further held that he could not claim *pro rata* for his work to the time of breach "as he was bound to give a whole year's service before claiming any wages and broke his contract by leaving that service before the year's end."

Section 2 of the Apportionment Act 1870 allows of apportion- **187**
ment of all "rents, annuities, dividends and other periodical payments in the nature of income" on a day-to-day basis. There is considerable doubt as to the applicability of this section to the remuneration of employees. Apart from the section, an employee may now have a remedy where his non-performance was prevented by the employer or where non-performance was attributable to some external event, such as death, which frustrates the contract and founds a claim under the Law Reform (Frustrated Contracts) Act 1943. So far as the section is concerned, the term "annuities" has been held to include emoluments payable to a Clerk of the Crown in Ireland (*Treacy* v. *Corcoran* (1874)), and a director's salary (*Moriarty* v. *Regent's Garage and Engineering Ltd.* (1921)). It is uncertain whether or not section 2 extends beyond salaries to include wages which do not appear to be *ejusdem generis* with the other types of income specified in the section. Dicta in the *Moriarty* case (above) indicate that wages should be included because of the impossibility of distinguishing the two forms of remuneration. Also

doubtful is the position where the employee fails to complete performance because of his own act, *e.g.* misconduct resulting in dismissal, or improper departure. Lush J. in the *Moriarty* case doubted if he could claim on the basis that he must be taken to have forfeited his claim by reason of misconduct. McCardie J., in the same case, whilst recognising the force of the argument that a servant ought not to be allowed to rely on his own misconduct as a reason for invoking a remedial Act, was not entirely satisfied as to the justice of denying to a servant who has been rightly dismissed after five-and-a-half months of service the apportioned part of his salary to the whole of which he would have become entitled after six months' service.

Under the Employers and Workmen Act 1875, jurisdiction is given (a) to county courts, which may in disputes between master and servant "adjust" claims on either side, *e.g.* to "set-off" damages against a claim for wages (s. 3), and (b) to courts of summary jurisdiction, which may make orders in disputes where the sum involved does not exceed £10 for each claim, *i.e.* more than £10 may be claimed where it represents the total of claims each under £10 (s. 4).

Effect of absence from work

188 The unauthorised absence of the employee from work is prima facie a breach of the duty to furnish personal service, rendering the employee liable to summary dismissal. As regards absence outside the employee's control, caused by sickness, injury or some external event, a distinction must be drawn between absence of a nature inconsistent with the continuance of the relationship and absence not having this grave effect. The former operates to determine the contract without more ado, although employers are well advised to take the safer course and give proper notice. In other cases the relationship continues. Can wages still be claimed? In those cases concerning absence through sickness it has been held that the question is one of contractual intent to be ascertained from the terms of the contract or by invoking the aid of the "innocent bystander." A distinction has been drawn in one case, and it has received some support, between cases where the employee's consideration is work and cases where it is readiness to work, *i.e.* in the former case no wages during sickness are claimable, whereas in the latter they are. The decline in piece-work and, even where it exists, its underpinning by the "guaranteed week" have made this distinction increasingly unreliable as a universal test. In *Orman* v. *Saville Sportswear Ltd.* (1960), Pilcher J. formulated the following rule (at p. 1064 of the report):

> "Where the written terms of the contract of service are silent as to what is to happen in regard to the employee's rights to be

paid whilst he is absent from work due to sickness, the employer remains liable to continue paying so long as the contract is not determined by prior notice, except where a condition to the contrary can properly be inferred from all the facts and evidence in the case."

This presumption is displaced by express provision in the contract, *e.g.* where the employee signs an agreement to join a friendly society to which the employers pay contributions, or where there is an established trade custom that wages are not payable of which, or of the existence of which, the employee was aware (*Petrie* v. *Mac Fisheries Ltd.* (1940)).

Suspension without wages

This is sometimes used as a method of disciplining employees **189**
guilty of industrial misconduct such as absenteeism. In the absence of express contractual provision or of an established trade practice, an employer has no common law right to withhold wages during the period of suspension. In *Hanley* v. *Pease & Partners* (1915), it was held that a worker suspended for one day without wages for one day's absence was entitled to 6s. 2d. withheld by his employers. Absenteeism may (i) justify dismissal and (ii) permit of a claim for damages whilst continuing the contract, but it cannot (iii) allow the employer to withhold sums due as a form of liquidated damages. Indeed, in the *Marshall* case, below, the view was expressed that there was no such thing as the suspended contract and that cases of suspension were really dismissals and re-engagements.

Suspension without wages may clearly operate where there is contractual agreement either express or implied. In *Bird* v. *British Celanese* (1945), suspension for disobedience was validated by the contract, with the result that, since nothing was to be paid during the suspension, no infringement of section 1 of the Truck Act 1831 had occurred. (The section prohibits deductions from any sum contracted to be paid—"You cannot deduct something from nothing" said the judge.) Nor is suspension unlawful where it is incorporated into the contract from trade custom as in *Marshall* v. *English Electric Co. Ltd.* (1945), in which Lord Goddard C.J., referring to *Sagar* v. *Ridehalgh & Son Ltd.* (above, para. 46) held (at p. 380 of the report) that "an established practice at a particular factory may be incorporated into a workman's contract of service, and whether he knew of it or not, it must be presumed that he accepted employment on the same terms as applied to other workers in that factory." But du Parcq L.J., dissenting (at p. 382 of the report), was doubtful of this mode of incorporation: "A workman who knows of a so-called practice, according to which he may enter into a new bargain, is certainly not binding himself to make a new bargain."

190 It goes without saying in a managerialist society like ours that the employee for his part cannot, except in the unlikely event of a term to that effect, suspend his contract of employment. If, however, he participates in a strike after giving due notice under section 147 of the 1971 Act, he is not to be regarded as having committed a breach of contract, unless there is agreement, express or implied, to the contrary. Whether one regards such participation in a strike as suspending the contract of employment, or as conferring certain immunities, the contract of employment continues during the strike until such reasonable time as the employee returns to work or the employer dismisses him (which he may do: see section 147 (4)).

The Employers and Workmen Act 1875, s. 11, prohibits the deduction of sums from the wages due of children, young persons or women because of absence or leaving work, except to the extent of the damage suffered by the employer. Section 136 of the Factories Act 1961 provides a more general prohibition of deductions by occupiers of factories.

Lay-off

191 Occasionally an employer lays off workers because he has no work for them. Applying Greer J.'s criticised dictum in *Browning* v. *Crumlin Valley Collieries Ltd.* (1926), at p. 528 of the report that—"The consideration for work is wages, and the consideration for wages is work," it would appear on first impression that an employee laid off work for a period has no right to remuneration during that period. This indeed was the finding in the *Browning* case itself (see para. 48, above) where the mine had been closed because of its dangerous conditions. Because the dangerous condition of the mineshaft could not be attributed to the fault of the employer, Greer J. fell back on an implied term to the effect that where work is interrupted by reason of some event outside the employer's reasonable control, such as a landslide, a breakage of machinery or a failure of supplies, the loss must be borne by both employer and employee: the employer forfeiting the lost production and profit, the employee losing his wages on the basis that he has provided no work and therefore no consideration, as opposed, presumably to "staff" who provide consideration in the form of "readiness to work." If the lay-off is due to the "fault of the employer" it has been suggested that the employee ought not to suffer a loss. This proposition has been supported by reference to *Devonald* v. *Rosser* (1906), where it was held that, during their period of notice, piece-

workers were entitled to wages from their employers, who could not fall back on the excuse that trade was slack.

However easy it may be to state the distinction between closure due to external causes and closure due to "fault" of the employer, it must frequently be difficult, if not impossible, to allocate a closure to its proper category. The dilemma posed by the *Browning* and *Devonald* cases has not, despite its importance, attracted much case law. No doubt the explanation for the lack of case law can be found in the practice of including provision for such eventualities in the terms of collective agreements, such as those relating to the "guaranteed week" or "fall-back" pay. Another reason can be found in the practice of laying off workers by dismissing them. Finally, there may be a contractual term, express or implied, including one sanctioned by custom, whereby the employer can suspend the contract by laying-off his employee. Cases of the latter are likely to be rare, although *Puttick* v. *John Wright & Sons Ltd.* (1972) (discussed below at para. 302) is a recent example of a "no work, no pay" contract of employment.

II. The Collective Bargain

Britain is *par excellence* the country of collective bargaining in **192**
that the great majority of workers in this country work on terms and conditions of employment which have been settled by collective negotiation. Indeed, when it is recollected that of the 18 million or so workers affected in some way or other by collective bargaining less than 10 million belong to trade unions, it will be apparent that the collective agreement has an effect on the terms and conditions of non-unionists.

Because of its importance, Chapter 8 is devoted exclusively to the collective agreement in its consensual aspect. The impact of collective bargaining upon individual contracts of employment has been discussed above at paras. 49 *et seq.* The *de facto* effect of the collective agreement is undoubtedly greater than its legal effect, whether consensual or normative. It is undoubtedly true of the collective agreement that "the best way *not* to know a country is to read its laws."

III. Statutory Regulation

1. Regulation of the mode of payment

We are not here concerned with statutory regulation of the **193**
amount of remuneration; such regulation, which began with the Trade Boards Act 1909, will be examined in the following section (below, paras. 201 *et seq.*). But, since 1464 (when the first statute

recited that workers "have been driven to take a quarter part of their wages in pins, girdles and other unprofitable wares"), statutory regulation has been invoked to control the *mode* of payment, although it was not until the nineteenth century that the practice of "trucking" became a fairly common practice in the industrialised conditions of that century. In the same way legislation was required in certain industries, to meet the demand for some "check-weighing" system for those paid by weight produced, and also to provide piece-workers, *e.g.* those in the hosiery trade, with some system showing the method of computation used for wages.

The Truck Acts

194 "Trucking" is a practice whereby employers pay their employees in kind or require them to expend their wages in goods bought from the employer's "tommy shop" at prices which exceed their cost value; such goods might be supplied by the employer or made available to him in a similar way, although good employers were able to pass on genuine savings in goods, tools and so forth to their workmen. The practice is subjected to "a very thorough system of inspection" (*per* Lord Atkin in *Pratt* v. *Cook* (1940)) in the form of the Truck Acts 1831–1940, to which must be added the Payment of Wages Act 1960.

Before summarising the effects of the legislation, it should be noted that the Acts only apply to the "artificer," the definition of which was however extended in 1887 to include manual labourers generally, with the exception of domestic or menial servants and of agricultural workers in regard to certain payments in kind. The distinction between manual and non-manual labour has produced some esoteric case-law, but the test in borderline cases is to determine whether the manual part of the employee's work is subordinate to the intellectual part or vice versa. Using this test, the bus conductor, the tram driver, the shop assistant and the girl making wreaths have been held, on the facts, to be non-manual workers. In the same way a lithograph artist or a typist is a non-manual worker despite the constant use of hands. But the television engineer who repairs television sets has, in a case under the Factories Act 1961, been held to be engaged in "manual labour" (see *J. & F. Stone Lighting & Radio Ltd.* v. *Haygarth*, below at para. 350).

195 The 1831 Act provides that contracts to pay an artificer other than in current coin of this realm are to be "illegal, null and void" as are contracts providing directly or indirectly in regard to the place where, the manner in which or the persons with whom the whole or part of wages shall be laid out or expended. The entire amount of the artificer's wages must be paid in the current coin of

this realm or in Bank of England notes (payment by bearer drafts or orders drawn on bankers within fifteen miles of the place of payment is still possible but of no practical interest now that the Bank of England is the only note-issuing bank). Civil redress is provided by enabling the artificer to recover to the extent that the whole of his wages are not paid in current coin of the realm. The House of Lords decided in *Pratt* v. *Cook*, above, that a deduction of 10s. dinner and tea-money from the weekly wages of a packer in a wholesale drapery firm was illegal and outside the protection of section 23 which authorises certain deductions with the written and signed authority of the artificer (see below, para. 197). (In view of an apparent widespread disregard of the Act, the Truck Act 1940 was passed, which made no change in the law but gave an amnesty to employers in relation to claims arising before the date of the Act, and also clarified the position, by declaring that infringement of the Truck Acts does not render the whole contract of employment void.)

The 1887 Truck Act made certain amendments to the law; the **196**
practice of "subbing" received statutory blessing and protection; the employer was prohibited from making any set-off or counterclaim for goods in respect of a claim for the recovery of wages; conditions of employment relating to the place or manner in which, or the persons with whom, wages are to be expended are prohibited —it is interesting to note that dismissal for breach of any such conditions appears to be prohibited. This Act was followed by the Truck Act 1896, which deals chiefly with fines and other deductions. The 1887 Act introduced an effective enforcement of the Acts by giving the factory inspectorate powers similar to those which it enjoys in relation to mines and factories including the power to commence prosecutions (of which there have been surprisingly few). In 1883, the payment of wages to any workman at or within any public house, beershop or like premises, save to workmen bona fide employed by the owner or occupier of such public house, was singled out for Victorian disapproval (Payment of Wages in Public Houses Prohibition Act 1883).

Permitted deductions

Prima facie, all deductions are illegal, since the artificer must **197**
receive "the entire amount" of his wages in current coin; but there are statutory and common law exceptions to this rule. Section 23 of the 1831 Act allows of deductions for medicine, medical attention, fuel (in relation to miners), materials, tools or implements, hay, corn or other provender to be consumed by any horse or other beast of burden (elephant?) employed by any such artificer in his trade or occupation, rent of premises let and "victuals" provided on the

premises. Deductions for such goods or services must not exceed their "real and true value" and must further be authorised by a written agreement signed by the workman. Apart from some minor provisions in the 1887 Act (dealing with deductions for education and the sharpening of tools), the next important statute is the Truck Act 1896, which regularises deductions for disciplinary fines, for damaged goods and materials, subject to complex and stringent requirements as to form (written contract or notice prominently displayed), particulars and occasions (for damaged goods, the acts or omissions in respect of which the deduction is made must be disclosed), and amount (*e.g.* fines must be "fair and reasonable"). Deductions authorised by separate legislation are obviously valid, *e.g.* income tax, national insurance and statutory superannuation.

198 In accordance with the principle that workmen ought not to have their wages diminished at source without their agreement, the Wages Attachment Abolition Act 1870 forbade the attachment of wages in respect of any servant, labourer or workman by the judge of any Court of Record or inferior court. This Act is of negligible interest for two reasons. First, the phrase "servant, labourer or workman" has been interpreted narrowly to denote persons of small means who require their wages for daily subsistence. Secondly, the principle of non-attachment has been eroded by a succession of statutes—the Affiliation Orders Act 1914, the Maintenance Orders Act 1958, the Criminal Justice Act 1967, the Administration of Justice Act 1970 and, most comprehensively of all, by the Attachment of Earnings Act 1971. Under the last-named Act, which consolidates the law on attachment of earnings, an attachment order may be made by the appropriate court in relation to maintenance, a judgment debt or administration order, requiring the person who appears to the court to have the debtor in his employment to make periodical deductions from the debtor's earnings and to pay the same to the court's collecting officer. The "earnings" which are attachable under the Act include, with certain exceptions, remuneration by way of wages or salary (including fees, bonuses, commissions and overtime pay) and pensions, although provision is made to leave the debtor with an income adequate to meet his needs.

The Payment of Wages Act 1960 allows an employer to pay an employed person by cheque (in addition to payment into a bank account and by postal or money order) if the person in question makes a request in writing to the employer and the latter agrees. The arrangement may be cancelled by a request in writing from either side giving at least four weeks' notice, and there are provisions permitting the employer to pay absent workers by postal or money order, subject to certain restrictions. Although the Act appears to make an inroad on truck legislation, the indications are that it has not brought about any extensive changes in the mode of wage payment.

Critics of truck legislation have suggested its repeal on the **199**
grounds that it is archaic and obscure. The doubt concerning the Acts may be illustrated by reference to *Hewlett* v. *Allen* (1894), in which the House of Lords held that the deduction by the employer of 2½d. a week from a woman's wages, to be paid over with her signed agreement to the employer's sick club, did not infringe the 1831 Act. Provided the money is paid over to an independent person (the club treasurer in the above case) it is as though current coin of the realm had been given to the person making the request; if the money is not paid over, *e.g.* it is kept and handed over at long intervals, it is doubtful if the exception applies. It clearly does not apply where the employer, at the request of the employee, deducts from the latter's wages sums owing in rent by the employee's father with whom the employee is residing (*Penman* v. *Fife Coal Co. Ltd.* (1936)), nor where the sum deducted is a sum owed to the employer whether as a simple or as a judgment debt. Again, the wide definition of wages given in section 25 of the 1831 Act has, in some cases, been held to render illegal payments in the forms of shares, *i.e.* co-partnership agreements and even gifts habitually given which can be deemed to be "recompense, reward or remuneration for any labour done."

The Karmel Committee on the Truck Acts recommended in 1961 that the Truck Acts 1831–1940 should be repealed and replaced by "legislation adapted to modern conditions" which should permit of greater freedom in the provision of benefits in kind and in regard to reductions to which the worker freely consents. So far, its recommendations have not become law.

Other statutes

The Truck Acts are the chief, but not the sole Acts dealing with **200**
mode of payment. Other examples are the Hosiery Manufacture (Wages) Act 1874 (providing for the payment of wages in full to those engaged in labour in the hosiery trade and imposing civil and criminal sanctions for deductions in respect of frame rents); the Stannaries Act 1887 (which regulates the payment of wages to certain miners); the Shops Clubs Act 1902 (which makes it an offence for an employer to make it a condition of employment that any workman shall discontinue his membership of any friendly society or shall not become a member of any friendly society other than the shop club); Acts dealing with checkweighing in coal mining and in

other industries; the Factories Act 1961 (*e.g.* section 135, requiring particulars of rates of wages to be given to persons employed in textile factories, and section 136, prohibiting deductions by the occupier of a factory in respect of anything to be done or provided in pursuance of the Act); and the Mines and Quarries Act 1954 (section 51 prohibits mine owners from charging workers for support materials).

2. Control of the amount of wages

201 Statutory control of minimum rates will be discussed here; prices and incomes legislation, which is more concerned with limitations on the maximum rates, will be discussed in the last section of this chapter (below, paras. 219 *et seq.*).

Despite the spread of collective bargaining, it was found at the beginning of the twentieth century that certain occupations, such as the "sweated trades," catering, agriculture and (later) road haulage, remained open to exploitation in the form of long hours, poor wages or bad conditions. The smallness of the unit (often a "one-man" business), the difficulty of unionising workers in scattered establishments and the employment of casual or female labour made it necessary for Parliament to intervene. The main forms of this intervention were wages councils legislation, legislation applying to agricultural workers and legislation to enable workers to obtain recognised terms and conditions of employment.

(1) *Wages councils*

202 The forerunners of the modern wages councils were the trade boards established by the Trade Boards Act 1909 (the first modern Act to interfere in the "wages-contract"). Initially confined to four sweated industries (ready-made tailoring, paper-box making, chain making, and lace and net finishing), the trade boards were extended to other industries, including road haulage, so that now there are over fifty wages councils (the trade boards were retitled "wages councils" in 1945) laying down minimum rates of remuneration for 3½ million workers employed in some half-a-million establishments (see generally M.O.L. Handbook on Industrial Relations, 1961, Chap. X). The relevant Act is the Wages Councils Act 1959, consolidating previous legislation.

The Secretary of State may establish a wages council, (1) on his own initiative "if he is of opinion that no adequate machinery exists for the effective regulation of the remuneration of workers"; (2) on the recommendation of the C.I.R. (which takes over the functions of the old commissions of inquiry) on a reference to them of an application from a Joint Industrial Council (or representative organisations of employers and employees) based on the cessation or inadequacy of existing machinery; and (3) on the recommendation of the C.I.R., to which he has referred the question of establishing a wages council because he considers that existing machinery to regulate remuneration of any workers is likely to cease to be adequate for that purpose and a reasonable standard of remuneration will not otherwise be maintained.

A wages council may submit "wages regulation proposals" to **203**
the Secretary of State, fixing the minimum remuneration, either generally or for any particular work, to be paid to all or any of the workers covered by the council, and may also fix the holidays and holiday remuneration for all or any such workers. Such a proposal cannot refer to "conditions of employment," although section 10 of the Act empowers a council, either on a reference from the Secretary of State or on its own motion, to make a report or recommendation concerning "industrial conditions." On receipt of a wages regulation proposal, the Secretary of State may (1) make an order by way of statutory instrument, or (2) refer back the proposal to the council for reconsideration (if it is then sent back unchanged the Secretary of State must give effect to the proposal by making an order).

In common with other wage increases, including agricultural wages orders, temporary powers to defer the operation of wages councils orders were taken under the Prices and Incomes Acts 1966–68 and, more recently, under the Counter-Inflation (Temporary Provisions) Act 1972, although in neither case could the Secretary of State amend or reject a proposal.

The statutory minimum remuneration may (1) be lowered, with **204**
the permission of the council, in the case of infirm and incapacitated persons; and (2) allow of stated deductions, *viz.* income tax, national insurance contributions, statutory superannuation, contributions to thrift schemes at the written request of the worker or for any purpose in which the employer has no beneficial interest, direct or indirect, and reductions in respect of fines, damaged goods and materials under the Truck Act 1896. Specified benefits or advantages may be reckoned as payment of wages if authorised by the order and not otherwise illegal under the Truck Acts.

It is provided that the orders shall have effect (1) civilly, in that the statutory minimum remuneration, etc., is incorporated into the worker's individual contract of employment thus enabling the worker to sue, if necessary, for amounts illegally withheld, and (2) criminally, in that an employer who fails to observe the terms of the order commits an offence punishable on summary conviction and, where he pays less than the minimum, is liable to be ordered to pay the employee the sums withheld for a period not exceeding two years. Wide powers of enforcement, *e.g.* to enter premises, to examine records and to receive complaints from workers, are conferred upon the wages inspectorate.

205 The hope that wages councils would wither away, as the Whitley Report envisaged, has not been fulfilled. The Donovan Commission made criticisms of the wages councils system for its failure, (1) to extend voluntary collective bargaining, (2) to raise the pay of lower paid workers, and (3) to acquire information on earnings in the industries affected by the system. Several unions have also criticised the wages councils for their narrow terms of reference and for the way in which they act as an impediment to the assertion of negotiating rights by unions (some 3 per cent. of workers in the Catering Wages Council are unionised). This low level of union organisation at the place of work "can only be lifted" said Mr. J. L. Jones (General Secretary of the Transport and General Workers Union) "by vigorous recruitment, and vigorous trade union pressure on a free trade union basis with the undertakings concerned. This, you will remember, we tried to do in the Torquay area. For our trouble we were brought into the law courts, and it cost the union £27,000 to try to organise the people who wanted to be organised" (*Post-Donovan Conferences of T.U.C., Wages Councils Sector*, p. 37). Other unions are dubious as to the practicability of unionising industries which have, on average, only seven workers per establishment, for which reason they are reluctant to forego the services of the wages councils inspectorate.

206 The Secretary of State may abolish a wages council under section 4 of the Act either—(a) to give effect to an application to that effect by a joint industrial council, conciliation board or other joint organisation representing substantial proportions of the workers and employers affected, or jointly by organisations of workers and organisations of employers (similarly representative, as above), or by an organisation of workers representing a substantial proportion of the workers affected (a new form of unilateral application introduced by the Industrial Relations Act 1971); or (b) on a report by the C.I.R. to which he has referred the question. Although a few wages councils have been abolished, progress has been disappointingly slow. The "vigorous trade union pressure on a free trade union basis" to which Mr. Jones referred (above) does not include use of the agency shop or sole bargaining procedures for which the Industrial Relations Act 1971 provides. Quite apart from the reluctance of unions to invoke these procedures, non-registration creates difficulty in these respects, and indeed as regards the right given to invoke section 8 of the Terms and Conditions of Employment Act 1959, which is now somewhat theoretically available in respect of workers in a wages council industry.

(2) *Agricultural workers*

The Agricultural Wages Act 1948 is a consolidating Act which regulates the wages of agricultural workers in a manner roughly similar to the wages councils legislation. The Agricultural Wages Board for England and Wales may lay down a national minimum wage and may prescribe holidays (and minimum holiday pay) for agricultural workers employed under a contract of service or apprenticeship. The County Agricultural Wages Committees have certain powers, *e.g.* the issuing of permits for the employment of certain workers (disabled or infirm persons) at special rates, and the revaluing of houses, the occupation of which may be taken into account against wages. Whilst the Act uses both civil and criminal sanctions (like wages councils legislation), greater latitude is shown towards payment in kind, *e.g.* in the form of cottages, food and intoxicating liquor, the provision of which to agricultural workers is outside truck legislation, although the Agricultural Wages Board can designate benefits or advantages, decide the value at which they shall be reckoned and restrict their amount. An inspectorate, provided by the Ministry of Agriculture, enforces the Act. **207**

(3) *Terms and Conditions of Employment Act 1959*

Leaving aside the somewhat academic possibility of legal enforcement of the collective agreement by a party thereto (on which see Chapter 8, below), we have seen that observance of recognised terms and conditions of employment can sometimes be secured by invoking section 8 of the Terms and Conditions of Employment Act 1959 (see para. 57, above). Although pay figures large in claims brought before the Industrial Arbitration Board, the terms and conditions of employment on which the Board can make an award extend to other matters, such as hours of work, the grading of work and so forth. **208**

The system of unilateral arbitration in respect of claims under the section contains certain distinctive features. First, the procedure may only be set in train by a claim duly reported in writing to the Secretary of State "by an organisation or association which is registered as a trade union or an employers' association under the Industrial Relations Act 1971" which is, or is represented by, a party to the collective agreement or previous voluntary award. Neither an individual worker nor, more importantly, an unregistered organisation may report a claim. Since nearly all the unions affiliated to the T.U.C. have preferred to stay unregistered under the 1971 **209**

Act, it will be seen that the utility of section 8 is reduced in practice. The reduced role of the Board under section 8 ought not to be exaggerated. In contrast to the large number of cases settled by autonomous machinery within industry itself and by the conciliation and arbitration machinery operated by the Department of Employment (see Chapter 9, below), only 108 awards were made by the Board in the years 1946–1966. Whilst references to the Board have stopped so far as unregistered organisations are concerned, the latter may still invoke the procedures made available in several Acts of Parliament dealing with specific industries, *e.g.* Civil Aviation Act 1949. In one respect the ambit of section 8 has been widened by the Industrial Relations Act to allow claims in respect of workers affected by the Wages Councils Act 1959 (on which see paras. 202–206). The organisation which is party to the agreement or previous award must be sufficiently representative of the employers and workers in the trade, industry or section to which the agreement or award relates.

210 Secondly, if the Board is satisfied that the claim is well founded, it must (unless satisfied that the employer is observing terms and conditions not less favourable than the recognised terms and conditions) make an award requiring the employer to observe the recognised terms and conditions as respects all workers of the relevant description from time to time employed by him. It will be seen that whereas the non-unionist is unlikely to have his claim taken up, he becomes a "free loader" once an award has been made, provided he is a worker of the "relevant description." This is in line with the tradition that the collective agreement in this country is a code applicable to trade unionists and non-unionists alike.

The third characteristic of the procedure, namely, its enforcement through individual contracts of employment, has already been discussed.

(4) *The Fair Wages Resolution of the House of Commons*

211 The present Fair Wages Resolution of the House of Commons (1946), like its forerunners, the 1891 and 1909 Resolutions, is based on the belief that the government ought to use its economic bargaining power to ensure that contractors with the public service provide wages and conditions of labour not less favourable than those established for the trade or industry in the district where the work is carried on, or, if not so established, which are not less favourable than the general level of wages, hours and conditions observed by other comparable employers. The "normative" effect of the Resolution is considerable since, apart from the great increase in the trading and industrial activities of central government since

1946, the Resolution has been applied, with or without slight changes, by local authorities and the nationalised industries.

Although the Resolution does not, of itself, confer actionable 212
rights upon individuals (*Simpson* v. *Kodak Ltd.* (1948)), it is the practice for complaints to be received by the Department concerned or the Secretary of State, who, if the claim is not otherwise settled or disposed of, may refer it to an independent tribunal (in practice, the Industrial Arbitration Board). As regards non-statutory references of this description, the awards of the Industrial Arbitration Board have no executive effect, it being left to the Department concerned to take such action as may be necessary. The Fair Wages Clause, or some similar formula, has been included in several Acts and thereby given statutory force (the four main ways in which these Acts operate are described in K. W. Wedderburn and P. L. Davies, *Employment Grievances and Disputes Procedures in Britain*, pp. 199–203). Many of these Acts provide for the reference of complaints to the Industrial Arbitration Board and for the incorporation of the Board's award in the individual contracts of employment of those covered by the award, although it is interesting to see that the Road Traffic Act 1960 made observance of the award a condition of the licence, thus showing that other sanctions can be used.

Contractors are required to display a copy of the Resolution for the information of workpeople and to ensure that sub-contractors observe its terms. In the *Simpson* case (above) there was no evidence that the employee had seen the notice: even if he had seen it, Sellers J. doubted whether the employee could have recovered wages by relying on the notice unless "certain things were done and said with regard to it."

The Resolution also states that "The contractor shall recognise the freedom of his workpeople to be members of trade unions," which is in line with the United Kingdom ratification of two Conventions of the International Labour Organisation (No. 87, Freedom of Association and Protection of the Right to Organise, and No. 98, Right to Organise and to Bargain Collectively).

(5) *Equal pay*

The Equal Pay Act 1970 is the culmination of a long campaign 213
for the equal treatment of men and women in employment. The T.U.C. recommended the adoption of the principle of equal treatment in 1888, but apart from some recommended improvements in the public sector (later implemented), the reports of the Atkin Committee in 1919 (Cmd. 135) and the Royal Commission on Equal Pay in 1946 (Cmd. 6937) were unable to propose any broad reform for non-industrial employments.

The 1970 Act imposes a requirement of equal treatment in terms and conditions of employment as between men and women engaged on like work or on work rated as equivalent without regard to any special statutory protection accorded to women. This requirement of equal treatment operates via an implied term in the contracts of employment of those affected (normally these will be women, although men are at liberty to invoke the Act). The title to the Act is misleading since it also applies to terms and conditions of employment other than those relating to pay. One of the rocks on which the Royal Commission (1944–46) had foundered was the difficulty in equiparating what it termed "disparate employments," such as nursemaid and coalminer. The 1970 Act, however, overcomes this difficulty by including in addition to "like work" (*i.e.* work which is broadly similar), "work rated as equivalent" (*i.e.* work rated as equivalent under a job evaluation exercise). The essence of a job evaluation exercise is that it evaluates the job, and not the person doing it, by reference to certain impersonal criteria which, because of their universal applicability, enable disparate employments to be measured one against the other. It is significant, however, that the Act does not (as one might have expected) impose a duty to carry out a job evaluation exercise.

214 Since the National Board for Prices and Incomes finding some years ago that only 10 per cent. of companies utilised job evaluation (very few of which covered women workers), job evaluation has become the rule, at least for large firms. Even so, in its first report on Equal Pay (1972), the Office of Manpower Economics found that these large firms still recognised wage differentials between men and women, whereas amongst smaller firms ignorance of the Act was widespread. If a firm does not carry out some job evaluation scheme, women will be driven to base their claims on the ground of "substantial similarity," which will often be difficult to prove. Even where job evaluation schemes are undertaken, the O.M.E. thought that it was "conceivable that as a result of equal pay job evaluation schemes will tend in future to be more heavily weighted against women by the choice of factors and the relative importance attached to them, *e.g.* by giving greater weight to certain physical requirements than to manual dexterity."

215 Only those who are employed under a contract of service or of apprenticeship, or who are employed under a contract personally to execute any work or labour, are covered by the Act, and the requirement only operates as between men and women employed by the same employer (or associated employer) at the same establishment (or establishments in Great Britain which include that one) and at which common terms and conditions of employment are observed either generally or for employees of the relevant classes. The term "establishment" as used in other legislation has caused some difficulty and the use of different criteria such as autonomy, the *locus in quo* of the headquarters of a firm, and the notion of "a staff of employees," have been variously pressed into service by the courts and tribunals. Claims arising out of an "equal pay clause," express or implied under the Act, are entrusted to the industrial tribunal, which, subject to a two-year period of limitation, may award arrears of remuneration or damages in respect of a breach of such clause. To deal with those cases in which a woman lacks union support, either because she is not a member of a union or her union officials are "no more than lukewarm" (O.M.E. Report, above, para. 97) on the subject of equal pay, power is given to the Secretary of State to refer apprehended breaches of the equal pay clause to the tribunal. Whoever claims, it is incumbent upon him or her to prove entitlement to equal treatment, whereupon the employer has to show that an advantage given to employees of the opposite sex is not the result of more favourable terms and conditions of employment but is genuinely due to a material difference between the claimant's case and the other employees. The Act will not necessarily result in equality of *earnings* between men and women. Men (or women) may earn more than employees of the opposite sex because they avail themselves of overtime work or because they produce more under a payment-by-results scheme.

The requirement of equal treatment applies without regard to **216**
laws providing for the special protection of women in employment, such as factory legislation (see Chapter 5, below) or any special treatment given to women in connection with the birth of a child. There are signs that women themselves are coming to have doubts concerning the retention of many of these laws at a time when social attitudes to working women are changing and when work needs less and less "muscle." There is evidence that the retention of some protective laws serves to achieve the disguised labelling of jobs as "tough" or "soft" and, therefore as "male" or "female." Indeed, an OECD Report criticises the notion of bringing women up to parity with men as regards terms and conditions of employment and suggests the use of objective job evaluation in order to arrive at a rate of pay to be paid without regard to the sex of the worker.

Collective agreements and employers' pay structures may be amended by the Industrial Arbitration Board (acting on a reference from the Secretary of State) to bring them into line with the principle of equal treatment under the Act. In so far as the terms and conditions of a person's employment are dependent upon a collective agreement, they are to be ascertained by reference to that agreement, as amended by the Board, and the same applies to an award of determination of the Board under section 8 of the Terms and Conditions of Employment Act 1959 (which operates subject to the amendment). The Act also enables wages regulation orders and agricultural wages orders to be brought into line with the principle of equal treatment.

217 Although many agreements and orders are now moving towards the elimination of discrimination in terms and conditions of employment, the O.M.E. in its first report found that in 1972 only a fifth of the companies examined had introduced equal pay for manual or white-collar workers with only 10 per cent. of these companies affording equal pay to both categories of employees (female manual workers lagging noticeably in this respect).

It was originally intended to include equality of pension provision in the Act, but the promise to deal with that matter in a later Act was frustrated by the outcome of the General Election in 1970. The Act does not come into force until December 29, 1975, although it may be implemented partially before that date. Collective agreements, pay structures, wages regulation orders and agricultural wages orders may be referred to the Industrial Arbitration Board for "advice" as to the amendments required in each to render them conformable to the new requirement.

The Act brings British law, if not practice, into line with international commitments such as the European Social Charter (ratified by the United Kingdom) and Convention No. 100 of the ILO which affirms "the principle of equal remuneration for work of equal value" (also ratified by the United Kingdom). Most important of all it is conformable to the principle of equal remuneration for "un même travail" contained in Article 119 of the Treaty of Rome. Pending the official translation "même travail" has been translated as "the same work" and as "equal work"—which do not carry the same meaning. In *Peregro* v. *Marzotto* (1965), an Italian court held that considerations, whether qualitative or quantitative, of the value of the work to the employer must be disregarded in applying Article 119. If an employer feels that women are of less value to him because they marry, have babies, decline responsibility, refuse overtime and so forth, he may only discriminate against them by not employing them at all.

218 Apart from the refusal of employment by reason of race, the exercise of trade union rights under section 5 of the Industrial Relations Act 1971 or disablement under the apparently unenforced Disabled Persons Acts, the refusal of employment to women is still permissible. Once in employment, however, a woman would presumably be able to claim that her dismissal on grounds of sex

was unfair under section 22 of the 1971 Act (such dismissal was a "disqualified reason" in clause 36 of the Labour Government's Industrial Relations Bill of 1970), unless the dismissal was founded on her lack of "capability," a term which is construed to refer to health, physical or mental quality, *e.g.* pregnancy. It will be seen, therefore, that the British Act seeks to achieve equality of treatment as between men and women *in employment*, unlike other countries in Europe as well as the United States and Canada where equality of *access* to work is also emphasised. Convention No. 111 of the ILO affirms the principle of "equality of opportunity and treatment in respect of employment" and prohibits discrimination in either form which is based on sex. The subject of discrimination against women has been examined by a Select Committee of the House of Lords. Until such time as the Government takes up the subject, private members' bills seem unlikely to achieve a reform.

(6) *Prices and incomes legislation*

Since the Second World War, Britain has experienced recurrent **219**
economic crises caused by inflation. Inflation not only erodes the real value of money wages: it creates a social problem for those on low or fixed incomes and international difficulty for sterling as a trading and reserve currency. The traditional governmental response to economic crisis was a mixture of hopeful exhortation and the use of monetary and fiscal measures. Although wages had been controlled by the Statute of Labourers and by justices under the Elizabethan law, the Prices and Incomes 1966 marked a new departure in modern times because it used the law as a complementary method of controlling the problem of inflation. The Prices and Incomes Acts 1966–68 were intended to be the statutory precursors of a régime of self-administered, voluntary restraint by Government, Industry and Labour. Experience since the Statement of Intent in 1964, and more recently, indicates that even if the will to tackle the problem were present, neither Industry nor Labour have the means to translate desire into action. The 1966–68 legislation was remarkable for the range of prices and incomes which it covered, for the use which (apart from the period of "freeze") was made of the National Board for Prices and Incomes and for the forbearance which the country as a whole showed. Because the policy was unpopular with the unions it was allowed to lapse and the National Board for Prices and Incomes, which in six years had issued 170 reports, several of lasting importance, was wound up on March 31, 1971.

After yet another lengthy bout of abnormal inflation, and fol- **220**
lowing upon the breakdown of talks between the government, the

C.B.I. and the T.U.C., the law was again invoked in the form of the Counter-Inflation (Temporary Provisions) Act 1972. Section 2 of that Act imposes a standstill on the following:

1. Prices and charges. These must not exceed during the period of standstill the prices or charges for transactions of the same description effected by the same person in the course of business before November 6, 1972.

2. Remuneration of an employee for work during the standstill. This must not exceed the rate of remuneration paid to him for the same kind of work before November 6, 1972. According to the White Paper *A Programme for Controlling Inflation: The First Stage* (Cmnd. 5125) the standstill applies not only to basic pay but also to pay for overtime, week-end work and piece-work. Also included are "other improvements in the terms and conditions of employment, *e.g.* hours and holiday," but not occupational pensions. Arbitrators, independent review bodies and statutory wage-fixed bodies are expected to take account of the standstill.

3. Company dividends.

4. Rents (but increases are not made criminal).

221 The standstill operates for ninety days from the date of enactment (November 30, 1972) but may be extended for a further sixty days by Order in Council. As in the case of the earlier legislation, the 1972 Act does not automatically render criminal all breaches of the standstill, but only those increases to which the standstill has been applied by ministerial order (which may also prescribe the degree of invalidity attaching to proscribed increases). Fines are imposable on those who contravene section 2, as applied, and upon any organisation of workers or employers, or other organisation, or person guilty of taking, or threatening to take, any action with a view to compelling, inducing or influencing a person to contravene any of the provisions of section 2. The consent of the Attorney-General is required for proceedings for an offence under the Act in England and Wales.

222 Section 3 affects existing contracts of employment by limiting the rate of remuneration payable to an employee in respect of work done when section 2 is in force to the highest rate payable to him under the agreement for work of the same kind before November 6, 1972. Increases in remuneration in respect of age and seniority are not affected. This exemption has been criticised as undermining the principle of equality of sacrifice. Work outside the United Kingdom, except on British ships or aircraft, is also excluded. At the time of writing, the Act is seen as an interim measure pending the introduction of legislation embodying agreement on long-term measures to contain inflation.

The two essays in statutory control since 1966 are novel for the 223
way in which, unlike the other forms of statutory control of wages described in this chapter, they seek to control maximum rates and earnings, albeit on a temporary basis, so that inflation may be contained. During such periods of limitation, the bipartite system of collective bargaining between management and labour is in danger of being replaced by a tripartite system in which the government is the third, and possibly, unwelcome guest in the bargaining process. The collective bargain must not only serve the two parties—it must also not harm the "public interest," *i.e.* the consumer. The same consideration applies to those who discharge arbitral functions. There is little doubt that the increased bargaining power of labour (on which full employment and the welfare state have played a part), the shift (with some notable exceptions) from industry-wide bargaining to plant bargaining (carrying with it lack of control and "wages drift"), and the growing secularisation of a society obsessed by reified interests to which it is conditioned by advertising and the like, have all contributed to an emphasis upon money wages rather than real wages. Sir Stafford Cripps warned that "It is time for us finally to renounce and to denounce that easy-going, get-rich-quick attitude to life that in all levels of society has found its post-war devotees and which prides itself on the smallness of its own effort and the largeness of its personal gain." One wonders if these remarks, uttered during the sterling exchange crisis of 1949, are, perhaps, even more relevant today.

CHAPTER 4

TERMINATION OF THE RELATIONSHIP

224 IN recent years, the decline of traditional industries and the accelerating pace of technological change, to which must now be added the mobility of capital and labour for which the Treaty of Rome provides, have led to a much greater emphasis upon "the right to work" and, once work has been obtained, to the "property in the job." The "sit-in" (perhaps copied from the students) and the "work-in" (particularly that in the Clydeside shipyards threatened with closure) are symptomatic of the fears of workers for their economic survival in a competitive society. At the national level, Britain seeks to achieve "as a major goal, an active policy designed to promote full, productive and freely chosen employment" in accordance with ILO Convention No. 122, although she has in practice fallen short of that ideal in some respects. The Industry Act 1972, although not as "employment-orientated" as the Local Employment Acts which it repeals, seeks to soften the economic and social effects of structural change. At the more personal level of employer and employee, the exercise of the so-called managerial prerogative to "hire and fire" has (despite criticism) been left intact but rendered increasingly expensive to exercise. It is the purpose of this chapter to examine the ways in which the employment relationship may end, and, in particular, to deal with unlawful termination, unfair dismissal and dismissal by reason of redundancy.

I. DURATION OF THE RELATIONSHIP

225 Lord Reid (in *Ridge* v. *Baldwin* (1964)), dealing with the application of the rules of natural justice to dismissed persons, named three chief categories, *viz.* (1) the ordinary master–servant relationship, (2) those who hold office at pleasure, such as civil servants, and (3) office-holders who discharge functions laid upon them by law, *e.g.* police officers. The latter two categories apart, the duration of the relationship is a matter of contractual intent and need not be the same as other periods, *e.g.* of notice (if required) or of the period after which wages or other remuneration are paid. Nor need the duration of the relationship be the same thing as the duration of the contract, which may be of two kinds, namely (1) a contract for a fixed period or (2) a contract of indefinite duration.

1. Contracts for a fixed period

Examples of the first category are contracts to last for a fixed term, *e.g.* five years certain, or for the completion of a particular piece of work, or even for life, although this will necessarily be rare despite the use of expressions such as "permanent employment" in the contract. In *Salt* v. *Power Plant Co. Ltd.* (1936), it was held that a contract which, after an initial period of three years terminable by notice, was to last permanently subject to the satisfactory performance of duties, was a contract for life. A similar conclusion was surprisingly drawn in *McClelland* v. *Northern Ireland Health Board* (1957), in which it was held that, despite a redundancy situation, the respondents could not dismiss the appellant for reasons other than those expressly set out in her conditions of service governing her "permanent and pensionable" post. In the *McClelland* case, the House of Lords, whilst not giving conclusive effect to words like "permanent" gave some evidentiary value to it in finding that the express conditions in the plaintiff's contract of service militated against terminability by notice. The decision was not followed in an Irish case, *Walsh* v. *Dublin Health Authority* (1964), in which it was held that "permanent" merely meant for an indefinite period subject to reasonable notice, and it is respectfully submitted that the decision might well be confined to its facts. **226**

A fixed term may be inferred from custom, *e.g.* "the run of the play" for an actor. A troublesome legacy from former rural England was the presumption of a general (or yearly) hiring, defined thus by Lord Coke: "If a man retaine a servant generally without expressing any time the law shall construe it to be for one yeare, for that retainer is according to law." However practicable such an inference might be for agricultural hands hired for "the revolution of the seasons," it was of questionable relevance in modern society, with its preference for the short-term contract. Nevertheless the presumption was applied to non-agricultural callings such as that of buyer's assistant, clerk to an army agent, a sales manager, a warehouseman, a coal owner's servant operating a "tommy shop," an engineer and a horsekeeper. In some of these cases the payment of salary or commission at annual intervals was seized on to support the application of the presumption. The continued existence of the presumption "would probably surprise a good many people" said du Parcq L.J. in *Jackson* v. *Hayes Candy & Co.* (1938), at p. 589 of the report, although the same judge accepted that it might be displaced by custom or other evidence for which the court would cast around, "sometimes rather eagerly." In a case which concerned a café manageress employed at an annual salary, payable **227** monthly, the Court of Appeal with robust common sense removed the excrescence of the yearly hiring from our law. "The time has now come" said Lord Denning M.R. "to state explicitly that there is no presumption of a yearly hiring. In the absence of express stipulation, the rule is that every contract of service is determinable by reasonable notice" (*Richardson* v. *Koefod* (1969), also holding that, even if the presumption existed, it had been excluded by the terms of the contract).

2. Contracts of indefinite duration

228 This second category of contracts may raise a situation which is quite common where the duration of the relationship is longer than the duration of the contract at any given time. An industrial worker on a weekly contract has at any given moment a fixed-term contract but his, and his employer's, expectation is that the relationship will continue beyond one week, *i.e.* there will be an expiry and a rehiring (*relocatio*) for the following week. As Pennycuick J. said in *Re Mack Trucks* (*Britain*) *Ltd.* (1967), at p. 787 of the report, dealing with the meaning of "continuously employed" in the Contracts of Employment Act 1963:

> "It must frequently happen in the case of a long period of service with a single employer that employer and employee enter into a whole succession of new contracts, *e.g.* on promotions or for other reasons. In ordinary speech one would in such circumstances treat the period of employment as dating from the commencement of the first of these contracts and not from the commencement of the contract currently in force at the date of its termination."

II. Termination by Events Other than Termination with or without Notice

1. Agreement to determine or vary

229 The parties may agree to dissolve their contract, the mutual relinquishment of rights thereby constituting valid consideration. It is common in the case of the premature determination of fixed-term contracts for the employer to give compensation for the unexpired term—the so-called "golden handshake."

A contract of employment may be dissolved expressly or impliedly by a new contract. *Strange* v. *Mann* (1965) is an example of such a "novation." M was appointed manager of a bookmaking and commission company subject to a restrictive covenant against competition after leaving the firm. After some disagreement, M was appointed manager of the credit department, and was later dismissed without notice. It was held (1) that the restrictive covenant was not binding upon him since the earlier contract containing the covenant had been replaced by the later contract, which contained no such covenant; (2) that he was entitled to three months' notice.

The replacement of a contract, in whole or in part, must be consensual. That the employer who wishes to vary the terms of service must be careful is shown by two cases. In *Dorman Long & Co. Ltd.* v. *Carroll* (1945), a rearrangement to enable two-shift working on Saturdays was held to be a purely temporary arrangement, which did not vary the contract, so that the men were entitled to go back to the old system on giving notice. In *Cowey* v. *Liberian Operations Ltd.* (1966), the employer sent round a notice, which was initialled by employees, purporting to vary the contract by making the period of notice to be given on termination one month. The plaintiff, who was a port engineer, had entered the defendant's employment without any period of notice being specified, although a period of three months had been specified in his previous (similar) employment. It was held that the employer could not unilaterally vary the terms of employment in this way.

An important development over the last few years has been the **230**
manner in which the courts have construed a unilateral variation by the employer as ineffective and, subject to the extent of the purported variation, as a repudiation of the contract ranking as "constructive dismissal" of the employee. The difficulty in distinguishing between a consensual variation or rescission on the one hand, and a repudiatory and abortive variation on the other hand, is typified by the vicissitudes of the *Marriott* case in which the Court of Appeal finally held that the demotion of a foreman and the reduction of his wages amounted to a constructive dismissal which had not been waived by his continuance under protest for a time in his employment as varied (*Marriott* v. *Oxford & District Co-operative Society* (*No. 2*) (1970)—a redundancy case).

No particular form is required to dissolve or vary a contract of employment even though initially reduced to writing or a deed. Where one party has performed the contract, he may take a substituted consideration or the promise thereof in satisfaction of his original claim ("accord and satisfaction").

Sadly, the complaisant employee who falls in with his employer's offer to dissolve their relationship by mutual agreement loses possible claims for compensation in respect of unfair dismissal, or dismissal by reason of redundancy, each of which postulates a dismissal *in invito* the employee.

2. Performance

231 Performance of the contract, as by the efflux of the agreed time or the completion of a particular task, discharges the contract. We have seen that performance must normally be personal in the case of contracts of employment, a rule which precludes both the employee from delegating his office in the absence of agreement and the employer from transferring the benefit of his workers' contracts to a third person. In *Re Foster Clark Ltd.'s Indenture Trusts* (1966), Plowman J. held that the sale of a company's business to another company, by the receiver and manager appointed by a debenture-holder, terminated the employment of employees of the former company. With the exception of certain classes of public servants, an employee may assign his salary or wages, *e.g.* as security.

3. Impossibility or frustration

232 Performance of the contract may be excused by the occurrence of some events supervening after the formation of the contract where such events render the contract impossible to perform (either physically or legally), or where further performance would be purposeless. Impossibility or frustration automatically discharges the contract without any need for one or both of the parties to take any formal steps (*cf.* fundamental breach where the contract is not discharged unless the "victim" accepts the breach as discharging the contract). From the middle of the nineteenth century the so-called Rule in *Paradine* v. *Jane* (1647) (to the effect that a person must perform what he has contracted to do) was clearly modified to allow of certain excuses for non-performance. This Rule (criticised by certain writers who doubt if *Paradine* v. *Jane* did in fact impose an absolute rule) produced harsh results in *Cutter* v. *Powell*, which we discussed above, at para. 186. Since its modification, the death of the employer or of the employee, the conscription of either, the internment of a party, the outbreak of war and changes in the law itself are all possible examples of impossibility or frustration.

233 In the same way, the incapacity of the employee, whether caused by sickness or injury, discharges the contract of employment if the employee cannot perform his obligations or such performance as he is able to provide is something radically different from that originally undertaken by him. Amongst the factors to be considered are (a) the terms of the contract, including provision for sick-pay; (b) the likely duration of the employment; (c) the nature of the employment; (d) the nature of the incapacity, including its past and likely future duration; and (e) the period of past employment (*Marshall* v. *Harland & Wolff Ltd.* (1972)). This last-named case is

not untypical of the sympathetic tenor of the cases towards the afflicted employee. Although the employee in that case had been absent from work without sick-pay for eighteen months because of *angina pectoris*, the Industrial Court held that his contract had not been frustrated. The employers, upon whom lay the burden of proving frustration, had adduced no medical evidence as to permanent incapacity. Similarly in *Farmer* v. *Willow Dye Works Ltd.* (1972), the Industrial Court declined to infer a frustration because of lengthy absences from work over a period of three years culminating in an absence upon which the frustration was based. "The contract had survived previous enforced absences" said Sir John Brightman (at p. 228 of the report) who held that the employee had been dismissed by reason of ill-health and not, as in the *Marshall* case, by reason of redundancy.

Much depends upon the facts of the case: a pianist who loses a hand would have difficulty in playing a two-handed concerto, and a pop star who collapses as the result of the frenetic life style common to that profession may thereby disclose his unsuitability for that way of life (*Condor* v. *The Barron Knights* (1966)). The employer may, of course, dismiss his sick employee by giving him the requisite period of notice, and might be well advised to do so rather than rely on the operation of the doctrine of frustration which is so uncertain both in its application and its timing. The employee dismissed by reason of redundancy while he is away sick may obtain a redundancy payment (as in the *Marshall* case, above). It is not impossible that, alternatively, he might be able to obtain compensation for unfair dismissal if, despite his lack of "capability," his employer is regarded as having acted unreasonably in treating his sickness as a sufficient reason for dismissing him (see unfair dismissal, below at paras. 279 *et seq.*).

4. Dissolution of partnership

A change in the firm may not only operate as a termination of **234**
the employee's contract but may also constitute wrongful dismissal. In *Brace* v. *Calder* (1895) it was held that the retirement of a partner worked a dissolution of the firm and thereby ended the plaintiff's contract of service without notice, although it might be added here that nominal damages were awarded since the plaintiff had failed to mitigate the loss when he refused new employment on the old terms with the new firm. The effect of other forms of dissolution has yet to be decided, and it remains to be seen if a distinction will be drawn between dissolution occasioned by the act of the partners (when presumably they should give adequate notice) and other acts, *e.g.* death or war (when notice, in the absence of a prophetic faculty,

could hardly be given!). *Phillips* v. *Alhambra Palace Co.* (1901) was a case in which the plaintiffs, who had been engaged to appear in music-halls, succeeded in an action for wrongful cancellation of their second engagement (they had performed the first), which, the defendants claimed, was justified by the death of one of the three partners (could the plaintiffs have been sued if *they* had withdrawn after the death of the partner?). *Lindley on Partnership* (13th ed., at p. 42) states that the contract will be determined "if the contract is of a personal character, to be performed by the individuals who have entered into it, or is dependent on the personal skill or honesty of the individual partners"—this "personal character" was lacking in the *Phillips* case.

5. Liquidation of company

235 If such a distinction applies in cases of dissolution of partnership, it is difficult to reconcile it with the rule that, however remote and impersonal a *corporate* employer, contracts of employment between such employer and employees have been held sufficiently "personal" to preclude the assignment of employees when, for example, a registered company transfers its undertaking to another company (*Re Foster*, above, para. 231). A court order for the compulsory winding-up of a company (and the same would appear to apply to a voluntary winding-up) operates as formal notice of dismissal to employees of the company. However praiseworthy it may be to stay on the sinking ship, employees who accept employment under the liquidator put at peril any claims to a redundancy payment which they may have. According to some tribunal decisions, and the view of Professor Grunfeld, the continued employment is considered to be fresh service under a new contract with a new employer (see *Golding & Howard* v. *Fire, Auto & Marine Insurance Co. Ltd.* (1968): *Law of Redundancy*, p. 53). The industrial tribunal in *McEwan* v. *Upper Clyde Shipbuilders Ltd.* (1972), preferred the more "sensible result" produced by treating the service under the company and the liquidator as continuous for the purposes of section 3 (2) of the Redundancy Payments Act 1965. It might, however, be unwise to accept the view that the liquidator can offer continued employment *in the company*'s name, however sensible and fair to employees such a view may be, until such time as a higher authority has settled the matter. If, as would appear, the appointment of a receiver and manager, other than as a short-term measure, has the effect of discharging the company's employees, it has now been decided that the appointment of a receiver and manager *out of court* does not have this effect where the receiver and manager continues the business as agent of the company.

6. Bankruptcy

The bankruptcy of the employer does not *ipso facto* terminate employment contracts, but the employee who "soldiers on" may have difficulty in obtaining his salary or wages, although it is provided in section 33 of the Bankruptcy Act 1914 that the wages or salary of a clerk or servant, workman or labourer, not exceeding £200, may be claimed for services rendered during the four months next preceding the receiving order. Such a claim is a preferential debt provable in the bankruptcy before ordinary debts, *e.g.* trade creditors. It covers only persons employed under contracts of service (*Re C. W. & A. L. Hughes Ltd.* (1966)), and not, *e.g.* men working on a building site employed on a "labour-only" basis. **236**

The bankruptcy of the employee does not determine his contract of employment, although circumstances can be imagined in which the fiduciary nature of the employment or the employee's conduct, *e.g.* conviction of a bankruptcy offence, might justify dismissal.

III. Termination with or without Notice

The private relationship between employer and employee terminates in the manner that the parties intend. In a contract for a fixed period or for the execution of a particular task, the contract prima facie ends upon the expiry of the period or the completion of the task. There is, however, no rule of law which prevents the parties from agreeing that the contract is to end before these events if they so wish. Contracts of indefinite duration are normally terminable by the giving of notice on either side. Lord Alverstone C.J. formulated the principle: "The general principle applicable to contracts of service is that, in the absence of misconduct or of grounds specified in the contract, the engagement can only be terminated after reasonable notice" (*Re African Association* (1910), at p. 399 of the report). In that case, a person had been employed as a trade assistant under a two-year contract in Africa, on terms that (a) his employment was to be terminable summarily in certain events, and (b) it should otherwise be terminable at any time within the two years at the absolute discretion of the employers. It was held that dismissal under (b) required due notice. **237**

We have seen that an employee, whether employed on a contract of fixed or indefinite duration, may be summarily dismissed. If the employee (or the employer) has broken the terms of the agreement, whether express or implied, such breach, if sufficiently fundamental, entitles the "innocent" party to treat the contract as ended. But, whether the summary dismissal (or wrongful departure) is lawful or not, we shall see that in either case it normally severs the employer–employee relationship. If it is wrongful, a claim for damages will lie. This is discussed separately below. But first it is proposed to discuss termination with notice (subject now to important minimum requirements as a result of the Contracts of Employment Act 1972) and then termination without notice.

1. Termination with notice

(1) *At common law*

238 "Notice" has two meanings. It may denote the formal intimation that the relationship is to end. In this sense it only takes effect when it has been served on the person to whom the notice is given (*Clark* v. *Coronel Ltd.* (1972)). It may also signify the period of time between the intimation and the time when the notice expires, a usage implicit in the expression "working out one's notice." The two meanings have caused some confusion in determining the meaning of "dismissal" or "termination" in certain statutory contexts. This confusion has been ended by the Court of Appeal in *H. W. Smith* (*Cabinets*) *Ltd.* v. *Brindle* (1973) in which it was held that a notice of dismissal given before the unfair dismissal sections of the Industrial Relations Act 1971 came into force, but expiring after that date, was only effective to terminate the employee's contract of employment at the expiry of the notice, thus enabling the employee to invoke the unfair dismissal sections. The court denied that a retrospective effect was being attributed to the 1971 Act by making a dismissal, which was not unfair at the time when notice was given, unfair in the light of the law in operation when the notice expired (*cf. Nicolson* v. *Imperial Chemical Industries Ltd.* (1972), where the tribunal had held that such a case came under the unfair dismissal sections but that the unfairness must be judged at the time when the notice was given). Lord Denning M.R., in the *Smith* case, doubted if employers could get round the Act by summarily dismissing persons before the operative date of the unfair dismissal sections. *Morris* v. *C. H. Bailey Ltd.* (1969), is a useful reminder that employers who inform a trade union that existing working rules are to be terminated do not thereby give notice of dismissal to employees who work under those rules. Even if the letter to the trade union were such a notice, Salmon L.J. was far from satisfied that the district delegate of the union was a proper agent to receive it on behalf of the employees.

There is no rule of law which requires notice to be given on a particular day or to expire on a particular day, although it is usual for the notice to take effect at the end of the contractual period.

As to what notice must be given, the first rule is that resort must be had to the contractual provision dealing with notice. The statutory notice of particulars of employment may in time help to "concretise" terms which are often taken for granted. Contractual notice will not apply where it does not come up to the minimum periods of notice applicable under the Contracts of Employment Act 1972. If there is no contractual provision concerning notice, the customary notice must be given, *e.g.* by custom, judicially noticed, domestic servants' contracts are, in the absence of agreement to the contrary, terminable by one month's notice (or one month's wages in lieu of notice) even though there is a yearly hiring. If the custom has not been judicially noticed, it must be proved and the parties must be shown to have contracted against the background of such custom. In *Fisher* v. *W. B. Dick* (1938), the court defined custom as "a set of terms which is notorious, which is reasonable and which is certain so that parties contracting with reference to it may know exactly what the terms of the contract which are imported by the custom will be" (at p. 469 of the report). **239**

If no custom, judicially noticed or otherwise, is adduced, the rule is that the notice must be reasonable in the circumstances. Factors relevant in this respect are the nature of the employment, the remuneration (including the intervals when paid) and the length of service. The widely held view that the interval of payment is necessarily the period of notice is unsupported by law; many factory workers are paid weekly and dismissible with one week's notice, but the coincidence of the two periods is not a matter of law. It would appear that whilst an employee has no right to depart summarily by forfeiting his wages, an employer may give wages or salary in lieu of notice (see *Austwick* v. *Midland Ry.* (1909), in which it was held lawful to give wages in lieu of notice to an employee, who in his capacity as trade union official, had written a strong letter to a fellow-employee). **240**

In *Devonald* v. *Rosser & Sons* (1906), it was held that a pieceworker who had received a month's notice was impliedly entitled to be given reasonable work. The case is interesting for two reasons. The first is a rare flash of judicial empathy for working people—"the workman has to live *de die in diem*" so that he cannot support himself and his family without regular income, unlike the employer whose resources enable him to weather bad periods. Secondly, because the works had been closed down, the plaintiff was entitled to average earnings over a period before the closure—a device which is now common under the 1972 Act, as we shall see.

(2) *Under the Contracts of Employment Act 1972*

241 This Act, which applies to Great Britain only, lays down minimum periods of notice to be given to employees (a term which includes ex-employees) who have the requisite period of continuous employment with the same employer as follows:

Period of continuous employment	*Minimum notice*
Under 2 years but not less than 13 weeks	1 week
Under 5 years but not less than 2 years	2 weeks
Under 10 years but not less than 5 years	4 weeks
Under 15 years but not less than 10 years	6 weeks
15 years or more	8 weeks

It was originally envisaged that the obligations with regard to notice would be reciprocal, as they are at common law, but the 1963 Act, now replaced by the 1972 Act, merely obliges an employee who has been continuously employed for thirteen weeks or more to give notice which is not less than one week. As we have seen, contracts of fixed duration expire without any need for notice, unless otherwise agreed. The present Act, however, covers any contract of employment for a term certain of four weeks or less as though it were a contract of indefinite duration, subject to the requirement that the employee has not less than thirteen weeks of qualifying employment.

242 The calculation of the length of a period of employment, and the determination whether or not it is continuous, are made in accordance with the provisions of Schedule 1. It is important to distinguish between the *counting* of weeks of employment and the *continuity* of weeks of employment: a week may not count yet not rupture continuity, as in the case of participation in a strike (see *Bloomfield* v. *Springfield Hosiery Finishing Co. Ltd.* (1972)). Unless otherwise stated, the following periods count for the purposes of calculating continuity of employment, any period which does not count in the following categories breaking the continuity of employment.

(a) Any week in which the employee is employed for twenty-one hours or more, including any week in which the employee's relations are governed by a contract of employment which normally involves employment for twenty-one hours or more.

243 (b) Any week during which the employee is (i) incapable of work in consequence of sickness or injury, or (ii) absent from work on account of a temporary cessation of work (excluding strikes in which an employee takes part), or (iii) absent from work in circumstances such that, by arrangement or custom, he is regarded as continuing in the employment of his employer for all or any purposes. Not more than twenty-six weeks of incapacity caused by

sickness or injury may count between any two periods falling under (i) above. All of the periods in this category are ones in which there is *no* contract of employment. Thus, a welder who was dismissed, along with other welders, because of a shortage of work in a shipyard, but who returned to work after a lay-off of nearly eight weeks, was held to have suffered merely a "temporary cessation of work" which counted for the purpose of computing his period of employment (*Fitzgerald* v. *Hall, Russell & Co. Ltd.* (1970)). In that case, Lord Morris of Borth-y-Gest considered that any temporary cessation of work necessarily involves a process of looking back from the individual employee's standpoint. Rejecting the argument that the cessation of work must affect the employer's business together with the argument that other employees should also be laid-off, Lord Morris, whilst accepting that the expectations of the employer and the employee at the time of the lay-off were relevant factors, did not accept that the absence of these latter factors was decisive (*cf. Hunter* v. *Smith's Docks Co. Ltd.* (1968)). In short, all three situations under this heading concern *de facto* breaks in employment which are notionally treated as not being breaks in employment.

(c) A week in which an employee takes part in a strike does *not* **244**
count for the purposes of reckoning the period of continuous employment but, as already indicated, does *not* break continuity of service.

(d) Periods of employment before call-up into the services.

(e) Periods spent with different employers may exceptionally count, *viz.* as the result of the transfer of a business or undertaking, because of a modification of an employee's contract of employment with a body corporate by or under an Act of Parliament which substitutes some other body corporate as the employer, where the personal representatives or trustees of a deceased employer take his employee into employment, or where there is a change in partners, personal representatives or trustees employing him, and, finally, where an employee is taken into the employment of an associated company.

Because the phrase "transfer of a business" has caused no little **245**
difficulty both in relation to the present Act and in relation to section 13 of the Redundancy Payments Act, it may conveniently be discussed here. Widgery J. considered that "the vital consideration is whether the effect of the transaction was to put the transferee in possession of a going concern the activities of which he could carry on without interruption." In deciding whether this has occurred his lordship was prepared to ignore the absence of a "formal and empty phrase purporting to include goodwill"—*Kenmir Ltd.* v.

Frizzell (1968). In that case, despite the absence of any express transfer of goodwill, it was held that the respondents, who were furniture manufacturers, had, by selling their premises, fixtures and fittings, plant and machinery to the appellants (who also manufactured furniture, although of a different kind), transferred their business within the meaning of section 13 of the 1965 Act. A similar conclusion had been reached in *H. A. Rencoule* (*Joiners and Shopfitters*) *Ltd.* v. *Hunt* (1967), on similar facts, except that in this last case the agreement expressly negatived a transfer of the business or of the transferor's business name. As Widgery J. put it in the *Kenmir* case, the question is one of substance rather than form, consideration being given to the whole of the circumstances by weighing the factors *pro* and *contra* a transfer of the business.

246 A transfer of assets, as such, does not necessarily connote a transfer of the business which uses those assets (*Dallow Industrial Properties* v. *Else* (1967)) although sometimes the assets will be inseparable from the business in which they are employed, as in *Lloyd* v. *Brassey* (1969), where a farm was transferred to another farmer. The self-contained part of a business may be transferred as a separate "going concern." In *Woodhouse & Staton* v. *Peter Brotherhood* (1972), the Industrial Court re-affirmed the test of transfer of "the whole working environment of the employees" which would rank as a transfer of the business itself, even though the latter had later been carried on elsewhere by the transferor. In that case PB Ltd. had purchased a factory from C Ltd., together with much of the latter's plant and equipment. PB Ltd. used the factory to make spinning machines but allowed the employees to finish off some diesel engines which C Ltd. had not completed at the time of the transfer. The Industrial Court held that factors such as the absence of a sale of goodwill, or of any transfer of customers or contracts, had no direct or necessary effect upon the working environment of the employees, correcting the industrial tribunal below for equating business with the species of commercial activity carried on by C Ltd. and for ignoring the production activity carried on at the premises which had been transferred. The Court of Appeal disagreed with this approach, holding that what had taken place was only a transfer of physical assets and not a transfer of a business. Unlike *Lloyd* v. *Brassey*, the transferee carried on a business different in nature from that carried on by the transferor. In its turn, the Court of Appeal corrected the Industrial Court for ignoring the nature of the business in which the employer is engaged. "If the new owner does not take over the business as a going concern, but only takes over the physical assets—using them in a different business" then there is no transfer of a business.

Even where continuity of employment is established under Schedule 1, the employee may not be entitled to the minimum periods of notice for the following reasons: 247

(1) Either party can still terminate without notice if the conduct of the other would have enabled him to do so before the Act was passed. Thus, the somnolent signalman who falls asleep over his controls can still be summarily dismissed.

(2) Whilst any provision for notice shorter than that stipulated only takes effect under the Act, there is nothing to "prevent either party from waiving his right to notice on any occasion, or from accepting a payment in lieu of notice" (s. 1 (3))—thus, though an employee cannot bind himself by agreeing in the contract to shorter notice than that stipulated in the Act, he can waive his rights "on any occasion." The provision in regard to the giving of payment in lieu of notice is odd since we have seen that it seems employees cannot free themselves from their contracts by proffering a sum representing the wages they would have otherwise earned. Needless to say, periods longer than those stipulated may be agreed. If no period of notice is agreed, the employee, it is submitted, is entitled to reasonable notice (as described above), where this exceeds the statutory notice (by at least one week in the case of notice from the employer if section 2 is to apply: this section furnishes a statutory measure of damages under the Act). In *Phillips* v. *M. L. Alkem* (1969), a senior female clerical worker who had worked for the firm for eighteen years at a monthly salary under a contract which contained no provision as to notice, was held to be entitled to three months' notice by the county court. The Court of Appeal reduced this to one month, but whether this latter period was arrived at by reference to the test of reasonable notice or by reference to her monthly salary or her statutory entitlement to notice under the 1963 Act, which happened to be four weeks' notice, does not appear from the report. The purpose of the 1963, now the 1972 Act, is to provide minimum periods of notice, and not to replace longer periods of agreed *or inferred* notice by the statutory notice.

(3) Certain categories are excluded by the Act, such as civil 248
servants, registered dock workers engaged in dock work, certain seamen and fishermen, and employees who have certain relationships of consanguinity and affinity with their employer. Employment in work wholly or mainly outside Great Britain is excluded, unless the employee ordinarily works in Great Britain and the work outside Great Britain is for the same employer. The application of the Act to those who normally work for twenty-one or more hours in any week clearly places many part-time employees outside the protection of the Act.

2. Termination without notice

249 Subject to what is said below, the relationship of employer and employee ends on the summary dismissal of the employee or his summary departure. Leaving aside summary departure by the employee (on which there is a paucity of cases), a distinction must be drawn between two types of dismissal by the employer, *viz.* (1) lawful, and (2) unlawful dismissal. A dismissal is lawful if—

(i) effected in accordance with the contract, subject to the Contracts of Employment Act 1972, discussed above;

(ii) the employment is treated by law as terminable without notice, as in the case of civil servants who hold office during "Her Majesty's pleasure." Certain chief officers of local government, *e.g.* the clerk to a county council formerly held office "during the pleasure of the council," although the Draconian severity of such a rule was substantially modified by the requirement of ministerial consent to dismissal. Officers appointed under section 112 (1) of the Local Government Act 1972 "hold office on such reasonable terms and conditions, including conditions as to remuneration, as the authority appointing him think fit" (s. 112 (2));

(iii) most importantly of all, the employee has broken a term in his contract, express or implied, justifying summary dismissal. Whereas the express terms are to be found in the employee's contract, the implied terms, such as those relating to obedience, competence, fidelity and behaviour, have been discussed in an earlier chapter.

Effect of breach of contract

250 A breach of contract does not necessarily discharge the contract. In order to have this effect the breach must (a) be "fundamental" and (b) be "accepted" by the party not in default.

(a) Fundamental breach is a breach which, by depriving the innocent party of substantially the whole benefit of the contract, entitles him to treat the contract as ended. It has been suggested that certain breaches which were considered to be "fundamental" in old cases might not now be so considered.

(b) The "acceptance" of the breach by the party not in default operates as a rescission of the contract, or, perhaps more correctly, as a discharge from his primary responsibilities under the contract. If the party not in default "waives" the breach, *i.e.* condones it, the contract continues in full force.

251 It is a matter of some difficulty, perhaps more theoretical than real, to apply (b) above, to the contract of employment which has,

at least in this respect, been treated as *sui generis*. "Normally, and apart from the intervention of statute, there would never be a nullity in terminating an ordinary contract of master and servant. Dismissal might be in breach of contract and so unlawful but would sound only in damages"—*per* Lord Keith in *Vine* v. *National Dock Labour Board* (1957), at p. 507 of the report. The view that a wrongful summary dismissal is effective *per se* to terminate a contract of employment, however difficult it might be to reconcile with principle (b) above, has been reiterated in several cases, notably *Denmark Productions Ltd.* v. *Boscobel Productions Ltd.* (1969) (Winn L.J. dissenting).

More recent cases have, however, tended to re-establish the **252**
orthodox contract principle. "I doubt whether a wrongful dismissal brings a contract of service to an end," said Salmon L.J. in *Decro-Wall* v. *Practitioners in Marketing Ltd.* (1971), at p. 223 of the report, adding that "no doubt in practice it does." Although the courts in the nineteenth century did flirt with the idea of "constructive service," so that the wrongfully dismissed servant was treated as notionally continuing in service until the proper termination of his contract (see *Gandell* v. *Pontigny* (1816), at p. 376 of the report), thus allowing of a quasi-contractual claim for wages which would otherwise have been earned, it was later feared that "a doctrine would be sanctioned that would be of pernicious consequence" (*Elderton* v. *Emmens* (1848), at p. 178 of the report). The upshot was that the employee was reduced to his claim for damages for breach of contract, the courts refusing to grant specific performance and showing themselves reluctant to grant declarations.

In effect therefore, whilst it may be true that "an unaccepted **253**
repudiation is a thing writ in water," the inability of the employee to obtain specific performance or a declaration means that in practice he normally has no choice but to accept both the dismissal and the duty to mitigate his loss which thereupon arises. The case of *Hill* v. *C. A. Parsons & Co. Ltd.* (1972), shows that in exceptional circumstances, where the mutual confidence between employer and employee remains intact, the courts may adjudge a dismissal without the requisite notice as abortive to terminate the employee's contract and consequently may grant the employee an injunction or a declaration on that footing. These latter remedies are discussed below (paras. 273 *et seq.*).

Boston Deep Sea Fishing & Ice Co. v. *Ansell* (1888) is instructive **254**
as regards *lawful* summary dismissal. A, who had been appointed managing director of a company for five years at an annual salary, was summarily dismissed at an extraordinary meeting of the company. It was found that he had accepted commission from ship-

builders, to whom he had given contracts on behalf of the company to build fishing smacks. It was held that his breach of the duty of fidelity justified immediate dismissal without any right to *pro rata* payment for the part of the year which he had served. Bowen L.J. pointed out (at p. 365 of the report) that "rescission" applies in a peculiar sense to employment contracts:

> "It is either a determination in conformity with the rights of the master which arise under the contract itself, there being . . . in every contract of service an implied condition that if faithful service is not rendered the master may elect to determine the contract, and the determination takes place on that implied condition; or you may regard it under the more general law, which is not applicable to contracts of service alone—you may treat it as the wrongful repudiation of the contract by one party, being accepted by the other, and operating as a determination of the contract from that time, that is, from the time the party who is sinned against elects to treat the wrongful act of the other as a breach of contract, which election on his part emancipates the other party from continuing further."

A's dismissal was held to be justified notwithstanding that he had been dismissed by a resolution of the extraordinary meeting on *other* grounds which had not been substantiated.

255 Summary dismissal for a sufficient reason is therefore valid at common law, irrespective of the fact that no reason, or the wrong reason, was given for the dismissal. "I think it is enough to shew a justification existing in point of fact," said Coleridge J. in *Ridgeway* v. *Hungerford Market* (1835). Despite criticism, this peculiar rule has been given a fresh lease of life by *Cyril Leonard & Co.* v. *Simo Securities Trust Ltd.* (1971), which re-affirmed it in the interests of *stare decisis.* Although a new trial was refused in *Cowling* v. *Matbro Ltd.* (1969), on the ground that the employer in that case should have investigated further charges of misconduct brought to his knowledge before judgment in the action which he had lost, Lord Denning M.R. did not rule out the possibility of a new trial to hear fresh evidence of misconduct by an employee, other than that of which he had already been acquitted. Whilst failure to give a reason and absence of knowledge of the misconduct of the employee at the time of dismissal do not *per se* render a dismissal unlawful, both of these factors may be relevant in cases of unfair dismissal, discussed below.

Effect of rescission

256 It will be seen, therefore, that rescission is an extra-judicial act whereby a contractual relationship is ended—dismissal by the employer, departure by the employee (it would seem, however, that an employee may have to wait, *e.g.* a miner cannot demand that the cage be sent down especially for him if he wishes to leave his employment). The consequences of rescission are seen in *General Billposting Co.* v. *Atkinson* (1909). The appellants, who had wrongfully dismissed the respondent, endeavoured to enforce a restrictive covenant against him. The House of Lords, dismissing the appeal, held that the unlawful dismissal constituted a repudiation of the contract which disabled the appellants from enforcing the covenant concerning competition. Quite apart from the exercise of the extra-judicial power to rescind, and whether it is exercised or not, a breach of contract entitles the party sinned against to claim damages if loss has resulted. We shall see that in *National Coal Board* v. *Galley* (below, para. 259) the plaintiffs, in an unusual action, tried to deal with the problem of absenteeism by an action for damages rather than by rescission, *i.e.* by dismissing the men.

IV. Remedies

The extent to which breach of contract justifies use of the extra- **257**
judicial remedy of rescission has been discussed above. The chief judicial remedies are the action for damages, and the injunction, but ancillary remedies, such as the declaration, arbitration and the statutory jurisdiction of inferior courts under the Employers and Workmen Act 1875, will receive brief mention.

1. Damages

Subject to some statutory exceptions—notably section 5 of the **258**
Conspiracy and Protection of Property Act 1875 (para. 574, below), breach of contract is a civil wrong. The breach may be either *anticipatory* or *actual*; the former occurring before the date set for performance, the latter on or during the time set for performance. Thus, where a person had agreed to act as courier for three months from June 1 and the employer repudiated the contract before that date, it was held that the employee might sue for damages without waiting until June 1 (*Hochster* v. *De la Tour* (1853)). The employee, in that case, could, if he so wished, have waited until June 1 and sued for an actual breach. In a remarkable decision of the House of Lords (*White and Carter* (*Councils*) *Ltd.* v. *McGregor* (1962)) it was held that since the "innocent" party need not accept the repudiation, he may, where he has a substantial interest, perform the contract and sue for the whole contract price. Lord Keith, dissenting, queried whether it was right that a person whose contract to go to Hong Kong for £10,000 has been repudiated can nevertheless set off and claim the £10,000. No doubt the principle enunciated in the

White and Carter case can produce results which are "grotesque," but it should be borne in mind that the courier referred to by Lord Keith, could perform his obligations without the assent of the contract-breaker, a circumstance which will not normally be present in ordinary contracts of employment, where the co-operation of the employer will be needed. The statement in Brooke's Abridgment that the labourer "*ne poet server contra voluntatem magistri*" is as true now as when written.

Liquidated and unliquidated damages

259 In most cases the breach complained of will be an actual breach. The damages claimed may be (a) liquidated, *i.e.* agreed and quantified by the parties in advance of a breach, or (b) unliquidated, *i.e.* left at large for the court to determine. Agreed damages clauses are not common in employment contracts, although there is nothing to stop the employer from obtaining the employee's agreement whereby the latter forfeits wages already due, *e.g.* "lying-on money." If an agreed or liquidated damages clause is not a genuine pre-estimate of the likely loss but is meant to penalise the contract-breaker, it will be a "penalty" and, as such, irrecoverable, although the party not in default may still prove and recover his actual loss.

Unliquidated damages are awarded on the basis of trying to put the plaintiff in the position that he would have held had the contract been duly performed, subject to the qualification that only loss which naturally flows from the breach may normally be recovered, since such loss is foreseeable by the contract-breaker—as one judge put it, it is "on the cards." Any special loss can only be recovered if it was in the contemplation of the parties, so that liability for such loss was clearly undertaken. Thus, in *National Coal Board* v. *Galley* (1958), deputies who had broken their contracts of employment by refusing to work on alternate Saturdays were held liable to pay damages measured by the net value of the work missed and not for the disruption of production. Loss of output was held to be an inappropriate measure for supervisory workers and the fact that the loss had been greater because the deputies had acted in concert was ignored. It has been suggested that where employees strike to inflict the maximum loss on their employers (and this is normally the case), they ought to be liable in contract for loss which was both foreseen and intended. Although it is open to the House of Lords to reconsider the *Galley* principle, it is doubtful if this particular nettle will be grasped.

Restitutio in integrum

Damages for wrongful dismissal are awarded on the *restitutio* principle, which carries with it the corollary that the worker cannot be better off as the result of the breach than he would have been had the contract been performed in accordance with its terms. 260

> "If there be a dismissal without notice the employer must pay an indemnity; but that indemnity cannot include compensation either for the injured feelings of the servant, or for the loss he may sustain from the fact that this having been dismissed of itself makes it more difficult for him to obtain fresh employment" (*per* Lord Loreburn L.C. in *Addis* v. *Gramophone Co. Ltd.* (1909), at p. 491 of the report).

To give the employee damages for difficulty in finding new employment would put him in a better position than an employee dismissed with notice in scarce employment conditions; despite the views of writers to the contrary, it is submitted that Lord Loreburn's dictum represents the current position. The special position of the apprentice was discussed at paras. 84 *et seq.*, above.

Loss

The loss suffered by the employee is a question of fact; the most frequent claim is for wages or salary during the period of notice or for the remainder of a fixed-term contract, but other items have been recovered, *e.g.* bonus, tips, commission (*cf.* fixed-term contract, where commission is not part of salary), board and lodging and even a promised gift. Each case must be construed on its facts and a review of the authorities reveals that there is considerable doubt where the employee sues for loss of a "chance." In *Bold* v. *Brough, Nicholson & Hall Ltd.* (1964), a director, who had been wrongfully dismissed, was held entitled to a sum representing the diminution of pension rights which he would otherwise have enjoyed even though the company's minutes showed that it could discontinue the contributory pension scheme at any time. "Is it likely," asked Phillimore J. (at p. 212 of the report), "that [the company] will take a step so disastrous [*i.e.* discontinue the pension scheme] to its relations with all its employees solely to defeat a claim by this plaintiff, an old employee of the company?" On the other hand, where, upon a director's wrongful dismissal, the company ended his participation in its non-contributory pension scheme by giving the director about £10,000, it was held that it was entitled to do so under the scheme, and a claim for the larger sum of approximately £27,000, which the director would have obtained had he served to the age of 65 years, was ignored: *Beach* v. *Reed Corrugated Cases Ltd.* (1956). 261

262 A more recent illustration of the difficulty attendant upon assessing an employee's loss is *Lavarack* v. *Woods of Colchester Ltd.* (1967). L, who was employed by W from 1962 on a five-year contract at £4,000 per annum, plus "such bonus, if any, as the directors should from time to time determine," was wrongfully dismissed by W in 1964. Immediately afterwards he obtained a post with a French company at £1,500 per annum and bought half of the shares in that company. In 1965, W discontinued the bonus scheme and replaced it with a fixed salary scheme under which it was estimated that L would have received £1,000 more per annum than his salary under the old scheme. The court held (Lord Denning M.R. dissenting) that L's claim for £2,000, in respect of the increased salary he would have earned during his last two years, failed, since it arose out of what was the employer's voluntary acceptance of new contractual obligations after L had left their employment; L had mitigated the loss by taking new employment promptly so that this should be taken into account with the increase in the value of his shareholding.

Reduction of damages

263 The damages claimable on the lines outlined above are a *maximum* and may be reduced by two important factors. First, we have seen that the plaintiff in an action for breach of contract (and the same applies to actions in tort) must mitigate his loss so far as he is reasonably able to do so (see *Brace* v. *Calder* (1895)). The employee who is wrongfully dismissed cannot, as one judge put it, "sit in the sun," but must take reasonable steps to mitigate his loss by seeking out suitable alternative employment. Conditions of full employment tend therefore to depress the already modest damages awarded by the courts. Injured feelings cannot be a ground for claiming a *solatium*, although the courts indirectly take account of this factor when a breach of contract occurs, *e.g.* where a person is constructively dismissed by demotion, notwithstanding that his remuneration remains unaffected. As Blain J. expressed it—"personal factors clearly are more likely to be of weight or are likely to be of greater weight in cases of personal services than in what I call (for want of a better word) soulless cases of sale of goods contract where money may often be the only important factor." (*Yetton* v. *Eastwoods Froy Ltd.* (1967)—a case which incidentally illustrates the manner in which the long-term contract shelters its holder from the chill winds of the market).

264 The second important factor which may reduce the maximum amount of damages is the principle of the *Gourley* case, whereby damages must take into account the tax element when such damages are not taxable in the recipient's hand—a principle which has since been extended to include damages for wrongful termination of contract occasioning loss of earnings (discussed in this latter context at paras. 118, 119, above).

Quantum meruit

Finally, it may be added that, instead of an action for damages, an action for a reasonable sum (*quantum meruit*) may be brought for work done, as in *Planché* v. *Colburn* (1831), where the plaintiff was unable to complete his contractual obligation because of the defendant's breach; we have seen earlier that a reasonable sum may be awarded where the contract itself is void (*Craven-Ellis* v. *Canons Ltd.* (1936)) or where the contract omits to specify the remuneration (above, para. 185). **265**

2. Damages under statute

(1) *The Contracts of Employment Act 1972*

The manner of assessing damages at common law for breach of contract, described above, may be modified by sections 2 and 3 of the Contracts of Employment Act 1972. Section 2 (read in conjunction with Schedule 2) regulates the liability of the employer during the period of statutory notice where the employee has been continuously employed for thirteen weeks or more; section 3 provides that in proceedings against an employer the measure of damages must take into account the liabilities established by section 2 (and Schedule 2). **266**

The statutory liability of the employer during the period of notice applies whether it is the employer or the employee who gives notice, and, in so far as a contract purports to exclude or limit the obligations imposed on the employer by this section, it is void. The section does not apply to a notice given by the employer or the employee, if the notice to be given *by the employer* "*must* be at least one week more than the notice required by section 1 (1) of this Act" (s. 2 (3)). It is clear that where, for example, an employee, who has served thirteen weeks, is entitled to two weeks' notice by virtue of an *express* term in his contract (*i.e.* one week more than his statutory entitlement), his rights during notice are governed by common law. The position is not so clear where the contract leaves the question of notice at large (which may still occur, since the statutory notice under section 4 may contain a "nil return" on this point). Perhaps a period of notice evolved by custom and judicially noticed (*e.g.* the month's notice for domestic servants) would be outside section 2; but it is dubious whether other forms of notice (*e.g.* dependent upon custom *not* judicially noticed or "reasonable notice") would be outside the section, since the word "must" appears to require that the period of notice is capable of being predicated in advance (*cf.* para. 247 above, as regards position under s. 1 of the Act).

267 Schedule 2 lays down the following rules concerning the employee's rights during notice.

(a) An employee who has *normal working hours* (which includes compulsory overtime) will, in the normal case, if given notice, simply work off such hours, so that no problem arises. If, however, (i) the employer provides no work although the employee is ready and willing to do work, or (ii) the employee is incapable of work owing to sickness or injury, or (iii) he is on holiday, then the employee is entitled to a guaranteed minimum pay. If his pay in normal working hours does not vary with the amount of work done, *e.g.* the employee on an "upstanding" weekly wage, he is entitled to an amount as much as he would have earned if he had been employed during the hours lost during (i), (ii) and (iii) above. If, on the other hand, the employee's pay varies with the amount of work done, complex provisions apply, whereby his earnings are averaged over the four weeks before the notice is given. The harassed employer called upon to apply these provisions will no doubt rely on the advice of his employers' association or of his legal advisers; the Department of Employment produce helpful explanatory leaflets on this Act and on the Redundancy Payments Act and their officers are extremely co-operative (as the author can testify).

268 (b) An employee who has no normal working hours is guaranteed a sum not less than his average weekly rate of remuneration in the period of twelve weeks, ending with the last complete week before the notice was given. Weeks during which the employee worked for less than twenty-one hours are ignored, but if this results in less than eight weeks on which an average can be based, then previous weeks must be brought in to bring the total up to eight. The employee must be ready and willing to do work of a reasonable nature and amount to earn the rate of remuneration mentioned above, although incapacity caused by sickness or injury, or absence on holidays will not preclude an employee from showing that he was ready and willing. If the employee gives notice, the employer is not obliged to make the statutory minimum payment, unless and until the employee leaves his service in pursuance of the notice.

Irrespective of whether the employee is covered by (a) or (b), above, it is provided that if the employee, having given notice, takes part in a strike on or before the termination of the contract, the employer is dispensed from the obligation to make the statutory minimum payment. As one might expect, he is also dispensed from making a payment for any time during which the employee is absent, with leave, at his own request. If, during the period of notice, the employee breaks the contract and the employer rightfully treats the breach as terminating the contract, no payment is due to the employee under the Schedule for the part of the period of notice falling after the termination of the contract. Conversely, the employer who breaks the contract during the period of notice is liable to pay damages at common law; but it is provided that payments received under the Schedule for the period of notice after the breach shall go towards mitigating the damages recoverable by the employee for loss of earnings during that period.

The cumulative effect, therefore, of these complicated provisions **269**
is to regulate the rights of the employee covered by them during the period of notice. The Act works out in detail the tentative principle applied by the common law in *Devonald* v. *Rosser & Sons* (1906) (discussed above, para. 240). Section 3 states that: "If an employer fails to give the notice required by section 1 of this Act, the rights conferred by the last foregoing section (with Schedule 2 of this Act) *shall be taken into account* in assessing his liability for breach of the contract" (my italics). From this, it is clear that the employee cannot recover damages twice over, *i.e.* under common law *and* under statute, for the same head of claim; nevertheless the words italicised indicate that the measure of damages under the section is not exclusive of other heads of damage which therefore remain claimable, *e.g.* for a promised gift, or the cost of a book purchased in order to obtain a job (see common law damages, above, para. 279). Damages for breach of the contract of employment, either at common law or under the 1972 Act, are at present recoverable in the ordinary courts (the county court has jurisdiction up to £750, or more if the parties so agree), pending the conferment of jurisdiction on the industrial tribunals under section 113 of the Industrial Relations Act 1971 which, however, excludes damages in respect of personal injuries.

(2) *The Employers and Workmen Act 1875*

The wide, but apparently little-used powers of the county court **270**
and the magistrates' court to settle disputes between employers and workmen remain, although curtailed in scope by recent Acts. Once the industrial tribunal becomes the chief single forum for the resolution of cases concerning the contract of employment (see above), there would appear to be little point in retaining the 1875 Act.

3. Other remedies

271 Rescission (above, paras. 249–256) and damages (above, paras. 257–269) are, *par excellence*, the chief remedies for breach of contract. Sometimes, however, other remedies may be available, such as the injunction, the declaration and arbitration. One remedy, "specific performance," is conspicuous by its absence, since the courts have steadfastly refused to enforce, directly or indirectly, contracts of a personal nature whether they be contracts of service or contracts for services. Various reasons have been ascribed for this state of affairs—the difficulty in effectively supervising the performance of such contracts, the possibility of putting the employee in "bondage," the adequacy of damages as a relief and the severity of the sanction (committal) for non-compliance (but in this case the same might be said of the injunction) have all been cited.

272 Trade unionists have argued for a right of re-instatement in certain cases, such as unfair dismissal or "victimisation," but the furthest the law has gone in this direction is to empower an industrial tribunal to *recommend* a reinstatement for the employee who has been unfairly dismissed (see below at para. 296). Cases such as *Ridge* v. *Baldwin* (1964) (the dismissed chief constable) and *Vine* v. *National Dock Labour Board* (1957) (the dock worker struck off the register) might appear to recognise some right of reinstatement for office holders or those employed under statutory schemes, but the remedies utilised in those cases were, respectively, the quashing of the dismissal as *ultra vires* and the granting of a declaration. If, conversely, the employee does not wish to work, section 128 of the Industrial Relations Act 1971 forbids the issue of any order by way of specific performance or for an injunction to compel an employee to do any work or attend at any place for the purpose of doing any work, and it matters not that the employee's refusal to work involves a breach of his contract of employment (*e.g.* where a "no-strike" promise is part of that contract), or that a "cooling-off" order or "balloting" order has been made under the 1971 Act, or that a state of emergency has been proclaimed under the Emergency Powers Act 1920.

Despite pressure for some right of re-instatement, the law at present reflects for better or worse a principle of mutuality by virtue of which no employer can be forced to accept a particular employee and no employee can be forced to perform service against his will.

(1) *The injunction*

In appropriate cases the courts are prepared to grant an injunction forbidding a person from breaking an independent negative stipulation in his contract, either during the currency of that contract (*e.g.* by singing at another's theatre) or after its termination (*e.g.* by breaking covenants against competition; see paras. 69 *et seq.*). Unlike specific performance, the injunction is not limited to breach of contract, although, like the former, it is a discretionary remedy. It is not necessary to show that damage will, or is likely to, result if the injunction is not issued, but the court may take the absence of likely damage into account in exercising its discretion. 273

If the result of the granting of the injunction would be, in effect, to bind a person to a particular contract, it will not be issued, since this would be an indirect way of granting specific performance—"I disclaim doing indirectly what I cannot do directly" (Lord St. Leonards in *Lumley* v. *Gye* (1853)).

The form of the stipulation is not conclusive. A stipulation 274 negative in form may be positive in substance, as in *Davis* v. *Foreman* (1894), where injunctive relief was refused to a manager who sought to restrain his employer from dismissing him with notice by relying on a term that he was not to be required to leave except for misconduct or breach of contract. Because a positive obligation carries with it a negative corollary, it does not necessarily follow that the latter will be enforced, as in *Whitewood Chemical Co.* v. *Hardman* (1891), where damages, and not an injunction, was considered to be the proper relief in the case of a manager who, having agreed to give "the whole of his time to the company's business," became interested in another company.

Negative stipulations and the like apart, can an employee obtain 275 an injunction to restrain his employer from dismissing him in breach of contract? Until *Hill* v. *C. A. Parsons & Co. Ltd.* (1972), it was generally thought that an injunction would not be claimable on the ground that to grant it would be tantamount to reinstatement. In the *Hill* case, the Court of Appeal, whilst accepting that in the ordinary course of things a dismissal in breach of contract, if insisted on by the employer, is effective to terminate a relationship in which mutual confidence has clearly disappeared, granted an interlocutory injunction to restrain Parsons from dismissing Hill with short notice. In special circumstances, however, the court would grant a declaration that the relationship still subsisted and an injunction restraining the employer from treating it as at an end. The *Hill* case itself raised such special circumstances in that Parsons had dismissed Hill, not because they had any quarrel with him, but because of industrial pressure from a trade union which Hill had refused to join. In granting a declaration and an injunction, the court was not foisting an unwelcome employee upon a hostile employer. Notwithstanding that the decision is limited to the peculiar "triangular" situation which existed in the Parsons works, it has not escaped criticism. What does seem odd about the decision is that one of the reasons given for granting the injunction was that the sections of the Industrial Relations Act dealing with trade union rights and unfair dismissal would shortly be in operation. The Court of Appeal was therefore influenced by *prospective* changes in the law and seems to have overlooked that even when those changes became operative there would be no power to *order* reinstatement, although there would be a power to *recommend* reinstatement. It would be a mistake to use this case as supporting the notion that declarations and injunctions are freely available in cases involving unlawful termination of contracts of employment.

276 Stigmatised as a "blacklegs' charter" by trade unionists, section 128 of the 1971 Act prohibits injunctions which, by restraining an employee from working in accordance with his lawful contract of employment, compel him to take part in a strike or in any irregular industrial action short of a strike. The employee who, by continuing to work, thereby breaks his union's rule against disobedience in relation to a direction to strike, cannot be restrained from continuing to work.

(2) *The declaration*

277 It may serve a party to a contract to obtain from the court a "declaration," *i.e.* a binding declaration of right, instead of, or in addition to, any other form of consequential relief. In consonance with the reluctance of the courts to grant specific performance of contracts of service, it has been stated that in cases of dismissal declarations "will rarely be made" (*Francis* v. *Municipal Corporation of Kuala Lumpur* (1962) at p. 1417 of the report). The *Hill* case, discussed above, is an exception to that rule.

A declaration may be made concerning a person's eligibility for office or his right to belong to an association. Thus, where a trade union official was employed under union rules during the will and pleasure of the executive council of the union, a declaration was given that the official, who had been dismissed in breach of the rules of natural justice, remained eligible for union office, but no declaration was made concerning the validity or otherwise of his dismissal from the employment of the union (*Taylor* v. *National Union of Seamen* (1967)). Sometimes a declaration may be extremely useful in a "test case," since the ruling may affect large numbers of persons who are not parties to the action. Admittedly, a declaration affords no coercive relief but the likelihood is that responsible persons will observe its terms. In *Price* v. *Sunderland Corporation* (1956), a declaration was granted that a resolution of a local education authority, requiring schoolteachers to collect "dinner money" under pain of dismissal, was unlawful, although the teachers might be required to supervise school meals.

(3) *Arbitration*

Finally, it is open to the parties to submit disputes to arbitration, **278** *i.e.* either to an independent arbitrator (sometimes chosen through the good offices of the Department of Employment, *e.g.* for apprenticeship agreements) or to a person within the employee's firm. If the arbitration agreement is in writing, the Arbitration Act 1950 applies. Such an arbitration agreement does not necessarily bar legal proceedings, but normally the courts will stay an action brought by a party to the agreement on the application of the other party, unless there is a sufficient reason for the court to entertain the dispute itself. The "claims procedure" under section 8 of the Terms and Conditions of Employment Act 1959 has been dealt with in the preceding chapter (see above, paras. 208 *et seq.*). Industrial arbitration and conciliation raise collective issues which are not germane here.

V. Unfair Dismissal

Over the past decade or so there has been mounting pressure for the **279** introduction of a new remedy which would be available to the employee who has been *unfairly* dismissed, and which would not turn upon the question of notice (as with unlawful dismissal at common law), or upon redundancy (as with dismissal by reason of redundancy). The new remedy was created by section 22 of the Industrial Relations Act, thereby bringing our law more closely into line with that of several continental countries (which had recognised a remedy for "abusive" dismissal) and, more importantly, with Recommendation No. 119 of the ILO on Termination of Employment (ratified by the United Kingdom, with reservations, in 1964). Recommendation No. 119 recognises termination by the employer where this is connected with the capacity or conduct of the worker or is based upon the operational requirements of the undertaking, but then goes on to list examples of invalid reasons for termination, such as those relating to union membership or activity, complaints of violation of laws, race, colour, sex, marital status, religion, political opinion, national extraction or social origin.

Unlike the provisions in the still-born Industrial Relations Bill of the Labour Government in 1970, the 1971 Act departs somewhat from the wording of the Recommendation.

280 In every employment to which it applies, section 22 of the 1971 Act confers upon an employee the right not to be unfairly dismissed and, if this occurs, the right to complain of an unfair industrial practice to the industrial tribunal (in exceptional circumstances, the Industrial Court may take up the complaint). The main features of this new statutory wrong (which is already producing a considerable number of cases) are as follows.

1. Dismissal

281 It is for the employee to show that he has been dismissed either (a) by the termination of his contract, whether with or without notice, or (b) by the non-renewal of his fixed-term contract. If the employer gives notice to the employee, and the employee then gives notice in writing to the employer to terminate his contract of employment within the "obligatory period of that notice," such employee is taken to be dismissed by his employer. The "obligatory notice" means the minimum period of notice required by law or otherwise to terminate the contract of employment (see paras. 238 *et seq.*, above). Conspicuous by its absence is any reference to "constructive dismissal" under which the employee is taken to have been dismissed where he leaves as the result of the employer's repudiation of the contract. The Redundancy Payments Act 1965 covers dismissal of this sort and the growing number of cases on constructive dismissal indicates that its omission from the present Act may constitute a serious limitation on the ambit of the section (*cf. R. Middlemass* v. *Greenwood & Batley Ltd.* (1972)). As to the time when notice is effective, see para. 238, above.

2. Unfairness

282 It must also be shown that the dismissal was unfair. In this respect two hurdles are erected by the Act, the first of which the employer must clear.

The first hurdle requires the employer to show that the reason for the dismissal fell within the following list of reasons or some other substantial reason of a kind justifying dismissal (the latter showing that the list is not exhaustive). The reasons listed in section 24 (2) are those which:

(a) related to the employee's capability or qualifications in relation to the work which he was employed to do; or

(b) related to the employee's conduct; or

(c) related to the redundancy of the employee; or
(d) prevented the employee from continuing work in the position which he held without contravention of statutory requirements.

"Capability" is assessed by reference to skill, aptitude, health or other physical or mental quality, whereas "qualifications" refer to any degree, diploma or other academic technical or professional qualification relevant to the position held by the employee. It may occasionally be a matter of difficulty to distinguish between capability and qualifications on the one hand and "conduct" on the other as in *David James Davis* v. *Swift Automobiles Ltd.* (1972), where the failure of a service manager to complete job description cards for eleven employees was, in the event, put down to lack of capability and qualifications.

The employer who has surmounted the first hurdle is not yet "home and dry." It still remains to decide whether the dismissal was fair or unfair.

The second hurdle. Subject to two exceptions, determination of **283**
the question of fairness or unfairness, having regard to the reason shown by the employer, depends on whether the employer acted reasonably or unreasonably in the circumstances in treating that reason as a sufficient reason for dismissing the employee; and that question is determined in accordance with equity and the substantial merits of the case. The industrial tribunal has, therefore, considerable latitude to determine questions of fairness by relying on notions of "reasonableness," "equity" and "substantial merits." Thus, where the manager of a butchery department was dismissed because there was disharmony between himself and another man brought in over his head in order to improve turnover in the department, the tribunal found that the employer had cleared the first hurdle on the ground that the reason for the dismissal was a substantial one. The tribunal however went on to find that the dismissal was not in accordance with equity or the merits of the case since the dismissed employee had not been shown to be responsible for the disharmony at work and had not, in any case, been warned in accordance with the Code of Practice (*Wood* v. *Louis C. Edwards & Sons* (*Manchester*) *Ltd.* (1972)).

Dismissals held to be not unfair include those based upon **284**
repeated absences due to ill health (*Clark* v. *Coronel Ltd.* (1972)—only van driver in a small staff); annoyance of customers (*Houston* v. *G. H. Zeal Ltd.* (1972), where the employer had given a warning); unsatisfactory conduct and assault on fellow-employee (*Neefjes* v. *Crystal Products Co. Ltd.* (1972)—previous warning given); trade union official working for a third person during his holidays (*Gibson*

v. *National Union of Dyers, etc.* (1972)—official's conduct prejudicial to union negotiations aimed at longer holidays); refusal to clean canteen (*Simmons* v. *Tom Garner Motors Ltd.* (1972)); serious negligence (*J. P. Comerford* v. *Swel Foods Ltd.* (1972)); conviction for theft (*Andrew Robb* v. *Mersey Insulation Co. Ltd.* (1972)—the employee was a shipwright working at various docks); and loss of driving licence (*B. Appleyard* v. *F. M. Smith (Hull) Ltd.* (1972)).

285 The following are examples of dismissals held to be unfair—dismissal of a service manager for incompetence, but employers largely to blame for shortcomings in the running of the business (*F. Burrows* v. *Ace Caravan Co. (Hull) Ltd.* (1972)); dismissal of placing broker absent because of knee injury (*M. J. J. Field* v. *Leslie Godwin Ltd.* (1972)); dismissal of illiterate for failing to put fertiliser *around* the roots of plants and to shoot bullfinches attacking pear trees (*W. Butler* v. *J. Wendon & Son* (1972)—applicant not solely to blame and given no opportunity to state his case); refusal to accept new work on new terms (*L. J. Wallace* v. *Bigg's Wall & Co. Ltd.* (1972)); bad language (*A. Rosenthal* v. *Louis Butler Ltd.* (1972)—no warning or opportunity to apologise); driving company van off specified route and having an accident (*A. F. Young* v. *E. Thomas & Co. Ltd.* (1972)); unsubstantiated allegations of drunken behaviour against teacher at language school (*J. H. Beaton* v. *Anglo Continental School of English Ltd.* (1972)); absence on one occasion in six years and no warning (*C. Dixon* v. *John Laing Construction Ltd.* (1972)); conviction for incest (*J. G. Bradshaw* v. *Rugby Portland Cement Co. Ltd.* (1972)); and absence from work for four days without permission and no warning given (*G. Clapton* v. *Ketton Foundry Co. Ltd.* (1972)).

286 Unlike the case of the first hurdle, it is not clear upon whom falls the burden of proving reasonableness or unreasonableness as the case may be. Section 9 (2) (*b*) of the Redundancy Payments Act 1965 raises a statutory presumption that a dismissal is attributable to redundancy unless the contrary is proved, but there is no comparable presumption in the present section. Indeed, where the same proceedings concern both redundancy and unfair dismissal, Schedule 6, para. 8 to the 1971 Act, excludes the statutory redundancy presumption in relation to the complaint of unfair dismissal. Experience with the 1965 Act has shown a tendency on the part of the courts and tribunals to accept a subjective reason on the employer's part that the dismissal was for a non-redundancy reason. Since the reasons for dismissal lie peculiarly within the knowledge of the employer, it has been suggested that the burden of proving that the dismissal was fair (in the terms of section 24 (6)) should be made into a second hurdle for the employer.

As indicated above, there is no second hurdle in two cases. First, the dismissal of an employee is regarded as unfair if the reason or principal reason for it was that the employee had exercised, or had indicated his intention to exercise, any of the trade union rights conferred on him by section 5 (1) (see paras. 145 *et seq.*, above). We have seen that there is overlap between the unfair industrial practice of unfair dismissal and that relating to denial of trade union rights under section 5 (see para. 147, above). Secondly, a dismissal by reason of redundancy is regarded as unfair if the employee was selected for dismissal because of his exercise, proposed or actual, of the rights conferred by section 5 (1), or because he was selected for dismissal in contravention of a customary arrangement or agreed procedure relating to redundancy and there was no special reasons justifying a departure from that arrangement or procedure in his case. 287

Ideally, all employers ought to have comprehensive redundancy agreements on the lines advocated in the Department of Employment's booklet *Dealing with Redundancies* (1968). A redundancy agreement may work to the disadvantage of particular employees, as in *A. Taylor* v. *Conveyancer Ltd.* (1972), in which dilutees were properly selected for dismissal in preference to time-served men in accordance with a redundancy agreement between the employer and a union. Even the presence of a redundancy agreement does not preclude the employer from falling back on a "special reason" for departing from that agreement. The person selected for dismissal may hold a position *sui generis*, or lack the skill and versatility of a junior employee who has been retained. In one case, the tribunal upheld a departure from the seniority principle set out in a redundancy agreement where the employer had yielded to the importunities of shop stewards who were asking for the retention of certain employees on compassionate grounds. The plea of "selective dismissal" is more difficult to sustain where there is no customary arrangement or agreed procedure to deal with redundancies, particularly in the light of the present tendency of tribunals to accept managerial judgments based upon principles of commercial effectiveness. 288

The Industrial Court and the tribunals have already demonstrated that they are prepared to hold that a dismissal will be treated as unfair if the employee is not given notice of alleged misconduct and a chance to state his case. "This was a case," stated one tribunal in connection with a complaint from a dismissed employee who had been afforded no opportunity to state his case or to appeal, "which was an unfair dismissal because of the way in which it was effected" (1972 I.T.R. 324). In *Earl* v. *Slater & Wheeler* (*Airlyne*) *Ltd.* (1973), 289 the Industrial Court held that a dismissal justifiable by reason of the employee's conduct, *e.g.* embezzlement will be unfair if the suspected employee is given no opportunity to state his case. This contrasts with the position at common law (see para. 255, above). However, it must be remembered that the complainant in the *Earl* case received no compensation. Failure to apply natural justice is therefore something more than mere procedural irregularity. The Code of Practice lays down certain rules to be followed in cases of disciplinary action, such as those providing for warning, first "offences" and the like (*ibid.* paras. 130–133). The rules are relevant in proceedings for unfair dismissal, a fact which does not appear to have been perceived by those employers who still operate a "hire and fire" régime.

290 Dismissal of an employee by means of a lock-out is not unfair, provided that he is offered re-engagement, either in his former position, or in a different position which is reasonably suitable to him. If such an employee is not offered re-engagement, he is at liberty to complain that his non-re-engagement constitutes unfair dismissal and this will be determined in the ordinary way described above.

Although the employer may dismiss an employee for participating in a strike or irregular industrial action short of a strike, such dismissal will be regarded as unfair if the employee was selected for dismissal from among the participants because he had exercised or had proposed to exercise, his rights under section 5 (1). To the extent that rights under section 5 (1) are not infringed, as where a striker has asserted a "right" to join an unregistered union, the employee may be subjected to what trade unionists term "victimisation."

3. Excluded cases

291 The remedy for unfair dismissal is only available to the "employee" and not to the "worker" (a term of wider import: see above, paras. 33, 35). Even so, certain employees cannot invoke the unfair dismissal provisions, *viz.* those—

(a) with less than two years of continuous employment with the same employer;
(b) employed in undertakings with fewer than four employees who have been continuously employed for not less than thirteen weeks;
(c) related to the employer as husband, wife or other close relative;
(d) who are registered dock workers, share fishermen, or teachers subject to section 85 of the Education (Scotland) Act 1962;

(e) employed for less than twenty-one hours per week;
(f) who have reached retiring age;
(g) who ordinarily work outside Great Britain;
(h) employed under a fixed-term contract for two years or more who, before the expiry of that term, have agreed in writing to forego any claim for unfair dismissal (fixed-term contracts for two years or more entered into before February 28, 1972 are excluded regardless of any waiver of claim).

Dismissal of a person in any of the categories (a) (b) and (f) is, however, unfair if the reason for dismissal relates to that person's exercise, or proposed exercise, of his rights under section 5 (1) (see para. 145, above).

4. Remedies

Complaints of unfair dismissal (or infringement of trade union **292**
rights under section 5) lie at the suit of the complainant to the industrial tribunal. If the tribunal finds that the complaint is well-founded, it may, if it considers it to be just and equitable to do so, grant either or both of the following remedies to the employee (leaving on one side for the moment the question of re-instatement):

(a) An order determining the rights of the complainant and the employer as regards the matter in dispute.

(b) An award of compensation to be paid by the employer to the complainant. The maximum sum payable under the Act is the amount representing 104 weeks' pay, or £4,160, whichever is the less. By virtue of section 116, the compensation will be such amount as the tribunal considers just and equitable in all the circumstances, having regard to (i) the loss sustained by the aggrieved party, in so far as that loss is attributable to the action of the party in default. Expenses reasonably incurred by the complainant are included, as is any loss of benefit which the complainant might reasonably be expected to have had but for the action taken, subject, however, to the duty to mitigate loss. Where the complainant is found to have caused or contributed to any extent to the unfair dismissal (or infringement of trade union rights) the amount of compensation may be reduced to such extent as is just and equitable.

In the relatively few cases reported so far decided, the tribunals **293**
have taken into account the following factors—loss of future earnings, without any "penal" element for unfairness as such, but taking account of the difficulty which an older man may have in finding new employment; social security benefits, income tax and union benefit; loss of continuity of employment, so that the employee is back to "square one" as regards entitlement to notice and redundancy payment; sum paid in lieu of notice; employee's

rejection of offer of fresh employment; loss of tied cottage or flat; loss of hotel expenses and use of car; compensation for past services which, as it was put in one case "should be in excess of the figure to which he would otherwise have been entitled as a redundancy payment" (*sed quaere?*).

294 It will be apparent from the foregoing that the guidance given by the Industrial Court in *Norton Tool Co. Ltd.* v. *Tewson* (1972) comes at a most opportune time. Stressing that the tribunal must at least give some indication of the principles upon which it is assessing compensation, the Industrial Court explained that the object of the Act is to compensate fully, without giving a bonus (save possibly where the employer fails to comply with a recommendation for reinstatement), and without proceeding by analogy to the common law rules for assessing damages for wrongful dismissal. In substituting an award of £375 for that of £200 given by the tribunal, the Industrial Court took account of (1) loss of earnings during the six weeks of notice to which the complainant was entitled under the Contracts of Employment Act, ignoring actual earnings during that period and unemployment benefit already paid, and (2) loss of protection in respect of unfair dismissal or dismissal by reason of redundancy. Because the complainant was aged fifty and could not now build up the maximum of twenty years' service under the redundancy scheme, and because of the chances of a dismissal by reason of redundancy in his new employment (and in his old employment had he stayed in it), the court awarded approximately one-half of his accrued protection in redundancy. Future loss of wages was ignored in the absence of evidence to suggest that his new employment was less secure than his former employment, as was compensation for wounded pride or feelings arising out of the manner of his dismissal where this did not make him less acceptable to potential employers or exceptionally liable to selection for dismissal.

At the moment unfair dismissal is a new colossus bestriding wrongful dismissal and redundancy. If redundancy is to be taken into account when awarding compensation for unfair dismissal, added point is given to section 150 of the Industrial Relations Act 1971 which empowers the Secretary of State to make regulations whereby claims in respect of both redundancy and unfair dismissal may be adjusted.

295 It is not difficult to recall situations in which an employer has dismissed an employee, not because he wanted to, but because pressure has been brought to bear on him by a trade union or other group. *Rookes* v. *Barnard* in 1964 claims pride of place in this line of cases. If such a dismissal ranks as an unfair industrial practice, either because it interferes with the employee's trade union rights under section 5 (1), or is unfair under section 22, the hopeful philosophy of the 1971 Act is that the employer ought to stand firm against such pressure. If he succumbs to the pressure, *he* commits an unfair industrial practice and may be made to pay compensation to the employee. Section 119, however, contains provision for the joinder of a third party who uses certain forms of pressure (basically the strike or irregular industrial action short of a strike, or threat of either—see section 33), and for the payment of a contribution by that third party to the compensation which the employer has to pay (on joinder see Industrial Court Rules 1971, r. 52; Industrial Tribunals (Industrial Relations) Regulations 1972, reg. 5). The third party who uses the forms of pressure, described above, for the purpose of knowingly inducing the employer to commit the unfair industrial practice in question, himself commits an unfair industrial practice (s. 33 (3)).

(c) The third possibility is that the tribunal may make a recom- **296**
mendation for re-instatement in a case of unfair dismissal where it considers that it would be practicable and in accordance with equity for the complainant to be re-engaged. Such a recommendation has been made in a few cases, but in the great majority of cases the tribunal has found that re-engagement would be impracticable, bearing in mind the possible failure of conciliation before the case and the exacerbated feelings which the hearing may leave in its wake. The absence of any power to *order* re-instatement has been criticised by trade unionists (for a view favouring compulsory re-instatement in certain situations, see the late G. de N. Clark's, *Remedies for Unjust Dismissal*, P.E.P., 1970).

VI. Redundancy

The Redundancy Payments Act 1965 was intended to achieve two **297**
objectives—one social and the other economic. The social object of a redundancy payment is to compensate the employee for the loss which he *has* suffered because of one of the vicissitudes of employment, *viz.* redundancy. It was never the intention of the Act to give relief against the hardship which might follow dismissal by reason of redundancy. If the redundant employee remains unemployed, he can claim unemployment or other benefit. If he obtains fresh employment, he is not called upon to restore any of his redundancy payment. The latter is given to compensate him for the loss of security which he has suffered. The triplet of remedies now available for wrongful dismissal, unfair dismissal and dismissal by reason of redundancy serves to protect the job security of the modern employee. The cases in which the employer can escape the financial

incubus of a dismissal, although still possible, are now considerably diminished. In addition to its social objective, the Act was designed to secure the economic *desideratum* of greater labour mobility in a time of rapid change. At the same time, the need for the Act is a testament to the preoccupation of British trade unions with the traditional issues of pay and conditions of service.

298 The Act obliges an employer to make a redundancy payment to an employee (for definition, see para. 33, above) who has been dismissed by reason of redundancy, laid-off or kept on short-time and who has served that employer for the requisite period of continuous employment. The three main ingredients of a redundancy claim are, therefore—

(1) dismissal (including lay-off and short-time);
(2) redundancy; and
(3) continuous employment.

1. Dismissal

299 For the purposes of Part I of the Act and subject to certain provisions in that Part, an employee is taken to be dismissed by his employer, if, but only if—

(a) the contract under which he is employed by the employer is terminated by the employer whether it is so terminated by notice or without notice, or
(b) where under that contract he is employed for a fixed term, that term expires without being renewed under the same contract, or
(c) the employee terminates that contract without notice in circumstances (not falling within section 10 (4)) such that he is entitled so as to terminate it by reason of the employer's conduct (section 10 (4) relates to termination without notice by the employee where he is entitled to do so because of a lock-out by his employer).

The nature and effects of "dismissal" have been discussed above, at para. 238; it has been held that the term does not include an unspecific warning of impending redundancy or a mutual agreement to dissolve the contract. In normal circumstances the employer will expressly dismiss his employee with or without notice, but a dismissal of type (a) occurs when, without such communication, the employer closes down his business. Under section 22 of the Act, a termination of the contract of employment by operation of law, such as that caused by the death of the employer, the dissolution of a partnership or company, and frustration, is treated as a termination of the contract by the employer.

Similarly, if the employer gives notice of dismissal to his employee, and within the obligatory period (*i.e.* the minimum period required whether by law or otherwise to terminate the contract) of that notice, the employee gives notice in writing to terminate his contract on a date earlier than that on which the employer's notice expires, the employee, notwithstanding his notice, is taken to have been dismissed by his employer (s. 4). Professor Grunfeld has drawn attention to two traps in section 4, namely, the requirement of a written notice, and the requirement that the employee's counter-notice must be given within the obligatory period of notice from the employer, so that where the latter generously gives more than the obligatory notice a counter-notice given *before* such obligatory period is ineffective for the purposes of section 4 (*Law of Redundancy*, p. 47). 300

Regulations made under section 50 may provide that termination of certain employments by statute is to be treated as equivalent to dismissal (as has happened with chief constables and chief or assistant chief fire brigade officers: S.I. 1965 No. 2022).

Dismissal (b) is really a notional dismissal because, in the ordinary course of events, a fixed-term contract comes to an end on the date fixed (whether or not terminable by notice before that date), and its non-renewal would not ordinarily be termed a dismissal. Contracts for two years or more made before December 6, 1965, other than contracts of apprenticeship, are not covered by the Act.

Dismissal (c), sometimes termed "constructive dismissal," arises where the employee rightfully terminates the contract without notice because of his employer's conduct. From the already considerable accretions of case-law on constructive dismissal, it can be seen that the employee who refuses to accept demotion, the reorganisation of work, or a change in the place of work, will be able to claim a redundancy payment if these changes are not justified by his contract.

Lay-off and short-time

The Act contains provisions to deal with those employers who might otherwise feel tempted to avoid the incubus of the Act by laying-off workers for a time or putting them on short-time. Unless caused by an industrial dispute, an employee who has been laid-off (*i.e.* receives no pay where this depends on work performed), or who has been put on short-time (*i.e.* receives less than half his weekly pay), may be able to claim a redundancy payment if he has been laid-off or put on short-time, as defined, for four or more consecutive weeks, or where he has been laid-off or put on short-time for a broken series of six weeks within a thirteen-week period. 301

The two forms which lay-off may take are, (1) dismissal followed by re-engagement, and (2) suspension of the contract until such time as a return to work is possible. Two of the cases which have come before the tribunals, *viz. Sneddon* v. *Ivorycrete* (*Builders*) *Ltd.* (1966), and *Jones* v. *Harry Sherman Ltd.* (1969), concerned form (1). The Act is concerned only with form (2) because, as we shall see, there is provision for the employee to give notice to terminate his contract. In the *Jones* case (above), the manager of a betting shop who had been "stood off" during a ban on racing was held to have been dismissed by reason of redundancy.

302 The statutory lay-off, however, only applies, where, in the words of section 5 (1), "an employee is employed under a contract on such terms and conditions that his remuneration thereunder depends upon his being provided by the employer with work of the kind which he is employed to do"; an application which has caused some difficulty in the cases. The tribunal in the *Jones* case (above), whilst awarding a payment on the ground of dismissal, went on to express a narrow view as to the scope of statutory lay-off, limiting it to those rare contracts in which remuneration is dependent on the provision of work by the employer and suggesting that the employer would have no right to stop the wages of an employee at a fixed weekly wage or a guaranteed minimum wage at hourly rates, short of terminating the contract. *Puttick* v. *John Wright & Sons Ltd.* (1972) is a recent example of such a rare contract, for in that case a boiler scaler was employed to do specific jobs between which he was laid-off. In February 1971, he became ill and was unable to work, but claimed a redundancy payment in accordance with the statutory procedure. The tribunal were held to have decided rightly that his illness had not frustrated the contract, but their decision that there was no continuing contract after February 1971 because of lack of mutuality was overruled by the Industrial Court, which thought that it was "quite possible to envisage circumstances in which A may consider it in his best interests to undertake to do such work of a particular kind as B provides for him, A holding himself available to do such work as required and being paid only for the work he actually does, while B undertakes to make available to A such work of that particular kind as from time to time comes to hand." Even so, cases in which the contract contains a term, express, or (as in the *Puttick* case) implied, empowering the employer to suspend the employee by laying him off temporarily, must necessarily be rare, with the consequence that the statutory lay-off provisions are likely to be invoked only infrequently.

The determination of what is "less than half a week's pay" for the purposes of short-time is arrived at in accordance with Schedule 2 to the Act (which draws on Schedule 2 to what is now the Contracts of Employment Act 1972). The spread of the "guaranteed" week is likely to render redundancy by means of short-time something of a rarity.

Once a lay-off or short-time, as defined, is established, ritualism 303
of a kind not always appreciated by the secular mind creeps into the Act. In order to obtain a payment, the employee must given written "notice of intention to claim" as required by the Act, and must also give notice to leave. Even then he is not "home and dry," since the employer may return fire in the shape of a written "counter-notice" given within seven days of the employee's notice to claim, announcing that he will contest the claim because he considers that there is a reasonable prospect of the employee entering upon a period of employment with him, without lay-off or short-time, for not less than thirteen weeks, such period commencing not later than four weeks after the date of the employee's notice to claim. The further employment must relate to the contract of employment in relation to which the employee is laid, *i.e.* it cannot be *different* employment. If the notices are not withdrawn, the matter is resolved by the tribunal and, it might be added, no payment may be made unless the employee has left the employment, whether or not the case is contested. One wonders if this statutory mumbo-jumbo with its carefully modulated timetable (only parts of which have been mentioned here) is the best way of engendering respect for law. It seems to typify the British preference for particularity and certainty at the price of comprehensibility.

2. Redundancy

The second main requirement is that the dismissal must be 304
attributable wholly or mainly to redundancy as defined in the Act. Whereas the onus of proving dismissal lies upon the employee, the onus of proving on a reasonable balance of probabilities that the dismissal was not attributable to redundancy lies upon the employer because of the statutory presumption raised by section 9 (2) (*b*) that a dismissal is presumed to have been caused by redundancy "unless the contrary is proved" by the employer. It follows that a dismissed employee will be entitled to a redundancy payment if the tribunal receives no evidence to show why he was dismissed or if the evidence supports equally redundancy and non-redundancy reasons.

Redundancy may arise in a number of ways: cyclical change, contraction, structural decline and automation may all involve redundancies. The coal industry has simultaneously experienced decline and automation. The Act draws a screen over the reason for redundancy. The employer's motive in dismissing persons for redundancy is irrelevant. In *MacLoughlan* v. *Alexander Paterson Ltd.* (1968), the employer dismissed his employees in preparation for a re-organisation of staff from which he hoped to have a better employer–employee relationship. In *Dutton* v. *C. H. Bailey Ltd.* (1968), a boilermaker was dismissed because he had refused to accede to new working arrangements which, it was hoped, would arrest the decline in the employer's business. In both cases the employer's motive was treated as irrelevant and redundancy payments were given. No doubt it is hard that the firm in chronic decline is treated in the same way as the expanding firm which decides to use labour-saving technology, but it would be impossible to treat redundancy according to its causes. In the case of the coal industry the problem of rapid decline has been met by a special redundancy scheme for redundant mineworkers. Under the general scheme of the Act, the parlous condition of those whose employers cannot meet the amount of redundancy payments because of insolvency is remedied by section 32 of the Act, which enables the Minister to make the payments himself.

305 There are indications that the tribunals will pierce the veil of redundancy where the redundancy is "self-induced," as in *Marsland* v. *Francis Dunn Ltd.* (1967), where the demise of the firm had been caused by the refusal of the employee to work pending his departure to New Zealand. The tribunal in that case, speaking *obiter*, considered that self-induced redundancy was outside the spirit and intendment of the Act and this view is surely right? In a society supposedly dedicated to the concept of managerialism it would be dangerous to lift the veil too far, since if this were done it would be possible to say that in certain cases (*e.g. Dutton*, above) the employees had, by clinging to outmoded working practices and the like, caused their own redundancy.

It has been held that an employee dismissed by reason of "displaced redundancy" may claim a payment. This occurs in a situation in which redundancy occurs in one section of a business but a redundant employee in that section is not dismissed but transferred to another section from which another employee is dismissed. In *W. Gimber & Sons Ltd.* v. *Spurrett* (1967), the displaced employee was awarded a redundancy payment.

306 Redundancy may take one of three forms.

(i) There may be a cessation, actual or intended, of the business for the purposes for which the employee was employed. Such a cessation need not be permanent, nor is it necessary in the case of a registered company that it should be dissolved since if its memorandum so permits it may close down a particular business and engage in some fresh business for which the skills of its existing employees are ill-adapted.

(ii) There may be a cessation, actual or intended, of the business in the place where the employee was employed. Two possibilities need to be borne in mind in cases where the place of business is moved. First, the employee may be contractually mobile, so that a refusal to move to a new place of work may well rank as disobedience to a lawful order, entitling the employer to dismiss him. In such a case, no question of a redundancy payment arises. The second possibility is that upon a consideration of the employee's contract, including customary or collective terms included therein (see paras. 43 *et seq.*, above) it appears that the employee cannot lawfully be ordered to work in some new place to which he has been ordered. In such a case, the employee may refuse to accede to his employer's order and may claim a redundancy payment. This is what happened in *O'Brien* v. *Associated Fire Alarms Ltd.* (1968), where the Court of Appeal held that an electrician who had been engaged in installing fire alarms in the Liverpool area could lawfully refuse to work in Barrow some 120 miles away. Although the company's work in the Liverpool area had fallen off, the electrician's contract did not oblige him to travel beyond a commutable distance of his home. **307**

(iii) The third (and, despite indications to the contrary, final) **308** possibility is that the requirements of the business for employees to carry out work of a particular kind, or to carry out work of a particular kind in the place where they were employed, have ceased or diminished, or are expected to cease or diminish. Changes in technology, such as those involving automation, new materials and new products, changes in fashion, and the re-organisation of work (perhaps involving the re-structuring of work) may render certain kinds of work superfluous to the requirements of a business. Without progress we would still have the charcoal burners of the New Forest. But the price of progress may be heavy as is shown in *Hindle* v. *Percival Boats Ltd.* (1969). There, a skilled woodworker, who had spent most of his time in boat-building, was held not to have been dismissed by reason of redundancy (notwithstanding the increasing use of fibreglass in the building of boats) but because of the thoroughness and consequent slowness of his work. There were, said Sachs L.J. in that case, two conditions precedent to entitlement, *viz.* a cessation or diminution in the requirements of the business for work of the employee's kind, and a dismissal of the employee wholly or mainly because of such cessation or diminution. The first test, said his lordship, is "purely objective."

However, even if the first condition is established, the employee is not entitled to a payment if he is dismissed because of some genuine but mistaken belief on the part of his employer, *e.g.* that the employee has committed grave misconduct or is not "paying for his keep." The fact that the employee has not been replaced, whilst entitled to due weight, does not raise a conclusive presumption that the dismissal was due to redundancy. The *Hindle* decision shows that, notwithstanding a redundancy situation, the employer may be able to convince the tribunal that he dismissed his employee for some non-redundancy reason, even a mistaken non-redundancy reason, such as a misapprehension by the employer that his daughter has been indecently assaulted by the employee.

309 It may be difficult to decide whether a re-organisation of work constitutes a change to which an employee is expected to adapt or is one requiring work of an entirely different kind. In *North Riding Garages Ltd.* v. *Butterwick* (1967), a long-serving workshop manager, who had been dismissed following upon a take-over, was held to have been dismissed because of his inability to meet the new standards imposed by his employer. A dismissal caused by age, physical disability or unsatisfactory work is therefore not a dismissal by reason of redundancy.

Redundancy may occur where the business, speaking loosely, continues to enjoy unabated (and possibly increased) requirements for work of a particular kind but not in the form provided by the employee. A builder who requires brickwork to be carried out may decide that self-employed bricklayers will be able to do the work more efficiently and economically than his employees and sack the latter for that reason. On such facts in *Bromley & Hoare* v. *Evans* (1972), it was held that the requirements (in the sense of "needs") of the business for bricklayer-employees had diminished.

310 The tribunals have shown a keen sense of refinement in identifying "work of a particular kind." A supermarket shelver who refused to work a thirty-five-hour week instead of her existing twenty-nine-hour week because of her domestic circumstances was held in *Pollock* v. *Victor Value* (*Holdings*) *Ltd.* (1967) to have been dismissed by reason of redundancy. To most of us a pastry cook is a pastry cook. Not so in *European Chefs* (*Catering*) v. *Currell* (1971), where a pastry cook, whose virtuosity in the production of meringues and éclairs did not extend to continental pastries, was held to have been dismissed by reason of redundancy when his employers decided to concentrate on the latter type of confection. On the other hand, the personal characteristics of an employee, or some incident to the job which he holds, may not be subsumed under the formula "work of a particular kind," as in *Vaux & Associated Breweries* v. *Ward* (1969), where a fifty-seven-year-old barmaid, dismissed because her employers wished to employ a younger, "Bunny-girl" type of barmaid, having greater attraction to the younger clientèle, whom they wished to draw into their premises (converted to include a discotheque), was not considered to have become redundant by the Divisional Court, although that court did not rule out that there might be a difference in work as between a conventional barmaid's work and that involved in "shaking cocktails and the like" in a different or altered establishment. Again, in *Arnold* v. *Thomas Harrington* (1969), a garage fitter, who had been required to help in the operation of an emergency breakdown service out of normal working hours, and to live in a flat adjacent to the garage, was refused a redundancy payment on the grounds that he had been dismissed because his employers wished to obtain possession of the flat and not because of any cessation or diminution in the requirements for a fitter's services. It was held that his emergency breakdown work did not qualify as work of a particular kind.

Offer of new employment

An employee, otherwise entitled to a redundancy payment, will **311**
be disentitled to receive a payment if (1) he unreasonably refuses an offer from his employer to renew his contract on the same terms as his former contract and that renewal will take place so as to follow on the termination of the former contract, or (2) he unreasonably refuses a written offer from his employer to renew his contract on different terms, if such offer is an offer of suitable employment in relation to the employee and the renewal would take place on or before the termination of the former contract or not later than four weeks from that date. In both cases the employer's offer must be made before the termination of the employee's contract of employment, except that in situation (2) the offer must be in writing. It is not surprising that situation (2) has occupied the tribunals more than situation (1).

In both cases the terms of the offer must be sufficiently specific to **312**
enable the employee to make an informed decision whether or not to accept them. Vague, cryptic and monosyllabic offers are likely to be struck down as affording the employee too little guidance. This is particularly true of offers which contain different terms and which must therefore be written to enable the employee to make an informed judgment as to the nature of the employment which is being offered. Understandably enough, the redundant employee may insist on some "guarantee" as to the grade, remuneration, location and duration of the new employment. The tribunals have realised that to put employers under obligations of this sort would be to force them to give "copper-bottomed" guarantees which could not have been given under the former employment. Thus, an

employee may refuse an offer of purely temporary employment, but not an offer of regular (but not indefinite) employment. In the case of an offer required to be in writing, it is not necessary that the terms should be set out in one formal and specific document; the terms may be contained in several documents, the last of which need not expressly incorporate the contents of earlier document. The written offer may reduce to writing terms which have been orally discussed or may be put on a notice board addressed to the employee (*McCreadie* v. *Thomson & MacIntyre* (1971)).

313 There has been considerable case law in applying the concepts of (1) "suitable employment" and (2) "unreasonable refusal" in relation to offers of alternative employment on different terms. Suitability of employment was discussed in the leading case of *Taylor* v. *Kent County Council* (1969), where Lord Parker C.J. considered that it meant "conditions of employment which are reasonably equivalent to those under the previous employment, not the same, because then subs. (2) would apply," his lordship adding, "it does not seem to me that by 'suitable employment' is meant employment of an entirely different nature, but in respect of which the salary is going to be the same." In that case, an offer to the headmaster of a boy's school (which was to be amalgamated with another school) to work in a mobile pool of teachers at the same salary was held to be an offer of employment not suitable to a person of the headmaster's qualifications, experience and status. Suitability, said his lordship, is "almost entirely a matter of degree and fact for the tribunal." The court declined to draw a distinction made by some tribunals between the objective test of suitability in relation to the employee and the subjective test of reasonableness in refusing the offer of employment.

Clearly employment may be suitable in relation to the employee but nonetheless reasonably refused by the latter. In determining the reasonableness or unreasonableness of the employee's refusal it is undeniable that a wide range of "personal" or "social" factors, extraneous to the employment as such, have been taken into account.

314 Amongst the factors which the employee has successfully invoked are—his health and that of his family, the educational prospects for his children, marital opposition to move, mortgage commitment, distance and expense in travelling to the new job, and lack of leisure. At the same time, factors relating to the new employment have been taken into account in determining the reasonableness or otherwise of the employee's refusal, such as pay, status and the nature of the job. In fact there does seem to be some overlapping between the so-called objective test of suitability and the subjective test as to the reasonableness of refusal. Lord Parker C.J.

in the *Taylor* case (above) declined to pass upon the validity of the distinction, and a similar reticence is to be found in the decision of the Industrial Court in *Universal Fisher Engineering Ltd.* v. *Stratton* (1972). If, as seems likely, it will be impossible to separate the two criteria into separate, water-tight compartments, it does seem that "reasonableness" allows of a much freer-ranging inquiry into subjective "personal" factors than does "suitability."

Obviously, if the employee accepts the new employment in accordance with section 2, whether on identical or changed terms, it is obvious that he cannot obtain a redundancy payment, although he will be able to add the new employment to the old for purposes of reckoning continuous employment.

Finally, section 13 applies the rules concerning renewal or re- **315**
engagement to those cases in which a change occurs (whether by virtue of a sale or other disposition or by operation of law) in the ownership of a business and the offer of renewal or re-engagement comes from the new owner of the business. The problems inherent in the concept of a change in the ownership of a business (discussed at para. 245, above) are with one exception, common to both the present section and Schedule 1, para. 9, to the Contracts of Employment Act 1972. The exception is the inclusion of transfer of *part* of a business in section 13 and its omission from Schedule 1 to the 1972 Act, an omission which had unfortunate results in *Meadows* v. *J. Stanbury Ltd.* (1970), in which an employee who had served a business for a period of years and later, on a division of the business into two parts, had served one of the parts, was unable to add the service in the part of the business to the service in the undivided business for purposes of reckoning the amount of his redundancy payment.

Misconduct

Subject to an exception discussed below, an employee who is **316**
dismissed for misconduct is not entitled to a redundancy payment, whether or not full notice is given, except that in the former case the notice must be accompanied by a statement in writing that the employer would be entitled to dismiss without notice because of the employee's conduct (s. 2 (2)). As Lord Parker C.J. put it, "A man may be wholly redundant yet if his employer is justified in dismissing him summarily for his conduct he is not entitled to a redundancy payment" (*James Stott & Son (Elec.) Ltd.* v. *Stokes* (1971) at p. 52 of the report). The subsection is something of a puzzle. If an employee is dismissed because of misconduct he is not dismissed by reason of redundancy, and the failure of the employer to give the written statement, referred to above, cannot work the

magic alchemy of converting the former type of dismissal into the latter. Lord Parker's dictum (above) shows that the subsection is a residual provision to deal with cases in which the dismissal is attributable to redundancy *and* misconduct, including misconduct discovered *after* a dismissal without notice but with wages in lieu of notice (*X.* v. *Y.* (1969)). If, in such a situation, the employer gives full notice, he must give the statement in writing referred to above.

317 The foregoing however is subject to the power given to the industrial tribunal to award all or part of a redundancy payment as it thinks just and equitable in a case where the employee is dismissed for misconduct in the circumstances described in the preceding paragraph *during* the proper period of notice for dismissal by reason of redundancy. The right of an employee to a redundancy payment who participates in a strike during notice of dismissal for redundancy is governed by section 40 which permits the employer to contest a payment if the employee fails without excuse to comply with the employer's notice to extend the notice by working the days lost by the strike.

3. Continuous employment

318 An employee is not eligible to receive a redundancy payment under the Act if he has not been continuously employed by the same employer for 104 weeks. Continuity of employment is also relevant in reckoning the amount of a redundancy payment (see below, para. 320). The rules governing continuity of employment are those set out in Schedule 1 to the Contracts of Employment Act, with some adaptations. We have already seen that in general continuity of employment is broken by weeks which do not count for purposes of enumeration but that in certain cases weeks which do not count for purposes of enumeration do not thereby break continuity of employment (paras. 242 *et seq.*, above).

4. Redundancy payment

319 Responsibility for making a redundancy payment is placed upon the employer, who is also obliged to give the employee a written statement indicating how the amount of the payment has been calculated. The employer who makes a redundancy payment under the Act to his employee is entitled in certain cases to claim a rebate from the Redundancy Fund which was set up by the Act and placed under the control and management of the (now) Secretary of State for Employment. Broadly, the amount of the rebate increases with the age and service of the employee. Without such a difference, employers would have been reluctant to dismiss older workers for fear of the potentially heavy payments which such workers may

involve. The scale of redundancies since 1965 has placed great strain on the Redundancy Fund which has regularly run into deficit. The Redundancy Rebates Act 1969 attempted to deal with this by reducing the amount of rebate from roughly 70 per cent. to 50 per cent., a measure which has not succeeded in meeting the increasing claims being made on the Fund. A feature of the rebate system is that it puts pressure on the employer to give advance notice of redundancy, for want of which the amount of his rebate may be reduced. The employer must claim a rebate within six months (or such further period as may be allowed) of making the redundancy payment to his employee. The rebate will only issue to an employer who has paid a redundancy payment which he was *legally* obliged to pay, and even then will be related to the amount of the redundancy payment as calculated in accordance with the Act.

As regards the redundancy payment itself, three criteria are **320** employed in determining its amount, *viz.* (1) length of continuous service in weeks, (2) age, and (3) earning capacity. The period of continuous employment (on which see paras. 242 *et seq.*) is reckoned backwards from the relevant date (normally the date on which notice of dismissal expires), subject to the overall maximum of twenty years. The age factor is reflected in the weighting given to the older worker. The earnings factor is reflected in the choice of a week's pay as the unit of payment for every year of qualifying service. The weighting according to age is effected by giving half a week's pay for each year of service from the age of eighteen years, replaced by a week's pay for service from the age of twenty-one years, in turn replaced by one-and-a-half week's pay for service from the age of forty-one years to retiring age, subject to "tapering" arrangements. The ascertainment of a week's pay is calculated in accordance with Schedule 1 to the Act, which in turn draws on and adapts with some strain Schedule 2 to the Contracts of Employment Act 1972, notwithstanding that the latter Schedule is concerned with an entirely different question. Earnings above £40 (a figure which may be reviewed upwards) are ignored, from which it will be seen that the maximum payment under the Acts is £1,200 (20 × £40 × 1½). The unit of a week's pay is also important in connection with short-time working (see para. 301 above).

An employer is not liable to make a redundancy payment, unless the employee claims in writing a payment from him not later than six months from the termination of his employment; there is no need to make such a written claim if the question of the employee's right to a payment, or the amount of such payment, has been transferred for decision to the tribunal, or a complaint of unfair dismissal has been presented under section 106 of the Industrial Relations Act 1971.

The Industrial Tribunal

321 Any question relating to the right of an employee to a redundancy payment, or concerning the amount of such payment, is determined by the industrial tribunal. In addition to the right to a payment conferred by section 1 of the Act, the tribunal may determine any question relating to a right to a redundancy payment contained in respect of which the Minister has made an exemption order under section 11. An exemption order does not preclude a reference under section 8 (1) of the Terms and Conditions of Employment Act 1959 (see para. 57) and does not preclude the Industrial Arbitration Board from making an award concerning the observance of the severance provisions in the collective agreement.

Despite the somewhat formalistic impression conveyed by its Rules of Procedure, the industrial tribunal is an informal, cheap and reasonably speedy forum for the settlement of a wide range of matters, quite apart from redundancy payments claims. It handles cases under the Contracts of Employment Act 1972, the Industrial Relations Act 1971, and in due course will take up equal pay cases and possibly all claims for compensation arising from breach of the contract of employment, excluding those involving personal injury. If the recommendations of the Robens Committee are adopted (Cmnd. 5034, paras. 273, 276), it will hear certain cases on industrial safety. In the past, the tribunal has been responsible for selective employment tax (now abolished) cases, and for cases involving statutory compensation. The decay of the industrial training levy system will presumably mitigate very slightly the increasing caseload to which the tribunals are, or are likely to be, subjected. Except where a party has acted "frivolously or vexatiously," costs are not normally awarded. The tribunals are attracting the attention of the legal profession as more and more claimants employ legal representatives to press their claims. Since the Industrial Relations Act 1971, appeals under the Contracts of Employment Act 1963 (now 1972), the Equal Pay Act 1970, and the Industrial Relations Act 1971 *quoad* complaints under that Act, lie on *questions of law* to the Industrial Court. As one might expect, the Industrial Court like its predecessor in these particular appeals, the Divisional Court, has not always been able to draw a "Mason–Dixon Line" between law and fact.

PART TWO
PROTECTIVE LEGISLATION

CHAPTER 5

PROTECTIVE INDUSTRIAL LEGISLATION

I. INTRODUCTION

THE transformed society produced by the Industrial Revolution **322** brought with it risks of injury and disease on a scale not previously experienced in this country. The distinctive response to these new risks has been the enactment of protective Acts starting with the Factory Acts. Later Acts brought most of the working population within the scope of legislation largely modelled on the factories' legislation, although the Robens Committee (the recommendations of which are summarised below at paras. 396 *et seq.*) found that some 5 million working persons were outside the scope of present-day occupational safety and health legislation. At the present day, there are three main systems which have relevance to industrial safety and health. These are as follows:

(a) The common law. The common law duty of the employer to provide for the safety of employees (see para. 102, above) is merely a particular emanation of the duty to take care, adumbrated by Lord Atkin in *Donoghue* v. *Stevenson* (1932), with the "reasonable man" replaced by the "reasonable employer." Although judges have claimed a preventive effect for the common law rules, the rules are mainly reparative in effect since they deal with accidents *after* they have occurred.

(b) Protective legislation dealing not only with the narrow **323** issue of safety, but encompassing hours of work, health and welfare. Judges have erected civil liabilities on much of this legislation, but its main function is to prevent accidents—hence the reliance on criminal sanctions and inspection. As will be seen, the Robens Committee were critical of its preventive functions.

(c) Social insurance under the statutory industrial injuries scheme (discussed in Chapter 6), which fulfils a reparative function with regard to industrial injuries and diseases but without the concept of "fault" on which the common law and much of the protective legislation is based. It has no preventive role, although the Robens Committee thought that the scheme could be given such a role by the use of differential rates of contribution from employers in the light of claims experience.

Before embarking on a discussion of protective legislation, something must be said of the relationship between that legislation and the other two systems, namely, the common law and social insurance.

Protective legislation, the common law and social insurance

324 Why is it then that protective legislation is needed at all when the common law affords protection to the worker? Many reasons may be given in answer to this question. The first is that the standards set by the common law were manifestly inadequate to meet the new risks which emerged in an industrialised society—the common law tended to fossilise the standards of reasonable employers at any given time, but was chary of dictating newer and more stringent standards; such duty as there was suffered emasculation at the hands of doctrines like common employment, the *volenti* defence (at least before *Smith* v. *Baker* (1891)) and contributory negligence—disfigurements which have been either removed or reduced in scope. Secondly, it was felt that employers should know precisely what was expected of them which, to the practical factory owner, was difficult in relation to the common law duty because of its generalised formulation (it will be seen that it is doubtful if the statutes in fact always put doubt at rest!). Thirdly, the common law was cast in narrow terms since, as indicated above, it merely covers the safety of the worker, whereas the wider issues of health and welfare were felt also to be relevant. Lastly, the common law is based upon the principle of risk distribution according to fault (*culpa*), *i.e.* it allocates responsibility for risk, *after* the risk has occurred, by reference to fault. Its role therefore is, as already indicated, compensatory.

325 The duty to take reasonable care not to injure those whom one can reasonably foresee are likely to be affected by one's acts or omissions remains enshrined in the common law. The failure of the common law to deal with the increasing numbers of fatalities which attended production and mobility in an industrial society were met by the Fatal Accidents Acts and the Law Reform (Miscellaneous Provisions) Act 1934 (see above at para. 124). In 1880, the Employers' Liability Act (since repealed) made employers liable to compensate workmen who had suffered personal injury by reason of the defective conditions of premises, plant or machinery, or as the result of the acts and omissions, or negligence, of certain persons in the service of the employer. The standard of care under that Act was essentially the common law standard of reasonable care in the circumstances, although the Act provided compensation, not by

reference to the damage actually suffered, but by reference to the estimated loss of earnings over the three years preceding the workman's injury. The Act also restricted somewhat the rule of common employment which precluded recovery of damages for an injury caused by the negligence of a fellow-employee in the course of employment. That little-loved rule was not finally exorcised from our law until 1948. The philosophy of Capability Brown has continued into this century, recent Acts such as the Employers' Liability (Defective Equipment) Act 1969 and the Employers' Liability (Compulsory Insurance) Act 1969 being attempts to adapt the common law to modern conditions.

A separate line of development began in 1897, when the first of **326**
the Workmen's Compensation Acts was passed. Under those Acts, the liability cast upon employers was no longer based upon fault but upon the now-familiar formula of a personal injury caused by accident arising out of and in the course of employment. If the appellant could bring himself within that formula, proof of fault was irrelevant. A claim at common law, which still depended on proof of fault, was possible but the workman or his representative was put to his election between pursuing a claim at common law or a claim under the Acts. Mining excepted, there was no duty to insure liability under the legislation, although employers might, with the approval of the Registrar of Friendly Societies, substitute insurance benefit schemes in place of the statutory liability. Compensation under the workmen's compensation scheme was limited in contrast to the theoretically open-ended nature of common law damages. Unfortunately, the Acts were turned by the courts into a mystique attracting its own types of lawyer, textbook writer and law reports, and abounding in subtle distinctions little to the liking of ordinary working folk. The Acts were replaced in 1946 by the statutory Industrial Injuries Scheme (below, Chapter 6) which still relies upon the formula (see above) used in those Acts.

The common law and the statutory codes complement each **327**
other. It is not unusual to join claims under each head in an action for damages, but judgment in one suffices to dispose of the action: damages cannot be claimed twice over. In *Smith* v. *National Coal Board* (1967), Lord Reid declined to accept the argument that a regulation dealing with coal mine sidings was intended to codify the whole common law duty of the employer for the sphere in which the regulation operated. It is dangerous to apply tests used in the statutory codes to common law claims and vice versa. In *Chipchase* v. *British Titan Products Co. Ltd.* (1956), the plaintiff, a painter employed at the defendant's factory, fell from some staging which was nine inches wide. The staging was six feet above the ground:

had it been six feet six inches above the ground, regulations would have applied and a staging not less than thirty-four inches wide would have been required. The Court of Appeal declined to interfere with the decision that the nine-inch plank was sufficient at common law and warned against the application of statutory standards by analogy. A defendant may comply with statutory standards and still incur common law liability. We shall see that it is doubtful if the "reasonable" standard of the common law means the same thing as the "reasonably practicable" standard used in certain statutory duties.

328 Both the common law and the industrial injuries scheme compensate persons who have suffered an injury. Because each deals with the results of accidents, neither purports to have prophylactic effect: such deterrent effect as damages may have is, in any case, reduced by insurance, now compulsory in relation to employer's liability. Protective legislation on the other hand is, as we shall see, supposed to have a preventive effect on industrial accidents and disease. Dissatisfaction with the *compensatory* role of the common law has led to the establishment of a Royal Commission on Civil Liability for Death and Injury (for terms of reference, see above, para. 121). The Robens Committee on Safety and Health at Work found the existing system of protective legislation to be seriously deficient in its *accident-prevention* role and made recommendations which are summarised at the end of this chapter. The relationship between social insurance benefits and damages has been noted above at para. 117.

The emergence of factory legislation

329 Although the factory system did not start in the nineteenth century, the technological innovations of that century, allied to improved communications and increased investment (facilitated by the limited liability company) resulted in the change to factory conditions and urbanised life described in such emotive terms by Engels in *The Conditions of the Working Class in England.* The first Act in 1802, 42 Geo. 3, c. 73, was aimed at the bad conditions produced by the Poor Laws and the Re-Settlement Acts, rather than at the evils of urban industrialism, which were yet to come. It was, by modern standards, a peculiarly paternalistic Act, providing, *inter alia*, for instruction in the Christian religion on Sundays at the employer's expense. In a century of *ad hoc* legislation, factory laws were no exception, and a piecemeal *congeries* of enactments was built up, applying mainly to textile factories and to specified categories of workers, and, from the middle of the century, reinforced by an inspectorate. Such laws were passed under pressure from

humanitarian reformers such as Shaftesbury and Owen who often encountered their fiercest opposition from workers themselves who feared that the new controls on female and child labour would diminish an already small "family wage." After 1867, when the urban artisan was enfranchised, the pressure came increasingly from trade unions desirous of using what the Webbs termed "The Method of Legal Enactment"; a method which was better suited to the achieving of uniformity in working conditions than collective bargaining.

From 1864, certain non-textile industries were brought within the scope of factory legislation, until in 1878 a measure of rationalisation was introduced by the Factory and Workshop Act, a consolidating and amending statute which, amongst other things, brought into use a definition of "factory" still in use to this day, with some changes. On the Second Reading of the 1878 Bill, it was said, "it is desirable, in the interests alike of employers and employed, that all trades and manufacturers employing the same class of labour should be placed upon the same footing, and under the same protective and restrictive regulations," to which was added the euphoric opinion that "it consolidates and simplifies the law beyond the possibility of misinterpretation." The 1878 Act was thereafter periodically amended and consolidated, a process which reached its consummation in the Factories Act 1961.

Role of legislation

Factory legislation has served as a paradigm for other forms of **330**
protective legislation, with the result that, today, we have four main "codes" dealing with industrial safety, health and welfare, *viz*:

(a) The Factories Act 1961, covering some 8½ million persons.
(b) The Mines and Quarries Act 1954, covering 345,000 persons.
(c) The Offices, Shops and Railway Premises Act, affecting 8 million persons.
(d) The Agriculture (Poisonous Substances) Act 1952, and the Agriculture (Safety, Health and Welfare Provisions) Act 1956, together affecting some 340,000 persons.

Under the parent Act in each case there are varying amounts of subordinate legislation which deal with detail. The codes are administered by separate departments and separate inspectorates, apart from the first two codes which come under the Department of Employment and its inspectorate (except for some inspection by local authorities).

In addition to the four main codes, there are special Acts to **331**
deal with particular problems, such as those involving explosives,

petroleum, nuclear installations and oil rigs. Indeed, in modern times it has become clear that industrial risks which formerly lay within the geographical confines of factories, mines and the like have become public risks by reason of the scale and mobility of modern productive methods. The use of radioactive substances, the emission of noxious gases and the deposit of poisonous waste have each led in turn to *ad hoc* legislation which, we are told, must suffice pending the arrival of a general statute dealing with the whole problem of environmental pollution.

To revert to the four main codes, there are two main themes running through the respective Acts. The first is the idea that the protective Acts will prevent accidents because of their strict standards, their criminal sanctions and their administrative techniques of enforcement. The Robens Committee found the Acts to be deficient in this respect (see below, para. 395). We shall see that sometimes the courts have managed to graft a civil action for damages onto the criminal breach of duty, and by so doing have given the Acts a compensatory role which, the Robens Committee thought, reacts unfavourably on their preventive aims.

332 The second theme is that "employers generally will know with certainty what is expected of them" (Minister of Labour commenting on the Factories Acts and court decisions thereunder when speaking on the Second Reading of the Offices, etc., Bill 1963). By contrast the Robens Committee in 1972 commented that: "The legislation is badly structured, and the attempt to cover contingency after contingency has resulted in a degree of elaboration, detail and complexity that deters even the most determined reader. It is written in a language and style that renders it largely unintelligible to those whose actions it is intended to influence" (Report, para. 29). The lawyer for his part does not always find the legislation to be "a well of English undefiled," and when he turns to judicial definitions of "dangerous part," "in motion" and "working place" he might well be excused for thinking he has strayed into some Kantian critique of pure reason. To the question of interpretation we now turn.

Interpretation

333 To the courts is given the unenviable task of interpretation. That they have experienced no little difficulty may be illustrated by some examples. In *British Railways Board* v. *Liptrot* (1967), the respondent was crushed between the body of a crane and one of the chassis wheels when the body of the crane slewed round. The crane in question was mobile and was mounted on rubber wheels. It was being used to lift scrap metal in a scrap yard. The respondent

claimed that he had been injured by reason of a failure to fence "a dangerous part of any machinery" under section 14 (1) of the Factories Act 1961. Two questions were involved, *viz.*: (a) did the fact that sections 22–27 of the Act dealt with cranes and other machines preclude an action under section 14 (1); (b) if the part in question was dangerous, was the crane a machine? The House of Lords, dealing with the first question, held that an action was not precluded under section 14 (1). On the second question, it found that the crane was a machine. Mobile equipment such as cranes may therefore be within the section although lorries and cars visiting the factory would not—in any case these last are dangerous as a whole and therefore outside the section. A similar problem arose in *Lovelidge* v. *Anselm Oldling & Sons* (1967), where a mason's tie became caught in the flexible driving shaft of a grinding tool. Widgery J. held that the mason was entitled to damages since the uncovered shaft was a dangerous part of machinery.

Another example of the difficulty inherent in interpreting statutory provisions is shown in the cases arising out of section 28 which, with section 29, deals broadly with the safety of premises. Section 28 (1) states that: "All floors, steps, stairs, passages and gangways shall be of sound construction and properly maintained and shall, so far as is reasonably practicable, be kept free from any obstruction and from any substance likely to cause persons to slip." Thus, where an employee slipped and fell on some metal plates covering pits, the plates being covered by slagdust, it was held that the "floor" was slippery: *Dorman Long (Steel) Ltd.* v. *Bell* (1964). A flue in the floor of a furnace which was being constructed on the defendant's factory premises has been held not to constitute an opening in the floor under section 28 (4); a floor of a gantry has been held to be within the section, unlike planks laid across the steel members of a crane gantry. The section has included things like a steep unfenced drop, objects lying on the floor and a ladder resting on a polished floor; "trivial" faults, *e.g.* slight unevenness in linoleum on the floor, have been excluded, as has an accident caused by the dangerous driving of a vehicle within the factory grounds. **334**

Section 29 states that:

> "(1) There shall, so far as is reasonably practicable, be provided and maintained safe means of access to every place at which any person has at any time to work, and every such place shall, so far as is reasonably practicable, be made and kept safe for any person working there."

This subsection has been held inapplicable to cases where a person slips on his way to the canteen or lavatory. It was held in *Dorman Long & Co.* v. *Hillier* (1951), that, under the 1937 Act, a person who fell whilst removing corrugated iron sheets from a roof, moving from point to point as he did so, was unprotected since the statute only applied to access to work as opposed to the place of work. This has now been remedied (by section 29 of the Factories Act 1961), since the latter is now included, although it has been suggested that the distinction may still be important on the ground that the duty to provide and maintain a safe means of access does not cover transient and exceptional conditions, *e.g.* grease on the floor, whilst the duty to make the place of work safe may include provision for such transient conditions. In *Boyton* v. *Willment Brothers Ltd.* (1971), demolition contractors were held liable to pay damages to one of their workmen who had fallen over the edge of a building which was being demolished. In demolishing the building, floorboards were taken up except for some which were left as passageways. These were held to be working places within the meaning of the relevant regulations; they were flat, confined areas used for work other than that of a purely transient nature, and the duty to fence them was mandatory, however unreasonable, absurd or unnecessary this might appear to some persons.

335 One final example to underline the need to approach the legislation with a healthy respect for the judicial interpretation of particular words is the House of Lords decision in *Price* v. *Claudgen Ltd.* (1967). The respondent, an electrician, received an electric shock, causing him to fall and injure himself, whilst repairing a neon lighting installation on a cinema. It was held that he could not claim for damages for breach of building regulations since the latter only applied to the "repair or maintenance of *a building*." Lord Morris of Borth-y-Gest said: "He was repairing something which was on a building" as opposed to the building itself.

The foregoing random examples of the technicality and particularity surrounding the statutory codes serve to show that in these contexts the only safe generalisation one can make is that generalisations are dangerous. Nevertheless, since microscopic examination of each statute and its supporting tier of subordinate legislation would involve many volumes, it is proposed to extract some general observations in the ensuing sections, which deal with the enforcement of protective legislation, the operation of such legislation in relation to places, processes and persons, the concept of strict liability in contrast to other less stringent standards (both in criminal and civil law) together with a discussion of foreseeability, types of injury, onus of proof, causation and defences.

II. Enforcement

Three features of protective industrial legislation which will be discussed here are (i) the imposition of criminal sanctions; (ii) the enforcement of the statutory duties by cadres of inspectors (from different Ministries); and (iii) the possibility of a civil remedy. **336**

1. Criminal sanctions

The word "shall" appears in most sections, imposing a statutory **337** duty. Every factory "shall" be kept in a clean state, no person "shall" use white phosphorus in the manufacture of matches, a person "shall not" be employed to lift, carry or move any load so heavy as to be likely to cause injury to him, and there "shall" be provided and maintained so as to be readily accessible a first-aid box (ss. 1, 67, 72 and 61 of the Factories Act 1961).

Section 155 of the Factories Act 1961 provides that any contravention of the provisions of the Act by the occupier (or where applicable the owner) is an offence. The same section also provides that an employed person upon whom a duty has been expressly imposed shall be guilty of an offence. Employees who wilfully interfere with health, safety or welfare appliances commit an offence under section 143, although this section has been interpreted to denote some perverse conduct. In *Wright* v. *Ford Motor Co.* (1967), an information was preferred against an occupier for failure to fence a dangerous part of machinery, when an employee was injured in machinery which was normally fenced but where the lock on the gate of the fence had been forced by some other employee. It was held that (i) the employer was not vicariously liable under section 155 (1) for the offence of the unknown employee under section 143, nor (ii) was he liable under section 155 (2) (which renders the occupier or owner liable, in addition to the employee committing an offence) since it had not been proved that he failed "to take reasonable steps to prevent the contravention" (a defence open to the occupier under section 155 (2)). Section 161 enables the occupier to escape liability by using "third party procedure," *i.e.* by showing that the offence was committed by someone else. According to a Law Commission Working Paper, the inspectorate rarely prosecute unless an occupier is at fault, even though he is thought to be in breach of a strict duty. The Robens Committee confirms that few infringements of the Act are prosecuted and that those which are prosecuted to conviction result in the imposition of only small fines. Save for those cases calling for exemplary punishment, the Committee considers that criminal sanctions are inappropriate for most of the offences arising from safety and health legislation.

338 In the Mines and Quarries Act 1954, contraventions of the Act in relation to any mine are attended by penalties exigible from the owner of the mine and others under section 152. The escape routes are more open than those in the Factories Act, since it is "a defence for the person charged [with any offence under section 152] to prove that he used all due diligence to secure compliance with the provision, prohibition, restriction or regulation as the case may be" (s. 156). Where a person is charged with an offence (excepting one providing expressly that a person is to be guilty) it is a defence for the person charged to prove that it was impracticable to avoid or prevent the contravention (s. 157). The Offices, Shops and Railway Premises Act 1963 imposes penalties upon those who commit offences under the Act (normally the occupier, unless responsibility is placed on some other person, either in addition to or instead of the occupier); the person actually committing the offence for which another person is liable is also rendered liable. It is a defence, however, for a person charged with a contravention of a provision of the Act or of regulations made thereunder, to prove that he used "all due diligence to secure compliance with that provision" (s. 67). There is a similar provision in section 16 of the Agriculture (Safety, Health and Welfare Provisions) Act 1956.

2. The factory inspectorate

339 The oldest and largest of the inspectorates is the Factory Inspectorate which is responsible for the inspection of some 400,000 premises affected by the Factories and Offices, etc. Acts, for which purposes it employs over 700 inspectors. These inspectors have extensive powers to enter, inspect and examine factories, to require the production of documents, etc., to ensure that the provisions of the Factories Act and of the relevant public health enactments are complied with, to require any person in a factory to give information within his power as to who is the occupier, to examine persons in a factory, to require them to sign a declaration of the truth of the matters respecting which they are so examined, save for self-crimination, and to exercise "such other powers as may be necessary for carrying this Act into effect." The occupier must assist the inspector in specified ways and anyone who obstructs an inspector in the execution of his duties under this Act is guilty of an offence. The inspectors also have the same powers in relation to warehouses, when they have reasonable cause to believe that young persons are employed there or have been employed there within the preceding two months. They may conduct proceedings in magistrates' courts if authorised in writing under the hand of the Secretary of State for Employment.

One can only hope that these statutory powers enable the inspectors to carry out their functions with greater ease than the sub-inspector who reported that the steam in the Turkey red dye-works "is so dense that he had to walk blindfold through the works, and to take hold of the coat-tail of the manager to guide him" (Second Reading of the 1878 Factory and Workshop Bill). The Robens recommendations concerning a unified inspectorate with greater powers are mentioned below at para. 398.

3. Civil enforcement

Are damages in general available?

One judge has observed that the civil sanction of damages, 340
possibly running into thousands of pounds, is a more coercive sanction to secure compliance with the terms of protective legislation than small fines. Against the deterrent effect of damages must be set the practice of insuring risks, now compulsory in relation to employers' liability (see para. 120, above). But is there civil redress in the form of damages? It is a peculiarity of protective legislation that in spite of its prolixity and detail on the various duties and their enforcement, it remains strangely silent on the question of civil redress. One exception is section 159 of the Mines and Quarries Act 1954, which, for the removal of doubts, declares that the owner of a mine or quarry is not absolved from liability to pay damages in respect of contraventions of that Act (including cases where the contravention is by an employee in respect of a duty imposed on him whereby another person is injured). Whether or not a civil suit may be brought for breach of a statutory duty has taken the courts into explorations of the intention of the legislature. The Law Commission's modest proposals for the reform of the rules and presumptions to be applied to the interpretation of statutes include the introduction of a presumption in favour of civil actionability. This idea has not been adopted, but one discerns a trend in recent Acts towards the explicit conferment of civil redress. Thus, section 11 of the Mineral Workings (Offshore Installations) Act 1971 expressly declares that breach of a duty under the Act, or regulations made thereunder, is to be civilly actionable to the extent that it causes personal injury. Because its terms of reference did not extend to accident compensation, the Robens Committee were unable to make any specific recommendations as to civil redress for breach of statutory duty, a topic which they felt merited separate investigation (see para. 328, above), but the Committee did take notice of criticisms that the compensation system disturbed the preventive function of protective legislation as well as having little deterrent effect itself because of the spreading of risk by means of insurance.

Damages available in particular instances

341 (i) *Safety provisions.* Fortunately it is quite clear that the courts construe protective industrial legislation as prima facie conferring actionable civil rights, at least where safety is concerned. In *Groves* v. *Lord Wimborne* (1898), a boy recovered damages for breach of a statutory duty to fence dangerous parts of machinery. That part or whole of the penalty also imposed *might* be diverted to the plaintiff or his family did not deter the court from awarding damages. Vaughan Williams L.J. said (at p. 415 of the report) that it could not be doubted that:

> "where a statute provides for the performance by certain persons of a particular duty and someone belonging to a class of persons for whose benefit and protection the statute imposes the duty is injured by failure to perform it, prima facie, and if there be nothing to the contrary an action by the person so injured will lie against the person who has so failed to perform the duty."

In 1951, Lord Normand felt able to say that there was support for the view "that all regulations made for the safety of employees in factories or coal mines under the relevant Acts should be construed if possible as imposing a direct obligation on the occupier of the factory or on the owner of the mine" (*Harrison* v. *National Coal Board* (1951) at p. 660 of the report). The connection between statutory offence and judicial remedy did not, as a matter of social policy, appear to be "logically plain" to Lord Hailsham L.C. in *F. E. Callow* (*Engineers*) *Ltd.* v. *Johnson* (1971), at p. 641 of the report, who, whilst conceding that an employer guilty of an offence under sections 12–16 ought to be liable to a workman injured by the statutory breach, did not think that the converse was so obvious, namely that the basis for the compensation of the injured workman should be the commission of a criminal offence. His lordship, however, accepted that the connection in question was now clearly law.

342 (ii) *Health provisions.* Outside the safety provisions, the position is less clear. It seems that a civil action will lie for breach of a health provision in Part I of the Factories Act 1961. A case against this view is *Ebbs* v. *James Whitson & Co. Ltd.* (1952). The plaintiff claimed damages for dermatitis, which he alleged he had contracted from scraping and sand-papering monsonia hardwood (at that time not known to give rise to the risk). He relied upon section 4 of the Factories Act 1937 (now s. 4 of the 1961 Act), which required the occupier to secure the adequate ventilation of the workroom and to render harmless, so far as practicable, all such fumes, dust and

other impurities generated in the course of any process or work carried on in the factory, as may be injurious to health. It was held that the section did not help the plaintiff, since it was directed at ventilation. Denning L.J. suggested that prosecution rather than civil action was the appropriate redress, although his view was *obiter*. Nevertheless, in *Nicholson* v. *Atlas Steel Foundry & Engineering Co. Ltd.* (1957), the House of Lords (without discussing the availability of a civil remedy at all) held that the widow and children of a deceased workman, who had died of pneumoconiosis, were entitled to damages for breach of section 4, since the respondents, by failing to provide adequate ventilation in the workshop, where siliceous dust was given off, had exposed the deceased to a greater degree of risk than would otherwise have been the case. Although their lordships were more concerned with the question of causation, *viz.* that on a balance of probabilities the presence of the dust had materially contributed to the deceased's affliction, than with the fundamental question of civil remedy (it was assumed throughout that such a remedy was available), it is submitted that the *Ebbs* case should be treated with care bearing in mind that the lack of knowledge concerning monsonia hardwood dust is relevant in determining "foreseeability" (dealt with below, para. 371).

(iii) *Welfare provisions.* As regards the welfare provisions in **343**
Part III of the Factories Act 1961 it is dangerous to generalise. As Lord Clyde pointed out in *Reid* v. *Westfield Paper Co. Ltd.* (1957) (dealing with the corresponding part of the 1937 Act), some of the provisions have "a purely welfare outlook; others, such as section 45, which deals with first-aid, seem to impinge substantially on matters of health and safety." It was held, in that case, that damages could be obtained for breach of section 42 (1)—which concerned the provision of adequate washing facilities (now s. 58 (1) of the Factories Act 1961)—if it could be shown that the pursuer's dermatitis could be attributed to the failure to provide the facilities. This case illustrates the benign construction put by the courts upon protective industrial legislation. See also *McCarthy* v. *Daily Mirror Newspapers Ltd.* (1949), in which a civil action lay for the theft of an employee's clothing, for which only a peg had, in his case, been provided. The occupier was under a statutory duty to provide *suitable* accommodation for clothing not worn during working hours and although this duty was not absolute, the risk of theft had to be considered in construing the word "suitable." It is interesting to note that it was assumed without discussion that a civil action could be brought. In many cases the question of civil redress will be purely academic, since it will be impossible for the employee to show that he has suffered loss or injury.

Nature of the tort

344 What is the nature of an action for breach of statutory duty? One thing is clear and that is that the action is not a statutory tort but a common law tort. "The statute does not in terms create a statutory cause of action," *per* Lord Atkin in *Caswell* v. *Powell Duffryn Associated Collieries Ltd.* (1940) at p. 164 of the report. Two main views have been expressed as to the common law nature of the action. According to the first, it is an action for the tort of negligence—"statutory negligence" as it has been termed—in which the standard of care is fixed or "concretised" by the statute. In the case of ordinary negligence the standard of care is found by the jury by referring to the mythical objective standard of the reasonable man, whilst in the case of "statutory negligence" breach of the statutory duty is conclusive of negligence—it puts the matter beyond controversy as a matter of law. In the *Caswell* case, however, Lord Wright considered (at p. 177 of the report) that an action for breach of statutory duty differs from common law negligence *simpliciter*: "It is a common law action based on the purpose of the statute to protect the workman, and belongs to the category often described as that of cases of strict or absolute liability. At the same time, it resembles actions in negligence in that the claim is based on a breach of a duty to take care for the safety of the workman."

The stringent standard of care set by certain statutory duties, the inapplicability of the common law to many statutory situations (see the *McCarthy* case, above) and the possibility that the relevant defences may be different make it desirable, it is submitted, to separate negligence and breach of statutory duty, the latter being a tort *sui generis.* We have, however, seen that, where claims under both heads of damage are conjoined in a single action, success in one necessarily disposes of the other. It is possible to succeed in one whilst failing in the other. Both types of claim were pressed in *Kilgollan* v. *William Cooke & Co. Ltd.* (1956), in which the plaintiff lost the sight of one eye when a small particle of wire flew out of a stranding machine which was not securely fenced. She was awarded damages at common law because in view of similar past accidents the risk of the harm in question was known to the defendants, but the defendants (and this was *obiter*) were considered not to be in breach of their statutory duty to fence since there was no duty to keep in the product on which the machine was working (see below, "Strict Liability").

III. Places, Processes and Persons

The common law rule in *Wilsons & Clyde* (above, paras. 103 *et seq.*) **345**
is limited to the issue of the employee's safety (and not his property), unlike protective legislative measures which encompass a wide range of matters of which safety forms only a part. There is nonetheless a generality about the common law duty which the industrial codes necessarily lack. The driver sent on a long journey in winter in an unheated van and the roving window-cleaner are as much within its provenance as the "wage-slave" in "some dark Satanic mill"; the one-eyed fitter, the epileptic and the young are covered by a duty at common law which is capable of infinite adjustments in relation to the especial vulnerability of particular workers.

The industrial codes lack the generality of the common law, since it was intended that they should display a particularity which would enable employers to know what was expected of them. It is possible to overstate their rigidity since the use of the "foreseeability test" (below, para. 371) allows of some flexibility in practice. Running through the codes, however, are the themes of geographical limitation in the form of places where certain processes are carried on. It was, for example, necessary to make special provision in section 116 of the Factories Act 1961 for young persons running errands and so forth who are employed in the business of a factory "wholly or mainly outside the factory." To a lesser extent the codes deal with particular persons, *e.g.* women, young persons and outworkers. Something will be said of these three themes—places, processes and persons.

1. Places

The most recent of the major codes, the Offices, Shops and Rail- **346**
way Premises Act 1963, uses spatial and functional criteria.

(1) *Offices, shops and railway premises*

By section 1 (2) of the Offices, Shops and Railway Premises Act 1963 "office premises" are "a building . . . the sole or principal use of which is an office or for office purposes"—the latter "include the purposes of administration, clerical work, handling money and telephone and telegraph operating"; "clerical work" in turn "includes writing, book-keeping, sorting papers, filing, typing, duplicating, machine calculating, drawing and the editorial preparation of matter for publication."

By section 1 (3) (*a*) "shop premises" means:

"(i) a shop;
(ii) a building . . . which is not a shop but of which the sole or

principal use is the carrying on there of retail trade or business; (iii) a building occupied by a wholesale dealer or merchant where goods are kept for sale wholesale . . . but not including a warehouse belonging to the owners, trustees or conservators of a dock, wharf or quay;
(iv) a building to which members of the public are invited to resort for the purpose of delivering there goods for repair or other treatment or of themselves there carrying out repairs to, or other treatment of, goods, or a part of a building to which members of the public are invited to resort for that purpose."

Further provision is made for fuel storage premises.

Buildings occupied with (i) (ii) (iii) and (iv) are treated as forming part of the shop or building as the case may be, as are premises maintained in conjunction with office, shop or railway premises for the purpose of the sale or supply for immediate consumption of food or drink wholly or mainly to persons employed to work in the premises in conjunction with which they are maintained.

By section 1 (4) "railway premises" means: "a building occupied by railway undertakers for the purposes of the railway undertaking carried on by them and situate in the immediate vicinity of the permanent way or a part (so occupied) of a building so situate, but does not include" an office or shop premises, premises used as living accommodation for employees, or hotel or electrical stations.

(2) *Mines and quarries*

347 As regards mines and quarries it is useful to remember that the word "mine" is not a definite term, but is one susceptible of limitation or expansion according to the intention with which it is used. The original or primary meaning of the word is "an underground excavation made for the purpose of getting minerals" whilst the word "quarry" implies "surface workings leaving no roof overhead" (Halsbury, *Laws of England*, Vol 26, 3rd ed., pp. 317, 318). These words have special meanings according to context, *e.g.* for rating, tax or nationalisation purposes. The Mines and Quarries Act 1954 gives the following definitions:

A mine is "an excavation or system of excavations made for the purpose of, or in connection with, the getting, wholly or substantially by means involving the employment of persons below ground of minerals whether in their natural state or in solution or suspension, or products of minerals" (s. 180 (1)).

A quarry is "an excavation or system of excavations made for the purpose of, or in connection with, the getting of minerals, whether in their natural state or in solution or suspension, or products of miners, being neither a mine nor merely a well or bore-hole combined."

In both cases, the surface and buildings surrounding or adjacent to the mine or quarry are included. The geographical emphasis in this type of legislation is shown by the provision for clear boundaries between two quarries.

Section 24 (1) of the Agriculture (Safety, Health and Welfare Provisions) Act 1956 states that: "agriculture" includes

> "dairy-farming, the production of any consumable produce which is grown for sale or for consumption or other use for the purposes of a trade or business or of any other undertaking (whether carried on for profit or not) and the use of land as grazing, meadow or pasture land or orchard or osier land or woodland or for market gardens or nursery grounds . . ."

(3) *Factories*

Statutory definition. The most complex definition is that of a "factory" in section 175 of the Factories Act 1961 which formulates a general definition and then specifically provides that certain premises shall be included, *e.g.* premises for the storage of gas in a gasholder. The general definition is as follows: 348

> "(1) Subject to the provisions of this section the expression 'factory' means any premises in which, or within the close or curtilage or precincts of which, persons are employed in manual labour in any process for or incidental to any of the following purposes, namely—
>
> (*a*) the making of any article or of part of any article; or
>
> (*b*) the altering, repairing, ornamenting, finishing, cleaning or washing or the breaking up or demolition of any article; or
>
> (*c*) the adapting for sale of any article; or
>
> (*d*) the slaughtering of cattle, sheep, swine, goats, horses, asses or mules; or
>
> (*e*) the confinement of such animals as aforesaid while awaiting slaughter at other premises, in a case where the place of confinement is available in connection with those other premises, is not maintained primarily for agricultural purposes . . . and does not form part of premises for the holding of a market in respect of such animals;
>
> being premises in which, or within the close or curtilage or precincts of which, the work is carried on by way of trade or for purposes of gain and to or over which the employer of the persons employed therein has the right of access or control."

The definition uses both geographical and functional tests. The factory may be a building, including open-air premises surrounding, adjacent or proximate to the building, or even be open-air premises, provided that there are "geographical boundaries" which need not necessarily be marked with a fence or wall.

349 *Interpretation through the cases.* A daunting number of cases, some of them dealing with rating questions, has been built up around the miniscule elements in the definition and each case, to a large extent, turns on its facts. An area within a factory need not itself be part of the factory, *e.g.* a works manager's house, an executive dining suite or an area cleared in a workshop for a Christmas party. A works canteen has been held to constitute part of a factory.

Section 175 (6) (and its forerunner in the 1937 Act), which provides that a place situate within the close, curtilage or precincts forming a factory, which is solely used for some purpose other than the processes carried on in the factory, is not to be deemed part of the factory (although it may itself constitute a separate factory), has caused some difficulty. In *Walsh* v. *Allweather Mechanical Grouting Co. Ltd.* (1959), the employee of contractors called in to break up and relay concrete on an apron near to a hangar (itself a factory, since aircraft were assembled and tested there) was held to be disentitled to damages for injury to his eye when a piece of concrete, dislodged by a pneumatic drill, struck him. It was held that, although the apron was within the close, curtilage or precinct of the factory, it was, at the relevant time, being used for some purpose other than the processes carried on in the factory, nor was the apron itself a separate factory. On the other hand, Megaw J. held that an administration block together with its courtyard and raised garden parterres was part of a factory in *Powley* v. *Bristol Siddeley Engines Ltd.* (1966), following *Thurogood* v. *Van Den Berghs and Jurgens Ltd.* (1951), in which a repair and testing shop for machinery in the curtilage of a margarine factory was deemed to be part of the factory: the activities in the administration block, namely, designing, drawing and technical work, were incidental to the making of aircraft engines so that section 175 (6) was inapplicable. This case, incidentally, highlights the difficulty in applying different Acts, since prima facie one would have said that the block was an office block concerned with administration and therefore covered by the 1963 Act dealing with offices and by the separate inspection arrangements provided for by that Act.

2. Processes

350 The functional criteria are more complicated, since it is essential that someone must be employed (a) in manual labour; (b) in a process for or incidental to any of five purposes (set out in the definition above, para. 348); (c) in premises in which work is carried on "by way of trade or for the purposes of gain."

With respect to (a), it is enough if only one person is engaged in manual labour, provided that such labour is the main purpose for which the place is used, *e.g.* the back room of a retail grocer's shop in which goods were unpacked and treated preparatory to sale and in which the plaintiff was injured by a bacon-slicing machine. But the employment of a porter to do manual work in a chemist's shop did not render the shop a factory in *Joyce* v. *Boots Cash Chemists* (*Southern*) *Ltd.* (1951). In *J. & F. Stone Lighting & Radio Ltd.* v. *Haygarth* (1968), in which a back room in which television sets were repaired and adjusted, was held to be a factory (this case was discussed in connection with truck legislation, above, para. 194), their lordships were more cogent in explaining what was not manual labour than in elucidating the essence of such labour. Lord Upjohn inclined towards a sociological test ("the ordinary conception of what is manual labour must be a weighty influence in reaching a conclusion"—at p. 186 of the report). Lord Pearson stated (at p. 190 of the report) the principle that: "A person is not employed in 'manual labour' for the purposes of any of the Acts if his occupation is primarily or substantially an activity of a different kind and the manual work that he does is merely ancillary or accessory to that activity." His lordship bore in mind the need to regard the Act "as a beneficial rather than a penal statute" adding that "Its object is to secure proper working conditions for persons employed to do manual labour in certain operations, and the penalties for failure to provide such conditions are merely incidental to that object" (pp. 187–188 of the report).

The five purposes in (b) (see above, para. 348) are not of equal **351**
difficulty and the two concerned with animals need not detain us. The first, which is concerned with "the making of any article," is directed to the process whereby "form value" is added to an article. It has been held that the filtration of water is within the section whereas the subjection of the water to pressure in a pump-house is undertaken in order to facilitate the *distribution* of the water—a purpose not covered in section 175 (*Longhurst* v. *Guildford, Godalming & District Water Board* (1963)—yet the pump-house within the curtilage of a textile factory used to pump water into the factory was held to be part of a factory (with a correlative duty to fence transmission machinery) in *Newton* v. *John Stanning & Son Ltd.* (1962)). The second purpose, *viz.* "altering, etc.," gives little difficulty (the mincing of meat in a hospital kitchen has been held not to be the "demolition" of an article, whilst the kitchen is outside section 175: *Wood* v. *L.C.C.* (1941)). The third purpose, is "adapting for sale"—the packaging of chocolates into boxes, the arranging of flowers into wreaths, the grading and sorting of furs into bales, the bottling of beer and the compression of paper into bales—have been brought within this rubric. In addition to the "tests" employed in

the general definition of a factory, certain premises are specifically endowed with factory status, *e.g.* dry docks; premises used for the sorting of articles as a preliminary to work being carried on in a factory; premises where there is washing or filling of bottles or containers, or packing of articles, if incidental to the purposes of any factory; hooking or plaiting, etc., of yarn or cloth; premises in which ancillary printing activities are carried on or certain types of theatrical "props" made incidental to the production of films or theatrical performances; off-site building and civil engineering workshops; a laundry ancillary to another business; and a gas-holder in which gas is stored.

352 The last requirement ((c), para. 350), *i.e.* trade or gain, represents two purposes since each is taken disjunctively. An indirect gain may suffice, as where a consulting engineer used premises for the testing of articles to destruction. Technical colleges (which, with the increase in higher and further education, often have large and dangerous workshops), hospitals and prison work-rooms are outside the ambit of the Act. Technical colleges do not employ persons since "employed" means employed under a contract of service and not just "occupied" or "busy." Some disquiet has been expressed at the exclusion of these and similar premises, especially those in the Health Service, since there seems to be little logical reason for putting them beyond the pale of protection. Nevertheless, the Act does apply to factories belonging to or in the occupation of the Crown (s. 173), even where the work carried on thereat is not carried on by way of trade or for purposes of gain.

3. Persons

Who owes the statutory duties?

353 Leaving places and processes, something must be said of persons. The common law is easy to state (though difficult to apply in marginal cases)—an employer must take reasonable care for the safety of his employee. Now, whilst it may generally be true to say that an employer must comply with statutory duties aimed at protecting his employees, this is not always the case since the person upon whom the statutory duty is cast *need not necessarily be the employer*. An instructive case is *Blakeley* v. *C. & H. Clothing Co.* (1958), which was discussed above, para. 36. Generally the statutory duties created by the Factories Act 1961 are imposed on "the occupier," an expression which is nowhere defined in the Act but meaning the person or firm having possession and control of the factory, or the right thereto. Occasionally duties are laid upon "the owner" (the person receiving the rackrent of the premises), as in the case of "tenement factories" (*i.e.* premises where mechanical

power from any prime mover is distributed, for use in manufacturing processes to different parts of the same premises occupied by different persons in such a manner that those parts constitute in law separate factories) where the owner is liable for the contravention of certain provisions in the Act (these are elaborated in section 121); similarly the owner may be liable in certain events under section 122, where part of a building is let off as a separate factory.

To whom are the statutory duties owed?

It is quite impossible to formulate any general rule which will **354**
serve to delineate the categories of persons covered by statutory duties. Each statutory provision must be separately construed in order to ascertain the range of persons who come within its protection. Section 14, which imposes a strict duty to fence in respect of "every person employed or working on the premises," includes not only the operator, but others working on the premises who need not necessarily be employees of the occupier. Independent contractors may be included, as in *Lavender* v. *Diamints* (1949), where it was held that the duty to provide a safe means of access to any place "at which any person has at any time to work" (s. 28) applied in relation to a window-cleaner. Again, where a painter, employed by independent contractors, was electrocuted whilst painting out a factory, it was held that ministerial regulations made under section 60 of the 1937 Act (which empowered the Minister to make regulations where there was a risk of bodily injury "to the persons employed") applied to the painter as a person employed. Lord Goddard C.J. stated that "there is no question about it that these regulations now are intended to protect, not only the servants of the factory occupier, but any other persons who may be called upon to do work in the factory, such as sub-contractors," adding that the latter need special protection because of their unfamiliarity with the hazards involved in working in strange premises.

On the other hand a regulation which imposes upon a person a **355**
duty in relation to "any workman employed by him" has been held not to extend to an independent contractor (*Herbert* v. *Harold Shaw Ltd.* (1959)), or to workmen employed by a building owner or a sub-contractor (*Claydon* v. *Lindsay Parkinson Ltd.* (1939); *Wingrove* v. *Prestige & Co. Ltd.* (1954)). In *Smith* v. *George Wimpey & Co. Ltd.* (1972), the Court of Appeal held that regulations, which require every contractor and every employer of workmen to comply with such requirements of the regulations "as affect him or any workman employed by him," did not impose any duty as regards employees of a sub-contractor, the insertion of the words "him or" in the regulation being held to indicate that a duty was being imposed on an

individual contractor to comply with the regulations for his own safety for the breach of which he would be liable to prosecution. A restrictive approach was taken in *Hartley* v. *Mayoh* (1954) in that the fireman who had been electrocuted because of a faulty switch in a factory to which he had been called, was held to lie outside the category of persons employed in the factory. This case was distinguished in the *Massey* case (above) on the ground that the fireman in quelling the fire was no more employed in the factory than a policeman called to quell a disturbance or to arrest a thief.

356 Semantic virtuosity is of little avail if a particular statutory provision sedulously avoids all mention of the clientèle coming within its terms. An example of such a situation is to be found in *Smith* v. *Supreme Wood Pulp Co. Ltd.* (1968), where a fencing provision in woodworking machinery regulations (silent as to the classes of persons covered) fell to be considered in relation to a driver who had used his employer's circular saw to cut up some firewood and who had suffered an injury thereby. It was shown that the work of sawing was normally performed by trained sawyers as independent contractors, although the employers were fixed with knowledge that some of their own men used the saw from time to time in order to make firewood from rejected wood. Melford Stevenson J. held that in the circumstances the injured driver must be included within the class of persons who enjoy the benefit of the regulations, rejecting the argument that by acting outside the scope of his employment the driver had put himself outside the ambit of the regulations.

Women and young persons

357 To many nineteenth-century employers women and young persons were a source of cheap and expendable labour. The reduction in their working hours and the prohibition of employing children in certain processes brought forth protests not only from manufacturers and mine-owners but also from parents who saw a dwindling in the family wage. Part VI of the Factories Act 1961 is devoted to regulating the hours and holidays of women and young persons (the latter are persons over compulsory school age, at present sixteen, but under eighteen years). Section 86 specifies the general conditions as follows:

(a) Total hours worked shall not exceed nine per day nor forty-eight per week; (b) the period of employment (this must generally be the same for all women and young persons in the factory) must not exceed eleven hours in any day nor commence earlier than 7 a.m. nor finish later than 8 p.m. on weekdays (the period was shorter for persons under sixteen and is longer for five-day-week factories);

the maximum spell of work is normally four and a half hours to be followed by at least one half-hour for meal or rest. No woman or young person may be employed during intervals for meals or rests which, with some exceptions, must be taken away from workrooms. The general conditions may be modified by ministerial exemptions under section 111, by a shift system under section 97, and by the exemption of certain trades or occupations. Women holding responsible managerial posts are excluded.

Section 89 permits of overtime working (statutorily defined as time worked over forty-eight hours per week) by women and young persons of sixteen or over when there is "pressure of work in any factory," subject to certain safeguards as to amount (not more than 100 hours in any year nor six hours per week) and incidence (overtime cannot prima facie take place on more than twenty-five weeks in a year and must generally conform to the period of employment rule described above). The overtime rules may be modified by the Minister who may prohibit or reduce overtime in certain events or increase it in certain other cases, *e.g.* for seasonal work. Sunday employment of women and young persons is, subject to some exceptions, prohibited.

Shift working may be permitted subject to restrictions, amongst which an important one is that prohibiting night-shift working (but even here there is predictably an exception in favour of male young persons employed in continuous day and night industries!).

The employment of women and young persons is regulated in **358**
matters other than hours of work and holidays. Women and young persons cannot be employed to clean any part of a prime mover or of any transmission machinery while either is in motion, and shall not clean any part of any machine if the cleaning would expose them to risk of injury from any removing part, either of that machine or of any adjacent machinery (s. 20). Section 15 (which permits the safety provisions of Part II to be left out of account where examination, lubrication or adjustment can only be carried out with the machine in motion) only applies where these operations are carried out by male persons who have reached the age of eighteen, as specified by the Minister in regulations. It is interesting to note that the prohibition, under pain of fine, relating to the employment of women within four weeks of giving birth to a child is only applicable to London and Scotland. The Maternity Protection Convention (No. 3, 1919) of the International Labour Organisation, as revised by Convention No. 103, has not been ratified by the United Kingdom.

Perhaps the most scarifying pictures of the exploitation of **359**
women and young persons to emerge from the last century were those showing their use as beasts of burden underground in mines.

The obliteration of those scenes is continued by the Mines and Quarries Act 1954, which completely proscribes the employment of female workers underground, although male young persons of sixteen and above may be so employed, subject to restrictions, *e.g.* the period of employment to be within the period 6 a.m.–10 p.m. Young persons under sixteen years may only attend instruction underground. Because of the different nature of the work processes involved there is no separate part of the Offices, Shops and Railway Premises Act 1963 dealing with women or young persons, although section 18 of that Act prohibits the employment of young persons in cleaning machines where there is a risk of injury from a moving part of those or adjacent machines; section 19 provides for training and supervision of workers (irrespective of age or sex) in connection with prescribed machines. Under the Equal Pay Act 1970, the right of women to equal treatment in terms and conditions of employment is not, and cannot be, affected by the special protection by law of women workers.

Outworkers

360 Finally, in the treatment of "persons," the decline of the "domestic system" has rendered the terms and conditions of the "home-worker" and the "outworker" less of a problem than it was during the nineteenth century when work was frequently "farmed out" to persons in their own homes where control and supervision were virtually impossible. Section 133 requires lists of outworkers to be kept in certain trades.

IV. Strict Statutory Liability

361 Protective legislation has been enacted in this country to meet the new and peculiar risks in an industrialised society. To some extent, such legislation was necessary because of the common law emphasis upon fault (*culpa*), an objective standard measured against the notional behaviour of the reasonable man. The common law did evolve torts of *strict liability*, but they had little application in the factories where negligence became the fertile mother of actions. Admittedly, the common law did formulate a rule of strict liability for the "escape" of dangerous things (*Rylands* v. *Fletcher* (1868)), *e.g.* flooding water from a person's land, filth from a neighbour's privy or a "chair-o-plane," but it is noteworthy that in *Read* v. *Lyons* (1947), the House of Lords were unable to use this form of strict liability to penalise ultra-hazardous activities in factories (in this case, the explosion of a shell in the defendant's munition factory) because there had been no "escape."

The duty is absolute

Starting in the last century, the legislature has created an increasing number of wrongs of strict prohibition, *i.e.* the person upon whom the duty is imposed *must* comply with it, so that it is no defence to say that he did not intend to break the duty or that he took reasonable care, objectively measured, to avoid breaking it. An employer who does all that he reasonably can may find himself in breach of a strict duty, *e.g.* that in section 28 (5) of the Factories Act 1961, which requires that "All ladders shall be soundly constructed and properly maintained." Thus if a ladder is defective, either because of bad construction or because an employee failed to maintain it properly, an offence is committed. It will, as we have seen, also constitute a tort if someone is injured. Although damage is a necessary ingredient of the action in tort, the duty with regard to the tort is commensurate with the criminal duty. 362

John Summers & Sons Ltd. v. *Frost* (1955) is often cited as instancing the Draconian stringency of the so-called absolute statutory duty. A workman, whose thumb was injured when it came into contact with a power-driven grinding machine whilst he was grinding the end of a bar of metal, was held entitled to damages under section 14 (1) (discussed below). It was held that the duty to fence was "unambiguously absolute" so that it was no defence to say that the defendants (who had fenced the machine leaving a seven-inch aperture to permit grinding operations) had done all that they reasonably could. There were no words qualifying the duty such as "so far as is reasonably practicable"; it must be complied with even though this necessarily means "the destruction of the machine as a working unit" (p. 776 of the report); see now the Abrasive Wheels Regulations 1970 which, *inter alia*, require the provision of a guard except when the use of a guard is impracticable by reason of the work being done on the abrasive wheel.

Dangerous machinery

The most important examples of absolute, or, to use the more acceptable word, strict, liability are contained in sections 12–17, inclusive, of the Factories Act 1961, which deal with dangerous machinery. More accidents are caused by people tripping over and falling off things than by becoming involved with dangerous machinery, but this may be a tribute to the efficacy of the fencing provisions. Sections 12–17 provide as follows: 363

Section 12. Prime movers

"(1) Every flywheel directly connected to any prime mover and every moving part of any prime mover, except such prime movers as are mentioned in subsection (3) of this section, shall be securely fenced, whether the flywheel or prime mover is situated in an engine-house or not.

(2) The head and tail race of every water wheel and of every water turbine shall be securely fenced.

(3) Every part of electric generators, motors and rotary converters, and every flywheel directly connected thereto, shall be securely fenced unless it is in such a position or of such construction as to be as safe to every person employed or working on the premises as it would be if securely fenced."

(A "prime mover" is defined as "every engine, motor or other appliance which provides mechanical energy derived from steam, water, wind, electricity, the combustion of fuel or other source" (s. 176). Two points may be noted: (i) the machinery named must be "securely fenced" whether it is dangerous or not—it will be seen that the distinction is of little significance (see "Foreseeability," below); (ii) alternatives to fencing are "safety by position" (but putting the types of machinery specified in subsection (3) near the roof will not suffice *quoad* an employee who is given a task which brings him near such machinery) and "safety by construction" (thus the crankcase of an engine provides security although part of the engine)). See section 15, below.

Section 13. Transmission machinery

364 "(1) Every part of the transmission machinery shall be securely fenced unless it is in such a position or of such construction as to be as safe to every person employed or working on the premises as it would be if securely fenced."

Section 13 further provides for devices to enable the power to be cut off promptly (subs. (2)); driving belts not to rest upon revolving shaft when not in use (subs. (3)); suitable striking gear or other efficient mechanical appliances to be provided and maintained to move driving belts to and from any loose pulleys forming part of transmission machinery, such gear or appliances to be so constructed, placed and maintained as to prevent the driving belt from creeping back on the fast pulley (subs. (4)); Minister empowered to relax requirements in certain cases (subs. (5)). The term "transmission machinery" is defined to mean specified mechanical devices whereby the motion of a prime mover is transmitted to or received by any machine or appliance. Safety by position or construction is permitted.

Section 14. Other machinery

365 "(1) Every dangerous part of any machinery, other than prime movers and transmission machinery, shall be securely fenced

unless it is in such a position or of such construction as to be as safe to every person employed or working on the premises as it would be if securely fenced."

The remaining five subsections make provision for the use of automatic devices which prevent the operator from coming into contact with the dangerous part in lieu of a fixed guard (subs. (2)); to enable the Minister to make regulations directing the use of safety devices in connection with certain classes of machinery (subs. (3)); to provide a defence in proceedings for a contravention of the foregoing subsection whereby it is a sufficient defence to show that a device at least equally effective as the prescribed device was being used (subs. (4)); for the fencing of a stock-bar projecting beyond the headstock of a lathe unless safe by position (subs. (5)); to enable the Minister to make regulations with regard to any machine or process in which a machine is used for the fencing of materials or articles which are dangerous while in motion in the machine.

We have already seen that section 14 does not require the fencing of a machine which is dangerous as a whole but which does not have dangerous parts (para. 333, above). A workpiece moving under power in the machine is not "part" of the machine and the same applies to other materials in the machine which are not parts thereof. In considering whether a part is dangerous within the meaning of section 14 regard must be had to the operation of the part while the machine is doing its ordinary work and not when it is stationary. "It may therefore be that a part can be dangerous because of its juxtaposition to another part of the machine or because of its juxtaposition to a moving workpiece or the material notwithstanding that in isolation it would not be dangerous and notwithstanding that when the machine is not in use the part itself would be innocuous" (Lord Hailsham L.C. in the *Callow* case, above, at p. 648 of the report).

Section 15. Provisions as to unfenced machinery

This section allows no account to be taken of (a) the examination, **366**
lubrication or adjustment of machinery in motion where unavoidable, and, (b) lubrication, mounting or shipping of belts in transmission machinery in processes specified in regulations being processes where, owing to the continuous nature thereof, the stopping of that part would seriously interfere with the carrying on of the process, where in either case it is necessary to determine whether any part of the machinery is safe by position or safe by construction.

Section 16. Construction and maintenance of fencing

This section requires that all fencing or other safeguards provided **367**
in pursuance of the foregoing provisions of this Part of the Act:

"shall be of substantial construction and constantly maintained and kept in position while the parts required to be fenced or safeguarded are in motion or use, except when any such parts are necessarily exposed for examination and for any lubrication or adjustment shown by the examination to be immediately necessary and all such conditions as may be specified in regulations made by the Minister are complied with."

The first part of this section clarifies the fencing requirements, whilst the second part permits those requirements to be left out of account for necessary lubrication and so forth.

It will be noted, however, that the requirements as to fencing only apply if the parts in question are "in motion or use." Motion and use are separate, so that a thing may be in motion without being in use and it has been held that it may be in use without being in motion, *e.g.* where it has stopped temporarily. Normally a machine or part thereof will be in use when it is running, as it was meant to run and it is doing the work it was intended to do. It is more difficult to ascertain what is meant by "in motion." A part may be "moving" without being "in motion." *Denyer* v. *Charles Skipper & East Ltd.* (1970) shows that a "moving part" in section 20 (see para. 358) has a meaning entirely different to that attaching to the words "in motion." In that case, the employer of a young person, whose hand had been injured in a printing machine which was being turned over slowly by means of an "inching button," was held liable for the injury. For the purposes of the present section, however, the rotation of part of a machine by hand or by means of an "inching button" would not be considered "motion," a term which carries with it the connotation that the part is running at or near its normal speed for an appreciable time (even for a very short time) whether or not such motion is accidentally started (*Horne* v. *Lec Refrigeration* (1965)). It is the character of the motion rather than its purpose which counts.

Section 17. Construction and sale of machinery

368 This section aims at prevention rather than cure. It penalises those who, either themselves or as agents, sell or let on hire, for use in a factory in the United Kingdom, any machine intended to be driven by mechanical power, which does not comply with certain precautions. In *Biddle* v. *Truvox Engineering Co.* (1951), a workman, who was injured by a machine containing toothed gearing which was not completely encased as required by section 17, sued the occupier of the factory for damages. The latter joined the manufacturer as third party, but it was held that the latter owed no duty to the workman for which an action for damages would lie. "Under the

present Factories Act, legal requirements concerning the design and construction of plant, machinery and equipment are limited, and very few of them bear directly upon the manufacturer" is the comment of the Robens Committee, which, however recognised that fuller control existed with regard to the design and manufacture of machinery for use in mining and agriculture. Nevertheless, the Committee felt that the design and manufacture of plant, machinery and equipment should be subject to general statutory obligations and more detailed obligations to be set out in special regulations, together with obligations to comply with standards and approval arrangements established by independent quality control bodies (Robens Report, paras. 346–354).

How absolute is "absolute"?

The foregoing sections of the Factories Act are often chosen **369**
to illustrate the "absolute" nature of the obligation cast upon the occupier. The gravamen of the discussion which follows is aimed at showing that such an obligation is not as Draconian as might at first appear. We have seen that in sections 12–17 inclusive, there are statutory exceptions to the absolute duty, such as safety by position or safety by construction or the substantial qualification introduced to section 17. Other restrictions have been discussed, *e.g.* the definition of the person upon whom a duty is placed or to whom the duty is owed. Apart from these qualifications, the absolute duty is further qualified by (i) standards of criminal liability, (ii) standards of civil liability, in this case substantially relaxed by the operations of "foreseeability," "type of injury" protected, onus of proof, causation and the defences open to the defendant. Of these something must now be said.

Criminal standards

We have seen that certain "escape routes" are open to a person **370**
charged with an offence under the Acts (above, paras. 337, 338).

Strict civil standards

"*Foreseeability*"

The manner in which the concept of foreseeability considerably **371**
reduces the absoluteness of a statutory duty may be illustrated by reference to the safety provisions given above. In sections 12, 13 and 14, for example, the words "securely fenced" are used—do these words mean that fencing must be installed and maintained to guard against *all* risks? The common law has recoiled from such a sweeping duty and has preferred instead to limit the duty and to require

provision only against those risks which are reasonably foreseeable. In the language of a logician, Lord Reid put the matter admirably in the *Summers* case (1955) at p. 769 of the report (above, para. 362):

> "If 'securely fenced' means fenced against all danger even if unforeseeable and an unforeseeable accident occurs then the event proves that the unfenced part was not as safe as if it had been fenced. As one cannot foresee the unforeseeable I do not see how on this view one could ever say in advance that any dangerous part left unfenced was as safe as it would be if securely fenced, because there would always be the chance of some unforeseeable accident happening, and proving that that part had not in fact been as safe as it would have been if fenced."

It is interesting to note that reasonable foreseeability has likewise been pressed into service in delimiting the meaning of the word "dangerous" as used in section 14 (1). In *Close* v. *Steel Company of Wales* (1962), in which the bit of an electric drill shattered, causing injury to the plaintiff's eye, one of the grounds of the decision, holding the defendants not liable, lay in the finding that the risk of grave injury was not reasonably foreseeable in the circumstances. In *Eaves* v. *Morris Motors Ltd.* (1961), the behaviour of a machine which repeated or performed "an uncovenanted stroke" was deemed to be unforeseeable. Not only the behaviour of the machine but the behaviour of persons needs to be taken into account since "you must not always assume that everybody will always be careful," *per* du Parcq J. in *Walker* v. *Bletchley Flettons Ltd.* (1937) at p. 175 of the report, adding "a part of machinery is dangerous if it is a possible cause of injury to anybody acting in a way a human being may be reasonably expected to act in circumstances which may reasonably be expected to occur." Lord Reid accepted this but felt that the words "a reasonably foreseeable cause of injury" should be substituted for "a possible cause of injury" (*Summers* case at p. 766 of the report).

372 There are signs of a *post hoc propter hoc* approach in two cases, namely, *Allen* v. *Aeroplane and Motor Aluminium Castings Ltd.* (1965) (discussed below at para. 382 in connection with onus of proof), and *Millard* v. *Serck Tubes Ltd.* (1969). In the latter case, the plaintiff was injured in a most unusual way by swarf which had dragged his hand into a machine through an aperture left by the fence, Danckwerts L.J. saying that, "if the fence had been effective the accident would not have occurred." Taken alone this statement might seem to conflict with Lord Reid's explanation of the scope of the duty to fence (above), but it should be borne in mind that the employer had already conceded that the machine was dangerous and ought to have been properly fenced. Salmon L.J. in the same case

did not deny that foreseeability is important in answering the questions "Was this a dangerous part of machinery?" and "Was the part securely fenced?" but considered that once these two questions had been answered in the affirmative, foreseeability was no longer relevant. The two questions had been answered in the affirmative in that case so that "the fact that the accident occurred in an entirely unforeseeable way [was] wholly irrelevant." Lord Hailsham L.C. in the *Callow* case (below) considered that each of these two cases involved a breach of section 14 and an accident occurring as a result of that breach (and in no other way) so that it did not matter that the plaintiff in each case was unable to establish exactly how the particular accident came about (p. 347 of the report).

In *F. E. Callow* (*Engineers*) *Ltd.* v. *Johnson* (1971), the House of **373**
Lords held that the employers were liable under section 14 to a workman, whose hand had become caught in a "nip" between an imperceptibly moving boring bar and a workpiece, held in position by the chuck on a lathe whilst he was squirting coolant onto the workpiece from a "squeezie" bottle. The employers knew of the lazy practice of using a "squeezie" bottle in preference to the automatic cooling system (which had to be emptied periodically of swarf), but disapproved of the practice because of the hazards which it involved. Not surprisingly, the House of Lords was not prepared to hold that a danger which was foreseen by both parties was unforeseeable.

The determination of reasonably foreseeable behaviour can **374**
produce not a little casuistry in the cases, which should always be confined to their facts and not elevated to the status of Acts of Parliament. A few cases illustrate this solemn warning.

In *Burns* v. *Joseph Terry & Sons Ltd.* (1951), a boy of seventeen, employed to clean up chocolate beans, leaned a ladder against a rotating shaft above a machine which had a four-foot fence in front of it. While on the ladder and trying to retrieve beans which had spilled on to a shelf, the ladder moved sideways and the boy was injured when his hand came between a pulley wheel and pinion. *Held*, applying the "test of reasonable foreseeability" that the defendants were not liable in damages for breach of section 13 (transmission machinery) since such an accident was not reasonably foreseeable. Dealing with the safety sections, Somervell L.J. considered that the test of foreseeability was the same for secure fencing and for dangerous parts, but that in either event it should be the foreseeability of the accident rather than of the plaintiff's behaviour which ought to be considered. Denning L.J. dissented on the ground that if fencing means a barricade preventing the worker from coming into contact, then there was no such fencing on the facts of this case. Foreseeability was a test of the exception in the section (position and construction) but could not be a test of the primary obligation. His lordship felt that foreseeability was relevant in determining the dangerousness of a part under section 14. This distinction would, however, necessarily mean that the duty to fence securely transmission machinery is stricter than the duty to fence dangerous parts of machines, but it is arguable that this view accords better with the intention of Parliament.

Contrast with this case *Uddin* v. *Associated Portland Cement Manufacturers Ltd.* (1965), which concerned section 14 (1). A workman ascended a vertical steel ladder to a platform (where he had no right to be) and suffered an injury while leaning over a dangerous unfenced revolving shaft to recover a pigeon which was sitting behind the shaft. *Held* that he could recover damages although these were reduced because of his contributory negligence. McNair J., at first instance, had found that the part was dangerous since it might injure someone acting in a reasonably foreseeable way, in this case doing an act of "extreme folly." The Court of Appeal agreed and also with the judge's finding that the plaintiff's conduct had not put him outside the protection of the section. Cases in which an employer is not vicariously liable for the servant who goes off on "a frolic of his own" ought not to be transplanted into the field of statutory liability.

Type of injury

375 *Narrow interpretation of statutory provisions.* Foreseeability, we have seen, places a limit on the ambit of the absolute duty. A further and at times artificial limit is placed on the ambit of such a duty by confining the duty to a certain type of injury *whether such injury was foreseeable or not.* Like the search for civil redress (above, paras. 340 *et seq.*), the search for the type of injury covered by a statutory provision takes us on a journey of exploration into the intention of Parliament. Thus, in *Rodgers* v. *National Coal Board* (1966), a civil action for damages brought by the administratrix of a colliery banksman who had (apparently) fallen down the shaft from the cage, failed, since section 31 of the Mines and Quarries Act 1954 only required the "surface entrance to every mine" to be provided with "an efficient enclosure or barrier . . . to prevent any person from accidentally falling down the shaft." Waller J. said (at p. 1563 of the report): "The mischief against which section 31 (2) is directed is the mischief of somebody accidentally falling down the shaft from the surface entrance . . . . This case was an accident which happened when the deceased fell down the shaft from inside the shaft." Similarly, a statutory requirement to take steps to prevent persons

from injury "in the event of a vehicle's running away" does not extend to the controlled running of a vehicle but only to "an unintended movement; it means that the vehicles are runaway vehicles" (*Jones* v. *National Coal Board* (1965) at p. 535 of the report).

In the much-criticised decision in *Nicholls* v. *Austin* (*Leyton*) **376** *Ltd.* (1946), Lord Simonds, dealing with the duty to fence, said that the fence is intended to keep the worker out, not to keep the machine or its product in, so that an employee injured when a piece of wood flew out of a circular saw could not recover damages. The dictum has caused some controversy. It was applied in *Carroll* v. *Andrew Barclay & Sons Ltd.* (1948), in which a person struck by a transmission belt which had broken was held disentitled to recover ("Fencing in my opinion means the erection of a barricade to prevent any employee from making contact with the machine, not an enclosure to prevent broken machinery from flying out": Lord Porter at p. 486 of the report). In *Kilgollan* v. *William Cooke & Co.* (1956), the Court of Appeal held that the defendants were not in breach of section 14 (1) when a particle of wire flew out of a stranding machine in the wire-rope factory even though such machine was not securely fenced, although they were accountable at common law for failure to take reasonable care (600 accidents involving wire flying out had occurred at this factory!).

The *Nicholls* idea did not receive its quietus in *Close* v. *Steel Co. of Wales Ltd.* (1962). It will be recalled in that case that the plaintiff was injured when the bit of an electric drill shattered and a piece entered his eye. We saw that the decision went off on the narrow ground that such a contingency was not reasonably foreseeable, so that there was no duty to fence. Their lordships, however, because of the desire of the Court of Appeal to have guidance on the matter, went on to deal with the *Nicholls* idea, which they affirmed. In so doing they overruled those cases in which it had been held that the duty to fence applied in relation to machines, or their products, having a known propensity to disintegrate or throw out pieces. It is suggested that the following points should be borne in mind when considering liability for machines which disintegrate or throw off pieces. (1) The observations in *Close* on this aspect were *obiter* since the case can be explained on the basis that the injury was not reasonably foreseeable. (2) Lord Denning and Lord Morris distinguished the *Nicholls* case which related to flying bits of the product on which the machine was working and not flying bits of the machinery. (3) Lord Goddard, whilst agreeing with the *Nicholls* case, did not rule out the possibility of a common law action where a machine has a tendency to throw off parts of itself or its products. In *Hindle* v. *Birtwistle* (1897), it was held that a shuttle which flew out and struck the plaintiff was a dangerous part since such an occurrence frequently happened and was therefore foreseeable.

377 But common law redress may be poor satisfaction for the plaintiff because of the onus involved in establishing an unreasonable lack of care. In a case such as *Rutherford* v. *Glanville* (1958), one of the cases overruled in *Close*, it would be difficult to attach common law liability since the machine, an abrasive carborundum wheel revolving at high r.p.m. *was* covered by a hood (which struck the plaintiff when the wheel disintegrated).

The manner in which the *Nicholls* and *Close* cases cut down the statutory protection of workers has been criticised both by judges and writers. The principle on which these cases rest is illustrated by the decision in *Eaves* v. *Morris Motors Ltd.* (1961), where an action, based upon injury caused by materials being worked on by the machine, failed. The power given in section 14, whereby the Minister may make regulations "requiring the fencing of materials or articles which are dangerous while in motion in the machine," fortified the court in its conclusion that section 14, does not, in the absence of such regulations, cover the case of flying materials. More recently, the House of Lords, whilst criticising the gap opened up in the protection of the Act, showed itself reluctant to exercise its power to have "second thoughts," saying that it was "too late for the courts to close the gap. The gap can only be closed by legislation or to some extent by the use of the regulatory powers of the Minister" (*F. E. Callow* (*Engineers*) *Ltd.* v. *Johnson* (1971), at p. 343 of the report). The artificiality of the position is heightened when it is considered that a tool held by a workman (which becomes enmeshed in machinery with consequent injury to the workman) is not deemed to be an extension of the operator's body (*Sparrow* v. *Fairey Aviation Co. Ltd.* (1964)—Lord Reid in that case, however, thought that clothing worn by the operator could be regarded as part of the operator).

378 *Wide interpretation of statutory provisions.* Decisions such as that in *Nicholls* constitute an invitation to counsel to argue for a narrow view of the intention of Parliament. Fortunately, the courts do not always take such a view. In *Grant* v. *National Coal Board* (1956), a mineworker was injured in a derailment when the bogie in which he was riding struck some stone which had fallen from the roof of the travelling road. Counsel argued that section 49 of the Coal Mines Act 1911, which required that the roof and sides of every travelling road should "be made secure," only envisaged injuries caused by falling materials *while they were falling*. This argument was rejected. Viscount Simonds said (at p. 655 of the report) that where damages were claimed for breach of statutory duty without

any allegation of negligence, two things must be established: "first, that the breach is intended, not only to be visited by a penalty but also to be the ground of civil liability to a class of persons of whom the pursuer is one, and, secondly, that the injury was one against which the legislation was designed to protect him." His lordship found that the first condition was satisfied and further held that the purpose of section 49 was the safety of miners and not just their safety with respect to falling objects. This wider (and, it is submitted, more sensible view) was also taken in *Donaghey* v. *Boulton & Paul* (1968), in which a workman fell through a hole in the roof while tugging at an asbestos sheet. It was held that the defendants were in breach of a building regulation which required crawling boards to be provided where work was being done on fragile roofs "through which" a person was liable to fall. *Gorris* v. *Scott* (1874) (in which the plaintiff, whose sheep were washed overboard from a ship, was held disentitled to damages since the statutory duty to provide penning was aimed at preventing the spread of contagion rather than at securing the safety of the sheep) was distinguished on the grounds that the regulation in the present case was aimed at preventing falls from roofs and should not be limited to falls *through* roofs. It is submitted that the broad approach to the "mischief" which a statute (or regulation) is intended to correct is preferable to pedantic adherence to the *ipsissima verba* of such provisions.

Causation

Whether he is suing for common law negligence or for breach 379
of a statutory duty, the plaintiff must prove (a) a duty owed to him, (b) breach of that duty and (c) consequent damage. Indeed negligence (including the so-called "statutory negligence") necessarily involves damage since there cannot be "negligence in the air," *i.e.* in the abstract and unrelated to harmful consequences. Prior to 1961 a distinction might be taken between the scope of the duty, the boundary of which was set by "foreseeability" and, once the duty and its breach had been established, the consequences for which the defendant was liable, *viz.* the direct, physical consequences. In that year the test whether consequences were reasonably foreseeable became the criterion of culpability *and* of compensation, *i.e.* foreseeability determined both the scope of the duty and the measure of the consequential harm for which the defendant was to be held accountable: *Overseas Tankship* (*U.K.*) v. *Morts Dock & Engineering Co. Ltd.* (1961)—*The Wagon Mound* (*No. 1*) case. Viscount Simonds said (at p. 422 of the report) that the authority of *Re Polemis* (1921) (in which the test of direct, physical consequence

was the measure of consequential harm) had already been "severely shaken," adding that "it should no longer be regarded as good law." The substitution of foreseeability for the *Polemis* test (*i.e.* direct, physical consequences) was not in any way impugned in *The Wagon Mound* (*No. 2*) (1967), although a different result was reached in the latter case.

380 *Hypothetical causation.* A peculiar twist to the rule that a defendant is only liable for the harm caused by his breach of duty was confirmed in the case of *McWilliams* v. *Sir William Arrol Ltd.* (1962), in which a new doctrine of "hypothetical causation" appeared (see Wedderburn, *The Worker and the Law*, pp. 194 *et seq.*). It would now appear to be open to a defendant *who has broken a statutory duty* to plead that even if he had complied with the statutory requirements the accident would still have occurred. In that case it was held that there was no liability for the death of a steel erector who had fallen to his death since, despite the employer's omission to provide a safety belt, the evidence indicated that these might not, on a balance of probabilities, have been worn. In the earlier case of *Nolan* v. *Dental Manufacturing Co. Ltd.* (1958), the doctrine had been applied to a toolsetter who had been injured when a chip flew off a carborundum wheel on which he was sharpening his tools, since no evidence was adduced to show that he would have worn the goggles which ought to have been provided *per* the regulations. It is curious that despite his failure in the claim for breach of statutory duty, the plaintiff succeeded at common law. Paull J. found that, although the risk was small as regards frequency, it was great in regard to seriousness and that therefore the employers should not only have provided goggles but ordered and supervised their use. Nor could the employer make out contributory negligence because "the plaintiff cannot be said to have been negligent in not using non-existent goggles." This case shows that it is desirable, wherever possible, to underpin a claim based upon statute with a common law claim, and also that the latter may be more "protective" of the worker than "protective" legislation!

Onus of proof

381 In conformity with the principle that he who alleges a wrong must prove it, the onus of proof in cases of breach of statutory duty, and negligence, lies upon the plaintiff. To succeed in this respect, the plaintiff does not have to show what Lord Kilbrandon has termed "an irrefragable chain of causation" (something that in the present state of medical aetiology might be impossible to prove), but only that only on a balance of probabilities the breach caused, or materially contributed to the injury. The leading case is *Bonnington*

Castings Ltd. v. *Wardlaw* (1956). There, a workman who had contracted a disease caused by the accumulation of harmful dust in his lungs, had been exposed to two sources of dust, one under the control of his employer, the other not under his control. The workman succeeded in that case, notwithstanding that the former source was not in itself sufficient to cause the disease: it sufficed that it had materially contributed to his injury. The *Bonnington* principle has recently been affirmed in *McGhee* v. *National Coal Board* (1973), where some of the Law Lords were disinclined to distinguish between something which contributes materially to a disease or injury and something which materially increases the risk of a disease or injury although Lord Salmon conceded that the distinction might be "a fruitful source of interesting academic discussion between students of philosophy." In that case, the House of Lords rejected the argument that the workman, who had contracted dermatitis after working in the abrasive dust of brick kilns, must show on a balance of probabilities that his having to bicycle home unwashed because of the employer's failure to provide adequate washing facilities had caused his injury; it was enough to show that such additional exposure had added materially to the risk of the disease.

It is not enough for the plaintiff to prove breach of duty and **382**
then to say that the thing speaks for itself (*res ipsa loquitur*). Proof is unnecessary where the *res ipsa loquitur* doctrine applies, but the latter is applied with stringency. Unless the plaintiff can bring his case within the confines of that doctrine, it is not enough to invite the court to speculate on questions of causation. Thus, where a plaintiff, who had slipped on a wet floor and caught his hand in unfenced belting, relied on breach of statutory duty, the Court of Appeal found that the judge had drawn an inference contrary to the weight of the evidence and reversed his finding that the accident had occurred owing to the defendant's breach of statutory duty. The burden of showing that the accident had occurred in circumstances sufficient to affix the defendant with liability had not been discharged (*Linton* v. *Colonnade Chrome Works* (1964)).

It is however difficult to be dogmatic, as is shown by *Allen* v. *Aeroplane & Motor Aluminium Castings* (1965), in which a boy's finger was injured in the "nip" of unfenced machinery. It was held that, despite the lack of evidence as to how the accident had occurred, the boy was entitled to damages and that the trial judge had erred in his inference that the boy had been engaged on a frolic of his own. Sellers L.J. said (at p. 1247 of the report): "It is often said that a plaintiff who cannot give an acceptable version of the accident which befell him or her really cannot ask the court to start to find where liability lies. This, however is an exceptional case; it is one where the facts show clearly that there was a breach of duty, and they show equally clearly that it was because of that breach, because of the dangerous nip, that this accident occurred." However "just" this finding may be, it is difficult to reconcile with the requirement that there is an onus upon a plaintiff to lead *some* evidence to show how the accident occurred. Where questions of "hypothetical causation" arise the burden is still on the plaintiff. Thus in the *Nolan* case, above, Paull J. asked himself the question (at p. 940 of the report): "Has the plaintiff shown that, if goggles had been provided in respect of this work, the probability is that he would have worn them?" His answer was emphatic—"I answer quite definitely 'No.' "

383 *Limitation of statutory liability.* It is a matter of some difficulty to decide where the onus lies when there is engrafted upon a statutory duty some limitation of liability under which the occupier, etc., can shelter. Breaches of statutory duty are summary offences and as such subject to section 81 of the Magistrates' Courts Act 1952, which places the burden of proving "any exception, exemption, proviso, excuse or qualification" on the defendant where he relies on such exception, etc. Although the weight of the burden of proof is different in a civil action (proof on a balance of probabilities and not, as in criminal cases, proof beyond reasonable doubt), the incidence of the burden of proof is the same in both types of case. Section 81, however, gives no guidance as to when a limitation on some primary liability is to be treated as an exception and when as part of the primary liability—"woven into the verb" of the primary duty, as one judge has put it (Lord Migdale in *Nimmo* v. *Alexander Cowan & Sons Ltd.*, below, when that case was before the Court of Session). Sometimes guidance is given, as in sections 157 and 158 of the Mines and Quarries Act 1954, in which expressions such as "It shall be a defence for the defenders to prove . . ." are used; in such a case no difficulty arises. But, as Lord Upjohn observed in the case of *Nimmo* v. *Alexander Cowan & Sons Ltd.* (1968), referring to the Factories Act 1961 and its several predecessors, these Acts "are notoriously badly drafted."

Not too much difficulty is caused by the so-called "absolute" sections. Thus, in a Scottish case, *Chalmers* v. *Speedwell Wire Co. Ltd.* (1942), section 13 (1) of the Factories Act 1937 fell to be considered. This section provided that "every part of the transmission machinery shall be securely fenced unless it is in such a position . . . as to be safe . . . as it would be if securely fenced." It was held that the phrase beginning with the word "unless" was an "exception" within the Scottish statutory provision corresponding to what is now section 81 of the Magistrates' Courts Act 1952, so that the burden of proving the exception fell upon the defendant.

Non-strict statutory liabilities. With non-strict statutory liabilities (discussed below, paras. 389 *et seq.*) the question of the onus of proof may be difficult. The suggestion that the onus of bringing himself within some exception, such as that contained in the words "so far as is reasonably practicable" in section 28 (1) of the Factories Act 1961, lies upon the defendant, receives some support from the *Nimmo* case (above, Lords Reid and Wilberforce dissenting) where the House of Lords was clearly influenced by (1) the superior knowledge of the employer as to what measures are reasonably practicable, and (2) the re-enactment of the relevant provision against the tenor of the cases. In most cases the onus of proof will not be critical, as in *Jenkins* v. *Allied Ironfounders Ltd.* (1970), in which the employer was held not to be liable to an employee who had stumbled over an obstruction; the evidence, scanty as it was, did not show that the employer had failed to take reasonable measures, short of having a man constantly on duty removing "gates" as they fell from castings in the process of being moved. It was there recognised that in rare cases the court might be unable to come to a definite conclusion on the evidence, in which event it would have to be decided who should suffer thereby. Just such a case occurred in *Garner* v. *John Thompson* (*Wolverhampton*) *Ltd.* (1968). The plaintiff in that case established that the ladder on which he had been standing and which had slipped was prima facie unsafe and succeeded in an action under section 29 (1) of the 1961 Act because the employer, on whom fell the onus of proving that reasonably practicable measures had been taken, did not discharge that onus. **384**

Defences

Contributory negligence and consent (*volenti non fit injuria*) have been examined in connection with the employer's common law duty (above, paras. 110 *et seq.*). Something must be said of the availability of these two defences and of delegation of duty in relation to breaches of statutory duty. **385**

(i) *Contributory negligence.* Where an employer is in breach of a statutory duty and such breach has had some material causative effect in relation to the harm, it is open to the employer to show (and the burden is on him) that the plaintiff's negligence has contributed to the harm. Thus in *Ross* v. *Associated Portland Cement Manufacturers* (1964), the House of Lords held that the employer was liable under section 29 (1) of the Factories Act 1961 for failing to provide a safe place of work, but that the plaintiff, who had used a ladder propped against overhead cables, which had slipped and caused him injury by falling, had been contributorily negligent. The defendants' claim that they had no blame because they were entitled to leave to the plaintiff the decision as to what to do and what to use, was rejected: "The occupier of a factory cannot delegate his duty to carry out the statutory requirements" (*ibid.* at p. 776). This dictum shows that those cases which rest upon a delegation of statutory duty by the employer need to be treated with care. In *Ginty* v. *Belmont Building Supplies Ltd.* (1959), Pearson J., in a statement approved in the *Ross* case, had said (at p. 423 of the report): "In my view, the important and fundamental question in a case like this is not whether there was a delegation, but simply the usual question: Whose fault was it?"

It may be, to apply Pearson J.'s simple question, that the plaintiff is the author of his own misfortune. In the *Ginty* case, the plaintiff had been instructed not to work on asbestos roofs without using boards. Since he knew that the roof upon which he was working was unsafe and that boards were available, it was held that he was entirely to blame for the harm which he had suffered. This case, and others, show that the worker who consciously disobeys or disregards a prescribed safety procedure may be entitled to *nothing*, as opposed to a reduction in damages under the Law Reform (Contributory Negligence) Act 1945.

386 At the same time, the simplistic question put in the *Ginty* case needs to be answered with caution. In the first place it is well to remember Lord Tucker's statement in *Stavely Iron & Chemical Co. Ltd.* v. *Jones* (1956), at p. 648 of the report, that "in Factory Act cases the purposes of imposing the absolute obligation is to protect the workman against those very acts of inattention which are sometimes relied upon as constituting contributory negligence so that too strict a standard would defeat the object of the Act." Once it is shown that the employer himself is in breach of statutory duty, it becomes meaningless to refer to a workman as author of his own misfortune, although his contributory negligence, judged by the more tolerant standards applicable to workmen, is relevant, not only to determine the question of liability, but also the question of apportioning culpability (*Stocker* v. *Norprint Ltd.* (1971); *Hawkins* v. *Ian Ross* (1970); *Mullard* v. *Ben Line Steamers* (1970)).

387 (ii) *Volenti non fit injuria.* As regards the *volenti* defence there were views, both academic and judicial, to the effect that consent cannot constitute a defence to breach of a statutory duty. These views, in relation to breach of statutory duty *by the employer*, would appear to stand, following the House of Lords decision in *Imperial Chemical Industries Ltd.* v. *Shatwell* (1965), in which the employer was held not to be vicariously liable for breach of statutory duty *cast upon an employee*. The case is, therefore, not directly relevant here but it will be convenient to discuss the views expressed. Two brothers, G and J, who were experienced shot-firers, broke their employers' rules and regulations which imposed on them the duty to take shelter when testing electrical circuits for shot-firing. G invited J to make a test in the open and both were injured when G touched a galvanometer with two wires given to him by J which led to a detonator. It was held in an action by G against his employers, based upon the vicarious liability of the latter for J's breach of duty, that the employers were not liable. The employers committed no breach of statutory duty themselves and any liability for J's breach was negatived by consent on the part of G who both knew of and accepted the risk. Lord Reid's account of *volenti* is instructive. After referring to the belief that *volenti* was a "dead or dying defence," he suggested that this belief might have arisen from the practice of pleading contributory negligence and, where this was 100 per cent., it mattered little whether one called it contributory negligence or *volenti non fit injuria*. But there is a distinction, since "there is a world of difference between two fellow servants collaborating carelessly, so that the acts of both contribute to cause injury to one of them, and two fellow servants combining to disobey an order deliberately, though they know the risk involved" (p. 672 of the report). The first involves the partial defence of contributory negligence—the latter is a case of consent. Lord Hodson, like the other Law Lords, did not doubt the validity of those decisions which treated as settled the proposition that the doctrine of consent affords no defence to a claim based upon breach of statutory duty (p. 682 of the report).

An employer in breach of his statutory duty cannot use the **388** defence of consent by showing that his employee had agreed to waive his rights (even for a higher remuneration, thought Lord Reid —see p. 674 of the report). Having said that, an employer who is not in breach of duty, *e.g.* where he has provided the safety equipment, goggles or protective cream required by the statute, can disclaim liability by showing that the plaintiff has deliberately chosen not to use the appliances provided. Whether one terms this *volenti non fit injuria* or the causative negligence of the plaintiff makes little difference.

V. "Non-strict" Statutory Liability

So far we have discussed the nature of strict statutory liability and **389** seen that the absoluteness of such liability is considerably eroded by common law requirements. It is important, however, to remember that not all statutory duties are couched in the severe language of strict liability.

The matter was put by Lord Reid with his customary clarity when, dealing with the variety of statutory duties, he said in the *Nimmo* case (1968) at p. 113 of the report:

> "Sometimes the duty imposed is absolute: certain things must be done and it is no defence that it was impossible to prevent an accident because it was caused by a latent defect which could not have been discovered—still less is it a defence to prove that it was impracticable to carry out the statutory requirement. But in many cases the statutory duty is qualified in one way or another so that no offence is committed if it is impracticable or not reasonably practicable to comply with the duty. Unfortunately there is great variety in the drafting of such provisions. Sometimes the duty is expressed in absolute terms in one section and in another section it is provided that it shall be a defence to prove that it was impracticable or not reasonably practicable to comply with the duty. Sometimes the form adopted is that the occupier shall, so far as reasonably practicable, do certain things. Sometimes it is that the occupier shall take all practicable steps to achieve or prevent a certain result. And there are other provisions which do not exactly fit into any classes. Often it is difficult to find any reason for these differences."

390 We have termed those sections in which the statutory duty is qualified as examples of "non-strict" liability. It should be remembered that the duty to comply with the objective standard of the reasonable man, at common law, or with the non-absolute standards of statutes is a "strict" duty since a defendant who fails to comply with those standards is liable whether he did his best or not. In this sense all common law and statutory duties are "strict." An example of a "non-strict" duty, in our sense, is *Braham* v. *J. Lyons & Co. Ltd.* (1962), which involved section 26 (1) of the Factories Act 1937 (now s. 28 of the 1961 Act—see above, para. 334). B, who was employed in the sausage department of the defendant's factory, slipped on some slippery substance on the floor. It was held that the defendants were not liable because their statutory duty was one to keep the floor free from any substance likely to cause persons to slip "so far as is reasonably practicable." The defendants had kept two persons employed in the cleaning of the floor and it was shown that the accident had been caused by B wearing rubber-soled shoes (an express warning had been given that the wearing of such shoes was dangerous). Lord Denning M.R. added that there was no breach of duty at common law which imposed a duty "no higher than" the statutory duty (p. 1052 of the report). The Master of the Rolls and Pearson L.J. (as he then was) agreed that it is not enough to install a safe system of cleaning if this is not, in fact, carried out—but this did not arise in the present case. Donovan L.J. reserved his opinion on whether a momentary lapse by an employee in cleaning up the floor would involve the employer in civil liability (p. 1053 of the report). The difficulty in ascribing a standard of strictness to such a statutory duty as that discussed in the above case is shown by Megaw J.'s opinion on the facts of the *Powley* case that "the statutory duty is higher than the common law duty" ((1966) at p. 732 of the report).

A statutory duty to make secure the roof of a gypsum mine **391**
"so far as may be reasonably practicable" does not necessarily involve a duty to shore up every piece of roof in every working place against rare and undetectable geological faults, *e.g.* "slickenside," even though this could be done without rendering the mine uneconomic (*Marshall* v. *Gotham Co. Ltd.* (1954)). As Lord Reid put it in a later case (*Jenkins* v. *Allied Ironfounders Ltd.* (1970) at p. 307 of the report), "On the one side, we must put any expense, delays or other disadvantages involved in adopting the preventive system and, on the other, the nature and extent of the risks involved if that system was not adopted."

Mindful of this warning, phrases such as "effective provision," "sufficient and suitable," "adequate," "as may reasonably be required" and so forth must be individually construed in the context of a particular factual situation. Indeed one cannot help wondering if protective legislation, far from letting employers "know where they stand," tends rather to obfuscate the employer's responsibilities in a tangle of semantic casuistry!

VI. Occupational Health

Protective legislation is concerned not only with safety in its narrow **392**
sense but also, as we have seen, with the wider issues of occupational health. Both the Factories Act and the Offices, Shops and Railway Premises Acts lay down general requirements concerning matters such as cleanliness, temperature, ventilation, lighting and first aid. Specific hazards, such as those arising from the use of toxic materials (*e.g.* asbestos, lead and radioactive substances) may be covered by special provisions, although ILO Convention No. 136, which deals with benzene poisoning, has not been ratified by the United Kingdom, avowedly on the ground that the Convention is wider in scope than that afforded by existing legislation. Enforcement of the statutory occupational health provisions fell to the inspectorate who were assisted by a Medical Branch until that was assimilated into

the Department of Employment as a separate Medical Services Division.

393 The Employment Medical Advisory Services Act 1972 overhauls the industrial health system. That Act provides for the establishment of an Employment Medical Advisory Service which will inform and advise the Secretary of State for Employment and others concerned with the health of employed persons. Instead of the present 1,500 "appointed factory doctors" (usually general medical practitioners), there will be a new cadre of full-time, specialised employment medical advisers, and these will have all the powers given to factory inspectors under the Factories Act 1961. The new E.M.A.S. will be responsible for the medical supervision of workers engaged in hazardous work; the supervision of young workers on a selective basis (in place of the time-wasting routine examination of all workers); the provision of medical assistance for those seeking work or training; and advice on the medical aspects of employment problems. The Robens Committee on Safety and Health at Work considered that occupational medicine should continue to be organised within the administrative arrangements for safety and health at work, and to that end should be articulated into the new Authority for Safety and Health at Work rather than the Department of Employment (Report, para. 374).

VII. Reform

394 Growing doubts concerning the efficacy of existing protective legislation in reducing accidents at work led to the appointment in 1970 of a Committee on Safety and Health at Work under the Chairmanship of Lord Robens. That Committee acknowledged the past trend towards the reduction of accidents per thousand employees, but feared that we might be reaching a "plateau" in that respect. Confronted with some 1,000 fatalities and some half million persons injured each year, the Committee was critical of the existing system and its legal framework.

395 The Committee found that the chief defects in the present system were:

1. Apathy at the place of work. The present system tends to encourage people to think of safety and health as primarily a matter of detailed regulation by external agencies.

2. An unsatisfactory statutory system, *viz.*

   (a) There is too much law in the form of statutes and subordinate legislation and this has begun to have a counter-productive effect. More law and more inspectors is not the answer.

(b) The law is intrinsically unsatisfactory because, it is—
(i) piece-meal,
(ii) haphazard,
(iii) intricate and difficult to comprehend, and
(iv) unprogressive.

(c) the administration of the system is excessively fragmented.

The Committee recommends that reform should be aimed at two fundamental and closely related objectives, *viz.* (1) improvement of the statutory system to increase the efficiency of the state's contribution to safety and health at work, and (2) a framework for a more self-regulating system at the place of work. Against the background of these objectives, the following are amongst the reforms which the Committee recommends.

(a) Replacement of the existing statutory arrangements by a **396** comprehensive and orderly set of revised provisions to be contained in a new enabling Act. This enabling Act should spell out the basic principles of industrial safety and health, apart from certain essential matters, such as those dealing with the proposed new Authority (see below), the power to make regulations and the like. The T.U.C., in its written evidence to the Committee, rejected the arguments of those who advocate replacing the specific requirements of existing legislation by a general duty of care, adding that the general common law duty of care "even if embodied in legislation, cannot provide adequate protection against a wide range of serious risks, particularly those which require positive preventive action." The Committee, in its turn, did not accept that the statement of basic principles which it recommends would be too general to be meaningful and helpful in practice. In any case, the generality of the proposed Act would be supplemented by detailed statutory regulations, and, voluntary standards and codes, couched in simpler style than present regulations and more amenable to periodic review.

(b) The new legislation should extend to all employers and **397** employees, subject to specific exclusions, and to those self-employed persons whose acts or omissions endanger other workers (employed or self-employed), or the general public. A novel feature is the recommendation that legislation should take account of the interests of the public in safety and health matters.

(c) A new Authority for Safety and Health at Work with com- **398** prehensive executive powers and functions should be set up. The existing separate safety and health inspectorates for factories, mines, agriculture, explosives, nuclear installations and alkali works should be amalgamated to form a unified service within the new authority. The new inspectorate would be used on a more selective basis to enable inspection to be concentrated on those areas where the resources of the inspectorate are most needed, although the basic function of the inspectorate would be to provide expert and impartial advice to industry.

399 (d) Although the Committee records that "any idea that standards generally should be rigorously enforced through the extensive use of legal sanctions is one that runs counter to our general philosophy," it makes certain recommendations with regard to sanctions and enforcement. Criminal sanctions are inappropriate for most offences and should be reserved for a minority of serious infringements which should have "exemplary punishment." There should be provision for higher penalties in cases of repeated offences and the liability of individuals in connection with offences by corporate bodies should be spelt out clearly.

400 (e) Greater emphasis should be placed on non-judicial administrative techniques. Where advice or persuasion fails, an inspector should have power to issue an Improvement Notice, which, if not complied with, would attract an automatic penalty in the courts. In particularly serious cases, the inspector should have the power to issue to a Prohibition Notice, which, if not complied with would require discontinuance of the use of specified premises, plant or machinery. Appeals in connection with Notices should lie to the industrial tribunals.

Finally, the Committee recommended an inquiry into the common law system of awarding damages for personal injury caused by a breach of duty, either at common law or under statute, a topic which lay outside the Committee's terms of reference. The Committee considered that prevention and compensation were two sides of the same problem and that concentration on the latter had reacted unfavourably on the former. As already noted (para. 121, above) it has been decided to establish a Royal Commission to examine the common law system of damages for personal injury.

CHAPTER 6

EMPLOYMENT AND SOCIAL SECURITY

I. INTRODUCTION

The Beveridge principles

01 During the forty-five years preceding the Beveridge Report of 1942, British social insurance was essentially piecemeal in nature, in that separate schemes dealt with particular aspects of social security such as health and unemployment insurance and workmen's compensation. The Beveridge Report brought together these different schemes in a largely unified system of social insurance providing against interruption and destruction of earning power and for special expenditure arising at birth, marriage or death, and, in so doing, laid the foundations for the post-war "Welfare State." The legislation which followed the Report, whilst it differs in some respects from the Report, is based on the six fundamental principles enunciated by Beveridge, *viz.* (1) flat rate of subsistence benefit; (2) flat rate of contribution; (3) unification of administrative responsibility; (4) adequacy of benefit; (5) comprehensiveness; and (6) classification (*i.e.* the division of the population into categories according to their needs). The legislation has since been modified and amended. For our purposes, the relevant current Acts are the National Insurance Act 1965 and the National Insurance (Industrial Injuries) Act 1965, the former containing the comprehensive scheme of national insurance, the latter according special treatment to the topic of industrial injuries on which the old workmen's compensation had made a contribution prior to its repeal after the Second World War. Both Acts have been successively amended either to revise contributions and benefits to keep pace with inflation and the raised expectations of the modern citizen or to make certain changes of principle. The three assumptions upon which the plan was based, *viz.* children's allowances, a comprehensive health service and the avoidance of mass unemployment have since, largely been translated into practice either by legislation or government policy.

Although Beveridge wrote much about unemployment, his plan is comprehensive in that it deals broadly with the whole population on a principle of classification worked out according to differing needs. In the treatment which follows, only those provisions affecting employment are singled out for general discussion.

New developments

402 Before discussing those provisions, some new developments may be noted, the first of which would undoubtedly have received Beveridge's support. The Ministry of Social Security Act 1966 gave belated recognition to Beveridge's preference for the term "social security" as opposed to "national insurance" in that the functions and responsibilities of the old Ministry of Pensions and National Insurance and of the old National Assistance Board were transferred to a new Ministry of Social Security (now part of the Department of Health and Social Security). The change of title reflects the feeling that in a generally affluent society, which is committed to a policy of full employment, the citizen has a right to security of income up to a certain minimum. This security is afforded in various ways. The basic risks are covered by the contributory insurance scheme. The supplementary benefits scheme is a non-contributory "long-stop" for those who are not in full-time work and whose income is insufficient for their needs. Over the last few years, the scale on which supplementary benefits is paid has escalated to the extent that far from assisting the few exceptional cases, the scheme now covers nearly 2½ million people, all paid for by the taxpayer. The family income supplement scheme endeavours to deal with the problem of low pay by bringing up the family income of those families with an income less than that prescribed by Parliament. Over the past decade there has been renewed pressure from some unions for the introduction of a national minimum wage, but a departmental committee which examined this proposal adverted to the serious problems which such an innovation might create in this country. The most recent proposal is that set out in the Green Paper, "Proposals for a Tax-Credit System" (Cmnd. 5116), under which tax would be deducted by the employer at 30 per cent., but would be offset by credits for single persons, married couples and those with children, so that, for example, a married man with three children who was earning £20 per week, would incur a tax liability of £6 but would be liable to £12 credits, *i.e.* would receive £6 net on top of his income of £20 per week. The advantage of such a "negative income tax," as it is termed, is that it unifies the plethora of special benefits at present payable to the low-paid worker and does so through the tax system. Finally, of course, there is for those who can afford it the possibility of something better than the minimum in the form of voluntary insurance through the market, something which Beveridge welcomed as perfectly compatible with his own plan. Beveridge would, most assuredly, not have welcomed the idea of voluntary insurance *instead of* rather than in *addition to* social

insurance, which is countenanced to some degree by the "contracting out" arrangements in connection with the state retirement pension scheme (see below, para. 416).

In 1961, two of the fundamental principles upon which the 403
Report was based, namely, flat rate of benefit and flat rate of contribution, were modified by the introduction of a graduated part of the national retirement pension linked to graduated contributions and payable in addition to the flat-rate retirement pension. In 1966, to the gratification of trade unionists, earnings-related supplements to unemployment and sickness benefit and a supplement to widow's allowance were introduced, the extra cost of which to the National Insurance Fund is met by additional graduated contributions. By April 1975, it is hoped that all employed persons will be making contributions by reference to their earnings at the rate of $5\frac{1}{4}$ per cent. instead of the present mixture of flat-rate and earnings-related contributions. Although contributions under the proposed scheme will be related to earnings, that scheme will retain flat-rate benefits with some modification of the earnings-related supplements.

II. National Insurance

In accordance with the principle of comprehensiveness the adult 404
population of Great Britain, consisting of all persons over school-leaving age and under pensionable age, is, subject to prescribed conditions as to residence, divided into three classes for the purposes of the National Insurance Act 1965, *viz.* (a) "employed persons," *i.e.* persons gainfully employed in Great Britain under a contract of service; (b) "self-employed persons," *i.e.* persons gainfully employed in Great Britain who are not employed persons; (c) "non-employed persons," *i.e.* persons who are neither employed nor self-employed persons (Beveridge did not like this description in relation to housewives). Only the first category of insured persons (Class I) is discussed here. Provision is made by means of regulations to include within Class I persons not engaged under contracts of service and to exclude those who might otherwise have ranked as Class I insured persons, *e.g.* those in employment of a casual or subsidiary nature.

Benefits and allowances fall into two groups, *viz.* (1) flat-rate 405
benefits—unemployment benefit, sickness benefit, invalidity benefit, maternity benefit, widow's benefits, guardian's allowance, retirement pension, child's special allowance and death grant; (2) graduated supplement to retirement pension and earnings-related unemployment and sickness benefit. Persons in each of the three classes of insured persons are, subject to exceptions and arrangements for the crediting of contributions, liable to pay the contribution

appropriate to their class. Provided other necessary conditions are satisfied, Class I flat-rate contributions carry with them entitlement to all flat-rate benefits. The employer is responsible not only for paying Class I contributions for each employee but also for ensuring that the employee's card is stamped, although the amount of the employee's contribution is deductible, subject to certain safeguards, from the employee's wages or other remuneration. During complete weeks for which sickness, unemployment or injury benefit or maternity allowance is received, the employee's card need not normally be stamped and the employee is credited with flat-rate contributions. Both the employer's and the employee's contributions are paid into the National Insurance Fund together with such moneys as are provided by Parliament.

406 In addition to flat-rate contributions, employed persons aged eighteen and over (and their employers) pay graduated contributions which are used to pay for the graduated part of the retirement pension (unless the employee is contracted out of the scheme, in which case the relevant contributions and graduated part of the retirement pension are not payable) and for earnings-related supplements to unemployment and sickness benefits or to widow's allowance. It is possible for larger employers to obtain a permit enabling them to pay flat-rate national insurance contributions for all their regular employees directly to the Ministry instead of using stamps. Graduated contributions are paid to the Collector of Taxes along with P.A.Y.E. income tax.

Of the flat-rate benefits, unemployment and sickness benefits alone are briefly examined here, followed by a summary of the chief graduated benefits.

1. Unemployment and sickness benefits

407 Subject to contribution requirements, and to additional conditions where he is over pensionable age, a person may receive unemployment benefit or sickness benefit for any day of unemployment forming part of a period of interruption of employment, or for any day of incapacity for work forming part of such a period, provided the claimant is under pensionable age or has not retired from regular employment on any such day. In order to qualify for the full rate of benefit, whether unemployment or sickness, the claimant must have paid not less than twenty-six contributions of the appropriate class since entry into insurance and have paid, or been credited with, not less than fifty contributions of the appropriate class, or their equivalent, in respect of the last complete contribution year before the beginning of the benefit year, which includes the day for which the benefit is claimed. The claimant's contribution year is denoted by a letter suffix (A, B, C or D) to his national insurance number. The benefit year commences on the first Monday of the month, five months after the end of the contribution year. Thus, the letter "B" denotes a contribution year running from the first complete contribution week in the month of June, *e.g.* June 7, 1971 to June 4, 1972, for which the benefit year runs November 6, 1972, to November 4, 1973.

(1) *Unemployment benefit*

This benefit is paid at a weekly rate for days of unemployment 408
forming part of a period of interruption of employment. Any two days of interruption of employment, consecutive or not, within a period of six consecutive days ranks as a period of interruption and any two such periods not separated by more than thirteen weeks is treated as one period of interruption. Limitations on the period of benefit are: (a) No benefit is payable for the first three days of any period of interruption of employment. These days, which exclude Sundays, are known as "waiting days." Under the old "twelve-day rule," benefit was payable in respect of waiting days if there were twelve days of unemployment, but this rule was abolished by section 7 of the Social Security Act 1971. The rule excluding benefit for the waiting days also applies to sickness and injury benefit. (b) Despite the Beveridge recommendation that unemployment benefit should be unlimited in duration, with certain qualifications, a limit has been imposed on the duration of unemployment benefit. A person who has been entitled to unemployment benefit for 312 days in respect of any period of interruption of employment is not entitled to further benefit unless he requalifies (which he may do by paying thirteen contributions for contribution weeks begun or ended since the last day of benefit). (c) Starting on January 1, 1972, flat-rate unemployment benefit is not payable for the first six days of any period during which the employee is *suspended* from employment by his employer, *e.g.* because of lay-off or short-time working (see para. 189, above). Provision is made for increase to the weekly rate of sickness benefit (and unemployment benefit) in respect of dependants, and like unemployment benefit, sickness benefit may be increased by an earnings-related supplement.

DISQUALIFICATION. A person may be disqualified from receiving 409
benefit for the following reasons:

(i) *Work stoppage.* Where a person has lost employment by reason of a stoppage of work due to a trade dispute at his place of employment, he is disqualified during the stoppage of work unless he has become bona fide employed elsewhere in the occupation which he usually follows or has become regularly engaged in some other occupation. A person is not disqualified if he proves that he is not participating in or financing or directly interested in the trade dispute which caused the stoppage of work and that he does not belong to a grade or class of workers of which, immediately before the commencement of the stoppage, there were members employed at his place of employment any of whom are participating in or financing or directly interested in the dispute.

The trade dispute disqualification goes back to 1911 and has caused controversy which the Blanesburgh Committee (1925–27) considered might never be ended however the provisions were framed. The rationale of the provision is that the National Insurance Fund should not be used to support workers during stoppages of work due to trade disputes. Section 10 of the Ministry of Social Security Act 1966 allows the payment of supplementary benefit (and a rent allowance) to meet the requirements of persons other than the breadwinner, such as his wife and children; in an urgent case, section 13 of the same Act permits the payment of benefit to those who fail to qualify for non-contributory benefit under the 1966 Act, such as single men.

The 1966 Act excluded persons in full-time employment from receiving supplementary benefit, but this rule was modified by section 2 of the Social Security Act 1971 which permits the payment of supplementary benefit to a person who returns to work after a stoppage due to a trade dispute subject, however, to the possibility that the benefit so paid may be recovered in certain cases.

410 The disqualification has also been defended on the grounds that (a) it is administratively convenient in that it enables the insurance officer confronted with possible thousands of claims to make speedy determinations, and (b) no satisfactory and workable alternative has been suggested. But, in the words of one Commissioner's Decision, the effect of the present section may be "to involve a person in disqualification because of acts and interests of others for whom he is not responsible." The disqualification, however, only applies if there is a stoppage of work due to a trade dispute at the claimant's place of employment—the latter two terms are defined in section 22 (6) (*a*) and (*b*).

Thus, if a worker is thrown out of work as a result of a stoppage at a place other than his place of employment he is not disqualified. In a strike of sewing machinists at one of the Ford plants at Dagenham, the Commissioner decided that the whole Dagenham estate, comprising different plants, was one factory and therefore one place. This shows that the word "place" may have a potentially wide ambit. "Participating" applies to those who strike or who by their conduct or inaction identify themselves with the disputants, *e.g.* those who comply with requests from picketers to abstain from work. "Financing" applies to those who give financial support in the dispute and includes membership of a trade union which is paying strike or relief pay to participants in the dispute at the place of employment, with the odd consequence that an official strike supported by the trade union may disqualify non-participating members, whilst an unofficial strike does not have this effect. The Donovan Commission recommend that membership of a trade union should not be considered to be a form of "financing" (para. 991).

"Directly interested" is a phrase which covers a situation in which **411**
a person's terms or conditions of employment stand to be affected by the settlement of the dispute, *e.g.* platers' helpers have been held to be directly interested in a stoppage due to a demarcation dispute between platers and shipwrights in that it appeared that the amount of work available to them would depend on the outcome of the dispute (*Punton* v. *Ministry of Pensions and National Insurance* (1963)). A person is directly interested if there is no act or occurrence to break the chain of causation between the dispute and the resulting change in terms or conditions of employment, so that if there is a need to amend the agreement on which those alleged to be directly interested work, the need for such amendment breaks the chain of causation and puts those workers outside the category of those who are directly interested. Since the magnitude of the interest is irrelevant, the possible loss of a tea-break suffices for this purpose.

Perhaps the most controversial exclusion is that contained in **412**
the "grade or class" disqualification, in that it is sufficient if *one* member of that grade or class is participating in, financing, or directly interested in the stoppage of work caused by a trade dispute at the place of employment. The extent of the disqualification can be seen from the Longbridge Strike involving the British Motor Corporation, in which 300 fitters stopped work but, after numerous test cases, between 16,000 and 17,000 workers were disqualified.

A more recent example is the strike of sewing machinists referred to above in which a repair-welder in a completely different plant in the Dagenham estate was disqualified. He had failed to show that he belonged to some other grade or class than that held by the machinists and the evidence showed that one member of the grade or class involved belonged to a union which had given the machinists financial support. In its Report, the Donovan Commission recommended that the whole grade or class provision should be abolished (paras. 980, 981).

(ii) *Misconduct, etc.* Where a person has (a) lost his employ- **413**
ment through misconduct or because he has voluntarily left his

employment without just cause; (b) refused or failed without good cause to apply for a situation notified to him or refused to accept that situation when offered to him; (c) neglected to avail himself of a reasonable opportunity of suitable employment; (d) refused or failed without good cause to carry out any written recommendations given to him by an officer of an employment exchange with a view to assisting him to find suitable employment, being recommendations which were reasonable having regard to his circumstances and to the means of obtaining that employment usually adopted in the district in which he resides; or (e) refused or failed without good cause to avail himself of a reasonable opportunity of receiving training approved by the Secretary of State in his case for the purpose of becoming or keeping fit for entry into or return to regular employment, he is disqualified for receiving unemployment benefit for such period, not exceeding six weeks, as may be determined. Section 1 of the Social Security Act 1971 provides for a reduction in the amount of supplementary benefit payable to a person who has been required to register at an employment exchange and is or is likely to be disqualified from receiving unemployment benefit by reason of (a) to (e) above. Employment is not to be deemed "suitable" for a person if, although in his usual occupation and in the district where he was last ordinarily employed, it is at a rate of remuneration lower or on conditions of work less favourable than he might reasonably expect or those generally observed in that district by agreement between associations of employers and employees or, failing that, those generally observed by good employers in that district. Nor is employment "suitable" if it is in consequence of a stoppage of work due to a trade dispute (*i.e.* no "scabs" or "blacklegs"). However, after an interval of time reasonable in the circumstances, employment is not to be deemed unsuitable by reason only of it being outside his usual occupation provided that the remuneration is not lower and the conditions less favourable than those collectively agreed, or recognised by good employers.

(2) *Sickness benefit*

414 Subject to the contribution requirements (set out above), sickness benefit is paid to employed persons (and, unlike unemployment benefit, to self-employed persons) for any day of incapacity for work which forms part of a period of interruption of employment. A day of incapacity for work is a day on which the claimant is incapable of work by reason of some specific disease or bodily or mental disablement. As in the case of unemployment benefit, sickness benefit is not payable for the first three "waiting days." If not less than 156 contributions of the appropriate class have been paid, benefit is

payable at the flat rate for 168 days; thereafter an invalidity pension becomes payable for subsequent days of incapacity for work forming part of the same period of interruption of employment. If the contribution tests already referred to are satisfied, but less than 156 contributions have been paid, sickness benefit continues to be payable up to a total of 312 days. Provision is made for increases to the weekly rate of sickness benefit (and unemployment benefit) in respect of dependants. Regulations provide for disqualifying a person from receiving sickness benefit for such period, not exceeding six weeks, as may be determined in accordance with the Act if (a) he has become incapable of work through his own misconduct, or (b) he fails without good cause to attend for or to submit himself to such medical examination or treatment as may be required, or to observe any prescribed rules of behaviour.

2. Graduated benefits

Reference has been made above to the modification of the **415**
Beveridge fundamental principles of flat-rate benefit and flat-rate contribution by the introduction of the graduated addition to flat-rate retirement pension in 1961 and the earnings-related benefits in 1966.

(1) *Retirement pension*

A person is entitled to a flat-rate retirement pension when he or she retires from regular employment at the minimum pension age of sixty-five (for men) and sixty (for women), if the relevant contribution conditions are satisfied. To qualify for the flat-rate pension at the standard rate the claimant must have paid at least 156 contributions and have a yearly average of at least fifty flat-rate contributions, whether paid or credited. A person who satisfies the first condition but has less than a yearly average of fifty contributions (but not less than thirteen) is entitled to a flat-rate pension at a reduced rate.

The graduated pension payable to the man or woman of pen- **416**
sionable age who has retired depends on the number of "units" earned since the graduated scheme began in April 1961. Each £7.50 paid by a man in graduated contributions (or £9 for a woman) earns a pension unit giving entitlement to 2½p a week graduated pension. Graduated contributions are paid by employed persons over the age of eighteen, and by their employers, on the employee's earnings. Except for those "contracted out," each pays 4·75 per cent. of that part of the employee's weekly pay which lies between £9 and £48 (or *pro rata* for those paid at other regular intervals). The contributions are related to the figure of gross pay which is

used for income tax under the P.A.Y.E. scheme. Although the rates of contribution of employer and employee are equal, both the rates of contribution and the "bands" of earnings over which the contribution is payable have been, and are likely to be, altered from time to time. Employees who are "contracted out" because their employers operate an acceptable occupational pension scheme, pay (like their employers) a rate of graduated contribution lower than those not contracted out, but both pay a higher rate of flat-rate contribution. Employees contracted out receive a graduated pension calculated in the manner described above. There is no contracting out of the earnings-related supplements described below.

(2) *Earnings-related supplements*

417 The National Insurance Act 1966 introduced earnings-related supplements to flat-rate unemployment and sickness benefits to cushion the better-paid worker against the effect of a serious drop in income in the event of unemployment or sickness. The supplements are payable to persons over eighteen and under pensionable age who are entitled to flat-rate unemployment or sickness benefit and who have "reckonable earnings" of at least £450 in the relevant tax year. The "reckonable earnings" are the gross earnings on which income taxed is assessed under Schedule E and which is payable through P.A.Y.E.; at the time of writing, this is normally the total for the tax year preceding the earnings-related benefit year in which the interruption of employment begins, such total being divided by 50 to give a weekly total. From January 1, 1973, income arising from self-employment and some other sources will not count as reckonable earnings, even though taxed under Schedule E and collected through P.A.Y.E., and, from the same date, there will be changes both in the earnings-related benefit year and in the method of establishing reckonable earnings (for which a computer will be used). The amount of the supplement is related to reckonable earnings between £450 and £1,500, *i.e.* between £9 and £30 per week on which, as a rough guide, one third is payable as a supplement. Thus, for a person earning £30 or more a week, the maximum supplement will be £7. By virtue of what is termed the "wage stop," the amount of both flat-rate and earnings-related benefits must not exceed 85 per cent. of weekly earnings. If the total of both benefits exceeds that limit, the supplement must be reduced, but not the flat-rate benefit, even where, as is possible, this exceeds the wage stop, although in such an event no supplement will be payable. The supplements are payable for a period not exceeding 156 days (excluding Sundays, the first twelve days of unemployment or sickness and the first six days of any *suspension* from unemployment)

in any period of interruption of employment. Spells of unemployment or incapacity caused by sickness and not separated by more than thirteen weeks are added together to form a single period of interruption of employment.

III. Industrial Injuries

Workmen's compensation

Under the system of workmen's compensation introduced in 418
1897 and made general in 1906, the employer was made liable to compensate the employee for loss of earnings attributable to accident or industrial disease arising out of and in the course of employment. Indemnification of the worker according to fault (*culpa*) on the employer's part was replaced by a division of loss between employer and employee in which, subject to a maximum, the latter's earnings were taken into account. The Beveridge Report acknowledged that the workmen's compensation scheme had conferred great benefits but nevertheless recommended its supersession by the inclusion of the industrial risks of injury and disease within the new scheme of unified social insurance, with some special adaptations. The Report referred to the disadvantages of the workmen's compensation scheme, *e.g.* the need for litigation, the initiative required of the employee in prosecuting his claim, the absence of compulsory insurance (except in mining), the undesirability of lump sum awards, the high administration costs (even of mutual insurance companies) in comparison with compulsory state insurance, and not least, the failure of the scheme to secure the restoration of the injured employee to the greatest possible degree of production and earning power as soon as possible. "The pioneer system of social security in Britain was based on a wrong principle and has been dominated by a wrong outlook" said the Report.

The present scheme

The new industrial injuries scheme, replacing the workmen's 419
compensation scheme, was enacted in the National Insurance (Industrial Injuries) Act 1946, which, after amendments, has been replaced by the National Insurance (Industrial Injuries) Act 1965, since further amended in minor respects.

The provision of a separate scheme for industrial injuries has been criticised on the basis that it is difficult and indeed needless to distinguish between industrial and non-industrial accidents. "If a workman loses his leg in an accident his needs are the same whether the accident occurred in a factory or in the street" (Beveridge

Report, para. 80). Nevertheless, despite a departure from the principle of treating equal needs equally, separate provision was made in a separate Act for industrial injuries for historical reasons and because of the failure of employers and employees to agree on a substitute for the workmen's compensation scheme. Today, an injured employee may have a claim (a) against his employer for breach of common law or statutory duty *and* (b) for benefit out of the Industrial Injuries Fund controlled and managed by the Secretary of State (subject to section 2 of the Law Reform (Personal Injuries) Act 1948, discussed above at para. 117). Social insurance, based upon a pooling of risks, contrasts with the common law emphasis upon fault and with the now obsolete allocation of risk between employer and employee in the workmen's compensation scheme.

420 The broad effect of the Act may be stated as follows—A person is entitled to the benefits of the industrial injuries statutory scheme if he can show that as an insured person he has suffered either (a) a personal injury caused after July 4, 1948, by accident arising out of and in the course of employment, or (b) a prescribed disease or a prescribed personal injury, not caused by accident arising out of and in the course of employment, but being a disease or injury due to the nature of that employment and developed after July 4, 1948. The scope of the Act will be examined as follows: 1. Insurable employment and contributions; 2. Risks covered by the Act; 3. Benefits provided by the Act.

1. Insurable employment and contributions

421 The most important category of persons insured under the Act is that of persons employed in Great Britain under any contract of service or apprenticeship.

This corresponds with the important category of Class I contributor in the main Act (accounting for more than 23 million of the 25 million contributors under that Act), except that certain persons not in Class I are covered by the industrial injuries scheme, such as children under school-leaving age in part-time employment (who pay no contributions), persons excluded from Class I because of the subsidiary or inconsiderable nature of their employment, seamen employed on British ships but ordinarily resident in specified countries, harbour and deep sea pilots, etc.

Several of the leading cases dealing with the legal attributes of a contract of service have arisen in connection with questions of classification under the Insurance Acts. These have been discussed in Chapter 1, to which the reader is commended. Categories other than those employed in Great Britain under a contract of service or apprenticeship are specified in Schedule 1, Part I, as insurable employments, some of them with great particularity, either in the Schedule, or in regulations made under the Act. Part II of Schedule 1 excepts certain employments from the Act. Under Part III of Schedule 1, the Secretary of State is given power to make regulations for the prevention of anomalies.

The Industrial Injuries Fund

The contributions of insured persons and their employers, plus **422**
a sum equal to one fifth of the aggregate amount of contributions from moneys provided by Parliament, are paid into a special Industrial Injuries Fund which is used to provide the benefits and to meet administration costs. The employer is liable in the first instance to pay both his own and his employee's contributions and has rights similar to those in the main Act permitting him to deduct or recover, as the case may be, the latter's contributions if these have been paid by the employer. Regulations provide for persons who are to be treated as employers in certain cases, *e.g.* the bailor of a taxi-cab. There are four rates of contribution payable by employer and employee, varying according to the sex and age of the insured person, *viz.* men aged eighteen or over, men under eighteen, women aged eighteen or over and women under that age. Contributions are normally payable in respect of each "contribution week" (*i.e.* period of seven days beginning with midnight between Sunday and Monday) during which, or part of which, the insured person is employed and such contributions are paid either by the affixing (or, in certain cases, impressing) of a stamp to the insured person's national insurance card (in the case of Class I contributors under the main Act one stamp suffices for contributions under that Act and the present Act) or by direct payment by the employer to the Ministry of flat-rate contributions instead of using stamps (employers employing at least 100 persons as regular employees may be allowed to use the latter method of payment).

With the exception of employment which is employed contri- **423**
butor's employment under the main Act, regulations may provide, in relation to persons in such insurable employment as may be prescribed, that contributions payable by the employer and employee at the appropriate rate shall be determined by reference to work actually done by the insured person or by a group of persons of whom he is one, or to remuneration paid to him or to such a group, instead of by reference to the weeks in which he is employed. Contributions are not payable by (i) persons (mariners and airmen) exempted by regulations made under section 75 from liability to contribute and persons in prescribed classes of subsidiary or inconsiderable employment who have been exempted from liability to

contribute, and (ii) by persons who normally are liable to contribute but are not liable to contribute for particular weeks because of incapacity by reason of some specific disease or bodily or mental disablement or because of holidays or service in the Forces. An employer or insured person who fails to pay at or within the prescribed times any contribution which he is liable to pay under the Act commits an offence. But right to benefit under the Act is in no way dependent upon contributions.

2. Risks covered by the Act

(1) *Personal injury caused by accident arising out of and in the course of employment*

424 (i) "PERSONAL INJURY CAUSED BY ACCIDENT." In contrast to the old Workmen's Compensation Acts, the words "injury" and "accident" are to be kept separate, although there must be a causal link between the two. "Personal injury" (which is a phrase used in connection with "prescribed personal injury"—see below, para. 438) denotes some physiological change in the living body of a human being, a formulation which excludes damage to some artificial appendage of the body such as spectacles, false teeth or an artificial limb, even though incapacity for work results. Nervous shock may constitute personal injury. Disfigurement is included in loss of physical faculty for the purposes of disablement benefit.

The word "accident," used in its popular sense, has been variously defined as "an unlooked for mishap or an untoward event which is not expected or designed" or as "any unintended and unexpected occurrence which produces hurt or loss." An occurrence which is "unintended" from the victim's standpoint may be an accident even though deliberately brought about by another person, *e.g.* the murder of a schoolmaster by his pupils. The accident need not necessarily be an "external" event as where a person feels something "go" inside him. Lord Diplock has, however, warned against treating the accident and the injury as the same thing, although his lordship concedes that an injury which is caused by some intentional bodily activity of the claimant himself may be difficult to separate as "injury" and "accident" respectively. The latter he defines as "something external which has some physiological or psychological effect on that part of the sufferer's anatomy which sustains the actual trauma, or some bodily activity of the sufferer which would be perceptible to an observer if one were present when it occurred. It is convenient," continues his lordship, "to call this external event or bodily activity the causative incident" (*Jones* case, below, at pp. 184–185 of the report).

In many cases it will be possible to separate the accident and the injury in the way which the Act envisages, *e.g.* (1) man inadvertently falls from ladder = accident; (2) he receives a fractured skull = injury; (3) he suffers loss of memory and power of concentration = loss of faculty. The causal link was expressed as follows by Scrutton L.J. in *Comery* v. *New Hucknall Colliery Co.* (1919) at p. 9 of the report, a case which involved death: 425

> "The result need not be a direct or a natural or even a probable consequence of the accident if in fact it is a result of the accident. It is enough that the accident caused or contributed to or accelerated death, and it appears from the authorities that the accident may contribute to the death if it causes such a state of things in the man's body that he is physically more susceptible to the cause which ultimately kills him."

In other cases, the courts recognise that it is impossible to separate the injury and the accident in this way. The case of *Minister of Social Security* v. *Amalgamated Engineering Union* (1967) shows how difficult it may be to separate causation in its legal and medical forms. The claimant, who had suffered a hiatus hernia after moving a heavy flagstone in the course of his employment, was held to be entitled to injury benefit by the deputy Industrial Injuries Commissioner. Subsequently in a claim for disablement benefit the medical appeal tribunal decided that it was not satisfied that the hiatus hernia was either caused or aggravated by the relevant accident. On appeal to the House of Lords, it was held that the decision of the deputy Industrial Injuries Commissioner was final and conclusive not only in relation to the claim for injury benefit but also in relation to the claim for disablement benefit.

In two decisions of the House of Lords (*Minister of Social Security* v. *Amalgamated Engineering Union* (1967); *Jones* v. *Secretary of State for Social Services* (1972)), the difficulty in separating legal and medical causation was further complicated by the finality of decisions by the "lay" or "secular" authorities under the Act, as to whether or not an industrial accident had caused an injury, on which the "medical" authorities, to whom might be entrusted the consequential question of disablement, were not competent to pass judgment. The question of "finality" is covered by section 5 of the National Insurance Act 1972. A decision by a secular (or lay) authority as to an industrial accident, or a reference to a medical authority concerning disablement, cannot now be taken to import a decision as to the origin of any injury or disability, whether or not there is an event identifiable as an accident apart from any injury that may have occurred, but (a) a decision that a person had an industrial accident by reason of an injury, when there was such 426 separate event, is to be treated as a decision that if the injury was suffered by accident, that accident was an industrial accident; and (b) a decision that an accident was an industrial accident may be given and a declaration to that effect be made without a finding that personal injury resulted from that accident. Section 5 also provides for the effect of a finding of fact (which is not to be conclusive for all purposes) and for the finality of a finding as to disablement for the purposes of death benefit.

427 The requirement that the accident must take the form of an "event" or "occurrence" has been held to exclude those situations in which a person suffers personal injury as the result of a "process," *i.e.* a series of events over a length of time. The line between an "accident" and a "process" may be difficult to draw. For example, the person who suffers fibrositis after driving a lorry with a broken window during a single morning, or after being twice soaked to the skin by the rain which entered a locomotive shed during a period of two weeks, has been entitled to benefit. But a workman who worked for twenty years as a slate-splitter in closed sheds was held to have contracted silicosis as the result of a process. However, a person who had been employed for eighteen years in the blasting department of a chemical factory, in which he had been more or less continually exposed to a particular substance, and had died after a week-end away from work, was held to have died as the result of a process rather than an accident.

428 (ii) "ARISING OUT OF AND IN THE COURSE OF EMPLOYMENT." This "composite expression" serves to demarcate the industrial from the non-industrial hazard. Although "arising out of" and "in the course of" are two aspects of a composite test rather than separate tests, it will be convenient for purposes of exposition to discuss them separately.

An accident arises out of employment if it is causally connected with employment or the incidents thereof. The link may be remote in that the "passive and inert surroundings" of the workplace may suffice to establish the degree of connection. "It is enough that the exigencies of the employment brought the workman within the range of the particular danger and exposed him to its impact whereas but for his employment he would not have been exposed" (*per* Lord Wright in *Cadzow Coal Co.* v. *Price* (*& Murphy*) (1943) at p. 233 of the report). Something which is not an industrial risk for one person may constitute such a risk for another. Thus the risk of being knocked down in the street by a vehicle would not ordinarily rank as an industrial risk *eo nomine*, so that the workman who is knocked down after leaving work has lost his identity as a workman and has become a member of the general public for this purpose. But the messenger boy or courier who is knocked down in this way runs a risk to which he is exposed by virtue of his employment. An accident occurs in the course of employment if it occurs at a time when the victim is doing that which he is employed to do or that which is reasonably incidental thereto. For the purposes of the industrial injuries scheme, the test is temporal, unlike the "arising out of" test, which is causal or connective in nature. "Course of employment" signifies the currency of a man's work and reasonable accompaniments thereof. It does not mean the period of actual work because, as will be seen, times during which no work is accomplished are included, such as meal-breaks.

As with many legal rules, difficulty occurs in a small minority of **429**
marginal cases. Cases decided under the now repealed workmen's compensation legislation are still relevant in elucidating the meaning of the composite expression, as are the decisions of the Commissioner under the new scheme. These decisions are not "precedents" but afford useful guidance as to the possible application of the statute in particular situations. Moreover, when such decisions come before the Divisional Court of the Queen's Bench Division they do so by way of "review" and not by way of "appeal," *i.e.* the decision is considered from the point of view of jurisdiction rather than merits.

For the purposes of the Act, an accident arising in the course of an insured person's employment is deemed, in the absence of evidence to the contrary, also to arise out of that employment. If, therefore, the insured person suffers an accident during employment, it is for the insurance officer to show that such accident did not arise out of the employment unless the facts themselves disclose such evidence. In *R.* v. *National Insurance* (*Industrial Injuries*) *Commissioner*, *ex p. Richardson* (1958), a bus conductor who had been attacked on the platform of his bus whilst wearing uniform was held disentitled to injuries benefit since the facts showed that he had not been singled out by his assailants because of his uniform: "If, however, the facts which are in evidence before the commissioner can amount to evidence to the contrary, then the presumption disappears, and it is then for the applicant to prove that the accident did arise not only in the course of but also out of his employment" (*per* Lord Goddard C.J. at p. 855 of the report).

Acts incidental to employment. The word "employment" covers **430**
not only the work which the insured person is employed to do, but also that which is reasonably incidental to such work. An act may be incidental in a narrow sense when closely implicated with the work, *e.g.* the operator of a machine who wipes his greasy hands on a cloth, or it may be incidental in a wider sense when the degree of

involvement with the work may be slight or even non-existent—the so-called "neutral acts." The notion contained in some older cases that such neutral acts only came within the sphere of employment if performed in pursuance of a duty owed to the employer was dispelled in *R.* v. *Industrial Injuries Commissioner*, *ex p. A.E.U.* (1966). "The idea that a duty is necessary is all wrong" said Lord Denning M.R. at p. 46 of the report. On the facts, the Court of Appeal agreed that the workman in question who had gone for a smoke was acting in the course of his employment although he had no duty in this respect. It was enough that the employer consented either expressly or impliedly to the activity, so that the workman had a right, privilege or prerogative to engage in the particular activity. But also on the facts, the court upheld the commissioner's decision that in staying for five minutes beyond the allowed ten minutes the workman had stepped outside his employment. Interruptions of work may have different effects, as Lord Denning M.R. pointed out in *R.* v. *Industrial Injuries Commissioner*, *ex p. A.E.U.*, at p. 48 of the report:

> "Take the first class where 'a man goes away from his work for purposes of his own.' An illustration is where a man goes from one end of a factory to the other to compare notes on football pools. He is not acting in the course of his employment. It would be different if he went to get a tool or to go to the lavatory.
>
> "Now take the next class, where a man 'at his place of work does something which has nothing to do with his employment.' An illustration was given by Lord Atkin in *Noble*'s case [*Noble* v. *Southern Ry. Co.* (1940)]. If the guard of a train takes it on himself to drive the train and is injured while driving, he is outside the course of his employment. Another illustration is the case . . . where a man was employed to hook goods on to a crane and, instead, took it on himself to drive a fork-lift truck. There he was outside the course of his employment.
>
> "Take the third class where 'being away from his place of work, he does not return to it when he should.' An illustration can be taken from *Knight* v. *Howard Wall Ltd.* (1938). Suppose the boy in the canteen, instead of going back to his work at the end of the meal, had stayed on for half an hour playing darts with the rest of the men in the canteen. By overstaying his visit to the canteen he would be taking himself completely out of the course of his employment because he would be doing something of a kind different from anything he was employed to do."

431 Like the categories of negligence, the list of incidental acts is not closed. The following are examples of acts which have, in particular circumstances, been held to have a sufficiently close

connection with employment—slipping on a step after a pithead bath, making and drinking tea, conversation (unless work is stopped in order to engage in conversation), relieving nature, reflexive or instinctive actions, *e.g.* catching at something thrown at one or bending down to tie a shoe-lace, accidentally falling asleep, handing a sweet to a boy seated on a potato digger (*cf.* handing a sweet across a circular saw table during a lull), smoking, and the use of medical services provided by or made available by the employer, including use of a chiropody service.

But the town clerk who makes a speech at a workmen's institute, the laundry worker who deposits her own washing in the sorting room (even though allowed to do so by her employer), and the worker who attends a meeting of a Joint Industrial Council, have all been held to be disentitled to benefit. The shadowy nature of the line between acts within, and acts outside, the course of employment is illustrated by the "hooker-on" case to which Lord Denning referred (above). In that case, a dock labourer who drove a fork lift truck (for which there was a skilled driver) in order to remove some pallet boards was held to have put himself outside the course of employment, whereas in a later case a dock labourer who had driven an electric truck in order to fetch some slings needed for loading operations was adjudged not to have stepped outside his employment by so doing.

Act in contravention of orders. An accident is deemed to arise 432
out of and in the course of employment notwithstanding that the insured person is acting at the time of the accident in contravention of a statutory or other regulation, or of any orders given by or on behalf of his employer, or that he is acting without instructions from his employer, as the case may be, if (a) the accident would have been deemed so to have arisen had the act not been done in contravention as aforesaid, or without instructions from his employer, as the case may be, and (b) the act is done for the purposes of and in connection with the employer's trade or business (s. 7 of the 1965 Act). As with vicarious liability, it is important to distinguish between prohibitions but for which the act would be within the scope of the employment, and prohibitions which limit the scope or sphere of the employment; disregard of the latter has the effect of altering the scope of the employment which cannot have been intended by section 7. The Commissioner has said that "a prohibition that has never been enforced or which has been more often broken than observed cannot be said to be a regulation applicable to a man's employment." It may be noted here, that a worker who *complies* with an order will normally act within the course of employment, unless the order relates to something which is either illegal or outside the terms of

the worker's contract of employment. The factory worker who complies with an order or request from his foreman to go strawberry picking, on the strength of the latter's assurance that his time-sheet will be "squared," does so *suo periculo* for the purposes of the industrial injuries scheme.

433 *Extension of the principle.* A desirable, if not completely logical, extension of the effect of the magical phrase "arising out of and in the course of" is embodied in section 10 of the Act, by virtue of which accidents which would otherwise have ranked as non-industrial occurrences are included, provided in each case that the accident arises in the course of employment and provided that the insured person did not directly or indirectly induce or contribute to the happening of the accident by his conduct outside the employment or by any act not incidental to the employment. The accidents in question are those caused by the misconduct, skylarking or negligence of another (including steps taken in consequence of the same), or caused by the behaviour or presence of an animal (including a bird, fish or insect), or accidents caused by or consisting in the insured person being struck by any object or by lightning.

The "course of employment" has been interpreted to include periods other than those of actual work but which are connected with the work or its incidentals. Thus a person who arrives at work or leaves the same a reasonable time before or after work is covered whilst on the premises and also during breaks, such as those for meals. In some occupations such as those of domestic servants, seamen on board ship, lighthouse keepers and resident nurses, a person may be "continuously employed," *i.e.* the employment extends beyond hours of work proper, in that the nature of the job determines physically where the worker must spend his off-duty time. The receipt of remuneration in respect of a particular period is not conclusive that the period is included in the course of employment, *e.g.* a bus conductress who was injured when stepping off a bus on her way back home during a "split-duty," for which she received half pay, was held to be disentitled to benefit.

434 *Geographical limitation.* In most cases, the course of employment will carry with it a geographical limitation in the sense that arrival at the employer's premises (rather than the actual place of work therein) will normally signify the commencement of the course of employment. The fact that the employee has entered his employer's premises for purposes of working there is not conclusive in that he may still have a distance to go before arriving at the premises which constitute his workplace, *e.g.* an engine driver who was injured whilst walking along a railway line was held to be disentitled to benefit in that he was half a mile from the depot at which he was

due to report. *Per contra*, a miner injured on a colliery railway line at a place 100 yards from the place at which he was due to start work in half an hour's time was held to have entered the course of employment.

There are two main exceptions to the general rule that time 435
spent travelling is outside the course of employment. The first, and obvious exception comprises those circumstances in which the employee is travelling on duty, *i.e.* in fulfilment of an express or implied term in his contract to that effect. Travelling has been adjudged to be an inseparable part of the duties of persons such as an agricultural advisory officer required to visit farms, an insurance agent, a commercial traveller and a chief fire officer. The last named of these in one case suffered an injury on his way to attend the annual dinner of a local fire brigade. The Commissioner did not think that the officer in question could be said to be travelling "to work"—he was travelling "on work" inasmuch as part of his general supervisory responsibility lay in fostering *esprit de corps* amongst fire brigades to which purpose the dinner was merely incidental. "His employment was peripatetic," said the Commissioner. Compare with this the case of the police officer cycling from his home to report for duty at the police station who was held to be travelling "to duty" rather than "on duty." Not all of the peregrinations of the peripatetic are necessarily included in the course of employment—the salesman on his way home for the week-end, the meter-reader on his way to the first house and the home-help with a similar destination have been held not to have entered the course of employment. The fact that the insured person is paid for travelling time or that he is paid for the interval in a "split-duty" is not conclusive in that the employer may well be indifferent as to what happens outside working hours. Nor does the fact that a person works at different places on different days have conclusive effect in that these places may each constitute the place of work for each day so that time spent in travelling to such place is spent in going "to work" rather than "on work." It is different, however, when an employee is travelling under his employer's directions, as when a workman is sent to a distant town to bring back some tool.

The second exception is statutory. Section 8 of the 1965 Act 436
brings time spent in travelling within the ambit of employment in that an accident happening whilst an insured person is, with the express or implied permission of his employer, travelling as a passenger (*note*—not driver or rider) by any vehicle to or from his place of work shall, notwithstanding that he is under no obligation to his employer to travel by that vehicle, be deemed to arise out of and in the course of his employment if (a) the accident would have

been deemed so to have arisen had he been under such an obligation, and (b) at the time of the accident the vehicle (i) is being operated by or on behalf of his employer or some other person by whom it is provided in pursuance of arrangements made with his employer, and (ii) is not being operated in the ordinary course of a public transport service.

That the words "arising out of and in the course of employment" (which are also used in road traffic legislation and employers' liability policies of insurance) have a special meaning in the present connection is shown by the remarks of Lord Denning M.R. in *Vandyke* v. *Fender* (1970) at p. 305 of the report. Standing alone, those words mean "that when a man is going to or coming from work, along a public road, as a passenger in a vehicle provided by his employer, he is not then in the course of his employment—unless he is *obliged* by the terms of his employment to travel in that vehicle. It is not enough that he should have the right to travel in the vehicle, or be permitted to travel in it. He must have an *obligation* to travel in it." The effect of (a), above, is that a man is *deemed* to be in the course of employment even though he is under no obligation to travel by that vehicle. "Vehicle," in this section, includes a ship, vessel or aircraft and has been held to include vehicles not adapted for the conveyance of persons, *e.g.* tractors. The words "travelling as a passenger" do not cover a person who is walking to or from the vehicle, although boarding the vehicle or alighting therefrom has been included. It is not necessary that the vehicle should take the insured person the whole way to his employment. The "arrangements" made by the employer need not be formal, contractual arrangements, but the alteration of a train or bus time of departure does not by itself constitute an "arrangement."

437 *Emergencies.* Finally, the course of employment is widened by section 9, which provides that an accident happening to an insured person in or about any premises at which he is for the time being employed for the purposes of his employer's trade or business shall be deemed to arise out of and in the course of his employment if it happens while he is taking steps, on an actual or supposed emergency at those premises, to rescue, succour or protect persons who are, or are thought to be or possibly to be, injured or imperilled, or to avert or minimise serious damage to property, *e.g.* the chauffeur injured in rescuing property from his employer's house which is on fire; the security guard assisting the police to investigate a light in a near-by building. The steps taken by the insured person must be reasonable and the onus is on him (*e.g.* a worker injured while climbing into a factory which had not been opened as usual was held to have acted unreasonably in the circumstances).

(2) *Prescribed diseases and prescribed personal injuries*

Those who are covered against personal injury caused by accident 438 arising out of and in the course of employment are also covered against any prescribed disease or injury not so caused being due to the nature of that employment and developed after July 4, 1948. The Minister is empowered to prescribe a disease or injury in relation to insured persons if he is satisfied that it ought to be treated as a risk of their occupations and not as a risk common to all persons and if such that, in the absence of special circumstances, the attribution of particular cases to the nature of the employment can be established or presumed with reasonable certainty. The general rule that a person suffering a disease or injury is at liberty to claim that such disease or injury is a personal injury caused by accident arising out of and in the course of employment is modified by the provision that a claim in respect of a prescribed disease or injury must be brought under that head (s. 56 (1)). If the disease or injury results in incapacity for work but does not qualify as either a personal injury or a prescribed disease it may still qualify for sickness benefit (see para. 414).

A claimant for benefit (other than death benefit) under section 439 56 (1) must satisfy three conditions. (1) It must be shown that the claimant is suffering from a prescribed disease or injury (which includes its *sequelae* or effects). Apart from the special provision made for pneumoconiosis and byssinosis, certain diseases have been prescribed by regulations. (2) The claimant must at some time since July 4, 1948, have been in insurable employment in one of the occupations listed against the relevant disease. In the case of "glanders," for example, the corresponding entry is "contact with equine animals or their carcases." (3) The disease or injury must be attributable to the nature of the work in insurable employment. The apparent harshness of this requirement is lessened by section 57 (3), which, *inter alia*, permits of the inclusion in regulations adapting Parts II and III of the Act of provisions for the presuming of a prescribed disease or injury to be due, unless the contrary is proved, to the nature of the employment. The benefits are broadly the same as those claimable for personal injury caused by accident. There is, however, no provision similar to section 48 by virtue of which a declaration that an accident was an industrial accident may be obtained notwithstanding that no claim for benefit is made.

3. Benefits provided by the Act

The three separate and distinct benefits payable under the Act 440 are injury benefit, disablement benefit and death benefit. In the words of Lord Diplock—"Each kind of benefit is payable in respect of a different period. There is no overlapping. Each kind of benefit is the subject of a separate and distinct claim. The conditions of entitlement to each kind of benefit are different. All that is common to them is that successive rights to each of the three kinds of benefit may arise from the same 'accident' " (*Jones* v. *Secretary of State for Social Services* (1972) at p. 1008 of the report).

(1) *Injury benefit*

441 This is payable at the appropriate rate for each day during the "injury benefit period" on which the insured person is incapable of work as a result of the relevant injury. "Injury benefit period" means, in relation to any accident, the period of 156 days, excluding Sundays, beginning with the day of the accident (or, in the cases of prescribed disease, the "date of development" of such disease). This is the maximum period, and the injury benefit period may be shorter where the insured's incapacity for work ceases within the 156 days and he claims disablement benefit.

Like unemployment and sickness benefits, injury benefit cannot be claimed for the three "waiting days." Nor can benefit be paid for a single day since there must be a period of interruption of employment, *i.e.* any two days of interruption, whether consecutive or not, within a period of six consecutive days ignoring Sundays. Any two periods of interruption of employment separated by not more than thirteen weeks are linked together to form one period of interruption of employment.

Normally the recipient of injury benefit cannot obtain certain national insurance benefits, notably unemployment or sickness benefit, but he is entitled to any earnings-related supplement which he would have received had he been receiving flat-rate sickness benefit subject to having reckonable earnings of at least £450 in the relevant tax year (see para. 417).

(2) *Disablement benefit*

442 This is payable to an insured person if he or she suffers as the result of the relevant accident from loss of physical or mental faculty (which phrase includes disfigurement without actual loss of faculty). Unlike injury benefit it is paid irrespective of any loss of earning capacity so that a person who has not stayed off work at all may be able to make a successful claim. Disablement benefit is not available to an insured person until after the third day of the period of 156 days (ignoring Sundays) beginning with the day of the relevant accident, nor until after the last day (if any) of that period on which he is incapable of work as the result of the relevant accident. If a claim for disablement benefit is made before the end of that period and is not withdrawn before it is finally determined, then if on any day of that period not earlier than the making of the claim the claimant is not incapable of work, the fact that he is or may be so incapable on a subsequent day of the period is disregarded. In Case R(I) 14/63 it was said that "The broad general purpose of these sections . . . appears to be to provide injury benefit during those days in that 156 days counting from the accident on which the claimant is incapable, and to provide disablement benefit in respect of the remaining days after the accident when he suffers from a relevant loss of faculty. The statute does not however make any such simple provision." The following summary, taken from Decision C.S.1 7/61, may help:

> Injury benefit is payable for a maximum period of 156 days. The injury benefit period may be shorter in that it will end when incapacity for work ends before the expiry of the 156 days. Two qualifications to this statement may be made: **443**
>
> (i) If within the 156 days the claimant again becomes incapable of work by reason of the relevant accident, and no claim for disablement benefit has been made, the injury benefit period in that case is not determined at the end of the first period of incapacity—it ends until the last day of incapacity within the 156 days.
>
> (ii) A person may wish to claim disablement benefit as soon as possible after the incapacity ends and this he may do within the 156 days. If such a claim is made, the effect is to terminate the injury benefit period on the last day of incapacity. This rule is however subject to the further qualification that the premature ending of the injury benefit period in this way may be cancelled and the injury benefit period restored if the disablement benefit claim is withdrawn before it is finally determined.

The disablement must amount to not less than 1 per cent. if **444**
benefit is to be claimed. The assessment is made by a medical board which decides whether disablement has resulted from the jury and, if so, the extent of disablement expressed as a percentage according to, or by comparison with, a defined scale, *e.g.* loss of both hands ranks as 100 per cent., whilst loss of an index finger is given as 14 per cent. (over 20 per cent. the percentage is expressed to the nearest multiple of 10). Flexibility is achieved by the device of final and provisional assessments. A final assessment may be reviewed if there has later been an unforeseen aggravation of the results of the relevant injury. A disablement assessed at less than 20 per cent. confers a right to a disablement gratuity which is prima facie a lump sum; an assessment of 20 per cent. or more attracts a disablement pension. Basic benefits are not affected by

the payment of other national insurance benefits, *e.g.* unemployment or sickness benefits.

Disablement benefit may, in proper cases, be increased by increases in respect of special hardship, unemployability, constant attendance, exceptionally severe disablement and hospital treatment. Both injury benefit and disablement pension may be increased in respect of dependants. The National Insurance Act 1966 made two changes which affect the industrial injuries scheme. First, an earnings-related supplement may be paid with injury benefit in circumstances in which flat-rate sickness benefits would have been payable instead. Second, a new allowance payable with constant attendance allowance was introduced in cases of exceptionally severe disablement.

IV. Administration: National Insurance and Industrial Injuries

445 A notable feature of both the Insurance Act and the Industrial Injuries Act is that the process of settling claims and questions arising under the Acts has been taken away from the courts, unlike questions arising under workmen's compensation legislation. Speed, cheapness and informality were the criteria which it was felt ought to apply in disposing of claims and questions under the Insurance Acts, in contrast to the slower, more expensive and ritualised procedure of the ordinary courts, to which recourse may only be had for certain appeals on law (*viz.* from Minister's decisions), or for review (as opposed to appeal) of other decisions by means of the prerogative orders.

446 Claims and questions arising under the National Insurance Act 1965 fall into two groups. First, certain questions are determined by the Minister of Social Security, relating to contributions, reckonable earnings, classes of insured persons and the person to be treated as maintaining a child or the family in which a child is to be treated as included. The Minister may, before determining any question, appoint a person to hold an inquiry and report to him. He may refer a question of law to the High Court. There is a right of appeal to the High Court against a Minister's decision on a question of law.

Secondly, any question concerning the right to benefit (including disqualifications not exceeding six weeks for misconduct, etc., under section 22) is determined by an insurance officer, unless he refers the claim or question to a local tribunal. If he does not so refer a question, the insurance officer may decide in favour of the claimant *or* decide adversely to the claimant, but if a Minister's question is in his opinion raised he must refer it to the Minister. Where the insurance officer has decided any claim or question adversely to the claimant, either by disallowing a claim or by not allowing it in full, the claimant for benefit may appeal to the local tribunal, with the qualification that the consent of the chairman of that tribunal is required where a Minister's question has arisen and been determined in connection with the decision of the insurance officer, who has certified that the decision on that question is the sole ground of his decision. From a local tribunal, appeal lies to the National Insurance Commissioner at the suit of the insurance officer, the claimant or an association of employed persons, *e.g.* a trade union of which the claimant is, and was at the time when the question arose, a member. Decisions of an insurance officer, a local tribunal or a National Insurance Commissioner may be reviewed in certain circumstances by an insurance officer, or on a reference by him, by a local tribunal, *e.g.* for mistake or change of circumstances.

Questions arising under the industrial injuries scheme fall into **447**
two groups and are determined in accordance with the National Insurance (Industrial Injuries) Act 1965 (as amended by section 8 of the National Insurance Act 1966). First, there are "special questions," *viz.* Minister's questions, certain questions as to child or family, and disablement questions, of which the first and last are most important. The Minister decides whether a person is or was in insurable employment, contribution questions, whether an increase in disablement benefit is payable for constant attendance, and how certain limitations on benefits payable on death apply. As in the case of national insurance, provision is made for references and appeals to the High Court. Disablement questions involve the determination of the question whether a relevant accident has resulted in loss of faculty and, if so, how the extent of disablement and its duration are to be assessed. The decision on these questions is taken by a medical board with a possible appeal to a medical appeal tribunal. Disablement questions may, with the consent of the claimant, be referred to a single medical practitioner, appointed by the Minister, from whom any appeal will lie to the medical appeal tribunal. In either event, appeal lies from a medical appeal tribunal on law to the National Insurance Commissioner at the instance of the claimant, an association of employed persons of which the claimant was a member at the time of the relevant accident, or of the Minister, but the leave of the medical appeal tribunal or the Commissioner is necessary for such appeal.

Secondly, there are "other questions" of which the most im- **448**
portant are those concerning claims for benefit. A measure of uniformity is introduced by section 8 of the 1966 Act which

assimilates with modifications the administration of such claims for benefit to the administration of national insurance benefit claims (see above). One difference which survives is the provision in the National Insurance (Industrial Injuries) Act whereby a person may obtain a declaration that an accident is an industrial accident without necessarily claiming benefit.

Chapter 7

THE COLLECTIVE ORGANISATION OF WORKERS AND EMPLOYERS

One of the legacies of the Industrial Revolution is the increasing **449** size of the business unit, a phenomenon largely explicable by the growth of the capital market (itself a product of the limited liability company) and by the desire for those economies which attend, or are supposed to attend, large-scale production. Since the Second World War we have witnessed the growth of multi-national companies and the growth of large markets such as that provided under the Treaty of Rome. The nineteenth-century proprietor-capitalist has been largely replaced by huge corporations and conglomerates managed, not by owners, but by the new breed of meritocrats produced by the so-called managerial revolution. British policy has been to encourage the growth of business units able to survive in modern conditions whilst still preserving the virtues of genuine competition. Competition does not, however, prevent employers from joining employers' associations in order to promote or defend certain of their joint interests.

On labour's side, trade unions have grown to match the size of **450** employers and their associations, although one of the features of recent years has been the tendency to replace monolithic national or industry-wide bargaining with plant bargaining (a development which is discussed in Chapter 8). The chief characteristics of British trade unions, apart from their structural features (discussed below), are (i) their defensive and oppositional role (defending the interests of their members by meanings of oppositional bargaining across the table); (ii) their preference for a system of bargaining unregulated by law and free of state intervention; and (iii) their "voluntary" nature as unincorporated associations, rather like the old ladies' tea-club to which the Webbs referred.

One of the general principles upon which the 1971 Act is based is that of "free association of workers in independent trade unions . . . so organised as to be representative, responsible and effective bodies for regulating relations between employers and workers." The freedom not to associate, the internal regulation of domestic affairs and the need for "responsibility" and public accountability are seen by trade unionists as part of an attack on free trade unions which has led the movement, with some exceptions, to have no truck with the Act or its institutions, and in particular with registration under the

Act and the unpopular Industrial Court (shunned except for purposes of legitimate self-defence).

The doctrine of restraint of trade

451 To the extent that they inhibit a member's freedom to contract with whomsoever he wishes and upon such terms as he can secure, trade unions were regarded as being in restraint of trade. Indeed, in the nineteenth century, the courts seem to have felt that any examination of the degree of restraint imposed on members was superfluous on the basis that "unions of whatever sort are in their nature contrary to public policy, and . . . their object in itself will vitiate every association and every transaction into which they enter" (Frederic Harrison in *Beehive*, January 26, 1867). Such an assumption entailed severe consequences for unions which were considered to be criminal, and later, civil, conspiracies, and, as such, disentitled to the assistance of the courts in the enforcement of their rules. This is shown in *Hornby* v. *Close* (1867), where one of the reasons for refusing relief to the plaintiff (who had taken proceedings against a branch treasurer for wrongfully withholding the sum of £24) was that the society had purposes which were in restraint of trade and therefore illegal for civil purposes.

452 Early in the twentieth century, the courts resiled somewhat from their view of unions as, so to speak, legal pariahs. Cozens-Hardy M.R., in *Gozney* v. *Bristol and Trade Provident Society* (1909), warned against the common mistake of supposing that every trade union was an unlawful combination at common law and allowed a claim against a registered trade union with objects which showed that it was "really a mutual insurance society" (see also *Swaine* v. *Wilson* (1889)). In two leading cases, *Russell* v. *Amalgamated Society of Carpenters and Joiners* (1912), and *Osborne* v. *A.S.R.S.* (1911), the unions concerned were held to be unlawful and lawful respectively. It is, therefore, open to the courts to examine the objects and rules of a union in order to evaluate the degree of interference with a member's freedom of trade, so that, for example, a distinction might be drawn between the power to *sanction* a strike and the power to *order* a strike. Even so, and notwithstanding the views of Cozens-Hardy M.R. in the *Gozney* case (above) that objects free of the taint of illegality might be advanced by rules unlawful as being in restraint of trade and that severance might take place between rules lawful and unlawful in this respect, it would appear that few unions will come through an examination unscathed. The courts seem to be reluctant to sever illegal rules on the scale used in contracts generally.

453 The Trade Union Act of 1871 freed trade unions from the

stigma of criminality (which had, according to some writers, survived the repeal of the Combination Acts in 1824) and also from the stigma of civil illegality. The old definition of a trade union in that Act had been framed explicitly on the assumption that, as the law then stood, unions generally, although perhaps not universally, acted in restraint of trade. To correct a situation in which a union had to prove its illegality from the standpoint of restraint of trade in order to register, the Trade Union Act of 1876 enlarged the definition to include trade unions lawful at common law in that respect, a definition which, as enlarged, the Donovan Commission were unwilling to overthrow, on the grounds that unions would probably prefer that definition to be retained as a precaution. Trade union fears on this score were not unfounded, as the *Edwards* case (discussed at para. 471, below) shows. Dealing with an automatic forfeiture of membership rule, Sachs L.J. asked in rhetorical fashion if such a rule could be valid in the light of, *inter alia*, the doctrine of restraint of trade. Whatever the merits of that case, it cannot but be a matter for surprise that a union rule should be struck down in 1970 by a doctrine which most lawyers and trade unionists considered had received its quietus in its application to unions by the Acts of 1871 and 1876. As *Fair Deal at Work* points out—"Rules can lay down provision for methods of working, people with whom members may or may not work, limitations on output, restrictions on number of apprentices, age limits, and so on." Problems of this sort are probably better handled, if they are to be handled at all, by some specialist body akin to the Restrictive Trade Practices Court. The Industrial Relations Act 1971 makes some tenative efforts in that direction, as we shall presently see.

Section 135 of the 1971 Act takes restraint of trade out of the **454**
definition of organisations of workers (and organisations of employers) and provides separately that—

> "The purposes of any trade union or other organisation of workers, of any employers' association or other organisation of employers or of any body to which section 35 of this Act applies (*voluntary joint negotiating bodies*) shall not, by reason only that they are in restraint of trade, be unlawful, so as—
>
> (a) to make any member of the organisation or body liable to criminal proceedings for conspiracy or otherwise, or
>
> (b) to make any agreement or trust void or voidable" (italics supplied).

I. ORGANISATION OF WORKERS

The old definition of "trade union" has gone with the trade union **455**
acts repealed by the 1971 Act which now vouchsafes to us a new

creature bearing the unfamiliar name of "organisation of workers." This is defined as an organisation, whether permanent or temporary, which either (a) consists wholly or mainly of workers of one or more descriptions and is an organisation whose principal objects include the regulation of relations between workers of that description or those descriptions and employers or organisations, or (b) is a federation of workers' organisations. The familiar term "trade union" is now reserved for an organisation of workers which is for the time being registered as a trade union, although one ventures to doubt whether these nuances of statutory meaning will ever pass into popular parlance.

456 Rather surprisingly, the new definition retains temporary combinations which, presumably, must have some regular structural form if they are to rank as *organisations*, a term which seems inapt to include any amorphous workgroup with an ephemeral complaint. In two respects the new definition differs from the old. First, the organisation must consist wholly or mainly of workers. Formerly, the nature of the membership was irrelevant—"The test of a trade union . . . is its objects, not its personnel," as Lord Hanworth M.R. put it in *Hardie and Lane Ltd.* v. *Chilton* (1928), which explains why employers' associations were capable of ranking as trade unions under the old dispensation. Secondly, if the principal objects include the regulation of relations between workers and employers, the organisation will qualify as an organisation of workers, in contrast to the old definition, which also included the regulation of relations between workmen and workmen, or between masters and masters, quite apart from the object of imposing restrictive conditions on the conduct of any trade or business. A committee of shop stewards may have organisation and may consist wholly or mainly of workers but fail to qualify as an "organisation of workers" if it does not exist to regulate employer–employee relationships. Such was the case in *Midland Cold Storage* v. *Turner* (1972), where the joint stewards' committee in the docks, which fulfilled the first two requirements as to organisation and composition, did not qualify as an organisation of workers in that it did not seek to bargain with employers, being purely an "influential pressure group" which recommended the taking or abandonment of industrial action in the London Docks.

457 The genus "organisation of workers" includes the species "federation of workers' organisations," the latter being an organisation, whether permanent or temporary, whose membership consists wholly or mainly (a) of constituent or affiliated organisations, each of which either fulfils the conditions specified in para. 455, or is an organisation for the time being entered in the special register (see para. 478), or consists wholly or mainly of constituent or affiliated organisations which fulfil the conditions referred to above, or are for the time being entered in the special register, or (b) of representatives of such constituent or affiliated organisations as are referred to in (a), and which in either case is an organisation whose principal objects include the regulation of relations between workers and employers (or the latter's organisations), or include the regulation of relations between its constituent or affiliated organisations.

II. The Guiding Principles

Under the old law unions had considerable freedom both in writing 458
and interpreting their own rules, and in conducting their own internal affairs. If, as was customary, a union chose to register, it merely had to comply with the very modest requirements of the old Acts. Whether registered or not, it had (and still has) to comply with the rules concerning the political fund set out in the 1913 Act (see para. 490, below). Section 4 of the Trade Union Act 1871, which stated that certain agreements between members were to be unenforceable, had been expressly designed to put the internal affairs of unions beyond the reach of judicial surveillance. Notwithstanding that section, it occasions no surprise that the common law, with its individualistic emphasis, contrived to erect a complicated edifice of law, both substantive and procedural, which limited the notion of complete union autonomy in domestic matters. First, the rule book was seen as a contract of association to which all, including the union, were bound. Second, in interpreting its rules and in exercising discretion under the rules, the union, or body to which the union had delegated its powers, must act fairly or, as it is said, in accordance with the precepts of natural justice. At first those precepts were applied to proceedings which imported some adjudicatory-type procedure, but later the duty to act fairly was extended to the exercise of discretion involving nothing in the nature of adjudication. Thus, the approval of a shop steward by a district committee was held in *Breen* v. *Amalgamated Engineering Union* (1971), to import the requirement of fairness, although the Court of Appeal's decision in that case (Lord Denning M.R. dissenting), upholding the district committee's refusal of approval, has rightly attracted criticism. In the *Breen* case, Lord Denning M.R. again re-stated his view that the contractualist approach to union rules does not reflect the true position, *viz.* that the rules are something more than a contract, being a legislative code to bind members, and as such subject to judicial control like the rules made by statutory bodies.

459 The 1971 Act attempts to put into procrustean form the guiding principles incumbent upon all organisations of workers (federation of workers' organisations excepted) whether or not they are registered. Those guiding principles have a particular significance for organisations of workers which wish to register, and for members of such organisations who wish to complain of unfair industrial practices involving breaches of those principles, apart from complaints concerning breaches of rules. If, as seems likely, it was intended that henceforth cases concerning trade union affairs should go to the agencies instituted or used by the 1971 Act rather than to the "ordinary" courts, it is doubted if this intention will be realised in practice, inasmuch as there would appear to be no section which abrogates or modifies the jurisdiction of the ordinary courts to determine cases concerning the contract of association. Whether or not cases of unlawful expulsion or improper disciplining will come before the ordinary courts remains to be seen. Much depends upon the attitude of the latter.

In pursuance of *Fair Deal at Work*, which had rejected the "absurd thesis" that trade unions and employers' associations should be treated in law rather like private clubs (something which should be "buried for good"), it is now required of all organisations of workers, other than federations of workers' organisations, that they must conduct their affairs in accordance with the following principles.

1. Admission

460 Any applicant for membership of the organisation who is a worker of the description covered by its rules, and who is appropriately qualified for employment as a worker of that description, must not be excluded from membership by way of arbitrary or unreasonable discrimination. Writing in 1894, the Webbs found that little use was made in practice of what they termed "The Device of Restriction of Numbers," a finding which has been more recently confirmed by others, including the Donovan Commission. Nevertheless cases do occasionally come to light, such as *Nagle* v. *Fielden* (1966), a case which concerned the exclusion of a female trainer from membership of the Jockey Club and which led Lord Denning M.R. to say that—"The common law of England has for centuries recognised that a man has a right to work at his trade or profession without being unjustly excluded from it. He is not to be shut out from it at the whim of those having the governance of it" (at p. 644 of the report). The primacy of the rules was however upheld in *Faramus* v. *Film Artistes Association* (1964), in which the House of Lords decided that the appellant's admission to the association was

of no effect under the rules of the association which rendered ineligible anyone convicted of a criminal offence, other than a motoring offence not punishable by imprisonment, an exclusion which applied to the appellant who had been convicted of "joy-riding" when he was seventeen and who was on that account disqualified. However much one may condemn the association's passion for legal *punctilio*, it might well be that the association, which was (and is) haunted by the spectre of oversupply, would now succeed in showing that its limitation of numbers is not "*unreasonable* discrimination."

2. Termination of membership

Every member has the right, on giving reasonable notice and **461** complying with reasonable conditions, to terminate his membership of the organisation at any time.

3. Membership rights

No member of the organisation may be excluded by way of **462** arbitrary or unreasonable discrimination from any of the following:

(i) Candidature for, or the holding of, any office in the organisation or a branch or section thereof. *Leigh* v. *National Union of Railwaymen* (1970) was a pre-Act case in which an interim injunction was granted to restrain the election of a president of the union, from which election, the plaintiff, as a Communist, had been excluded, Goff J. finding in the rules no express exclusion of Communists and declining to imply a term therein to that effect. If there were such an express exclusion of Communists (or Catholics or coloured persons) would it constitute arbitrary or unreasonable discrimination? Presumably each of these exclusions would have to be considered on its merits.

(ii) Nominating candidates for office.

(iii) Voting in any election for any office in the organisation or in any ballot of membership.

(iv) Attending and taking part in meetings of the organisation or of any branch or section thereof. An order requiring the defendant union to permit the plaintiff to attend branch meetings was made in *Goad* v. *Amalgamated Union of Engineering Workers* (1972), together with a declaration that the latter had been arbitrarily and unreasonably excluded from attendance at branch meetings, but since the defendant union had boycotted the proceedings of the Industrial Court, and earlier proceedings before an industrial tribunal (which had held that Goad was a member of the union), the value of the case as a precedent is somewhat doubtful as it tells us nothing as to the reasonableness or unreasonableness of the defendant's conduct.

4. Secrecy of the ballot

463 One of the defects of the old law lay in the impotence of the Registrar of Friendly Societies in connection with electoral irregularities in unions, a defect which drove complainants to fall back on either the rule-book (to the extent which this might regulate elections, if it did so at all) or the law of tort. In the E.T.U. "ballot-rigging" case of *Byrne & Chapple* v. *Foulkes, Haxell et al.* (1962), the complainants invoked successfully the tort of conspiracy in a trial which lasted forty-two days and cost some £80,000, quite apart from human "wear and tear." It causes little wonder that the Donovan Commission was led to conclude that what was needed was some "less difficult and less expensive method of redress." This is now provided by the requirement that the ballot shall be secret, with the further requirement that the member must have a fair and reasonable opportunity of voting on any motion in any ballot without interference or constraint.

5. Disciplinary action

464 No member of the organisation shall be subjected by or on behalf of the organisation to any unfair or unreasonable disciplinary action. In particular, no disciplinary action shall be taken against any member of the organisation by reason of his refusing or failing (a) to participate in any action which would be an unfair industrial action on *his* part (*e.g.* to join in a strike aimed at securing the dismissal of a non-unionist), or (b) to participate in a strike which his organisation, or any other person, has called, organised, procured or financed, otherwise than in contemplation or furtherance of an industrial dispute in circumstances constituting an unfair industrial practice on the part of that organisation or that other person, or (c) to participate in irregular industrial action short of a strike, organised, procured or financed by his organisation or other person. The rules stated above, meet the criticism made of the old law by *Justice* in its evidence to the Donovan Commission when it testified that "The law, as developed, to some extent protects the member against oppressive action by the organs of the unions which apply the rule, but it does very little to protect the member against the oppressive effect of the rules themselves." By bestowing upon the member the right to dissociate himself from certain actions of his union, the Act in this respect has been criticised by trade unionists for providing a "blacklegs' charter" aimed at dissolving the fraternal

bonds of solidarity which bind those who embark on industrial action. Be that as it may, the punishment must now be proportioned to the crime, whatever the rules may say.

6. Natural justice

Except in respect of non-payment of any contribution which under the rules he is required to pay, no member of the organisation may be subjected to any disciplinary action by or on behalf of the organisation unless— **465**

(i) he has had written notice of the charges brought against him and has been given a reasonable time to prepare his defence;
(ii) he is afforded a full and fair hearing;
(iii) a written statement of the findings resulting from the hearing is given to him; and
(iv) where under the rules of the organisation he has a right of appeal, his appeal has been heard or the time for appealing has expired without his having exercised that right.

A person's membership of the organisation must not be terminated except by reasonable notice and the reason must be given to him.

The hitherto opaque rules of natural justice are now objectified **466** in statutory form and provide a legal peg on which a member of an organisation can now hang his claim. The statutory rules will still require clarification for which it is likely that in the future recourse will be had to common law decisions, taking account of the general principles upon which the 1971 Act is posited. An illustration of rule (i) is furnished by *Lawlor* v. *Union of Post Office Workers* (1965), in which the plaintiff's expulsion from the union was held to be void because, *inter alia*, he had not received proper notice of the charges to be made against him. In this respect, it has been held that an invitation to a meeting to discuss a particular matter is not notice of a charge, notwithstanding that the member may have surmised correctly the purpose of the meeting (*Abbott* v. *Sullivan* (1952)).

The "full and fair hearing" required by rule (ii) has caused no **467** little difficulty. It is clear that the member must have a chance to put his case (*audi alteram partem—lit.* hear the other side) before a fair and impartial body (*nemo iudex in sua causa potest*—no one can be judge in his own cause) but cannot insist on all of the formalistic trappings of a court of justice. The degree of formalism will clearly vary with the nature of the case (*e.g.* whether it involves an adjudicatory-type proceeding, or the exercise of administrative discretion—see the *Breen* case, above) and the seriousness of its subject-matter. In the case of *Local Government Board* v. *Arlidge* (1915), Viscount Haldane L.C. indicated that there was no invariable right to an *oral* hearing, but that statement must now be read subject to Lord Denning's dictum in *Pett* v. *Greyhound Racing Association Ltd.* (1968), at p. 549 of the report, to the effect that in matters affecting a man's livelihood, or any matters of serious import, that man may speak by his own mouth. His lordship's further statement that, "He has also a right to speak by counsel or solicitor" did not commend itself to Lyell J. in the sequel to that case (1969), who came down on the side of informality and who would have reserved legal representation for those bodies which have reached "some degree of sophistication" in their affairs. Ideally, a full and fair hearing requires that strict impartiality of mind which one associates with the British judiciary, but for domestic bodies such as trade unions it is too much to ask, in Bowen L.J.'s words, for the "icy impartiality of a Rhadamanthus," a view which finds support in the pragmatic decision in *MacClean* v. *The Workers Union* (1929), where the expulsion of a member by the executive committee of the union, after a hearing before the latter, was held not to be vitiated by the fact that certain members of the committee had been involved in a long-standing dispute with the member, thus casting it in the role of "prosecutor"; the member's case, it was held, had been properly considered and the committee had come to an honest conclusion.

468 Admittedly, the *MacClean* decision can be rested on the contractual provision in the rules for expulsion by a defined body, but it is submitted that the statutory requirement of a full and fair hearing does not require that the hearing must be entrusted to some independent arbitral body outside the union: if it does, the rule ignores the strong feelings of corporate solidarity which animate trade unionists. A disagreement on policy between a member and a disciplinary body is one thing, but bias, malice and bad faith on the part of the latter is another thing altogether, and such elements would go to vitiate a decision in which they are found to be present. A failure of natural justice is not cured by the observance of the rules of natural justice at some later appellate stage as provided for by the rules (*Leary* v. *National Union of Vehicle Builders* (1971), where the participation of an outsider in the committee's deliberations and decision was held to constitute a further ground for avoiding the decision to expel).

Subject to what is said below (para. 471), a rule which purports to cause automatic punishment for breach of rules, or which purports to confer an unfettered discretion (the meaning of which and the application of which is reserved to the union or its committee), can no longer prevail against the new statutory rules. Even before the Act, decisions, such as *Radford* v. *National Society of Operative Printers, Graphical and Media Personnel* (1972), show that the courts were not averse to striking down union rules inimical to natural justice. In the *Radford* case, Plowman J. expressed the opinion that a rule providing for automatic forfeiture of membership would be *ultra vires* and void, but went on to find that the rules in the case before him imported some form of adjudication and *ergo* natural justice, for want of which the plaintiff's expulsion was held to be illegal and void.

The requirement in (iii), above, that a written statement of **469**
findings be given to the member, is novel and evocative of the similar innovation in relation to administrative tribunals, an innovation which facilitated easier review by the superior courts for error of law on the face of the record.

Requirement (iv) postpones the imposition of disciplinary **470**
sanctions upon a member until he has exhausted any right of appeal, or the time for any such appeal has expired. It is not unusual to find provision in union rules for some form of appeal against the imposition of sanction to some higher body within the union hierarchy, such as the executive committee, or to the annual conference itself (or a committee thereof). Notwithstanding *White* v. *Kuzych* (1951), several cases have since acknowledged that in proper circumstances a member may have redress from the courts without necessarily exhausting internal appeals machinery within the union, and this even where the rule is couched in *Scott* v. *Avery* (1856) form making recourse to the union's machinery a condition precedent to application to the courts. Redress is now, in any event, secured by the 1971 Act (see para. 472, below).

It will have been noted that disciplinary sanctions cannot be imposed unless requirements (i) to (iv), inclusive, are met, but that those requirements do not apply to the disciplining of a member for non-payment of any contribution which, under the rules, he is required to pay (discussed below).

A member whose membership is terminated is, as we have seen, entitled to receive reasonable notice and the reason for the termination.

It is not uncommon to find in union rules provision for "auto- **471**
matic cesser" of membership for non-payment of subscriptions. Unions usually make their own arrangement for the collection of dues so as to have, amongst other things, some minimal contact with members, but some unions have agreed to the "check-off" system under which the employer deducts dues from the member's wages, paying the dues so collected to the union. The arbitrary nature of an automatic forfeiture rule, and its still more arbitrary application by

a union, came in for censure from the Court of Appeal in *Edwards* v. *Society of Graphical and Allied Trades* (1971), a case unlikely to find its place in that select body of cases which make up the trade union martyrolatry. There, the plaintiff had been deprived of his temporary membership of the union under a rule providing for automatic forfeiture of membership for non-payment of dues. The irony of the situation lay in the fact that the plaintiff (who was coloured) had in truth authorised a "check-off," but owing to an oversight by his union official the authorisation had not been forwarded to the plaintiff's employers. Compounding its mistake, the union refused to re-admit the plaintiff in contrast to other members who had suffered from the same error, and indeed, the plaintiff was later dismissed because his workmates had threatened a strike because of his continued employment as a non-unionist! The Court of Appeal held the rule in question to be invalid because it was repugnant to natural justice and in restraint of trade. Statutory confirmation of the principle in the *Edwards* case, so far as it relates to natural justice, is now contained in the 1971 Act which prohibits "unfair and unreasonable disciplinary action." There is no need to go through the statutory ritual to ensure natural justice, described above, in cases of disciplinary measures arising from non-payment of a contribution required by the union rules, but unions relying upon "automatic cesser" of membership rules for non-payment of dues, are now subject to the requirement of reasonable notice and reasons, to which extent forfeiture of membership is something less than "automatic."

Access to the courts

472 No restriction, whether by the rules of an organisation or otherwise, may be placed on a member of that organisation in respect of his instituting, prosecuting or defending proceedings before any court or tribunal, or giving evidence in any such proceedings. Several cases bear witness to the sensitivity of unions when their members take part in legal proceedings, particularly where those proceedings seek to question the constitutionality of union behaviour in some matter. Such members are disciplined either under some rule forbidding participation in legal proceedings, or, more commonly, under some vaguely-worded rule such as those forbidding "conduct prejudicial to the interests of the association." "Schisms are not confined to religious bodies," philosophised Fletcher Moulton L.J. in *Osborne* v. *Amalgamated Society of Railway Servants* (1911), at p. 560 of the report, where, it will be remembered, Osborne was expelled from his union for his temerity in taking his complaint to the courts. The most recent example is *Radford* v. *National Society*

of Operative Printers, Graphical and Media Personnel (1972), in which the plaintiff had been expelled for "action taken against the union" in putting his claim to a redundancy payment in the hands of a solicitor contrary to a redundancy agreement between his employer and his union. Plowman J. in that case declined to infer from the plaintiff's refusal to disclose to the union his dealings with the solicitor any breach of rule. The right of redress to the courts is now reinforced by statute.

In the past, the courts undeterred by section 4 of the now-repealed Trade Union Act 1871, have granted relief to individual union members anxious to keep their unions on the paths of constitutional rectitude. Injunctions have been given to restrain the disbursement of strike pay *contra* union rules (*Yorkshire Miners' Association* v. *Howden* (1905)), to prevent a union from raising members' subscriptions (*Edwards* v. *Halliwell* (1950)) and, more recently, to prevent the executive council of a union from instructing delegates to a T.U.C. Conference to vote in favour of Britain joining the Common Market against the wishes of the union conference to which policy was confided by the union's rules (*Hodgson* v. *N.A.L.G.O.* (1972)). **473**

There are two limitations to temper the zeal of members with crusading inclinations. First, it should be remembered that the remedies of injunction and declaration (the remedies most likely to be invoked), are discretionary in nature. In *McNamee* v. *Cooper* (1966), Goff J. took a narrow view of the individual rights which a member could enforce in this connection, limiting them to rights concerning property and voting, and declining to grant an injunction to restrain a member's union delegation from voting in favour of a governmental incomes policy at a T.U.C. Conference. The second limitation is the Rule in *Foss* v. *Harbottle* (1843), according to which the proper plaintiff in an action concerning a wrong to a company or association is prima facie the company or association itself, with the corollary that if the wrong is one which can be ratified by a simple majority, no individual member may maintain an action in respect of that wrong. To yield to the member's request would render the court's decision an empty threat, in the event of ratification by a simple majority, quite apart from occasioning a multiplicity of suits at the instigation of what one judge termed the "cantankerous member." The court will, however, intervene if an act is *ultra vires* the company or association, a fraud on the minority, or an infringement of "individual corporate rights." In the *Hodgson* case (above), Goulding J. considered that the Rule in *Foss* v. *Harbottle* did not apply to an unregistered trade union, but that if it did apply it was no bar to the granting of urgent relief, in which connection **474** his lordship did not take the narrow view of individual rights taken by Goff J. in the *McNamee* case (above). The Rule is therefore an impediment to the individual member of a registered trade union, which is now necessarily a corporate body (see para. 479, below), but, if Goulding J.'s view prevails, no impediment to the member of an unregistered trade union. Since most unions have preferred to remain unregistered, the rights of individual members are to that extent enlarged in the present connection.

475 The "guiding principles" discussed above fulfil a three-fold function. (1) An organisation of workers, or a person acting on its behalf, commits an unfair industrial practice if it, or he, takes, or threatens to take, any action against any member of the organisation or other person in contravention of the guiding principles. (2) The principles play a critical part in the registration process, admitted by the Secretary of State to be the "heart of the Act." (3) Once registered as a trade union (other than a federation of workers' organisations), a member thereof is given the right to apply to the Registrar to complain of action taken by his union which constitutes an unfair industrial practice within (1), above, or which, with two exceptions, constitutes a breach of the trade union's rules. Moreover, the Registrar himself may initiate an investigation into trade union action alleged to constitute a contravention of the guiding principles or a serious breach of rules.

III. Registration

476 An independent organisation of workers having power to alter its rules and to control its property and funds without the concurrence of a parent organisation is eligible to register as a trade union. Company-dominated unions run counter to ILO Convention No. 98, and have created problems, not only in the United States (where such unions are a form of unfair employer practice under section 9 of the National Labor Relations Act 1935), but also in this country (as the reports of the Cameron Inquiry and the Donovan Commission reveal). It has already been alleged that some of the organisations which have registered under the 1971 Act are not "independent." If unions were minded to register (as few are at the time of writing), those with federal structures would encounter some problems. Under the old law, some unions had branches which were registered as separate trade unions. Under the new dispensation such branches are not eligible for registration unless they possess the autonomy required under the 1971 Act. A further difficulty is that a federation of workers' organisations cannot register, even though it is independent and autonomous, unless all of its constituent or affiliated organisations are either trade unions (in the technical sense) or organisations entered on the special register (para. 478, below).

Application for registration is made to the Registrar and must be accompanied by, *inter alia*, a copy of the rules and a list of officers. If the necessary formalities have been complied with, and the Registrar is satisfied that the body making the application is an organisation of workers and that it is eligible for registration as a trade union, he is bound to register it as a trade union and to issue to it a certificate of registration. The certificate of registration will specify whether the organisation is registered as a federation of workers' organisations or as an organisation of workers *simpliciter*, and will give the name of the organisation.

Types of registers

The Act provides for three registers: the permanent register (which deals with registration under the Act), the provisional register and the special register. The provisional register was used in order to prevent a hiatus between the lapse of registrations under the old Acts and the registration of organisations under the 1971 Act, and to enable the Registrar to "screen" the rules of such organisations before entering them in the permanent register. In fact, most unions registered under the old Acts have preferred to become unregistered under the new Act where their rules so permit; some of those not so permitted have called rules revision conferences in order to permit of de-registration. Provisional registration is not registration for the purposes of the Act, except for certain important provisions, such as those concerning trade union rights under section 5 and the unfair industrial practices in sections 96 to 98. 477

The special register deals with professional bodies which are not otherwise eligible to register under the Act. Provided it fulfils certain requirements, a corporate body registered before August 5, 1971, or incorporated by Charter or Letters Patent before or after that date, may apply for entry in the special register where its activities *include* the regulation of relations between workers and employers. Several corporate bodies with objects other than those required of trade unions, *e.g.* professional associations, have come, in the course of time, to extend their activities to include collective bargaining. In its original form, the Industrial Relations Bill would have excluded such bodies, both because they were corporate bodies (see section 157 (1) of the Act), and because they did not have principal objects which included the regulation of relations between workers and employers. As the result of an amendment to the Bill, such bodies may be registered in the special register, provided they 478 possess the requisite autonomy. Once registered, they are treated broadly as trade unions, except for certain administrative provisions, such as accounts and audit, for which in any case provision is made by companies' legislation or, possibly, the instrument of incorporation.

Entry in the permanent register is registration for the purposes of the Act and attracts the magical name of "trade union." Pursuant to the T.U.C. "instruction" to affiliated unions, the great majority of unions have resisted the magic and have chosen to de-register or remain unregistered.

The consequences of registration

(1) *Incorporation*

479 On receiving its certificate of registration an organisation of workers becomes a body corporate having perpetual succession and a corporate seal. So ends 100 years of speculation concerning the status of that legal conundrum—the registered trade union—termed with varying degrees of obfuscation "a *persona juridica* not previously known to the law," a "creature of statute," a "quasi-corporation" and a "*tertium quid*" which is "something"! It was because of such doubts that the Donovan Commission urged corporate status for *all* unions with a concomitant obligation to register, but the Industrial Relations Bill of the Labour Government in 1970, following its White Paper *In Place of Strife* (Cmnd. 3888), opted for unincorporate status, showing that second thoughts had prevailed. The effect of incorporation is to vest all property and funds for the time being held in trust for the organisation in the organisation itself without need of further assurance, and to transfer any liability or obligation of a trustee as such for the organisation to the organisation itself. The registered trade union therefore enters the jurisprudential stage as a new category of corporate body having separate legal personality and competent to hold and dispose of property, to sue and be sued, to enter contracts and to commit crimes, torts and breaches of trust.

480 The shades of the historic case of *Taff Vale Railway* v. *Amalgamated Society of Railway Servants* (1901) still hang heavily over the modern union, registered and unregistered. What had angered trade unionists generally was the fact that the damages of £23,000 and total expenses of £42,000, which the union in that case had to pay, came from funds used to provide mutual benefits to members. One of the recommendations of the Dunedin Commission, set up after *Taff Vale* (and boycotted by trade unions for its legal composition), suggested a division of funds as between those used for industrial action and those used for mutual benefits. In the event,

the 1906 Act mollified the trade unions by conferring upon them complete immunity in tort. Since then, the mutual insurance role of trade unions has to some extent been overtaken by the Welfare State, although that insurance role (including the provision of legal advice) remains important. The 1971 Act is "intended to protect non-militant funds from compensation claims" (H.L. Deb., Vol. 319, col. 1000), which it does by preventing the recovery of compensation, damages, costs or expenses from any fund which, under the rules of the organisation, cannot be used for the financing of strikes, lock-outs, or other industrial action. The immunity of such a fund is bestowed upon all organisations of workers (and organisations of employers), whether registered or not. The Dunedin idea (mooted under a Conservative Government) has come to roost under another Conservative Government over sixty-six years later.

Organisations entered in the special register apart, the new **481**
registered organisations, whether of workers or of employers, are ineligible for registration under the Companies Act 1948, and other Acts regulating friendly societies or individual and provident society. Admittedly, there *is* some legal regulation of trade unions in the 1971 Act affecting rules, finance, publicity and disclosure, but this hardly amounts to a comprehensive legal régime comparable to that regulating registered companies. A host of questions, such as the rights of corporators (particularly minority rights), the application of the *ultra vires* doctrine, and the circumstances in which the "veil of incorporation" will be lifted, remain to be clarified. It is significant that in New Zealand the granting of corporate status to industrial unions has tended to draw those unions more and more within the fold of a legal régime analogous to that applicable to companies.

It is convenient to interject at this stage that the unregistered organisation, like its pre-1971 forebear, would at first sight appear to be basically an unincorporated association. That forebear laboured under difficulties, both substantive and procedural. It could not, for example, own, dispose of, or receive property, or be privy to a contract. Its procedural near-impotence precluded it from bringing or defending actions in its own name; an impotence from which the clumsy device of the "representative action" gave only uncertain relief (see *Barker* v. *Allanson* (1937)).

Section 154 of the 1971 Act is an important innovation. It **482**
makes a compromise with pure principle to the extent that it permits any civil proceedings (including proceedings under the 1971 Act) to be brought by and against the unregistered organisation in its own name, and, subject to the protection of property used for non-militant purposes, permits of the enforcement of judgments, orders

and awards in respect of such proceedings (including punishment for contempt) against any property belong to, or held in trust for, the organisation as though it were a body corporate.

It is now clear that the unregistered organisation possesses quasi-corporate attributes to a much more marked degree than the pre-1971 registered union, the quasi-corporate status of which cannot be regarded as having been settled by the conflicting opinions given in *Bonsor* v. *Musicians' Union* (1956). Indeed, the cases have gone further and indicate that in relation to unfair industrial practices the primary method of redress is against the organisation, rather than individuals, or inchoate bodies, such as committees of shop stewards. It was this *tabula in naufragio* which enabled the Industrial Court to free the five dockers in 1972. In *Heatons Transport* (*St. Helens*) *Ltd.* v. *Transport and General Workers' Union* (1973), the unregistered organisation of workers was held to be vicariously liable for the unfair industrial practices of its members committed within the scope of their implied authority. The criminal liability of unions is discussed at para. 171, above. *Heatons*' case is discussed further at paras. 613, 614, below.

(2) *Advantages*

483 Underlying the Act is the theme that organisations which are not prepared to accept the responsibilities of registration ought not to enjoy the advantages which registration brings. Since most unions have complied with the T.U.C. "instruction" of 1971 not to register, few unions, the professional associations excepted, have therefore necessarily experienced either the responsibilities or the advantages attendant upon registration. The advantages of registration are as follows.

484 Only a registered union may be party to an agency shop agreement, an approved closed shop agreement, or an application for that "compulsory contract," as it has been labelled—the enforced procedure agreement. It alone can enjoy certain benefits connected with collective bargaining, such as the status of sole bargaining agent, the right to information from an employer for the purposes of collective bargaining, and the right to set in train section 8 of the Terms and Conditions of Employment Act 1959, as amended. It alone may invoke those provisions which deal with the unfair industrial practices arising out of agency shop agreements and collective bargaining (see also sections 125, 126). The "trade union" is given special protection in relation to the unfair industrial practices in section 96 (inducing breach of contract) and section 97 (3) (supportive action). If the union is liable to pay compensation for unfair industrial practices, section 117 places a "ceiling" according to the size of the union on the amount of compensation which it will have to pay. Trade union officials are protected from liability in connection with inducing breach of contract (s. 96 (1)), awards or orders of the Industrial Court (s. 101 (4)), "cooling-off" orders and ballot procedures (see ss. 139 (3), 143 (6)). More than once during the hot summer of 1972 judges were reported to have exclaimed in rueful fashion that difficulties arising out of fines on unions and the imprisonment of their members might never have occurred had the unions in question been registered. Other advantages attaching to the registered trade union are those relating to nominations by members concerning money payable on death, certain tax advantages and certain exemptions from insurance legislation. Last (but, to the member, not least) are the important individual rights given to workers to join (or not to join) trade unions in section 5, and the rights related thereto.

(3) *Disadvantages*

The benefits of registration must be taken with the burdens. **485**
Trade union hostility to registration goes beyond dislike of the registration provisions (repellent as these are to most unions) being based on an abhorrence of the whole Act as an attack on free trade unions.

(a) *Control of the rule-book.* Whilst it is true that *all* organisations **486**
of workers must act in conformity with the "guiding principles" discussed above, the "trade union" must submit to "Ordeal by Registrar," so that the latter may be reassured that the trade union's rules conform to those guiding principles, as well as to the requirements of Schedule 4, which makes detailed provision for the constitution and management of the organisation, the requirements concerning membership, and the property and finances of the organisation, all adding up to something decidedly more stringent than the old registration requirements.

If the Registrar finds that the rules are defective, either because they reveal inconsistency with the "guiding principles," or because they do not comply with Schedule 4, he must serve a notice on the trade union indicating necessary alterations in those rules, which, if not complied with, may cause the Registrar to apply to the Industrial Court to have the union's registration cancelled.

(b) *Administrative control.* Part of the price of registration is the **487**
obligation to comply with administrative requirements relating to accounts, finance, the register of members, the annual return, audit, annual reports to members (unless exemption is given) and superannuation schemes (on which disquiet had previously been expressed after one or two resounding "crashes"). The registered union must

keep the Registrar apprised of changes in rules, officers and other matters. If the Registrar considers that there are reasonable grounds for believing that an organisation is insolvent he may appoint an inspector to examine into and report on its affairs. If the inspector finds that the Registrar's suspicions are well founded, the latter may present a petition to the High Court for the organisation to be wound up under the Companies Act 1948. In *Keys* v. *Boulter* (*No. 2*) (1972), it was held that the High Court has an inherent power to wind up a trade union, a power which presumably continues to apply in relation to unions unregistered under the 1971 Act. Formerly a registered trade union had to provide in its rules for the manner of its dissolution; all that the previous Registrar could do was cancel its registration, *e.g.* where it had ceased to exist. How far the inherent jurisdiction asserted in the *Keys* case applies to registered unions in the light of the special winding-up procedure for insolvency specified in the 1971 Act remains unclear. Perhaps the High Court still has inherent jurisdiction to wind up such a union, except that a winding-up for insolvency must follow the procedure laid down in the 1971 Act. Unusually, the administrative requirements, referred to above, are enforced by means of criminal sanctions.

488 (c) *Appeals to the Registrar.* In addition to his functions already noted, the Registrar has become a sort of "ombudsman" for the individual member of a trade union. Any person who is a member of a "trade union" (other than a federation of workers' organisations), or who has ceased to be a member otherwise than by voluntary resignation, or who has sought and been refused membership or prevented from obtaining admission by other action taken by or on behalf of the organisation, may make an application to the Registrar that action has been taken against him which constitutes either an unfair industrial practice under section 66, or a breach of rules (s. 81). This new jurisdiction contrasts with the limited powers given under the old law to the Chief Registrar of Friendly Societies, who had no powers to deal with complaints by members, apart from those relating to mergers and political funds, which still remain.

Assuming that the application is a proper one, the Registrar will investigate it and, if he cannot promote a settlement, may, in a serious case, present a complaint to the Industrial Court, which may award to the original applicant one or all of the remedies of compensation, "declaration" or mandatory order. If, on the other hand, the Registrar does not conceive that the matter is sufficiently serious to warrant a hearing by the Industrial Court, he may present a complaint to the industrial tribunal, which is only empowered to award the remedies of compensation and the "declaratory" order.

As an alternative to a complaint to the Industrial Court or industrial tribunal via the Registrar, there is the possibility of direct complaint to the industrial tribunal under section 107. Two significant differences between the two "routes" are: (1) a "direct" complaint to the tribunal may be laid by a member of an organisation, whether registered *or not* (other than a federation), whereas only registered organisations (other than federal bodies) are affected by the indirect procedure. (2) the direct route can only culminate in compensation or a "declaration, in contrast to the indirect route which, if it ends in the Industrial Court, has the three remedies described in the previous paragraph as possible prizes. 489

Furthermore, the Registrar is given a new power to initiate investigations of (a) serious or persistent breaches of rules (other than those relating to mergers and political funds), or (b) serious or persistent contraventions of the "guiding principles," by trade unions. If his investigation reveals that either type of malpractice has occurred, the Registrar is obliged to give notice to the organisation of his conclusions and to endeavour to secure such action or undertaking as he considers appropriate to remedy or mitigate the consequences, and to prevent continuance or repetition, of the malpractice. As a last resort, he may, after notice, present to the Industrial Court a complaint. The Industrial Court is empowered to order the trade union to remedy the malpractice and to prevent its continuance or repetition.

IV. The Political Fund

The politicised nature of British unions should occasion no surprise 490 when it is recalled that in the nineteenth century unions had turned increasingly to the method of legal enactment as a means of correcting, on some uniform basis, particular evils such as "sweating" and excessive hours of work. It was largely as the results of the efforts of trade unionists that the Independent Labour Party had come into existence in 1893, as the biggest socialist society in the country, and the same can be said of the Labour Representation Committee, which was formed in 1900, and later became the Labour Party. In 1910, by a peculiarly restrictive interpretation of the Trade Union Acts, the case of *Amalgamated Society of Railway Servants* v. *Osborne* (1910), managed to put a severe restriction on such activities by holding that an amendment of union rules to allow of parliamentary representation which had been followed by a compulsory levy of 1s. 11d. from each member, was *ultra vires* those Acts. Lord Halsbury took the statutory definition of a trade union in the 1871 Act, as amended in 1876, to be a sort of "charter of incorporation" and rejected the notion that the statutory charter "legalises a combination for anything" (at pp. 92–93 of the report). This decision imprisoned unions within their statutory objects and rendered *ultra vires* not only political activities but other peripheral activities, such as running a newspaper. In fact trade unions were much more restricted by the *vires* doctrine than registered companies, for which the doctrine has proved in practice to be an illusory restriction.

The Trade Union Act of 1913, which is still law, was passed to settle the controversy provoked by the *Osborne* decision. Section 1 permits a union to have objects and powers other than the statutory objects and to apply its funds for any lawful objects or purposes for the time being authorised under its constitution, with one important exception, *viz.* political expenditure.

491 Section 3, as amended terminologically by the 1971 Act, provides that the funds of an organisation of workers shall not be applied directly or indirectly in the furtherance of certain political objects (but without prejudice to the furtherance of any other political objects), unless these objects have been approved by a resolution passed by a majority of the members actually voting. Where such a resolution is in force, the organisation must have rules, approved by the Registrar providing for a separate political fund to which a member may decline to contribute by "contracting out." Those who have "contracted out" must not be prejudiced by excluding them from any benefits or otherwise placing them at any disadvantage compared with other members, and contribution to the political fund cannot be made a condition of membership of the organisation (see *Birch* v. *National Union of Railwaymen* (1950)). The political objects to which section 3 applies are (a) the election expenses of parliamentary candidates and of candidates for other public offices; (b) meetings or the distribution of literature in support of candidates; (c) the maintenance of M.P.s or holders of public office (a union secretary, who has been elected as M.P., may receive his salary from the union's general funds in respect of his continuing union office); (d) the registration of electors or the selection of parliamentary and other candidates; and (e) political meetings of any kind or the distribution of political literature of any kind, except in furtherance of the union's statutory objects (given a narrow meaning, namely, to denote "party political" meetings or literature, so that T.U.C. support for the *Daily Herald* was outside the scope of the paragraph as not being "political literature"). An excellent analysis of the law and decisions is contained in Grunfeld, *Modern Trade Union Law*, Chap. 16).

492 The provisions of section 3, which apply to both registered and unregistered unions, do not inhibit political activities which involve no expenditure or which involve expenditure but fall outside the five categories in that section, although it should be borne in mind that an activity must be authorised by the rules. In *Bennett* v. *National Society of Operative Printers* (1915), expenditure on the shares of a company to publish a newspaper aimed at promoting the policy of the Labour Party was held to be *ultra vires* the union's rules. The Registrar of Friendly Societies has considerable control both over political fund rules, and claims alleging infringements of such rules. Although the "contracting out" procedure has been a bone of contention in the past (in fact "contracting in" was substituted for the years 1927–1946), the political parties now seem to accept it as a fact of political life. British unions are therefore much more political than their American counterparts (some of whom have a preference for "business unionism") and lack the political and religious differences of European unions.

V. The Trade Union Movement

Reformers have looked longingly at what the ILO, in a special study, termed the "sprawling structure" of the British trade union movement. **493**

Trade unions are at present both numerous and varied. At the end of 1971 there were nearly 500 unions with an aggregate membership (including Irish membership) of 10,935,000, although it needs to be remembered that some 77 per cent. of this membership was concentrated in twenty-three trade unions, some two hundred and fifty trade unions having fewer than 1,000 members and accounting for less than 1 per cent. of the total trade union membership. The Trade Union (Amalgamations, etc.) Act 1964 was passed in order to accelerate the slow but steady rate of either amalgamation between unions, or merger by transfer of engagements, each of which can be achieved by a simple majority of votes recorded by members, unless the rules impose some different requirement.

British unions fall into different categories, *viz.* (a) general **494**
workers' unions, (b) craft unions, (c) industrial unions and (d) occupational unions. In recent years one of the most striking developments has been the relative decline in so-called "cloth cap" unionism and the growth of "white-collar" unionism. The latter has made significant penetration amongst supervisory and technical workers, and has brought within its fold some levels of management, despite the individualistic philosophy of most managers and their psychological identification with the firm rather than with "labour" as such. Perhaps the most logical reform would be the formation of

unions on an industrial basis, as has been carried out in post-war West Germany, but such a reform is considered to be impracticable for historical and other reasons in this country. Certainly, the multiplicity of unions and the lack of any clear demarcation of memberships continues to create problems, particularly within undertakings. The problem of inter-union competition for membership is to some extent covered by the "Bridlington Agreement," at least for unions affiliated to the T.U.C. Under this Agreement, no one who is or has recently been a member of one trade union should be accepted into membership by another union without inquiry, nor should a union accept a member from another union if inquiry shows that he is under discipline, engaged in an industrial dispute or in arrears with his subscription. The Agreement does not prevent some competition, healthy or otherwise, for membership.

495 The Trades Union Congress is the chief central organisation for trade unions and is responsible for national policy and the co-ordination of trade union matters. Its "defensive" role on behalf of the trade union movement can be characterised by its policy towards the 1971 Act and, more recently, statutory incomes policy. Doubts, however, exist as to the efficacy of the T.U.C. in enforcing central control in controversial areas like industrial disputes (the CBI/T.U.C. Agreement of 1972 on independent conciliation and arbitration free of governmental interference is an example), or in controlling incomes. It cannot issue orders to member unions, but holds in reserve the sanctions of disaffiliation and suspension (the latter brought into use in 1972 when several unions, in defiance of T.U.C. policy, registered under the 1971 Act or otherwise invoked its machinery). The T.U.C. has regional offices and its co-ordinating role is seen in connection with Local Trades Councils upon which are represented branches of local affiliated unions. These Councils provide a useful forum for the resolution of matters of common interest which often transcend trade union affairs in the narrow sense.

The plurality of unions is to some extent lessened by confederal groupings of unions for certain purposes, such as the multi-union grouping in the Confederation of Shipbuilding and Engineering Unions. There were seventy-one federations of trade unions in 1971. C.I.R. Report No. 22 on Shipbuilding and Shiprepairing (Cmnd. 4756) shows that a confederation does not preclude the existence of independent action by employees of a "highly sectional character." National Joint Councils set up in the wake of the Whitley Report may have several unions on the union side, as may the sole bargaining agent under the Industrial Relations Act 1971.

VI. Organisations of Employers

Employers' associations were a natural, and perhaps inevitable response to the growing collective strength of trade unions. Their main function is the regulation of collective bargaining on the employers' side, not only in order to meet trade union claims on some uniform basis and to avoid the "picking off" of vulnerable employers by trade unions, but also to prevent unfair competition between employers by means of the undercutting of wages. Some associations have machinery for the resolution of disputes. In addition, employers' organisations provide advice and other services. Organisations formed to foster trade or technical interests are usually known as "trade associations," although the latter have increasingly extended their scope to encompass aspects of collective bargaining. Employers' organisations exhibit great variety in degree of formalism (although most have written constitutions), structure and functions, each reflecting the peculiar problems besetting a particular industry. **496**

Against the collective bargaining function of employers' associations must be set the trend towards plant bargaining (the central finding of the Donovan Commission), and the emergence of big corporations, often part of an international structure. The latter have not infrequently preferred to settle their own terms and conditions of employment at plant level, and have either declined to join the appropriate organisation, or have left it. In the result, many organisations have found their most effetive role in servicing and protecting the interests of small and medium-sized firms, and in giving a lead in non-wage matters such as the length of the working week, holidays and redundancies.

For the purposes of the Industrial Relations Act 1971, an "organisation of employers" means an organisation, whether permanent or temporary, which either (a) consists wholly or mainly of employers or individual proprietors of one or more descriptions and is an organisation whose principal objects include the regulation of relations between employers or individual proprietors of that description or those descriptions and workers or organisations of workers, or (b) is a federation of employers' organisations. An organisation of employers which is registered under the Act receives the accolade of "employers' association." **497**

As with organisations of workers, all organisations of employers must comply with certain guiding principles, in their case those set out in section 69 of the Act. Those which wish to register as employers' associations must show to the Registrar that their rules comply with the guiding principles.

Organisations of employers, to revert to the generic title, are regulated by the 1971 Act both in substantive matters, such as the commission of unfair industrial practices, and in procedural matters, such as proceedings and winding up. Comparatively little space has been accorded to them here, not because they are unimportant, but because they do not normally find themselves involved in the dramatic legal tussles which trade unionists sometimes encounter, a phenomenon which is probably ascribable not so much to the fact that employers are purer in heart than trade unionists but to the greater wealth and resources which they normally command.

CHAPTER 8

COLLECTIVE BARGAINING

I. THE BACKGROUND

498 The outstanding characteristic of the British system of industrial relations is the manner in which it has, from an early stage, come to rest on a tradition of autonomous bargaining between employers and trade unions with the minimum of state and legal interference. This traditional reliance upon autonomous bargaining can be attributed in large measure to early industrialisation and to the appearance of relatively strong trade unions at a time when the extension of the electoral franchise to non-property-owning workers had already taken place. In other industrial countries, where industrialisation took place at a time when universal male suffrage had already been conceded, there has been a tendency to enlist the aid of the state and of the law in order to bolster up collective bargaining and to support a weak trade union movement. In the United States, trade unions had to battle (often literally) against the constitutional doctrines of property and individual rights. In France, trade unionism is a minority movement divided into Christian, Marxist and other groupings. German trade unions, chastened by the collapse of the Weimar Republic, subjugation during the Nazi corporative State and defeat in the Second World War, have emerged, as the result of British influence, in a new form—that of industrial unionism. Australia and New Zealand rely upon a statutory system of conciliation and arbitration.

499 In this country the emergence of trade unions has been ascribed to the general dismantling of statutory controls over employment which began towards the end of the eighteenth century in response to the new economic dogma of individualism, to which any collective interference with individual contract was anathema. Trade unions came to protect the individual worker from the exploitation by the employer which resulted from the "higgling of the market." Through his "shop club," and later his trade union, the worker was able to present a collective front to the employer, who was to an increasing extent a limited liability registered company. Extended to include employers in a district, or even in a whole industry, the collective bargain established a "common rule" for terms and conditions of employment, which, as the Webbs showed, applied indifferently, on the one hand, to the wealthy employer and the

employer hovering on bankruptcy, and on the other hand, to the "superior craftsman" as well as the "starving man." "The practice of Collective Bargaining," wrote the same authors in 1897, "has, in one form or another, superseded the old individual contract between master and servant over a large proportion of the industrial field." Their conclusion is truer now than when made. Today, some 18 million workers, manual and non-manual, are covered by collective bargaining or statutory wage-fixing machinery (itself an embryonic form of collective bargaining) out of a total of 23 million or so employees. If one recollects that there are 10 million trade unionists, it becomes evident that collective bargaining has a normative effect on the remuneration and conditions of large numbers of non-unionists. Although trade unions pressed for statutory reforms and acted as provident societies in relation to their members, their chief *raison d'être* was, and still is, collective bargaining. One of the concomitants to the workplace bargaining which had taken place over the past few decades is the enhanced role of workplace representatives such as the shop steward. Much attention has been directed to the problem of articulating informal workplace bargaining into a structure in which responsible unionism plays its part.

II. Characteristics of Collective Bargaining

500 The chief characteristics of collective bargaining as it has developed in this country are as follows.

1. Freedom from legal regulation

501 A remarkable feature of collective bargaining is the manner in which it has generally escaped legal regulation. To some extent this phenomenon is ascribable to the principle upon which the Whitley Report during the First World War was founded and which has applied throughout industry, namely, that both sides of industry ought to settle their own agreements and patch up their own differences. British unions have set as their goal that of "100 per cent. unionism" rather than a statutory "closed shop" so that, from a position of strength, they might bargain as equals with employers. Where the parties are unequal, the aid of the law may be invoked "to hold the ring," as has happened in the case of weakly unionised industries (such as those covered by the Wages Councils Act 1959), or in the case of agriculture (the Agricultural Wages Act 1948). There is nothing comparable to the French device of "extension" of collective bargains by ministerial decree so as to include employers and workers who were neither themselves, nor through their associations, privy to a particular collective agreement, the nearest

analogy in this country being the enforcement of "recognised terms and conditions of employment" under section 8 of the Terms and Conditions of Employment Act 1959, as amended. In the background to bargaining under a system of "countervailing" power is the strike and the lock-out. "Where the rights of labour are concerned," said Lord Wright in the *Harris Tweed* case, "the rights of the employer are conditioned by the right of the men to give or withhold their services. The right of workmen to strike is an essential element in the principle of collective bargaining" ((1942), at p. 463 of the report). This preference for industrial sanctions rather than legal sanctions is, in part, due to a traditional suspicion of the judiciary. "In the past working men have," stated the 1963 *Rule Book of the Boilermakers' Union*, "been ground down and held by laws made and administered by those who have been called 'The Ruling Class'." Winn L.J. took the opportunity in *Morris* v. *C. H. Bailey Ltd.* (1969), of pointing out that the plaintiff in that case had no occasion to feel that he was being ground down by a decision which, in effect, left the men in full possession of their restrictive practices.

The preference for industrial rather than legal solution, the **502**
suspicion of law and lawyers of which the *Morris* case is fairly typical, and the way in which collective bargains are at present drafted, have cumulatively produced what Geoffrey Lane J. termed a "climate of opinion" in which the collective bargain is seen as lacking that "intention to create legal relations" which textbook writers have seen as a necessary, separate ingredient for an enforceable and binding contract. To that prevailing "climate" the parties to a collective agreement were held to be subject by that judge in *Ford Motor Co. Ltd.* v. *A.E.E.F.W. & T.G.W.U.* (1969), a case which set the seal of judicial approval on the conventional wisdom. In that case, where an *ex parte* injunction was sought to restrain breaches of a procedure agreement and a substantive agreement concluded between the plaintiffs and a national joint negotiating committee of trade union representatives, Geoffrey Lane J. declined to give the relief sought on the ground that the agreements were not contracts in the legal sense because of their vague and aspirational language (but not necessarily because of uncertainty), and because of the "climate of opinion voiced and evidenced by the extra-judicial authorities" which was adverse to enforceability. The decision is remarkable for the freedom with which the judge ventured into extra-judicial sources such as the Donovan Report, the Ministry of Labour Evidence to the Donovan Commission, the Ministry's Industrial Relations Handbook, the Report of a Court of Inquiry and the articles of a leading labour law writer. The *Ford* case was decided at a time when section 4 of the Trade Union Act 1871

expressly precluded the direct enforcement of an agreement between one trade union and another, as would have been the case in an action for damages. This section, as interpreted by the courts, did not preclude "negative enforcement" of such an agreement by means of a declaration or injunction given to preserve the *status quo ante*, and, of course, it left undecided the enforceability of an agreement between a trade union and an employer. The *Ford* case has not escaped criticism both for the way in which it rests on some subjective or objective "intention to create legal relations" rather than on the notion of "bargain," and for its reliance on some amorphous body or climate of opinion—something which the Industrial Relations Act 1971 might possibly change, although this is extremely doubtful.

503 Still, other countries *are* prepared to attach contractual effect to the collective bargain quite apart from its normative function. Recommendation No. 91 of the International Labour Organisation defines collective agreements as "all agreements in writing regarding working conditions and terms of employment" between management and labour and goes on to state that such agreements "should bind the signatories thereto and those on whose behalf the agreement is concluded." The same Recommendation provides for the compulsory normative effect of the collective agreement on individual contracts of employment, the terms of which are null and void to the extent that they conflict with collectively agreed terms, save where the former are more favourable than the latter. In the United States most of the cases on section 307 of the Taft-Hartley Act 1947 (which authorises Federal District Courts to entertain "suits for violation of contracts between an employer and a labor organisation") have turned on the enforceability of grievance and arbitration terms in collective bargains. It is fair to add that in these other countries the normative function of the collective agreement seems to play a more significant part than the contractual function, which is seen as fulfilling the role of a treaty or code, as opposed to a static contract of exchange.

504 To the panacea of enforceable collective agreements (see below, para. 537) a plethora of objections has been given. Collective bargains are often formless, consisting of "understandings" rather than written agreements, and even where they are written, many of them, as the late Lord Donovan has said, "would fail for uncertainty." Enforceability would require a lawyer at the negotiator's elbow—practical, perhaps, in national negotiations, but impractical in shop-floor bargaining. Collective bargains require to be flexible to deal with the dynamics of labour relations, or the "daily accommodations," as they have been termed, and cannot be compared to a contract for the sale of goods, or a lease which regulates a continuing relationship upon reasonably static terms. Whilst it is generally true that trade unions negotiate with employer as principals (the so-called "corporate theory") and not as agents for their members (the "agency theory"), agency problems can still arise (see below, para. 536). Above all, there is the traditional antipathy towards enforceability which labour and (until recently) management have generally shared. That the aversion to enforceability has not always been one-sided is shown by the ten-year struggle of workers in the boot and shoe industry, with T.U.C. support, to secure the legal enforceability of National Agreements (*History of the National Union of Boot and Shoe Operatives 1874–1957*, A. Fox, at p. 450).

2. Lack of formalism

In pursuit of their aim of a "common rule" it was natural that trade unions should seek to extend collective bargaining from the single employer to the locality, and, ultimately, to the industry as a whole. The growth in the size of unions, and in the size of employers (often grouped together in employers' associations), and the institutional machinery of national and regional joint industrial councils set up after the Whitley Report, were amongst the factors which produced the "model" of the formal national agreement upon which much of British industrial relations practice has been based. This model is centralised, narrow in scope (concentrating on pay and conditions of work) and consensual in nature. It aims to have regulative effect, particularly with regard to wages, over an entire industry. Perhaps the central finding of the Donovan Commission was that besides the formal, centralised system of bargaining there had sprung up in many cases, an informal system of autonomous and fragmented "plant bargaining." This latter system derives its authority from the shop floor. In it, national rates of pay are seen as minima upon which local bargainers can build by negotiating higher rates and special payments—the result is that earnings often bear no relation to nationally agreed rates of pay—a phenomenon which the economists have termed "wages' drift." 505

Not only is the potential range of bargaining wider in the plant bargain, it is also less "consensual" in nature, not infrequently consisting of an amorphous amalgam of tacit arrangements and inarticulate practices subject to short-term change, particularly under pressure from shop-floor "militants." "The formal and informal systems are in conflict" said the Donovan Commission (Report, para. 149). Since 1968, attention has been directed towards the formalisation of the informal system. The larger firms have voluntarily agreed to register their "factory agreements" with the

Department of Employment. The Commission on Industrial Relations considers and reports on references to it concerning collective bargaining arrangements generally or in relation to particular firms. The Industrial Relations Act 1971 is clearly aimed at producing, *inter alia*, a more structured and formalised system of collective bargaining to cope with the problem of unregulated shop-floor power, and to make that system socially accountable.

506 Unlike several other industrial countries, the British collective bargain does not formally reflect the distinction between "conflicts of interest" and "conflicts of right," *i.e.* between disputes as to new terms, and disputes as to the application or interpretation of existing terms. Thus in Sweden and the United States, it is frankly acknowledged that conflicts of interests are essentially power confrontations which cannot be settled by some adjudicatory process. However, in Australia and New Zealand, a system of statutory conciliation and arbitration exists to resolve just such disputes. Even so, there is general acceptance of the notion that "conflicts of rights" lend themselves more easily to some form of settlement by a quasi-judicial or arbitral procedure (such as the grievance arbitration system in the United States). In this country we have a somewhat vague division between "substantive" agreements, *i.e.* agreements which lay down terms and conditions of employment, and "procedural" agreements, *i.e.* agreements which lay down rules, whether general or particular for the settlement of disputes and sometimes termed "peace-keeping treaties." "The tendency in the British industrial relations system for the parties to treat issues arising more as grievances than as conflicts of rights is logically reinforced by the attitude of employer and trade unions to voluntary *substantive* agreements about terms and conditions of work. The characteristics of such agreements are such that they are rarely intended to establish in detail a corpus of rules which can, or should, be applied to each situation in which disputes between the parties at various levels are likely to arise. . . . In fact, in most industries, *procedures are very little used in the application or interpretation of substantive agreements*" (Research Paper 2, Pt. 2, para. 67, by A. I. Marsh, prepared for the Donovan Commission).

3. Variety

507 To contrast the formal and informal systems of collective bargaining is to oversimplify. Within each of these systems there is a bewildering diversity of bargaining structures, levels, units, scope and form. These are set out in the Industrial Relations Handbook, published by the Department of Employment (H.M.S.O.). Superimposed on this diversity is the increasing complexity in the bar-

gaining process itself, no longer an "annual wage-round" but an attempt to deal with problems of productivity and job evaluation. This complexity is reflected in the pressure for the appointment of specialist personnel directors and of trade union negotiators possessing these new skills.

III. Reform of Collective Bargaining

The Donovan Commission was clear that collective bargaining still 508
represented the best way of conducting industrial relations in this country, but that the central defect in collective bargaining in Britain was the disorder accompanying factory relations and pay structures which stemmed from the conflict between the formal and informal systems discussed above. Industry-wide agreements, the Commission felt, ought to be limited to those matters which they could effectively regulate, leaving a wide area to the factory agreement. Boards of companies were exhorted to review industrial relations with six objectives in mind, *viz.* comprehensive and authoritative bargaining machinery; joint procedures for the rapid and equitable settlement of grievances in a manner consistent with relevant collective agreements; regularising the position of shop stewards; redundancy agreements; effective rules on disciplinary measures; and, regular joint discussion of measures to promote safety at work. Since 1968, the Department of Employment has requested companies employing 5,000 or more persons in an establishment to register details of their company agreements and can, if necessary, utilise the power in section 58 of the Industrial Relations Act to make regulations requiring employers to notify their procedure agreements. This Register and the C.I.R. (to whom references may be made) are obviously designed to play a central part in the reform of collective bargaining in Britain, although the policy of non-cooperation on the part of unions has proved to be something of an obstacle in this respect.

Although one of the general principles upon which the 1971 Act is based is "the principle of collective bargaining freely conducted on behalf of workers and employers and with due regard to the general interests of the community," the provisions for trade union rights at the workplace, recognition of unions and enforceability are an attempt to contain free collective bargaining within legal constraints, to which must now be added the effect of a statutory incomes policy.

IV. The Agency Shop

509 A trade union, or its representatives, cannot bargain in a vacuum. To do so, it or its representatives must secure some form of recognition from the employer. Recognition disputes take two forms. First, there is the recognition dispute *simpliciter* in which the employer declines to recognise a union (or perhaps all unions) as having rights to negotiate on behalf of members. Second, there may be an inter-union recognition dispute in which there is dispute, not on the principle of recognition, but as to which of two or more unions is to carry off the accolade of bargaining rights. The whole question of recognition is clearly linked with the degree to which an employer's workers have been unionised and his attitude to that fact. The 1971 Act, as we shall see, attempts to fit the intractable recognition dispute into a statutory mould, notwithstanding trade union preference for "100 per cent. unionism" without the aid of the law and for the resolution of inter-union disputes through T.U.C. machinery.

510 The employer's attitude to the "union shop" varies. At one extreme, he may require his workers, possibly as a term of their contracts of service, to forego all claim to union membership—the so-called "yellow-dog contract" of American labour law. Employer hostility to the union shop is not unknown in this country, particularly amongst the smaller employers, as is testified by the need in certain industries for minimum wage legislation. Other employers tolerate or even favour trade union membership in their members, either on some formal basis, or by means of "understandings." At the other extreme, is the employer who concedes the "closed shop," estimated in 1964 to cover to some $3\frac{3}{4}$ million workers. In the public sector, both the civil service and the nationalised industries recognise and encourage membership of the appropriate union.

511 Clearly, a union which succeeds in establishing a "closed shop" is particularly well placed to conduct collective bargaining. The 1971 Act proclaims "the principle of free association of workers in independent trade unions" and does so by conferring upon the worker the right to join, or not to join, a trade union as he sees fit (the exercise of this right is discussed above, paras. 145 *et seq.*). The individualistic philosophy of the Act has been criticised for creating a false antinomy by purporting to equate the right to join a trade union with the right not to join a trade union. Indeed, most of the arguments about section 5 are philosophical rather than legal.

512 The worker's freedom of association under the Act is considerably restricted where (1) he elects to join an unregistered union (see para. 146, above), and (2) where either an "approved closed

shop" (para. 144, above) or an "agency shop agreement" exists. The latter is defined as an agreement between an employer (or employers) and a trade union (or trade unions) under which it is agreed in respect of workers of one or more description specified in the agreement that their terms and conditions of employment shall include that every worker must either (a) be, or become, a member of that trade union or of one of those trade unions, as the case may be, or (b) agree to pay appropriate contributions to that trade union (or one of those trade unions) or, where permitted, agree to pay equivalent contributions to charity. As in the past, so in the future, it is likely that employer and union will be able to agree on the rights and duties of the employer's workers with regard to trade union membership. Indeed, such traditional understandings and agreements must necessarily continue if organisations refuse to register as trade unions.

However if an employer is unwilling to enter into an agency shop **513**
agreement despite the wishes of one or more trade unions (or of a joint negotiating panel), either he or the trade union side may apply to the Industrial Court so that the C.I.R. may arrange a ballot of workers concerned. Provided that there has not in the preceding two years been an adverse ballot or a ballot adverse to the continuance of an agency shop agreement, and provided that the trade union side has been recognised by the employer as having negotiating rights (or rights corresponding thereto) in respect of workers as described in the application, the Industrial Court must request the C.I.R. to take a ballot. If the result of the ballot, as reported by the C.I.R. to the Industrial Court, shows that either a majority of the workers eligible to vote, or not less than two-thirds of those who voted, have voted in favour of an agency shop agreement, it then becomes the duty of the employer to take all such action as is requisite on his part to enter the agency shop agreement in respect of the workers comprised in the ballot, and thereafter to implement that agreement whilst it remains in force. If the employer contravenes his duty, the employee may present a complaint to the Industrial Court which may, if it finds that the complaint is well-founded, and it would be just and equitable to do so, make one or more of the orders, *viz.* (a) a "declaration" as to the rights of the parties, (b) an order directing the employer to take implementary action (s. 13). Industrial action by any person (including a trade union or other organisation of workers or official thereof) knowingly to induce or attempt to induce an employer not to perform his duty under the present provision is an unfair industrial action in respect of which a complaint will lie to the Industrial Court. Industrial action involves either the calling, organising, procuring or financing

of a strike (or threat thereof) or the organising procuring, or financing of any irregular industrial action short of a strike (or threat thereof). On the other hand, if the required majority of votes is lacking, the Industrial Court must make an order directing that no agency shop agreement be made in respect of workers comprised in the ballot for a period of two years from the reporting of the result of the ballot, and that any agency shop agreement during that period shall be void.

514 Where it exists, the agency shop agreement makes a substantial inroad upon the generality of the rule in s. 5 conferring upon the worker the right not to join a trade union. It is not an unfair industrial practice for an employer to whom an agency shop agreement applies to (a) dismiss, penalise or otherwise discriminate against a worker, or (b) to refuse to engage a worker, if the worker in question is not, or refuses to be, a member of the trade union, or refuses to pay appropriate contributions to the trade union in lieu of membership of it. A worker who has conscientious objection to both membership of the trade union and the payment of contributions to such union in lieu of membership may propose to the trade union that he pay an equivalent contribution to a charity. The industrial tribunal has jurisdiction to determine disputes concerning the genuineness of the worker's conscientious objection to paying contributions to the trade union, the charity to which the contribution should be payable, and the amount of the contribution to the charity. The same tribunal may also entertain claims from workers that a contribution is not payable or that it exceeds the permitted limit (s. 10).

515 Finally, section 14 seeks to achieve a balance between the stability of an existing agency shop agreement, and the desirability of reviewing such an agreement where it no longer represents the wishes of the workers, by allowing any worker covered by the agreement to apply to the Industrial Court for a ballot to ascertain whether the agreement should continue. The Industrial Court cannot entertain such an application unless it is satisfied that, (1) not less than one-fifth of the workers to whom the agreement applies have signified in writing their concurrence in the application, and (2) the application is not made within two years of a previous ballot (s. 14). If the result of the ballot, as reported by the C.I.R. to the Industrial Court, shows that neither a majority of those entitled to vote nor two-thirds of those actually voting supports the continuation of the agency shop agreement, then the Industrial Court must rescind the agreement and direct that no agency shop agreement shall be made by the parties to the old agreement in respect of workers comprised in the ballot for a period of two years from the

reporting of the result of the ballot. During those two years, any purported agency shop agreement is void and any application for such an agreement is not receivable by the Industrial Court (s. 15). Were the employer to continue to implement the old agreement, or an organisation of workers or other person to take or threaten industrial action to force the employer to enforce the agreement, an unfair industrial practice would be committed. Needless to say, if a majority (as defined) votes in favour of continuance, then the agency shop agreement continues, with the further feature that no application for such an agreement may be entertained by the Industrial Court for two years from the date when the result of the ballot is reported.

V. The Sole Bargaining Agent

It was estimated in 1965 that 18 million out of 23 million employed 516
persons had their terms and conditions of service settled by voluntary collective bargaining or statutory wage-fixing machinery. Since less than 10 million workers were trade unionists, it is clear that trade union bargaining has had (and still has) a normative effect over the greater part of industry, including the public sector. Accepting that Britain is, perhaps, the most highly unionised country in the world, the fact remains that considerable numbers of workers, mostly in the private sector, are not affected directly by collective bargaining. The employer may enforce a "non-union shop" either on the basis of an "understanding" to that effect, or by stipulating for a term of employment prohibiting trade union membership—the "yellow-dog contract" of American labour law. The union may seek to unionise workers so that it can claim recognition from the employer of its right to engage in bargaining on behalf of those workers; if a union claim is resisted, one has a "recognition dispute." Apart from recognition *simpliciter*, a recognition dispute, as we have seen, may arise where two or more unions with overlapping membership (one of which may have been recognised by the employer) claim the right to represent workers. The fact that Britain has, subject to some important exceptions, failed to evolve "industrial unions" (*i.e.* unions representing workers in an industry as opposed to an occupation or craft), and the present multiplicity of British trade unions have given rise to the possibility of recognition disputes which are in essence inter-union disputes. The law reports alone show that the "Bridlington Agreement," under which the poaching of members is discouraged, has not resulted in the complete elimination of inter-union conflicts, particularly between white-collar and manual unions. Borrowing from the United

States, the 1971 Act seeks to provide "electoral" machinery for the settlement of recognition disputes of both types as an alternative to reliance upon trials of industrial strength. This view of a legalistic, industrial democracy does not accord with the traditional trade union preference for autonomous and unregulated industrial democracy. The Act will not affect the great majority of employers who have stabilised the negotiating rights of unions and who do not have recognition disputes. In those cases in which the parties cannot agree on recognition and negotiating rights, the purpose of the Act is, in the words of the President of the Industrial Court "to help parties to enter into voluntary agreements for the creation of sole bargaining agencies, or, if that fails, to provide machinery which will resolve a dispute in which one party seeks, and the other party rejects, a sole bargaining agency, or the parties are unable to agree upon the scope of the agency or the identity of the bargaining agent" (*Car Collection Co. Ltd.* v. *Transport and General Workers' Union* (1972), at pp. 137–138 of the report). The fact remains, however, that the effectiveness of the Act in this respect depends largely on the willingness of unions to register.

517 The Industrial Court is far from being a mere conduit for the transmission of references to the C.I.R. It must be satisfied that the parties have endeavoured to settle the dispute themselves and have made adequate use of conciliation facilities. It must also feel that a reference to the C.I.R. is necessary to promote a satisfactory and lasting settlement of the dispute. Thus, in *C. A. Parson & Co. Ltd.* v. *A.U.E.W.* (1972), it was clear that the long-drawn out dispute between unions had resisted all the efforts of several "honest brokers" and that the last chance lay in a reference to the C.I.R. The "screening role" of the court is illustrated by the refusal of a reference in *U.K.A.P.E.* v. *Rolls Royce Ltd.* (1972), where an unregistered union sought a reference on behalf of four hundred or so senior engineers, scientists and technologists. The Industrial Court considered that the interests of the four hundred were adequately served by the recognised union. The latter was unregistered, unlike the applicant, thus showing that registration confers no particular advantage in securing the prize of statutory bargaining rights. On the other hand, the court will not allow the recognition procedure to be used as a means of questioning the propriety of registering a union, something which lies within the province of the Registrar of Trade Unions. *Car Collection Co. Ltd.* v. *Transport & General Workers Union* (1972) shows that a union or other body cannot invoke the recognition procedure in the Act in order to gain protection from industrial action which is being taken against it (see below, para. 526). The court is not obliged to make a reference if a similar dispute con-

cerning substantially the same group of employees has been before the C.I.R. in the previous two years and a further reference would be unjustified, and it must be satisfied that recognition has not been withdrawn by order within the previous two years.

In the event of disagreement as to negotiating rights, an application may be made to the Industrial Court for a reference to be made to the C.I.R. to examine (a) whether a group of employees should be recognised (or continue to be recognised) as a bargaining unit, (b) whether a sole bargaining agent should be recognised by the employer for that bargaining unit, and if so, (c) what body should be the sole bargaining agent. The application may be made by one or more trade unions, or one or more employers, or jointly by both. Before making an application, notice must be given to the Secretary of State, who may make an application himself, provided he has consulted the employer and union involved. The Industrial Court has given some guidance on these difficult provisions. First, it is not the concern of the applicant to frame the statutory questions but to specify the group of workers to which question (a) refers. This should ideally be wide enough to include all possible bargaining units, leaving it open for the applicant in argument to press for a smaller bargaining unit, a procedure which obviates the time-wasting requirement of extending the reference to the C.I.R. The size of the unit requires a careful balancing between the avoidance of both over-fragmentation and the creation of a unit comprising inconsistent interests and standards. In a multi-plant company the overall position may have to be taken into account. A union may have support in one establishment and none in the other ninety-nine of the same employer's establishments. Where the only negotiating body is a national body, such as the National Joint Council in the electricity supply industry, and local bodies may only recommend measures to the national body or implement the latter's decisions, there is no room for a reference under the present provisions. This was the position in *Electricity Supply Union* v. *Central Electricity Generating Board* (1972), where Sir John Brightman was also clearly unimpressed by the claims of a union with a small membership, practically no funds and a part-time general secretary who worked in the horticultural industry. His lordship indicated that the statutory machinery was not to be a charter for breakaway unions—something on which the late Lord Donovan had expressed disquiet. **518**

On a reference, the C.I.R. may be able to recommend that the reference be withdrawn because of a satisfactory and lasting settlement of the dispute. It may propose that the scope of the reference be widened, giving notice to those affected who may, in turn, apply to the Industrial Court within two weeks of such notice **519** for a consideration of the need and expediency of the proposed extension. On such an application, the Industrial Court may extend the scope as recommended by the C.I.R., extend its scope to a lesser extent, or direct that the scope shall remain unchanged. If there is no such application, the Industrial Court must extend the scope of the reference as proposed by the C.I.R. However, if the reference is not withdrawn, the C.I.R. will examine the questions as to bargaining with the unit and sole bargaining agent as raised in the reference (including a reference enlarged in scope) and report thereon, transmitting copies to the Secretary of State, the employer (or employers, where there are "associated employers," as to which see s. 167 (8)), and every trade union or other organisation of workers appearing to be directly concerned. As regards the bargaining unit, the C.I.R. must consider the homogeneity of a particular group of employees from the points of view of nature of work and training, experience, professional or other qualifications. It must also consider, *inter alia*, whether the sole bargaining agent recommended will command substantial support and the necessary resources to act as an effective representative of employees in the bargaining unit.

520 Within six months of the C.I.R. report, the employer or trade union side may, in the absence of voluntary acceptance of the recommendations by the parties, apply to the Industrial Court for a ballot on the C.I.R.'s recommendations concerning the bargaining unit and the sole bargaining agent therein. It may be noted here that an unregistered organisation of workers may be recommended as sole bargaining agent, but such an organisation cannot apply for a ballot if it does not register, and the employer cannot apply on its behalf. Subject to compliance with any conditions imposed in the C.I.R.'s recommendations, the Industrial Court must request the C.I.R. to make arrangements for a ballot of the employees in the bargaining unit on the question whether the C.I.R.'s recommendation should be made binding.

If a majority of employees voting in the ballot support the C.I.R. recommendation, the Industrial Court is required to make an order defining the bargaining unit and directing that the trade union or joint negotiating panel shall be recognised as the sole bargaining agent in that unit. The order will cease to have effect if the trade union ceases to be such, or the joint negotiating panel ceases to be a joint negotiating panel of trade unions.

521 It will be seen, therefore, that the whole purpose of the statutory process is to have a single focal point of union recognition in the bargaining unit, whether such unit comprises employees of one employer or two or more associated employers. The process cannot be used to regularise negotiating rights on a larger scale, *e.g.* industry-wide bargaining between an employers' association and a confederation of trade unions (see para. 495, above). Because bargaining is often conducted at different levels, *e.g.* the national agreement which fixes minimum rates of pay and the plant bargain which fixes the plant rate, the C.I.R. may recommend that matters which come within the provenance of what are termed "more extensive bargaining arrangements" shall be excluded from the competence of the sole bargaining agent; if it does this, the order of the Industrial Court conferring bargaining rights must make the necessary reservation as to such arrangements. The C.I.R. however is not constrained to protect the "primacy of negotiations at the higher level."

Once appointed by an order of the Industrial Court, what then are the rights of the sole bargaining agent? Apart from its right to object to negotiations with another organisation of workers, the sole bargaining agent is entitled to expect that the employer will take such action by way of, or with a view to, carrying on collective bargaining with the agent, as might reasonably be expected of an employer ready and willing to carry on such collective bargaining.

In the United States, it is an unfair employer practice under **522**
section 9 (a) of the National Labor Relations Act 1935, for an employer to refuse to bargain collectively with the accredited bargaining agent. As interpreted, this provision imposes an obligation on both the employer and the bargaining agent to bargain in good faith, but stops short of insisting that the parties must reach an agreement. Any agreement must be voluntary in the true sense of that word. Nevertheless, the Supreme Court has noted that "there is tension between the principle that the parties need not contract on any specific terms and a practical enforcement of the principle that they are bound to deal with each other in a serious attempt to resolve differences and reach a common ground" (*NLRB* v. *Insurance Agents' International Union* (1960)). It is also, perhaps, noticeable that the Supreme Court is less ready than the National Labor Relations Board to seize on a failure to agree as evidence of a lack of the necessary good faith. Another American problem which we are likely to encounter here, if the statutory procedures set out in the 1971 Act are utilised, is the question of what constitutes the proper subject-matter for collective agreement. Are we to have the American distinction between "mandatory" and "non-mandatory" subjects for bargaining, the latter including so-called "management rights"? It is significant that the managerialist reference to management's primary responsibility for industrial relations in section 2 (2) (*a*) of the 1971 Act is toned down in the Code of Practice to "the joint responsibility of management and of employees and trade unions

representing them" in which, however, management has the primary responsibility" and must take the initiative (*ibid.* para. 3).

523 The rights of a sole bargaining agent, whether established as the result of the statutory process described above or on the traditional ground of voluntary agreement, are not interests in perpetuity. Any employee in the bargaining unit is at liberty to apply to the Industrial Court, and to claim that the recognised sole bargaining agent does not adequately represent the employees in the unit or the particular section thereof to which he belongs. The application to withdraw recognition must have the support in writing of at least two-fifths of the employees in the bargaining unit. Even with such support, it cannot be made if the order granting bargaining rights has been made within the previous two years. A voluntarily-agreed sole bargaining agency can be questioned if one-fifth of the employees in the bargaining unit concur (in writing) in the application. If the C.I.R. (to which the question has been referred) is unable to secure a voluntary settlement of the dispute, there is, again, resort to the ballot, a majority of votes against the continuance of recognition obliging the Industrial Court to make an order directing the employer to withdraw recognition from the bargaining agent for a period of two years. Naturally, if the result of the ballot goes the other way, the *status quo ante* prevails. The procedure for a "testing ballot" permits the C.I.R. to consider whether or not the existing unit should be divided into separate units. Some unions, such as those representing civil servants, fear that the possibility of "testing ballots" will subject them to the threat of constant harassment from dissident elements. "The breakaway union formed by seceded dissidents is still a menace" said Lord Donovan, who felt that something akin to the Australian and New Zealand provision giving power to a registrar to refuse to register a union where he was satisfied that the workers concerned were already adequately catered for by some existing union might well have been introduced into the 1971 Act (H.L. Deb., Vol. 317, cols. 41–42).

VI. Unfair Industrial Practices

524 An "industrial dispute," as defined in section 167 (1) of the Act, includes both a dispute concerning negotiating rights, and a dispute concerning terms and conditions of employment involving a union to which recognition has been accorded. As already noted, it seems likely that unions will continue to unionise workers so that they can use their industrial strength to secure recognition and, thereafter, better terms and conditions of employment, rather than rely on the new statutory procedures described above, which are necessarily

stultified if, as at present, the unions obey the T.U.C. "instruction" not to register under the Act. Industrial action which interferes with the statutory procedures may involve liability for unfair industrial practices.

The types of industrial action are (a) the instituting, carrying on, 525
organising, procuring or financing of a lock-out or threat thereof, by the employer, and (b) the calling, organising, procuring, financing of a strike or irregular industrial action short of a strike, or the threat thereof, by any person (including a trade union, organisation of workers, or official of either). The following involve the commission of an unfair industrial practice:

(1) Industrial action, as defined above, taken in connection 526
with a question which is pending before the Secretary of State (*i.e.* after he has been notified), the Industrial Court or the C.I.R. (*cf.* para. 517, above). Once notice has been given to the Secretary of State of a proposal to make an application to the Industrial Court, the intention is that "there shall not be industrial warfare designed to bring pressure to bear upon those who are concerned with the investigation" (*per* Sir John Donaldson, President, in *Ideal Casements Ltd.* v. *Shamsi* (1972), at p. 412 of the report—unofficial strike action threatened after notice of proposal given).

(2) Where an employer is required to recognise a sole bargaining agent by order of the Industrial Court, he commits an unfair industrial practice if (a) he carries on collective bargaining with another organisation of workers in relation to the bargaining unit affected by that order, or (b) does not take the necessary steps to carry on collective bargaining with the sole bargaining agent (see para. 521, above). If the order of the Industrial Court has conferred recognition upon a joint negotiating panel, the employer may carry on collective bargaining with one or more of the trade unions on the panel if the panel so agrees.

(3) Furthermore, it is an unfair industrial practice if industrial action of category (b) (see para. 525, above) is taken knowingly to induce or attempt to induce an employer to commit either of the unfair industrial practices described in the last paragraph.

(4) Once the C.I.R. has reported to the Industrial Court, it is an unfair industrial practice for any person to take industrial action of type (b) (see para. 525, above) within the ensuing two years knowingly to induce or attempt to induce an employer to recognise as sole bargaining agent or to carry on collective bargaining with any organisation of workers not recommended in the report (s. 55 (6)).

(5) If the Industrial Court has made an order withdrawing recognition from a sole bargaining agent, it is an unfair industrial

practice for any person to take industrial action of type (b) (see para. 525, above) knowingly to induce or attempt to induce the employer not to comply with that order (s. 55 (7)).

(6) An employer who takes industrial action of type (*a*) above (see para. 525) so as knowingly to induce, or attempt to induce, any person to refrain from making an application relating to the recognition of a sole bargaining agent or the withdrawal of such recognition (s. 55 (8)).

527 If any of the actions constituting an unfair industrial practice described above, has been committed, "the person against whom the action was taken" may present a complaint to the Industrial Court which, with one exception, may make (a) an order determinative of rights, (b) an award of compensation, and (c) an order prohibiting repetition of the action in question (these remedies are discussed below, see para. 626). In the case of unfair industrial practice (2), described above, the trade union or joint negotiating panel concerned cannot seek the remedies just described; it may only obtain from the Industrial Court authorisation to present a claim to the Industrial Arbitration Board. The latter may make an award as to terms and conditions of employment, which are then statutorily implied into the individual contracts of employment of the employees affected, subject to any subsequent agreement between the employer and the employee or a subsequent award of the Board. It will be seen therefore that in the case of failure to negotiate with the employer (and also in the case of failure to disclose information) British law is prepared to enforce the duty to bargain to the extent that it gives a compulsory, normative effect to something upon which there is *dissensus*.

VII. Disclosure of Information

528 Knowledge is power. This is particularly true of collective bargaining which, like politics, is the art of the possible. Collective bargaining conducted on the basis of mistaken assumptions as to the realistic area of negotiation can have results which are damaging both for the contestants and the community at large. In a section which the Secretary of State has described as aiming at "equality of information," the Act obliges the employer to disclose to *trade union* representatives at all stages of collective bargaining such information relating to his undertaking as is in his possession (or the possession of an associated employer) and is both (a) information without which the trade union representatives would be, to a material extent, impeded in carrying on collective bargaining with him, and (b) information which it would be in accordance with good industrial relations practice that the employer should disclose to them for the purposes of collective bargaining. In determining what would be in accordance with good industrial relations, regard must be had to the principles relating to disclosure which are set out in the Code of Practice.

The Code itself, in paras. 96–98, is content to lay down pre- 529
scriptions of a somewhat transcendental nature. Thus, the parties should have "adequate information"; management should aim to "meet all reasonable requests from trade unions from information"; and, management need not disclose information "which would be of advantage to a competitor." Since the Code was promulgated, the C.I.R. has issued its own report on the matter ("Disclosure of Information": Report No. 31), and this purports to give further definition to the general concepts in the Code. The Report recommends that management and labour each need to formulate considered policies before attempting to reach joint agreement. The Report concedes that the amount of disclosure will depend upon the circumstances of the case, but offers guidelines as to the sorts of information which might be included, *e.g.* general background information about the organisation and its activities, manpower information, details of pay systems, conditions of service, financial information and prospects. Doubtless the Code will be amended in due course to take account of these recommendations. Even when amended, the Code will clearly not give guidance in all circumstances. In the United States, questions of disclosure have given rise to appreciable case-law and there is provision for recourse to the Industrial Court in this country in cases of dispute concerning disclosure. The trade unions who have decided to boycott the Industrial Court will be hoist with their own petard in this respect since they will wish to obtain an order enjoining the employer to part with the valued information but will not wish to contravene the T.U.C. "bull" against seeking the aid of the court! It should be added that evidence as to good industrial relations practice may be adduced from sources other than the Code or the Report.

To revert to section 56, the employer must disclose, or confirm, 530
the required information in writing, if so requested, but he cannot be required to (a) produce or allow inspection of any document other than that prepared for the purpose of conveying information, or to make a copy or extract from any document, or (b) compile information involving an unreasonable amount of work or expenditure out of reasonable proportion to the value of such information.

If the employer refuses or fails to disclose information (or to confirm such information in writing on request) to trade union representatives, the trade union may present a claim to the Industrial

Court, which may either, (a) make an order determining the rights of the parties and directing the employer to fulfil his duty under the section, or, (b) authorise the presentation of a claim for specified terms and conditions of employment to the Industrial Arbitration Board (which, in its turn, may make an award operating as an implied term *quoad* employees covered by the award: ss. 126, 127).

VIII. The Collective Agreement and the Procedure Agreement Defined

531 For the purposes of the 1971 Act, a "collective agreement" means any agreement which is for the time being in force and (a) is an agreement or arrangement made (in whatever way and in whatever form) by or on behalf of one or more organisations of workers and either one or more employers, one or more organisations of employers, or a combination of one or more employers and one or more organisation of employers, and (b) is either an agreement or arrangement prescribing (wholly or in part) the terms and conditions of employment of workers of one or more descriptions, or an agreement or arrangement relating to one or more of the matters contained in a procedure agreement (on which, see below) (s. 166 (1)). This statutory definition is wide enough on the one hand to encompass a workshop agreement between an employer and an organisation of workers and an industry-wide "treaty" between an employers' association and a confederation of unions on the other hand. The definition also includes "arrangements" which prescribe terms and conditions of employment. The term "arrangement" has been explained as indicating a practice which exists *de facto* and which has been accepted and acted upon. It might start from agreement, but generally arises from custom and practice (Lord Drumalbyn, H.L. Deb. 1971, Vol. 320, col. 448, on the Industrial Relations Bill). The definition is therefore wide enough to include not only new consensual agreements, but the "crystallised custom" and "inarticulate practices" which characterise much of British industry. The notion of the implied term permits such practices to be incorporated into individual contracts, although whether such incorporation rests upon the subjective intention of the parties or upon the objective inference from facts is an unsettled question. Such practices have not received much attention from the law, although the two Acts of 1942 and 1950 concerning the restoration of pre-war trade practices recognise the tip of the iceberg. Presumably the requirement that even an "arrangement" must be "made" by or on behalf of the parties is met by the notion of "making" an agreement which incorporates by implication trade custom.

In order to clear up doubt, the definition expressly includes the 532
decisions of joint bodies, such as Whitley Councils, where these relate to terms and conditions of employment or matters for which a procedure agreement can provide, provided that such decisions are intended to have effect as legally enforceable contracts (s. 166 (2)). Surprisingly, the definition includes the compulsory contract in the form of the procedure agreement enforced under s. 41 of the Act (below), as well as the "substantive agreement" (*i.e.* agreement regulating terms and conditions of employment) and "procedure agreement" (the "administrative" agreement as defined below). As to the substantive agreement, the Irish courts have drawn a distinction between *terms* of employment, *i.e.* contractual terms, and *conditions* of employment, *i.e.* the non-contractual, environmental conditions of work, such as physical conditions, or an "unofficial" tea-break. Section 167 (1) of the Industrial Relations Act 1971 gives the phrase "terms and conditions of employment" a narrow meaning by defining it as those "terms and conditions on which one or more workers are, or are to be, required to work for their employers." This is rather less explicit than the definition used in the Labour Government's still-born Industrial Relations Bill which referred to "terms and conditions on which one or more employees are, or are to be, *required by their contracts of employment* to work for their employers" (italics mine). That a substantive agreement need only regulate obligatory, contractual terms and conditions is an inference supported by the definition of an industrial dispute which relates, *inter alia*, to a dispute concerning "terms and conditions of employment, *or the physical conditions in which any workers are required to work*" (italics mine).

The "procedure agreement" is defined as that part of the col- 533
lective agreement which relates to any of the following matters:

(a) machinery for consultation with regard to, or for the settlement by negotiation or arbitration of, terms and conditions of employment;
(b) machinery for consultation with regard to, or for the settlement by negotiation or arbitration of, other questions arising between an employer or group of employers and one or more workers or organisations of workers;
(c) negotiating rights;
(d) facilities for officials of trade union or other organisations of workers;
(e) procedures relating to dismissal;
(f) procedures relating to matters of discipline other than dismissal;
(g) procedures relating to grievances of individual workers.

534 In practice, the functions of procedures are (1) to regularise trade union recognition, and (2) to establish some methods of resolving disputes. It is easier to recognise a union than to determine upon what matters a union is entitled to bargain. In the United States, considerable case law has accumulated on the distinction between "mandatory" subjects for bargaining (such as wages, hours, seniority, holidays, bonuses, working conditions, pensions, welfare, insurance, grievances, severance arrangements, lay-offs and so forth), and "non-mandatory" subjects of which the hard core is the central preserve of "managerial rights." It is likely that the provisions concerning "sole bargaining agent" in the 1971 Act will give rise to similar problems in this country. In addition to their functions as peace-keeping and war-avoiding treaties, procedure agreements may take different forms, such as (1) joint machinery on a standing basis composed of persons within and outside the individual firm; (2) *ad hoc* conferences convened as and when required.

535 Who, then, are the parties to the collective agreement? Where the agreement is made by representatives on behalf of two or more employers or of one or more organisations of employers (or a combination of the two) on the one hand, and by representatives on behalf of one or more organisations of workers on the other hand, then for the purposes of the Act each employer, organisation of employers and organisation of workers is to be regarded as a party to the collective agreement (s. 166 (4)). The omission of the single employer is presumably justified on the basis that a natural person or a corporate *persona* can act by himself—in the latter case, through the "primary organs" of the company, such as directors and managers. However, companies frequently act through persons acting as agents rather than as those with whom the company is identified. It remains to be seen how the term "representative" will be interpreted. If, as seems likely, representation denotes agency, the application of ordinary principles of agency law would mean that the "principal" may be bound by the unauthorised act of the agent acting within the scope of "apparent" or, alternatively, "usual" authority. The provision underlines the need to define the authority of the agent, particularly the shop steward who negotiates an agreement with management at plant or even shop level.

536 It is interesting to note that the Act lends support to the "corporate theory" of collective bargaining, *viz.* that the union (albeit acting through agents) is a "principal" to the bargain. English law generally renounces the so-called "agency theory" under which a union is seen as the agent of its members, a theory which is often difficult to reconcile with reality, and even were it not, would raise

difficulty in ascertaining the "principals," *i.e.* the members, particularly in large organisations with a changing membership. Where the union is registered and becomes a corporate body it clearly acts on its own behalf, just as a company is a right-and-duty-bearing subject in its own right and does not act on behalf of its corporators. Where the union is not registered, it still has quasi-corporate personateness for certain purposes, although remaining an unincorporated association (see para. 482).

However, in *Edwards* v. *Skyways* (1964), an agreement between representatives of the defendants and representatives of the association (to which the plaintiff belonged) concerning the payment of *ex gratia* sums to redundant employees was held to constitute an agreement affecting legal relations, but there was no discussion of the agency aspect, Megaw J. contenting himself with the conclusion that the association's representatives were the "duly authorised agents of the plaintiff."

IX. Enforceability of Agreements

A. The collective agreement

Whatever the position may be at common law (on which see **537**
para. 502, above), section 34 creates a conclusive presumption that every collective agreement which is made in writing after the commencement of the Act (December 1, 1971, for the purposes of this section) is intended by the parties to it to be a legally enforceable contract, unless it contains a provision (however expressed) stating that a part of the agreement is intended not to be legally enforceable, in which case the agreement will be enforceable save for the unenforceable part. The ramifications of this section are, as yet, not completely clear. Thus it would seem to include not only a consensual agreement in the ordinary sense, but a "codification" of working practices which have been acted on for some time (see the term "arrangement" in s. 166 (1), above, para. 531). The "conclusive presumption" in favour of enforceability is curious in that, whilst it may be rebutted by express provision to the contrary, it seems not to be *impliedly* rebuttable as would be the case with an ordinary presumption. Moreover any express exclusion of the presumption as to enforceability must be *contained* in the collective agreement, so that a general agreement between an organisation of workers and an employer, providing that all subsequent agreements between them shall be presumed not to be legally enforceable, would appear to have no effect, unless the subsequent agreements were deemed to incorporate and thus "contain" the general agreement—which is doubtful. The difficulties involved in ascertaining

the "parties" to the agreement have already been noted (see para. 535, above).

538 Section 35 extends the conclusive presumption as to enforceability to the decisions of joint negotiating bodies established by or under a collective agreement in order to (a) regulate terms and conditions of employment, or (b) determine matters for which a procedure agreement can provide. Decisions of such bodies on either of these matters are conclusively presumed to have effect as legally enforceable contracts provided that they are "duly recorded in writing" and, as so recorded, do not contain a provision (however expressed) stating that the decision is intended not to be legally enforceable. This section covers joint bodies ranging, on the one hand, from national joint councils of the Whitley variety, to joint works councils. Although the Solicitor-General interpreted this section, when it was before Parliament, as allowing a joint body to decide "at the outset of its first proceedings" what sort of decision it will take, *e.g.* a "once-and-for-all" disclaimer of enforceability (H.C. Deb., Vol. 810, col. 1367) it is, with respect, extremely doubtful if this is possible and the D.E.P. Guide itself is unequivocal (and rightly so) in its view that such a once-and-for-all disclaimer is not possible but must be stated *ad hoc* as the occasion arises (para. 71). If a joint body keeps minutes of its decisions (as is normally the case), would such decisions be "duly recorded in writing" for the purposes of raising the presumption as to enforceability? Minutes are kept as a record of proceedings and not *animo contrahendi.* Even so, it is arguable that minutes recording agreement on terms or conditions or procedural matters should contain an entry excluding enforceability on each occasion if enforceability is not desired. Clearly, section 34 and the present section place a high premium on vigilance.

539 Breach of an enforceable collective agreement is not, however, confided to the jurisdiction of the ordinary courts. No court, other than the Industrial Court, may entertain proceedings to interpret, enforce, or claim damages for breach of the collective agreement (s. 129). Instead of breach of contract, we now have an unfair industrial practice which may take two forms—breach and vicarious breach. The first covers breach of the whole or part of a legally enforceable collective agreement (whether entered into before or after the Act) or part thereof. Vicarious breach arises where any party to the agreement does not take all such steps as are reasonably practicable for the purposes—

(a) of preventing persons acting or purporting to act on behalf of that party from taking action contrary to an undertaking given by that party and contained in the collective agreement;

(b) where the party is an organisation, of preventing members of the organisation from taking any such action; and
(c) of securing the discontinuance of action in either (a) or (b) above.

The "policing" function of the organisation of workers has excited predictably hostile reactions from unions who are both reluctant to undertake such a function and fearful that, if they did, it would act as a stimulus to "blue unions." Nor are they entirely sure of what is expected of them. Is an official's exhortation to the members to refrain from action which puts the union in breach sufficient? Would the payment of strike pay or other assistance be taken as showing that the union was encouraging the breach? Is the union expected to discipline recalcitrant members, perhaps even expelling them from the union? The doctrine of implied authority as elaborated in *Heatons* case (see para. 614, below) would appear to render exhortation and advice insufficient if liability is to be escaped.

Breach in either of its forms of an enforceable collective agree- 540 ment, is, as already noted, an unfair industrial practice and as such may be the subject of complaint to the Industrial Court (see para. 626 for the three-fold remedies available to that court). A party to a collective agreement in writing may apply to the Industrial Court for a declaration with respect to any question relating to any provision of the agreement, save such as have been expressed to be not legally enforceable by a provision contained in the agreement. The Industrial Court, on such application, may make a declaration with respect to the question raised in the light of its findings of fact and its interpretation of the agreement (a seminal "conflict of rights" procedure). In the case of a breach of the non-vicarious variety relating to a collective agreement which was made before the date on which section 4 of the Trade Union Act 1871 was repealed (December 1, 1971) and was a legally enforceable collective agreement made by or on behalf of parties which must include an organisation of workers or of employers, the sole remedy available to the Industrial Court is an order determining the rights of the complainant and the respondent. Although a collective agreement is likely to be a contract "binding in honour" only (see the *Ford* case, discussed at para. 502, above), this is not necessarily so, *e.g.* a union and an employer may have provided expressly for enforceability.

B. Procedure agreement

Much attention has been directed to the problem of the "un- 541 constitutional" strike, *viz.* the strike in breach of agreed procedure for the settlement of disputes. Breach of an *enforceable* procedure agreement is now an unfair industrial practice and, as such, is remediable in the manner described above in connection with breach of an enforceable collective agreement (para. 539, above). More controversial, is the suggestion that individual workers commit breaches of contracts where they strike, or take other industrial action in breach of a procedural clause, *e.g.* a "no-strike" clause, which has been incorporated either expressly or impliedly, into their individual contracts. In *Rookes* v. *Barnard* (1964), the defendants were held liable for threatening breaches of contracts of service, *viz.* breaches of a "no-strike" agreement. Others have doubted if such individual liability can attach to workers on the grounds that (a) *Rookes* v. *Barnard* was not conclusive in that it was *conceded without argument* that the "no-strike" clause had become part of the workers' contracts, and (b) breach of a no-strike clause is essentially a collective breach and is therefore not an apt provision to be incorporated into *individual* contracts.

542 Hitherto, it has been generally recognised that until proper procedures have been drawn up any law which purports to enforce defective or non-existent procedures will be *lex imperfectus.* Instead of the idea of Procedural Commissioners (put forward in Research papers for the Donovan Commission) who would oversee the reform of procedural agreements, a voluntary system for the registration of collective agreements with the D.E.P. has been instituted since 1968, and several references have been made to the C.I.R. concerning procedure agreements within particular firms. In the background is the statutory power given to the Secretary of State by section 58 of the 1971 Act, which enables him to make regulations for the compulsory notification of procedure agreements: this power has not, as yet, been invoked.

543 All of this was, however, not enough for the framers of the 1971 Act. Sections 37–43 of that Act describe the steps which must be taken in order to render selected procedural provisions enforceable—a result which possibly represents the biggest inroad upon the voluntarist thesis so far worked by the 1971 Act.

The main stages in the enforcement of a procedure agreement are as follows. The first step is for the Secretary of State, or the trade union involved, or the employer, to apply to the Industrial Court on the grounds that the unit of employment (or "composite unit" extending to two or more associated undertakings) has one or both of the following defects—

(a) no, or an unsuitable, procedure agreement;

(b) industrial action has been resorted to contrary to the existing procedure agreement.

Before applying to the court, the Secretary of State must consult with the parties. For their part, the parties must give notice to the Secretary of State; such notice enables the latter to offer assistance or to refer the matter directly to the C.I.R. Once seised of the application, the Industrial Court is something more than a mere conduit for the transmission of the application to the C.I.R. If it has reasonable grounds for believing that either or both of the defects noted above have seriously impeded industrial relations in the unit or that there have been substantial and repeated losses of working time therein, it will refer the application to the C.I.R. If the C.I.R. considers that the scope of the reference ought to be extended, it may request the Industrial Court to extend the scope of the reference.

If the C.I.R. cannot obtain voluntary acceptance of the revised **544**
procedures, it reports to the Industrial Court on the new or revised provisions which are required and which could take effect as a legally enforceable contract. Within six months of the report, the employer or trade union included among the parties to the reference may apply to the Industrial Court for an order defining the unit of employment to which the C.I.R.'s provisions apply and specifying the parties on whom they are to be binding. Unless the Industrial Court is satisfied that an order is not necessary to secure acceptance with the recommended provisions, it must make the order, which then gives effect to the provisions "as a legally enforceable contract." Such a "contract" has effect as if it were a contract containing those provisions between consenting parties. Of course the parties are not in truth consenting, a state of affairs which has occasioned criticism of the "notional" or "compulsory" contract to which persons are deemed to have consented.

Procedure agreements are only enforceable in relation to a **545**
particular bargaining unit or, at the most, a composite unit; they cannot, for example, be enforced over a complete industry. It is likely that the reform of procedures will proceed under section 131 of the 1971 Act which permits the Sectetary of State, acting alone or jointly with any other Minister, to make references to the C.I.R. on industrial relations questions either generally or in relation to particular firms, including, in particular, the following questions—

(a) the organisation of employers or workers for the purposes of collective bargaining;
(b) procedure agreements;
(c) any matter for which a procedure agreement can provide;
(d) recognition and negotiating rights;
(e) disclosure of information by employers to employees or officials of organisations of workers having negotiating rights;
(f) facilities for training in industrial relations.

However, any recommendations which the C.I.R. may make on any of the above matters remain unenforceable and rely on the force of publicity and public opinion. The C.I.R. has confessed that its work has been affected by the non-cooperation of trade unions since the enactment of the Industrial Relations Act.

CHAPTER 9

INDUSTRIAL CONFLICT

A fundamental cleavage of opinion exists as to the proper basis of industrial relations in this country. According to one view, both management and labour share a common interest in the prosperity of the business in which they are jointly engaged. This "common interest" may be recognised by devices such as profit-sharing, works councils (as in France, where all undertakings, save the smallest, are obliged by a law of 1966 to have a works council which must be consulted on a range of important matters), or worker-directors (as in Germany, where such directors serve on the supervisory boards of companies). The German co-determination laws have clearly influenced the form of the European Company proposed for the EEC but have had little effect here, apart from experimentation such as that with worker-directors in the British Steel Corporation. It is possible that some form of "participative management" involving labour will emerge from the long-awaited reform of British company law. **546**

According to the opposite view, conflict in industry is endemic and ineradicable in the present state of economic and social organisation in Britain. Frank recognition of this conflict will, it is said, enable realistic measures to be taken to keep the peace. This is the predominant view and is supported by government, management and labour (with some exceptions), all of whom generally adhere to a managerialist and unitary theory of management. British unions have expressed their fears of anything which might undermine their claim-making role in an oppositional system of collective bargaining. They have opposed co-partnership schemes and shown themselves to be suspicious of devices such as works councils on which they might have only a minor place. It is significant that the Labour Government's White Paper in 1968 opened with the assertion that "There are necessarily conflicts of interest in industry" and that the Code of Practice, issued in 1972 under the Industrial Relations Act 1971, also accepts the conflict thesis, but departs slightly from the unitary theory of management when it states that "Good industrial relations are a joint responsibility" in which despite management's "primary responsibility" the co-operation of unions, employers' associations and individual employees is needed. **547**

Conflict in industry may be settled peacefully or by resort to industrial action.

I. Peaceful Settlement of Disputes

Two types of dispute

548 Disputes may be said to denote any disagreement between management and workers (or those representing them). They fall into two categories, *viz.* (a) "conflicts of interests," and (b) "conflicts of right." The former arise where differing views are held as to what should be the terms and conditions in a collective agreement, such as, for example, the proper rate of pay under a new collective agreement. Even highly regulated systems of labour law, such as that prevailing in Sweden, have been constrained to leave the resolution of such disputes to the exercise of economic power by the disputants, rather than attempt to treat them as justiciable issues. The latter type of dispute, the conflict of right, concerns the interpretation or application of the substantive terms of an agreed bargain or working practice and, if drawn properly, is clearly better fitted to settlement by some adjudicatory process.

549 Unlike several other countries, this country is conspicuous for its failure to recognise the conceptual distinction between the two types of dispute. Here, grievance procedure is generally used to raise both types of conflict. "It is not usual for a distinction to be made between the process of applying and interpreting existing agreements, as against the process of formulating new ones," wrote A. I. Marsh in his Research Paper (No. 2, Part 1) for the Donovan Commission. Jurisdiction over the interpretation and enforcement of legally enforceable collective agreements is entrusted to the Industrial Court by section 129 of the Industrial Relations Act 1971. Although the definition of a "procedure agreement" in the 1971 Act shows that "procedure" may be utilised to settle terms and conditions of employment and to deal with other matters, such as individual grievances (see s. 166 (5), above, para. 533), the Code of Practice refers to the two types of conflict both of which, it states, can be settled by independent conciliation and arbitration if the parties so agree, adding however that arbitration "is particularly suitable for settling disputes of right" (*ibid.*, paras. 126, 129). No doubt, the hope is that parties to collective agreements will come to recognise the difference between the two types of conflict so that, at the least, conflicts of right can be settled by means of some adjudicatory process rather than by trials of industrial strength. The 1971 Act has, as one of its postulates, the "principle of developing and maintaining procedures in industry for the peaceful and expeditious settlement of disputes by negotiation, conciliation or arbitration, with due regard to the general interests of the community."

From the legal standpoint, the most important type of dispute is the "industrial dispute" which is defined in terms wide enough to accommodate both conflicts of interest and conflicts of rights (para. 566, below).

Voluntary settlement

The basic principle that industry ought to settle its own differ- 550
ences is in line with the voluntarist philosophy of British labour relations. The domestic machinery for the settlement of disputes is described in the Department of Employment's *Industrial Relations Handbook*, which refers to the "great complexity and variety in structure and organisation" exhibited by such machinery. Thus, some procedures, such as those in engineering, embody the principle of "employer conciliation" whereby employers or panels thereof determine whether or not a procedural claim is justified. The majority of procedures however utilise "joint conciliation" machinery involving employers and trade union officials, and these received the endorsement of the Whitley Committee, the five reports of which provide much of the basis for the modern machinery, both voluntary and statutory, for the settlement of disputes. Amongst the criticisms made of much British "procedure" are those relating to dilatoriness and scope. As regards the latter, the T.U.C. would like to see procedure widened to include managerial action such as the speed-up of work, manning arrangements, redundancy arrangements, and a "status quo provision" *i.e.* automatic reversion to the position prior to managerial action precipitating the dispute until such time as procedure has been exhausted. As regards delay, the Donovan Report recommended that one of the desiderata of a procedure agreement should be provision for the rapid and equitable settlement of grievances.

As a long-stop, it has been found necessary to make available 551
statutory procedures for (a) conciliation, (b) arbitration and (c) investigation in those cases where domestic machinery is either non-existent or has broken down.

Concern at the extent to which the government was being increasingly drawn into industrial dispute caused the C.B.I. and the T.U.C. to enter into an agreement in 1972 for the voluntary conciliation and arbitration of industrial disputes. The existence of large non-federated firms and the lack of T.U.C. control over members have occasioned some scepticism as to the effectiveness of this new voluntary machinery.

Conciliation

552 Where a difference exists or is apprehended between an employer or any class of employers and workmen, or between different classes of workmen, section 2 of the Conciliation Act 1896 empowers the Minister to take such steps as may seem expedient for the purpose of enabling the parties to meet together under a chairman with a view to the amicable settlement of the difference, or, he may, on the application of employers or workmen interested and after taking into consideration the existence and adequacy of existing conciliation machinery, appoint a conciliator or board of conciliation. The Minister may, therefore, offer conciliation on his own initiative or on request from *one* side to the dispute. In the absence of any definition of a "difference," the range of conciliation is potentially wide.

553 An overlapping provision is section 2 of the Industrial Courts Act 1919 which permits the Minister to "take such steps as seem to him expedient for promoting a settlement" of an existing or apprehended "trade dispute," an expression which is defined for the purposes of the Act as "any dispute or difference between employers and workmen, or between workmen and workmen connected with the employment or non-employment or the terms of the employment or with the conditions of labour of any person" (s. 8). The definition of "trade dispute" resembles that given in the now-repealed Trade Disputes Act 1906, except that the latter definition referred to workmen employed in trade or industry. The difference was noted in *National Association of Local Government Officers* v. *Bolton Corporation* (1943), where Lord Wright, concurring in the decision that the term "workman" included a local government officer, was averse to attributing a limiting effect to what he termed the interchangeable terms "trade or industry," pointing out that, etymologically, trade derived from "tread," denoting a way of life or occupation and wide enough to encompass the "commercial magnate" and the "professional worker."

It deserves mention here that much valuable work is performed behind the scenes by the conciliation services available from the Manpower Advisory Service of the D.E.P. Such services are unavailable in relation to "unofficial" industrial action on the ground that intervention in such circumstances would be seen as cutting across the authority of the trade union. Because of some criticism from the Donovan Commission, the D.E.P. has broadened its mandate since 1968 by taking the initiative, suggesting the use of independent persons to conciliate and making prompt informal investigations, apart from which the Department has not expressed any wish to have a mandate broader than that conferred by the 1896 and 1919 Acts.

Arbitration

In contrast to the system of compulsory legal conciliation and arbitration used in Australia and New Zealand, this country prefers to rely on the limited facilities for voluntary arbitration afforded by the Conciliation Act 1896 and the Industrial Courts Act 1919. Under the later Act, the Secretary of State may refer an existing or apprehended trade dispute to the Industrial Arbitration Board, or to one or more persons appointed by him, or to a board of arbitration representing both sides equally under an independent chairman. Arbitration in any of these forms can only take place if *both* parties consent—a requirement which underlines the voluntary nature of arbitration in this country. The Secretary of State cannot make a reference to arbitration unless there has been a failure to obtain a settlement by means of any existing, agreed conciliation or arbitration machinery within the industry concerned. Such a failure may be due to the refusal of one party to utilise the available machinery. Single arbitrators and boards of arbitration, the latter used in those trade disputes where the use of the Industrial Arbitration Board is not considered to be necessary, act on an *ad hoc* basis. The 1919 Act requires the Secretary of State to constitute panels of persons appearing to him to be suitable to act as members of a board of arbitration and the panels must include women. 554

The highest arbitral body is the Industrial Arbitration Board (formerly the Industrial Court) which is a permanent court free of departmental influence although its members are appointed by the Secretary of State. Its members comprise representatives of employers, workers and independent persons, although it is customary for the full-time President of the Board to preside with representatives of employers and workers respectively. If the members of the Board cannot agree (and this is unusual), the matter is decided by the Chairman acting as umpire. The Board may sit in public or in private (in practice preferring the latter) and may sit in London or elsewhere (its premises and secretariat are in London). Features of the Board's awards are the full presentation of the rival arguments and the absence of reasons in the decision itself. Economy in the matter of reasons is justified on various grounds—a terse decision cuts the Gordian knot in a clinical manner and ends arguments whilst preventing accretions of "case law." The Donovan Commission recognised the force of the reasons for this preference for the Delphic utterance, not only by the Board, but by arbitrators generally, but urged that "arbitrators should be encouraged to give reasons whenever they can." A theoretical defect in the awards of the Board is that, subject to some exceptions, they are not binding 555 upon the parties. That this is a theoretical defect is borne out by the testimony of the President of the former Industrial Court to the Donovan Commission when he stated that, to his knowledge, there had been only one case in the history of the court in which an award had been repudiated by a party to the reference.

556 The 1919 Act also permits references from the Secretary of State for advice in any matters connected with a trade dispute or trade disputes generally or in any other matter which the Secretary of State considers ought to be referred, but the power so conferred has been sparingly used and no use of it has been made since 1946. Clearly, the C.I.R. will pre-empt most, if not all, of such general references in the future.

In addition to its consensual jurisdiction under section 2 (2) of the 1919 Act (under which most important references are made), and in those cases in which industries have included in their own disputes procedures provision for the reference of unsettled disputes to the Board, the Board has certain important functions. First, it deals with references concerning non-observance of the "Fair Wages Resolution" of the House of Commons, including statutory applications of that Resolution (para. 211, above). Secondly, the Board deals with references concerning the application of recognised terms and conditions of employment under section 8 of the Terms and Conditions of Employment Act 1959, as amended by section 152 of the Industrial Relations Act 1971. Thirdly, the device of statutory implication of terms and conditions of employment into individual contracts of employment may also be used in awards of the Industrial Arbitration Board relating to the employer's failure to carry on collective bargaining with a "sole bargaining agent" or his failure to disclose information to employees. (See Industrial Relations Act 1971, s. 127.)

557 The unilateral arbitration provided for in section 8 of the Terms and Conditions of Employment Act 1959, as amended, and in section 127 of the Industrial Relations Act 1971, is all that remains of the war-time system of arbitration which allowed the then Minister of Labour to refer a dispute to arbitration at the request of *either* party to the dispute. To the protests of trade unions and the general satisfaction of employers (who felt that unilateral arbitration had been invoked more against them than by them), the Industrial Disputes Tribunal (which had been set up in 1951) was abolished in 1959 and the unilateral arbitration of disputes was, with one exception, taken away. The exception was the former "issues" procedure, now termed the "claims" procedure and set forth in section 8 of the Terms and Conditions of Employment Act 1959 (discussed at para. 208, above).

Investigation

If the matter is sufficiently important, the Secretary of State may feel inclined to use his powers under sections 4 and 5 of the Industrial Courts Act 1919 by virtue of which he can set up a court of inquiry to inquire into such matters concerning an existing or apprehended trade dispute (whether or not reported to him) as he may refer to it. If a reference is made, the disputants know that the merits of their respective cases will have to run the gauntlet of public opinion because of the requirement that a copy of the court of inquiry's report must be laid before both Houses of Parliament. A court of inquiry is, in practice, used to resolve an *impasse* when all else has failed, as in the case of the Miners' Strike of 1972. Another possibility is that the Secretary of State, either acting alone or jointly with another Minister, may refer any question relating to industrial relations in a particular industry or undertaking (or part thereof) to the C.I.R. and, indeed, this body has already issued several reports. The Chairman of the C.I.R. announced in 1971 that he saw the Commission's role as strategic rather than tactical or "fire-fighting," presumably on the assumption that prophylaxis is better than cure. **558**

At a less formal level, committees of investigation and committees of inquiry may be set up, the former under the Conciliation Act 1896, the latter by virtue of the Secretary of State's ministerial position.

II. Settlement of Disputes by Industrial Action

The background

It was one thing to accept trade unions and collective bargaining as lawful; it was another thing altogether to ascertain in law how far labour and management could go in the assertion of their interests. "The right of workmen to strike is an essential element in the principle of collective bargaining," said Lord Wright in 1942, recognising that the strike is collective bargaining carried on by other means. The "rules of the game" have evolved from judicial decisions and particular statutes (usually enacted to reverse a decision which had proved to be anathema to the trade union movement)—the *Taff Vale* case and the Trade Disputes Act 1906, *Osborne* and the Trade Union Act of 1913, and *Rookes* which led to the passing of the Trade Disputes Act of 1965. The result was a curious amalgam of common law and legislation, distrusted by trade unionists and described as a "disgrace" by witnesses to the Donovan Commission. In applying the law, the judges have repeatedly asseverated that their task is not **559** to adjudicate on merits or to calculate the effect of their decisions on the public interest, but to draw the line between what is lawful and unlawful. In so doing, they have been forced to manipulate the exiguous materials of the common law in order to deal with the complex problems of a modern industrialised society characterised by a high degree of interdependence. The Donovan Report of 1968 was essentially a gradualistic report aimed at reforming the existing law (although many of its suggestions related to industrial relations generally rather than to the law as such). After some vicissitudes, an Industrial Relations Bill (less the so-called "penal clauses") was introduced in 1970 but dropped with the General Election of that year. Thereafter reform took a different and much more radical path leading to the enactment of the Industrial Relations Act 1971, the antecedents of which are to be found not so much in Donovan, as in the pamphlet *Fair Deal at Work* and in American borrowings.

560 In contrast to the piecemeal treatment of the old Acts, the 1971 Act purports to surround industrial relations with a positive and coherent framework based upon the four principles in section 1 (see para. 13, above). The law of industrial conflict is therefore to be found in (a) the 1971 Act, and (b) the common law and statutes otherwise applicable. Introducing the Act, the government explained that the intention was that, generally speaking, legal cases on industrial relations matters should be heard by the new Industrial Court and the industrial tribunals. Nevertheless, the "ordinary" law of contract, tort and crime continues to co-exist with the unfair industrial practice and the line between the two is not always clear. It is not surprising that already some difficulties have occurred between the jurisdictions of the Industrial Court and the "ordinary" courts, although the former is clearly bound by decisions of the Court of Appeal.

561 It is proposed to discuss the present law in the following order:

(1) Forms of industrial action and the "industrial dispute."
(2) Criminal liability.
(3) Civil liability—
  (a) contract;
  (b) tort and picketing;
  (c) unfair industrial practices.
(4) Emergency procedures.
(5) The Industrial Court and industrial tribunals.

Whilst it may be true that the "economic torts" have been relegated to a subsidiary role in the field of industrial relations, they will be discussed before the unfair industrial practices both for historical reasons and, more importantly, because the latter bear the clear imprint, conceptual and verbal, of the economic torts. This is not to say that the unfair industrial practices are mere statutory forms of the economic torts applicable to the field of industrial relations. The new law of the unfair industrial practice is to be interpreted (1) in accordance with the four basic principles of the 1971 Act, and (2) against the background of the Code of Practice made under that Act. The Industrial Court has already revealed its unwillingness to apply the old cases to the new situation and has shown that it is prepared to call upon the industrial expertise of its lay members, who, in fact, outnumber the legal members.

What constitutes "industrial action"?

If the parties to an industrial dispute cannot reconcile their **562**
differences by negotiation, conciliation or, if necessary, arbitration, they may be tempted to resort to industrial "warfare," such as the strike or the lock-out. A "strike" is defined in section 167 (1) of the 1971 Act as "a concerted stoppage of work by a group of workers in contemplation or furtherance of an industrial dispute, whether they are parties to the dispute or not, whether (in the case of all or any of those workers) the stoppage is or is not in breach of their terms and conditions of employment, and whether it is carried out during, or on the termination of their employment." This definition is both wide and narrow. Wide, in the sense that it covers both a stoppage of work by persons who are parties to a dispute with their employer (the "primary boycott") and a stoppage by persons in order to bring pressure to bear *through* their employer on some other person (the so-called "secondary boycott") as occurred in the *Stratford* case. The definition also includes a "sympathetic strike" by workers not involved in a dispute themselves; taken to an extreme, such a strike may become a "national strike." The definition (unlike that of the "irregular industrial action short of a strike", on which see below) covers both stoppages in breach and not in breach of contracts of employment. At the same time, the definition is curiously narrow to the extent that a stoppage of work without any industrial dispute is not legally a strike for the purposes of the 1971 Act, so that the "Kill the Bill" stoppages which preceded the enactment of the 1971 Act would not have been strikes in the legal sense. A brave attempt to escape from the *circulus inextricabilis* of a restricted definition is to be found in section 65 (7) (*b*) of the Act which refers to "a strike . . . otherwise than in contemplation or furtherance of an industrial dispute"!

A "lock-out" involves the exclusion of workers from their place **563**
of work or the suspension of work by one or more employers in contemplation or furtherance of an industrial dispute to which that employer (or those employers) need not necessarily be a party

(s. 167 (1)). Lock-outs occasionally occur from time to time but less frequently than strikes, a state of affairs which is, no doubt, attributable to the employer's control of the work situation, which, in turn, obviates the need for resort to cruder forms of action.

564 Rather than use the strike weapon, workers have sometimes preferred to use other tactical weapons such as the "go-slow," the "work-to-rule" or the "overtime ban," on which there was until recently a conspicuous lack of legal authority. The 1971 Act introduces the concept of "irregular industrial action short of a strike," defined as "any concerted course of conduct (other than a strike) which, in contemplation or furtherance of an industrial dispute,—(a) is carried on by a group of workers with the intention of preventing, reducing or otherwise interfering with the production of goods or the provision of services, and (b) in the case of some or all of them, is carried on in breach of their contracts of employment, or (where they are not employees) in breach of their terms and conditions of service. The National Union of Railwaymen had contended to the Donovan Commission that an official "go-slow" or "work-to-rule" on the railways was legal since it was carried out "by the strict observation (*sic*) of Railway Rules and Regulations" but that argument failed in *Secretary of State for Employment* v. *Associated Society of Locomotive Engineers and Firemen* (1972), where railwaymen, who had complied with their union's ban on overtime and rest-day working and who had worked to rule, were held to have engaged in irregular industrial action short of a strike; notwithstanding that they may have complied literally with their contracts the concerted action was directed to the disruption of the railway system and such disruption involved breach of an implied term in the railwaymen's contracts of employment not to act in a wilfully obstructive manner. The legality of each of the tactical weapons mentioned above depends upon the facts of each case, *e.g.* overtime may be optional or compulsory, so that an overtime ban might be legal or illegal accordingly, subject to the paramount consideration explained in the railwaymen's case (above). Workers who, in furtherance of a dispute, refuse collectively to handle work coming to them from fellow-workers, or to work alongside the latter, may thereby commit breaches of their contracts of employment and be guilty of an irregular industrial action short of a strike (*U.K.A.P.E.* v. *A.U.E.W.* (*TASS*) (1972), where, pending the non-appearance of the defendant, an interim order was made).

565 A more recent phenomenon, borrowed perhaps from students, is the "sit-in" and its variant the "work-in" the latter used with great success in the Upper Clyde Shipyard dispute in 1971 and since repeated with varying success. Unless the employer gives permission to such action, the sit-in and the work-in will normally be trespassory, and injunctions to restrain such activities have been given, although most employers have declined to take legal action for politic reasons. Those who have felt inclined to take more direct action have no doubt been deterred by the danger lurking in the old statutes on forcible entry.

What is an "industrial dispute"?

As in the case of the former "trade dispute," the "industrial dispute" occupies a central place in the law of industrial relations. It is defined as "a dispute between one or more employers or organisations of employers and one or more workers or organisations of workers, where the dispute relates wholly or mainly to any one or more of the following, that is to say—(a) terms and conditions of employment, or the physical conditions in which any workers are required to work; (b) engagement or non-engagement, or termination or suspension of employment, of one or more workers; allocation of work as between workers or groups of workers; (d) a procedure agreement, or any matter to which in accordance with section 166 of this Act a procedure agreement can relate" (s. 167 (1)). Also included in the definition are disputes between a Minister of the Crown and workers or their organisation. Any doubt which may have surrounded the meaning of "workmen" in the old definition of "trade dispute" is dispelled by the definition of "worker" in the new Act. The latter term is wide enough to include not only "white-collar" workers, but also those who work under a contract other than a contract of employment. 566

The definition excludes disputes between employers and employers, or between workers and workers. It includes not only a dispute between an employer and his workers but a dispute between an employer and workers not in his employment, as was the case in the dramatic case of *Midland Cold Storage Ltd.* v. *Turner* (1972), where dockers, who had besieged a cold storage depot outside the "docks" (using that word in its technical sense) because they felt that the container work being carried out in that depot rightfully belonged to them, were held to have an "industrial dispute" with the proprietors of the cold storage depot notwithstanding that they were not employed by the latter and notwithstanding somewhat strained relations between the drivers who worked at the depot (whose jobs were threatened) and dockers chanting "You out, us in." 567

Sir John Donaldson in the *Midland* case adverted to the resemblances between the old "trade dispute" and the new "industrial dispute" but considered that it would be a mistake to regard the latter as an amended re-enactment of the former. Because of the 568 relatively limited purpose of the 1906 Act and the wider purpose of the 1971 Act, his lordship did not think "that the authorities on the meaning of 'trade dispute' under the Act of 1906 have any relevance whatsoever to problems of construction in relation to the words 'industrial dispute' in the Act of 1971." Nevertheless, this dictum needs to be taken with care in that it does not affect the attitude of the courts in cases involving issues outside the purview of the 1971 Act, and even in issues under the Act his lordship has acknowledged that the Industrial Court is bound by decisions of the Court of Appeal (which might be disposed to take more cognisance of the decisions relating to "trade dispute"). In rejecting the requirement of some nexus between the employer and the workers in dispute with him, the *Midland* decision rehabilitates Lord Denning's view in the *Stratford* v. *Lindley* (1965) case that an employer might have a dispute with a union claiming recognition even though he had no dispute with any individual workman—"Suffice it that the union, on behalf of all its members, desires to be able to negotiate terms of employment, and that the employer refuses to recognise it." Lord Pearce in the *Stratford* case placed importance on the absence of a formal request and refusal on recognition, despite the fact that the union had pressed for recognition over a period of years, and also on the lack of any "practical need" for representation by that union. The position would appear to be that a recognition dispute proper may be the basis of an "industrial dispute" if the union is making what Lord Pearce termed "a genuine claim on the employers for bargaining status," whereas a recognition dispute which is merely a "front" for some extraneous issue such as inter-union rivalry will be disregarded if it can be shown that the union in question has no (or possibly, relatively few) members working for the employer with whom the dispute exists.

569 A graphic (and—to the union—costly) illustration of the dispute not ranking as a "trade dispute" (and, presumably, "industrial dispute") is furnished by *Torquay Hotel Co. Ltd.* v. *Cousins* (1969) in which oil supplies to the plaintiff's hotel were threatened by picket action following upon certain remarks which the managing director of the company had allegedly made in connection with the efforts of the defendants' union to unionise hotel workers in another hotel in Torquay. Upholding the injunction to restrain the interference with oil supply contracts (considered below at para. 593), the Court of Appeal took the view that there was no trade dispute with the plaintiff who did not employ members of the defendants' union. There was no dispute concerning terms and conditions of employment. The defendants had acted "in furtherance of anger" in order to teach the managing director a lesson for his officious intervention.

Presumably, if the defendants' union had enjoyed appreciable union membership amongst the workers in the hotel it could have claimed that an industrial dispute existed even though another union had been accorded recognition so that, to that extent, inter-union rivalry could be said to exist. One of the main arguments advanced by the consultative document for the new Act was that it would avoid the "destructive conflict and breakdown" attendant upon recognition disputes by providing machinery for the accrediting of a sole bargaining agent. Once a question is pending concerning the recognition of such an agent, strikes, irregular industrial actions short of the strike and lock-outs may rank as unfair industrial practices under section 54 of the Act (see para. 526, above). Another sort of rivalry—the "who does what?" dispute—is clearly within the ambit of the definition.

The courts have shown themselves ready to pierce the veil of an **570**
"industrial" dispute in order to reveal a "non-industrial" dispute, as in *Conway* v. *Wade* (1909) where a vendetta against the plaintiff for failure to pay a union fine was revealed, or, as in *Huntley* v. *Thornton* (1957), where jealousy at a person's promotion and the ruffled dignity of a district committee at being designated "a shower" were the real causes of the dispute. As Lord Loreburn L. C. put it in the *Conway* case, "A mere personal quarrel or a grumbling or an agitation will not suffice—It must be something fairly definite and of real substance." The "meddler" who comes in and uses the trade dispute as a cloak for his nefarious designs, sectarian, political or purely mischievous, cannot shelter under the umbrella of what has been termed "the golden formula" of the "trade dispute." According to this view, political disputes are *dehors* the definition. Examples are not hard to find. The blacking of goods destined for the White Russians, dockers' strikes against the degree of nationalisation of the ports, strikes by postal workers against the dismissal of the chairman of the Post Office Corporation, stoppages against the Prices and Incomes Acts and the "Kill the Bill" stoppages of 1971 (on which see *Associated Newspaper Group* v. *Flynn* (1970), where an injunction was given), all exemplify disputes with a "non-industrial" purpose. *Non obstante* the objection of trade unionists (who see political awareness as the sure indication of enlightened industrial democracy), and the doubts of academic writers (who consider that "industrial" and "non-industrial" purposes cannot always be identified), the courts seem prepared to explore the real issue lying behind a dispute. It has been suggested that a "General Strike" aimed at defeating a government would rank as a conspiracy.

The words "in contemplation or furtherance" signify that a **571**
dispute is imminent and that action has been taken in expectation of

and with a view to it, or that the dispute is already in existence and action has been taken in support of it. What is required is the objective reality of a difference between the parties on some concrete matter as opposed to the subjective judgment of one party that he is in dispute with the other. For example, the refusal of workers to work alongside a non-unionist has been held to constitute a trade dispute (*Hodges* v. *Webb* (1920)), but this would not be so if the workers simply took action without communicating their grievance to the employer. Workers who pursue action against co-workers arising out of a previous trade dispute which has been settled are not acting in furtherance of a trade dispute (*Hutchison* v. *Aitchison* (1970)).

Criminal liability for industrial action

The retreat of the criminal law

572 As though to bear out Durkheim's thesis that progressive societies abandon penal sanctions in favour of restitutive sanctions, the tendency since 1825 has been to rely less and less on the criminal law as a mode of enforcing compliance with norms of industrial behaviour, although the prices and incomes legislation of 1966–68 stood out as a notable exception. The Combination Act 1825 legitimised the collective bargain as a method of settling wages and hours, but did not prevent the criminal law from being used to restrain industrial action, particularly where this took the form of conspiracy, obstruction and molestation. Today, the tendency has been to use reparative sanctions and to resort to criminal sanctions for special cases. The Industrial Relations Act 1971 accords with this fundamental philosophy.

573 Unions have been emancipated from the crippling application of the restraint of trade doctrine (see para. 451, above) in that the purposes of a trade union or other organisation of workers are not, by reason only that they are in restraint of trade, unlawful so as to make any member of the organisation liable to criminal proceedings for conspiracy or otherwise. The protection thus given by section 135 (*a*) of the 1971 Act (re-enacting s. 2 of the Trade Union Act 1871) is also conferred upon organisations of employers and voluntary joint negotiating bodies. *R.* v. *Bunn* (1872) (in which London gas stokers, who had threatened to go on strike unless fellow-unionists were re-instated, were convicted of criminal conspiracy) showed that agreements to commit certain acts in furtherance of union purposes could still be criminal conspiracies, subject now to section 3 of the Conspiracy and Protection of Property Act 1875 which, as amended, gives those who agree, or combine to do, or procure to be done, any act in contemplation or furtherance of an industrial dispute, immunity from liability for criminal conspiracy if the act when committed by one person would not be punishable as a crime (see the "conspiracy to injure," below, para. 600).

The criminal law has not, however, been abandoned as a form of **574** social control. It is true that section 4 of the Conspiracy and Protection of Property Act 1875 (which, as extended by section 31 of the Electricity (Supply) Act 1919, rendered criminal breaches of contracts of service by those employed in gas, water and electricity undertakings) has been repealed, but section 5 of the same Act remains in force and this makes criminal the wilful and malicious breach of contracts of service committed with the knowledge, or with reasonable cause for believing, that the probably consequences will be the endangering of life, or the causing of serious bodily injury, or the exposure of valuable property to destruction or serious injury. This section has been criticised by some as anachronistic (breach of a contract of service ceased to be a criminal offence in 1875), and by others for failing to deal with serious harm to the economy. Part VIII of the Act meets this latter objection to the extent that it provides for "cooling off" and balloting procedures in those situations where harm to the economy is apprehended. Like the earlier Prices and Incomes Acts, the present legislation to deal with inflation relies upon criminal enforcement not only against "persons" in the jurisprudential sense of that word but against organisation of workers and organisations of employers who, in wide terms, contravene the statutory provisions (see section 5 of the Counter-Inflation (Temporary Provisions) Act 1972).

Also retained is section 7 of the 1875 Act, unusual in that **575** it makes criminal acts previously only tortious. Every person who, with a view to compel any other person to abstain from doing or to do anything which such other person has a legal right to do or abstain from doing, wrongfully and without legal authority—(1) uses violence to or intimidates such other person or his wife or children, or injures his property; or (2) persistently follows such other person about from place to place; or (3) hides any tools, clothes or other property owned or used by such other person, or deprives him or hinders him in the use thereof; or (4) watches or besets the house or other place where such other person resides, or works, or carries on business, or happens to be, or the approach to such house or place; or (5) follows such other person with two or more other persons in a disorderly manner in or through any street or road—is liable to conviction for a criminal offence and may be fined (not more than £20) or imprisoned (for not more than three months). The offence is triable summarily. To the extent that s. 134 of the Industrial Relations Act permits peaceful picketing (on which, see para. 607, below), the crime of "watching and besetting" cannot be committed. The Industrial Relations Act has lived up to its description as a "civil Bill," except for a few provisions which provide for criminal sanctions, such as those concerning the notification of procedure agreements (s. 59), the disclosure of information (s. 158) and contempt of the Industrial Court or the industrial tribunal (paras. 27 (2), 28, Sched. 3, and para. 11 of Sch. 6, respectively). Had the Act relied generally on criminal enforcement by the state, it is possible (paradoxical as it might seem) that some emotional "confrontations" might have been avoided.

Civil liability for industrial action

576 For present purposes it is convenient to discuss civil liability under the headings—(1) contract; (2) tort; and (3) unfair industrial practice. The problem of breach of the rules of a registered organisation is discussed elsewhere (paras. 488 *et seq.*, above).

(*a*) *Contract*

577 A strike may or may not involve breaches of contracts of employment. For many years, the traditional view was that a strike after strike notice of duration not less than that required to terminate contracts was lawful. The traditional view was rudely disturbed by dicta in the *Rookes* and *Stratford* cases which appeared to indicate that a strike notice, whether preceded by notice or not, might frequently be construed as notice of impending breach of contract. The Donovan Commission doubted the construction put upon those dicta and in *Morgan* v. *Fry* (1968) at p. 725 of the report, Lord Denning M.R. himself had second thoughts on the correctness of an interpretation which threw the whole question of the legality of strikes into doubt. His lordship, clearly influenced by the acceptance of the rights to strike for some sixty years, rejected logic in favour of an implication to the effect that contracts of employment are subject to an implied term that a strike after notice, not less than that required to terminate contracts of employment lawfully, will suspend the rights and duties of the parties, which revive when the strike is over—a view which the Donovan Commission examined but then found too complex for immediate solution.

578 Section 147 is patently aimed at clearing up the difficulty hitherto experienced. It provides in negative fashion that due notice given by or on behalf of an employee shall not, unless it otherwise expressly provides, be construed as notice to terminate his contract of employment, or as a repudiation of that contract. Notice, it will be seen, may be given by either the employee or some other person authorised in his behalf, *e.g.* a union official or shop steward. A shop steward may give notice on behalf of union members by virtue of authority

vested in him by the union rules, or by virtue of the authorisation of those on whose behalf he gives the notice; if he gives notice unofficially without the authorisation of those whom he purports to represent, or without the sanction of the rules, such notice is ineffective for the purposes of section 147 (*Ideal Casements Ltd.* v. *Shamsi* (1972); for the implied authority of shop stewards see *Heatons Transport Ltd.* v. *T.G.W.U.* (1972), a case concerning the vicarious liability of the union for unfair industrial practices).

The employee who takes part in a strike after due notice is not 579
regarded as having committed a breach of his contract for certain purposes *viz.* proceedings in contract brought against him, proceedings in tort (whether brought against him or any other person), proceedings under section 5 of the Conspiracy and Protection of Property Act 1875 (see para. 574). No protection however is given in respect of breach of a "no-strike" term in the employee's contract of employment, whether such term is express or implied by reference to a collective agreement. Similarly due notice will not act as a magic talisman against dismissal or non-re-engagement.

No court or tribunal has power to make an order for specific performance, or to grant an injunction, to compel an individual employee to work (or remain at work), or refrain from working (or to participate in a strike or irregular industrial action short of a strike), against his will. No assistance is therefore given to the employer who seeks a legal order to force his employees back to work, or to the union which desires to compel employees to stop working.

There can be little doubt that contract has been given a nodal 580
position in the "economic torts," such as inducing breach of contract, unlawful interference, intimidation and conspiracy. Lord Radcliffe, speaking judicially, has doubted whether breach of contract in its tort manifestations provides a realistic dividing line between what the law forbids and what it permits, saying that an embargo (as in the *Stratford* case) should be treated "according to its substance, without the comparatively accidental issue whether breaches of contract are looked for and involved; and by its substance it should be either licensed, controlled or forbidden." The 1971 Act is an attempt to escape from narrow legalism—whether the attempt succeeds still remains to be seen.

Tort

To remedy the "legalism" inherent in the economic torts, the 581
1971 Act creates the unfair industrial practice, jurisdiction over which is entrusted to the Industrial Court and the industrial tribunals. Section 132 limits in certain ways, discussed below, tortious liability for inducing breach of contract, preventing performance of

a contract (including threats of both of the foregoing), interference with trade, business or employment, and conspiracy, subject in all of these cases to the requirement of an industrial dispute.

582 Section 131, possibly "drawn by an irresolute hand" as Megarry J. put it (below), deals with the jurisdictional question. It confers a discretionary power upon a court to stay proceedings in tort in respect of an act which has given rise to proceedings before the Industrial Court or an industrial tribunal, or is one in respect of which proceedings under the Act could be brought before the Industrial Court or an industrial tribunal. There is a similar provision for an act alleged to be threatened or intended. Megarry J. exercised this discretionary power to stay proceedings in *Midland Cold Storage Ltd.* v. *Steer* (1972), in which the plaintiff sought an interlocutory injunction from the High Court in respect of acts which the Industrial Court had already ordered to be discontinued (since they revealed, prima facie, the commission of unfair industrial practices), but which order the plaintiff had taken no steps to enforce. In the absence of some distinct cause of action in tort outside section 131, his lordship was not prepared to go against what he termed "the general drift of the provisions . . . towards restricting the exercise of the jurisdiction of the High Court."

583 Section 132 (4) imposes an obligatory stay on proceedings in tort relating to an agreement or combination to do or procure to be done an act in contemplation or furtherance of an industrial dispute not otherwise protected by subsection (3) of that section. This provision (below, para. 606) fortified his lordship in granting a stay in the *Midland* case on the ground that industrial disputes are seldom simple and do not lend themselves easily to the dissection of those portions in respect of which a discretionary stay may be given and those portions, showing agreement or combination, in respect of which a stay is obligatory. The law of tort and the jurisdiction of the "ordinary courts" remain important where there is a "distinct cause of action" apart from the unfair industrial practice, or where there is no industrial dispute. There is no "irresolute hand" in the provision which precludes the Industrial Court from entertaining proceedings in tort.

Be that as it may, section 131 (4) seeks to prevent evasion of the principle by providing that proceedings in tort brought against trustees, members or officials of a trade union or employers' association *virtute officii* in respect of acts done by or on behalf of the trade union or employers' association shall be treated as though they were brought against the latter bodies. Typically, those who act on behalf of unregistered organisations are left in an exposed position in the legal no-man's-land which such organisations have chosen to inhabit. They cannot claim the protection of the subsection nor that of section 101 (4) (*q.v.*).

Inducing breach of contract. The principle that the parties to a **584**
contract are entitled to have their contractual relations preserved inviolate from the intermeddling and wrongful acts of third persons finds its modern origin in the case of *Lumley* v. *Gye* (1853) where a person, who had persuaded a dramatic singer to depart in breach of her contract, was held liable in tort. Crompton J. said that: "It must now be considered clear law that a person who wrongfully and maliciously, or, which is the same thing, with notice interrupts the relation subsisting between master and servant by procuring the servant to depart from the master's service, or by harbouring and keeping him a servant after he has quitted it and during the time stipulated for as the period of service, whereby the master is injured, commits a wrongful act for which he is responsible at law." Since 1853, the tort has been enlarged to include interference with contract generally. Its importance for present purposes is the central place which it has come to occupy in the law of industrial conflict where the issues are more important than those raised by erratic opera singers.

The present position is that a person who knowingly, intentionally and without justification, induces or procures, whether directly or indirectly, another person to break his contract with a third party, so that loss ensues to such third person as a necessary consequence, commits a tort. The five elements in the tort are:

(i) KNOWLEDGE. The first requirement is that the tortfeasor must **585**
have acted knowingly, so that a master who harbours a servant only commits the tort from the time that he learns that the servant has left his previous employer in breach of contract. The requirement of knowledge has, however, been somewhat eroded since the case of *Emerald* v. *Lowthian* (1966), in which an injunction was granted to restrain union officers from procuring the breach of a "labour-only" sub-contract between a contractor and his sub-contractor, which was apparently terminable by the former in the event of the latter failing to maintain reasonable progress with the brickwork to which the sub-contract related. Referring to the union officers, Lord Denning M.R. said: "Even if they did not know of the actual terms of the contract, but had the means of knowledge—which they deliberately disregarded—that would be enough. Like the man who turns a blind eye."

(ii) INTENTION. Second, the tortfeasor must act intentionally. For **586**
example, if A should call upon an employer to dismiss an employee, or if he should call upon his union members to withdraw their services, it must be shown that A *intended* the employer to dismiss

the employee in breach of contract (*e.g.* without adequate notice), or the union members to withdraw their services in breach of employment contracts.

587 (iii) INDUCEMENT OR PROCURATION. The third requirement is that the induce must induce or procure a breach of contract. *D. C. Thomson & Co.* v. *Deakin* (1952), settles that there is a distinction between persuasion on the one hand and procurement, whether direct or indirect, on the other hand. This was a matter upon which Coleridge J., dissenting in *Lumley* v. *Gye*, felt obliged to say in prophetic words, "that to draw a line between advice, persuasion, enticement and procurement is practically impossible in a court of justice." The near-impossible seems to have been achieved in the *Thomson* case. Thomson & Co. dismissed one of their employees for breaking an undertaking not to join a trade union—the "yellow-dog contract" of American labour law. The dismissed man's union resorted to strike action at Thomson's where more than seventy men had been unionised clandestinely, and also sought the assistance of other unions. One of the defendants, Deakin (general secretary of a large union), acting through his local officials, put to Bowaters, one of Thomson's suppliers, the unwisdom of supplying a firm declared "black." Bowaters notified Thomson's that they would be unable to deliver supplies—supplies which the Bowater drivers would not in any case handle. Deakin and his co-defendants were held not liable for procuring breach of the commercial contract between Thomson's and Bowaters in that (a) Bowaters had themselves decided to stop supplies and no breaches of employment contracts by their drivers had been demonstrated (*e.g.* refusal to obey orders to deliver to Thomson's); and (b) Deakin's "advice" did not amount to inducement.

588 The case settles that the tort may be committed in three ways: (a) by "persuading" a person to break his contract; (b) by committing some wrongful act which prevents a person from fulfilling his contractual obligations, *e.g.* hiding his tools or physically restraining him, and; (c) persuading a third person to do an act in itself wrongful, or not legitimate, such as breaking his contract of employment, so as to render performance of the contract impossible. In (a), simple persuasion *per se* is enough. In (b) and (c), however, the means employed must be independently illegal (or not legitimate). As Jenkins L. J. put it: "acts of a third party lawful in themselves do not constitute an actionable interference with contractual rights merely because they bring about a breach of contract, even if they were done with the object and intention of bringing about such a breach" (at p. 693 of the report).

589 As Lord Diplock has pointed out, the common law is not a

motor-way, and this is borne out by the way in which the *Lumley* v. *Gye* tort took to some unclassified roads before returning to the road signposted by the *Thomson* case. In *Stratford* v. *Lindley* (1965), the House of Lords found that, prima facie, the facts revealed indirect procurement of breaches of contract, except for Lord Pearce, who dealt with the facts as disclosing direct inducement of breaches of contracts. Trade union officials, who had made little progress in unionising firm A (which had accorded recognition to another union), instructed their members to refuse to work barges hired by customers of firm B (which had the same chairman as firm A). The House of Lords granted an interlocutory injunction against the union officials, who were considered to have knowledge that the effect of the embargo would be to put the hirers in breach of the hiring contracts, the majority finding that the officials had, by inducing the watermen to break their contracts of employment, caused breaches of the hiring contracts. Lord Pearce considered that it was a case of direct inducement to the hirers to break the contracts of hire, so that it was unnecessary to decide whether the men's refusal to take barges to the appellants was a breach of their contracts of employment with the hirers.

Some confusion was introduced by the decision in *Daily Mirror* **590**
Newspapers Ltd. v. *Gardner* (1968), one of the grounds of which was the principle that it was unlawful for anyone without justification to procure or induce breach of contract, either directly or indirectly, *i.e.* it is of no moment whether or not the means used are illegal. Since then, Lord Denning has changed his mind, in *Torquay Hotel Co. Ltd.* v. *Cousins* (1969), where he confesses that the principle adumbrated in the *Daily Mirror* case would have obliterated the distinction between direct and indirect interference, and where he rehabilitates the requirement of unlawful means in the indirect form of the tort. Indeed, the *Daily Mirror* decision can be rested on the other ground given in that case, *viz.* that the defendants, by issuing the stop-notices, were imposing a restriction contrary to the public interest under section 21 of the Restrictive Trade Practices Act 1956. The Master of the Rolls explained the earlier case as one really involving direct inducement in that the newsagents had merely acted as agents of the association in sending the stop-notices.

(iv) BREACH AS A NECESSARY CONSEQUENCE. As Jenkins L.J. showed **591**
in the *Thomson* case, an inducer may prevail upon an employee to break his contract of employment, *e.g.* by refusing to obey an order to deliver goods to a particular person, without necessarily causing his employer to break his contract with that person—the employer may have other employees who are willing to deliver goods, or may have some other means of delivery available to him. Lord Pearce

introduced a refinement in the *Stratford* case. Conceding the present principle *quoad* the indirect form of the tort, his lordship, whom, we have seen, treated the facts in *Stratford* as disclosing direct inducement, considered that breach of contract as "a reasonable consequence" of the inducement was all that was needed for the direct form of the tort, dismissing the argument that the plaintiffs might have tried to employ men from other unions as "quite unreal" —"In *Lumley* v. *Gye* it was not necessary for Miss Wagner to break her contract; but the defendant was liable because he successfully persuaded her." With due deference to Lord Pearce's opinion, it would seem that to introduce a distinction between reasonable consequence and necessary consequence according to whether one is talking of the tort in its direct or indirect forms is to introduce a degree of refinement bordering on the sophistical.

592 (v) LACK OF JUSTIFICATION. With the benefit of hindsight it may be that the courts would have been better employed in working out a realist philosophy of justification than in producing the somewhat sterile legalism associated with this particular tort—a tort which the Donovan Commission found to have been enlarged in a manner which is both "complicated and irrational." Accordingly, the plea of justification has been admitted sparingly. Rather touchingly, judicial solicitude for the plight of chorus girls driven to vice by their low wages enabled the defendant in *Brimelow* v. *Casson* (1924) to sustain the defence that he was not liable for inducing theatre proprietors to break off their commercial engagements with the plaintiffs who employed the girls. But the economic interests of miners did not command the same judicial empathy as did the purity of chorus girls. In *South Wales Miners' Federation* v. *Glamorgan Coal Co.* (1905), the defendants, who had ordered miners to observe four "stop-days" in breach of contract, were held liable for inducing breaches of contract despite their desire to keep up the price of coal by restriction of supply. Similarly, in *Smithies* v. *National Association of Plasterers* (1909), the defendants were held liable for inducing their men to stay out in breach of contract by supporting them with strike-pay—their submission that they were justified in so doing by reason of the alleged breach of a national agreement by the management was dismissed on the basis that "the breach by B of his contract with A cannot . . . properly be held to justify or excuse A in procuring C to break an independent contract with B." If the contract between B and C is one which involves a breach by B of a prior contract with A, A may induce B to break the B–C contract, *e.g.* A may induce his servant B, who has been induced in breach of contract to enter into a contract with C, to return and fulfil his original contractual obligations.

Interference short of breach. In its original incarnation, the *Lumley* 593
v. *Gye* tort depended upon the inducing of a *breach* of contract. Lord Reid, however, in the *Stratford* case, treates as *res integra* the question of deliberate and direct interference with the execution of a contract short of causing a breach. The nettle exposed by Lord Reid's *obiter dictum* was firmly grasped in the important case of *Torquay Hotel Co. Ltd.* v. *Cousins* (1969), where interim injunctions, essentially *quia timet* in nature, were granted to restrain union officials from interfering with the supply of oil to the plaintiff's hotel. Although in fact no breach of contract took place, the significant feature for present purposes is that interruption of oil supplies to the hotel was covered by a *force majeure* clause in the oil-supply contract which included interruption ascribable to labour troubles. The case can be explained in two ways. Russell L.J. treated the clause as an exception to liability and not as a delimitation of contractual obligation—a view which accords with the traditional English approach to exception clauses. The suppliers would commit a breach of contract if they failed to supply because of the labour troubles, but the *force majeure* clause would protect them from the liability arising from such breach, Lord Denning M.R., who has consistently asserted the theme of the inviolable contract, was prepared to go further and to extend the *Lumley* v. *Gye* principle to interference short of occasioning a breach, as where a person prevents or hinders a party from performing his contract. The interference, said his lordship, must be deliberate (a term which includes the Nelsonian application of the telescope to the blind eye) and direct. If the interference is indirect, unlawful means must be employed such as the threat of breach of contract (as in *Rookes* v. *Barnard*), the inducing of breaches of contracts of employment (as in *Stratford* v. *Lindley*) or the aiding and abetting of another person in breaking an injunction and thereby committing contempt of court (as in *Acrow* (*Automation*) *Ltd.* v. *Rex Chainbelt Inc.* (1971)).

A wide meaning has been given to the word "inducement." "The fact that an inducement to break a contract is couched as an irresistible embargo rather than in terms of seduction does not make any the less an inducement," said Lord Pearce in the *Stratford* case. Winn L.J., in a music-hall example, shows that the line between inducing and informing is very thin when he says—"A man who writes to his mother-in-law telling her that the central heating in his house has broken down may thereby induce her to cancel her intended visit."

IMMUNITY UNDER SECTION 132 (1) (*a*) OF THE INDUSTRIAL RELATIONS 594
ACT 1971. "An act done by a person in contemplation or furtherance of an industrial dispute shall not be actionable in tort on the

ground only—(*a*) that it induces another person to break a contract to which that other person is a party or prevents another person from performing such a contract."

Granted the requirement of an industrial dispute, this enactment gives immunity in wide terms. Unlike the corresponding unfair industrial practice under section 96 (on which, see para. 611, below), protection is not confined to registered organisations or those acting with authority on their behalf. Nor is the protection limited to the inducing of breach of a contract *of employment* (as was the first limb of the now-repealed section 3 of the Trade Disputes Act 1906). Finally, by including prevention of performance as well as breach of contract, the protection covers the *Lumley* v. *Gye* tort, as enlarged by the *Torquay* case. The phrase "shall not be actionable in tort on the ground only" (section 3 of the 1906 Act did not contain the words "in tort") has proved troublesome. Clearly a person who induces breach of contract by independently tortious means, such as by assault or defamation, has no immunity as regards these independent torts. But as regards the "inducing" itself, some judges have concluded that what is not actionable is lawful. Other judges, construing the similar phrase in section 3 of the 1906 Act, considered that whereas the inducing of breaches of contracts of employment might not be actionable under section 3, such inducing might remain unlawful for the purpose of procuring breaches of commercial contracts by indirect means. For example, Lord Pearce, in the *Stratford* case, thought that section 3 availed against the employer but not against a third person. The omission of the words "of employment" in section 132 (1) (*a*) robs this latter view of its relevance and, indeed, the better view would appear to equate "not actionable" with "lawful."

595 *Intimidation.* This tort consists in the threat of an illegal act which causes loss to another person. The threat may be made to the person who suffers the loss, or to a third person. If the latter, it matters not that the third person is entitled to inflict the loss upon the plaintiff; it is a *non-sequitur* to say that because the third person is entitled to inflict the loss upon the plaintiff, the defendant is thereby entitled to coerce the third person into inflicting such loss. Prior to 1964, the scope of the tort beyond threat of a crime or tort (especially where violence was involved) was unclear. In deciding that threat of breach of contract constituted unlawful means for the purposes of intimidation, the House of Lords in *Rookes* v. *Barnard* (1964), equated an "economic club" with a "physical club." The three defendants (one of whom was not an employee of the airways corporation) were held liable for conspiring to intimidate the plaintiff by threatening to strike in breach of a "no-strike" promise, thus causing the airways corporation to dismiss the plaintiff with notice. Counsel conceded that the "no-strike" promise was part of the contracts of employment of the workers concerned—a fateful concession. Neither section 1 of the 1906 Act (dealing with conspiracy), nor section 3 of the same Act (giving protection against inducing breach of any contract of employment and against the putative tort of interfering with trade or business), afforded any protection against acts which were independently tortious as intimidation. A dangerous dimension was added by Widgery J. in *Morgan* v. *Fry* (1968) where a notice to the employer that the defendants would not work alongside the plaintiff (resulting in the latter's dismissal) was held to be intimidation, notwithstanding the absence of a "no-strike" promise. Strike action, whether after notice or not, was a breach of employment contracts and, such, sufficed for the tort of intimidation. Section 3 of the 1906 Act provided no defence to an action by the plaintiff (*cf.* the employer: above at para. 594). Fortunately, the decision was reversed on appeal or the great majority of strikes would, at a stroke, have been labelled as illegal. Emphasis was placed on the deliberate breaking of a solemn pledge not to strike as opposed to some "technical" breach as giving notice of a strike which is a day or two short of that required. The effect of a strike notice and of participation in a strike consequent upon such notice is discussed at paras. 577 *et seq.*, above.

The *Rookes* v. *Barnard* case was consigned to that select body of cases now a hallowed part of the trade union *manes*, by the Trade Disputes Act 1965 and, more recently and with some modifications, by section 132 of the 1971 Act.

> IMMUNITY UNDER SECTION 132 (1) (*b*) OF THE INDUSTRIAL RELATIONS ACT 1971. "An act done by a person in contemplation or furtherance of an industrial dispute shall not be actionable in tort on the ground only—. . . . **596**
> (*b*) that it consists in his threatening that a contract (whether one to which he is a party or not) will be broken or will be prevented from being performed, or that he will induce another person to break a contract to which that other person is a party or will prevent another person from performing such a contract."

Ignoring the substitution of "industrial dispute" for "trade dispute," this provision differs in certain respects from its precursor, section 1 (1) of the 1965 Act. First, it is not limited to contracts of employment but covers any contract. Again, it covers not only breach of contract, but also prevention of performance of a contract. In line with the 1965 Act, and Lord Denning's dictum in *Morgan* v. *Fry* that "a threat includes a threat to induce," both threats to break contracts and threats to induce others to break contracts are covered.

It is difficult to quarrel with Lord Dunedin's definition of a "threat" as a "pre-intimation of proposed action of some sort" (*Sorrell* v. *Smith* (1925) at p. 730 of the report). Attempts to distinguish between threats and warnings or advice have incurred merited judicial censure. Lord Hodson in the *Rookes* case seemed to disapprove of semantic juggling when he pointed out that the word "threat" is neutral and need not be contrasted with a warning; a threat in the *Sorrell* v. *Smith* sense can relate to proposed conduct, which will be either lawful or unlawful, so that the threat will be lawful or unlawful accordingly.

597 *Interference with business relations.* In a society animated by economic self-interest, the judges have striven to distinguish between what is lawful and what is unlawful and not to pontificate on what is fair or unfair. Even so, there seems to be some vaccillation as to the proper legal dogma behind the mask of Olympian objectivity. At the present time, there can be little doubt that the fertile common law has parturated a residual tort of interference with business relations.

One of the grounds upon which the *Stratford* case was decided consisted in the interference with *future* contracts into which Stratford might have entered. The action of the respondents had, in Lord Reid's words, "made it practically impossible for the appellants to do any new business with the barge hirers." Lord Denning M.R. accepted this ground in the *Torquay* case, and, more recently, Pennycuick V.-C. treated the latter case as establishing that "this tort of interference with contracts applies not only where there is interference with contracts already made but where there is interference with contracts to be made in accordance with a regular course of dealing" (*Brekkes Ltd.* v. *Cattel* (1972) at p. 114 of the Report). Neither section 132, which deals with the tort of inducing breach of contract, nor section 96 which deals with the corresponding unfair industrial practice, make any reference to the wrongful inducing of a person not to enter into a contract. On the authorities as they stood, Megarry J. was not prepared, in the interlocutory proceedings in *Midland Cold Storage Ltd.* v. *Steer* (1972) to hold that there was a tort of wrongfully inducing a person not to enter a contract, apart from conspiracy and the use of unlawful means, although his lordship saw no reason why an injunction should not apply to *both* an existing contract and any future contract, as in the *Stratford* and *Torquay* cases.

598 As Megarry J. indicated, interference of the kind under discussion is only unlawful if unlawful means are used. The proposition that "an act not otherwise wrongful always becomes so if it interferes with another's trade or employment and needs to be excused or justified" has been emphatically rejected. Those who fire at natives who have come out by canoe to trade with a ship, who commit fraud or violence, who fire guns to frighten wild fowl, who obstruct workmen, who commit breach of contract or intimidation utilise means which are unlawful if such means interfere with another's trade or business. Furthermore, conduct prima facie lawful is not rendered unlawful by improper motive. Lord Dunedin referred to the "leading heresy" that a lawful act done by one is unlawful if done with intent to injure (in *Sorrell* v. *Smith* (1925)).

"It often takes a long time to determine what is heresy and what is orthodoxy," commented Lord Reid in the *Rookes* case and, certainly, there has been some dalliance with the notions that (a) there is a tort of interference with business relations *simpliciter* not requiring unlawful means (a heresy into which Lord Denning temporarily lapsed, as we have seen, in the *Daily Mirror* case), and (b) intent to injure might render conduct otherwise lawful unlawful (a possibility which Lord Devlin was not prepared to reject out of hand in the *Rookes* case). Some of the confusion may be laid at the door of the second limb of section 3 of the old 1906 Act which seemed to give protection to interference with trade, business or employment in the circumstances of a trade dispute, but Lord Reid, and later the Donovan Commission explained the insertion of the second limb as a form of statutory insurance against a putative tort of interference without justification.

IMMUNITY UNDER SECTION 132 (2) OF THE INDUSTRIAL RELATIONS ACT 1971. **599**

> "For the avoidance of doubt it is hereby declared that an act done by a person in contemplation or furtherance of an industrial dispute is not actionable in tort on the ground only that it is an interference with the trade, business or employment of another person, or with the right of another person to dispose of his capital or labour as he wills."

So, interference *simpliciter* is "not actionable" in the circumstances of an industrial dispute. But even in the absence of such a dispute, it is now established that interference will only be actionable if it is (1) deliberate, (2) unjustifiable, and (3) achieved by unlawful means, *i.e.* by means which the defendant was not at liberty to use.

Conspiracy. Defined as an "agreement of two or more to do an unlawful act, or to do a lawful act by unlawful means" by Willes J. in *Mulcahy* v. *R.* (1868), conspiracy is both a crime and a tort; a tort if the conspirators damage the plaintiff in pursuance of the agreement. Conspiracy may take two forms, *viz.* (1) the conspiracy **600** to injure (the wide form), and, (2) conspiracy to commit an unlawful act (the narrow form).

(1) CONSPIRACY TO INJURE. In this, its wide form, the tort marks a departure from the fundamental principle that damage done intentionally, even malevolently, does not, of itself afford grounds for complaint in the absence of interference with another's legal rights. The House of Lords rejected the proposition that the defendant in the case of *Allen* v. *Flood* (1898) was liable for securing the dismissal of shipwrights because of "malice" stemming from resentment which the boilermakers (whom the defendant represented) entertained for the shipwrights (who had previously executed ironwork on another ship). Assuming "malice," the defendants had done nothing which interfered with the legal rights of the plaintiffs. The boilermakers were entitled to withdraw their labour at the end of the day without breach of contract, so that the defendant, by instructing them to do this, had done nothing which constituted an invasion of the plaintiffs' rights. No question of conspiracy was before the House of Lords.

601 That the conspiracy to injure stands on an altogether different footing appears from Lord Cave's dictum in *Sorrell* v. *Smith* (1925) at p. 712 of the Report: "A combination of two or more persons wilfully to injure a man in his trade is unlawful and, if it results in damage to him, is actionable," immediately qualified by the exception that "if the real purpose of the combination is, not to injure another, but to forward or defend the trade of those who enter into it, then no wrong is committed and no action will lie, although damage to another ensues." It is the joining together which constitutes the unlawful means, since we have seen that it is not unlawful to injure another if the latter's legal rights are not affected.

602 The manner in which the dangerous potentialities inherent in the first part of Lord Cave's dictum are circumscribed by his exception is shown in *Crofter Harris Tweed Co.* v. *Veitch* (1942), where it was recognised that workers, like traders, can combine to advance or defend their interests even though a possible consequence may be commercial ruin for another. In Lord Wright's words, English law "has for better or worse adopted the test of self-interest or selfishness as being capable of justifying the deliberate doing of lawful actions which inflict harm so long as the means employed are not wrongful". In the *Crofter Harris Tweed* case itself, the appellants (producers of tweed cloth on the island of Lewis who used mainland-spun yarn) sought an interdict to restrain the respondents, union officials, from continuing an embargo which dockers, in response to union instructions, had placed on the movement of such yarn, without committing any breach of contract. The respondents were not guilty of conspiracy to injure since their actions had been prompted by a desire to further the interests of their members and of the employers who used island-spun yarn. In other words, to do acts not otherwise unlawful which cause harm to the plaintiffs is not an actionable conspiracy to injure if the object is to further legitimate interests. The legitimate interests in this case included the interests of employers who, with their workers, had a common interest in the prosperity of the island industry, which interests did not become illegitimate because they might be said to be "uneconomic." It sufficed that there was a sufficient community of interest—a "complete identity of interest" is not required. The same notable judge left open the categories of interests, other than those arising out of trade competition, labour disputes and professional matters, which the law might label "legitimate." The indications are that morality, political stability, religious freedom and racial tolerance are values which the law deems to be legitimate, just as their opposites are likely to be stigmatised as illegitimate. In *Hutchinson* v. *Aitchison* (see para. 571, above) workers who pursued a vendetta against another worker, whose dismissal they had procured, were held to have committed a conspiracy to injure.

Now that jury trials in civil cases have virtually disappeared, it **603** is for the court to determine as a question of fact whether the sole or predominant object (meaning ultimate purpose as opposed to immediate intention) is the advancement of legitimate interests. It is for the parties themselves, and not the court, to determine whether the measures taken are reasonable ways of effectuating the ultimate purpose. Once the ultimate object is accepted as legitimate, it matters not that malevolence or "glee at the adversary's expected discomfiture" is present. For an interesting illustration see *McKernan* v. *Fraser* (1931) as given in Wedderburn, *Cases and Materials on Labour Law*, p. 452. In recent years we have seen concerted action against employers (with whom there may be no dispute) aimed at the government and even the law and justified on the ground that the action has, as its ultimate purpose, the amelioration of terms and conditions of employment in a general sense. We have already seen that the courts are reluctant to accept political objectives as legitimate in the context of industrial conflict.

In the pursuit of their traditional objectives, the conspiracy to **604** injure does not place a serious obstacle in the path of unions or their members. Section 132 (3) goes even further and provides that:

> "An agreement or combination by two or more persons to do or procure to be done any act in contemplation or furtherance of an industrial dispute shall not be actionable in tort, if the act in question is one which, if done without any such agreement or combination, would not be actionable in tort."

In the context of an industrial dispute, the conspiracy to injure therefore is of academic interest only, although its importance remains in cases not involving such a dispute.

605 (2) CONSPIRACY TO COMMIT AN UNLAWFUL ACT. This type of conspiracy, which is narrower in scope than the type already discussed, arises where two or more persons combine to inflict damage upon a third party by unlawful means. Furthermore, the "unlawful means" is restrictively interpreted in that an agreement in restraint of trade is unlawful in the law of contract to the extent that the courts will not uphold a contractual term containing such a restraint, but it does not follow that an agreement by two or more which is restraint of trade will be an actionable conspiracy (see *Eastham* v. *Newcastle United Football Club Ltd.* (1964), at p. 445 of the report). "Unlawful" connotes a legal wrong, such as a crime or a tort. If there is a combination to inflict damage by means which are in themselves actionable wrongs, such as assault, deceit, inducing breach of contract, etc., there is usually little to be gained by framing the action in conspiracy since each conspirator can be sued for the actionable wrong which he has committed. Indeed, in criminal cases, the courts have deprecated the use of indictments for conspiracy if the illegal means constitute crimes in themselves, and similar indications have been given in relation to civil conspiracy. But *Rookes* v. *Barnard* (para. 595, above) shows that conspiracy may be used to ensnare someone who himself has not committed, and could not commit, the tort to which the conspiracy relates. Silverthorne in that case was a trade union official who could not have been sued for threatening B.O.A.C. with breach of contract since he held no contract with B.O.A.C. But it was held that he could be liable for conspiring with others who were employed by B.O.A.C. to threaten breaches of contract so as to cause loss to the plaintiff.

606 Is it conspiracy for two or more to combine to commit breaches of contract? Lord Devlin left this question open in the *Rookes* case. Others, however, recoiling from the subtlety that breach of contract is unlawful *quoad* intimidation but not unlawful *quoad* conspiracy, have suggested that strikers who break their contracts of employment in concert are doing something which is actionable, a conclusion which put them outside the protection of the now-repealed trade disputes legislation. Section 147 of the Industrial Relations Act (discussed above at para. 578) clarifies the position where due notice of a strike is given, but leaves unresolved the position where such notice is not given. Donovan L.J. noted in the *Rookes* case (in the Court of Appeal) that had a strike been considered unlawful in itself there would have been "countless actions against strikers before now, on the ground that they had conspired to secure their

ends by unlawful means." It would seem that there are weighty arguments against viewing a strike as a conspiracy in the narrow form purely because it involves concerted breaches of contracts of employment. It is instructive that the *Rookes ratio* has been limited to cases of "flagrant breach" of contract *e.g.* the breach of a "no-strike" promise—as opposed to the "technical illegality" involved in short notice (see *Morgan* v. *Fry*, para. 595, above). Secondly, it is open to an employer to sue individual strikers for breach of contract. Thirdly, it would further blur the already hazy line between contract and tort if concerted breaches of contract were to rank as also tortious. If, as is here suggested, breach of contract is not "unlawful means" for the tort in its narrow form, there is no reason why it should not remain unlawful for the purposes of the tort in its wide form where, in any case, the means need not be unlawful if committed by a single person. In the circumstances of an industrial dispute the difficulty does not arise, for the reason that participation by one person in a strike in breach of contract "would not be actionable in tort" under section 132 (3), above.

If proceedings in tort are brought in respect of an agreement or combination to do or procure to be done an act in contemplation or furtherance of an industrial dispute and section 132 (3) does not afford a defence, the court *must* stay the proceedings if the requirements of a stay are fulfilled (see para. 583, above).

Picketing. After a chequered history, the right to picket peace- **607**
fully was defined in section 2 of the Trade Disputes Act 1906 and is now to be found in section 134 of the 1971 Act, which defines pickets as those who, "in contemplation or furtherance of an industrial dispute, attend at or near—(*a*) a place where a person works or carries on business, or (*b*) any other place where a person happens to be, not being a place where he resides, and do so only for the purpose of peacefully obtaining information from him or peacefully communicating information to him or peacefully persuading him to work or not to work." The attendance of pickets in the circumstances and for the purposes specified above does not "of itself" constitute an offence under section 7 of the Conspiracy and Protection of Property Act (see para. 575, above), or a tort.

Two preliminary points may be made on section 134. First, it **608**
excludes attendance at or near a person's house or place where he resides. Second, the positive assertion "It shall be lawful . . ." in the 1906 Act has now been replaced by a negative formula. A more general point is the restriction of the statutory right to picket to the circumstances of an "industrial dispute" which, as we have already seen, is wide enough to encompass picketing of an employer's premises by persons who are not his employees, as in the case of

Midland Cold Storage Ltd. v. *Steer* (1972) (where the dockers were held to be in dispute with the owners of the container depot), or the case of the miners' strike of 1972, where the miners besieged power stations (with whom they had no dispute). It would seem that the attendance of pickets "at or near" the places mentioned in the section does not constitute a trespass to the highway (see the Irish case of *Ferguson* v. *O'Gorman* (1937): *aliter* picketing on private premises without consent—*Larkin* v. *Belfast Harbour Commissioners* (1908)).

609 The negative formulation of the right to picket indicates that no positive *carte blanche* is being bestowed; a view which the cases are quick to confirm. Clearly the section does not legalise separate nominate wrongs such as criminal libel or defamation. More controversially, pickets who ignore police instructions run the risk of being convicted of obstructing the police in the execution of their duty, as in *Piddington* v. *Bates* (1961), where the police apprehended a breach of the peace from the continuance of the picketing, and *Tynan* v. *Balmer* (1967), where ambulatory picketing (*i.e.* walking around, rather than standing still) caused the police to apprehend an "unreasonable user of the highway." In neither case were the accused charged with the offence of breach of the peace or nuisance, but with obstructing the police in the execution of their duty. Of course, the police have to satisfy the court as to the reasonableness of their opinion at the time so that it is not a case of "*post hoc, propter hoc.*" Even so, trade unionists view such cases, which put an uncertain restriction on what the Americans term "mass picketing," with some doubt, particularly against the additional hazard of a conviction for "watching" or "besetting" under section 7 of the Conspiracy of Protection of Property Act. A more recent restriction on the scope of section 134 appears from the decision of the Industrial Court that picketing which is otherwise permitted under section 134 will be unlawful if it involves the commission of an unfair industrial practice such as that involved in inducing persons to break their contracts with a third person (*Midland Cold Storage Ltd.* v. *Steer* (1972), distinguishing *Churchman* v. *Joint Shop Stewards' Committee* (1972)). Thus, unofficial picketing to induce lorry drivers not to enter premises so as to cause a breach of contract may rank as an unfair industrial practice under section 96 of the Act even though carried out peacefully. In the *Midland* case four types of breach of contract were discussed under section 96, quite apart from the unfair industrial practices in other sections of the Act.

An inquiry into the reform of the law of picketing was announced in 1972. Clearly, section 134 requires the inclusion of some immunity for unfair industrial practice if that section is to retain any general significance. Reforms which seek to restrict the premises which may be picketed or the persons who may attend as pickets are more controversial, and may raise more difficulties than they solve. The same is true of any attempt to proscribe "mass picketing" which, like a bald man, is difficult to define.

(*c*) *Unfair industrial practices*

The unfair industrial practice is a new, statutory wrong subject **610**
to civil redress in the Industrial Court or the industrial tribunals, and resting on notions of "fairness" as concretised in the statement of the four basic principles in section 1 of the Act and amplified in the Code of Practice. Some of its unpopularity with trade unionists may stem from the fact that it makes explicit "rules of the game" which formerly had to be elicited from piece-meal legislation and judicial decisions. The definitions of the unfair industrial practice utilise terms which have become familiar in connection with the "economic torts," but it would be dangerous, as the Industrial Court has indicated (see paras. 568, 625), to assume that the construction of these terms is the same in both contexts. In what follows, attention is mainly directed to those unfair industrial practices which are most relevant to industrial conflict in its collective aspect, except those connected with collective bargaining (which are discussed in Chapter 8), but mention is made of the unfair industrial practices connected with certain specific issues, such as infringement of trade union rights and unfair dismissal (discussed substantively in Part I of this book). The relevant unfair industrial practices are as follows:

(1) *Inducing or threatening to induce breach of contract.* **611**

> "It shall be an unfair industrial practice for any person in contemplation or furtherance of an industrial dispute, knowingly to induce or threaten to induce another person to break a contract to which that other person is a party, unless the person so inducing or threatening to induce the breach of contract—
> (a) is a trade union or an employers' association, or
> (b) does so within the scope of his authority on behalf of a trade union or an employers' association" (s. 96 (1))."

Unlike section 3 of the 1906 Act, all breaches of contract are **612**
covered and not merely contracts of employment, subject to the exclusion of collective agreements (unfair industrial practices connected with collective agreements are discussed in Chapter 8). A contract of employment is, however, covered by the section even though it contains terms implied or incorporated by reference to a collective agreement. Thus, a shop steward who calls out workers on strike without adequate notice (see section 147, discussed above

at para. 578), induces the workers to break their contracts of employment and thereby commits the unfair industrial practice in section 96. As we shall see, indirect inducing of breach of contract would appear to be covered by the section, as where the shop steward induces breaches of contracts of employment by workers of another employer so that the latter is unable to fulfil a commercial contract with the employer who is in dispute with his workers, provided that the shop steward has the requisite degree of knowledge (see below), and the complainant can show that he "is the person against whom the action is taken." The section is wide in that it encompasses all breaches of contract, but narrow in comparison to the cognate tort in that it does not refer to *prevention* of performance, as opposed to *breach* of contract.

613 In its narrow sense, it is clear that a person may be induced to break his contract by means of persuasion or encouragement—the direct form of the tort in *Lumley* v. *Gye* (see para. 588). Although it has been suggested that the word ought to be restricted to this narrow connotation, the cases so far indicate that a person who causes or procures a breach of contract indirectly may be said to induce such breach. Those cases turn upon the "containerisation" issue which dominated events in 1972. That issue was a "who does what" dispute between the owners of container depots and hauliers who served them on the one hand, and dockers on the other hand who claimed that the "stuffing" and "stripping" of containers was work which was properly theirs. Dockers who picketed a container depot in order to persuade drivers not to cross the picket lines and in order to note those lorries who did so (which would be "blacked" and refused entry to the docks on later occasions) were held in interim proceedings to have induced breaches of contracts, *viz.* breaches of their own contracts of employment, breaches by suppliers to the container depot, breaches of the container firm's contracts with its customers and breaches of contracts between the container firm and its hauliers (*Midland Cold Storage* v. *Steer* (1972)). The refusal of entry to "blacked" lorries was adjudged to have induced breaches of contracts between the hauliers and their customers as well as breaches of the contracts between the dockers and their employers (*Heatons Transport* (*St. Helens*) *Ltd.* v. *Transport and General Workers' Union* (1972) at p. 339 of the report). The requirement that the person who induces or threatens to induce a breach of contract must do so "knowingly" was added as an amendment to the Bill. The Court of Appeal gave the word the same meaning as it has in the *Lumley* v. *Gye* tort, so that it would appear to include those who know of the contracts and their contents and those who turn a blind eye to them (see para. 585 above). It is significant that the hindering or prevent-

ing of performance of a contract is not included, unlike section 132 (see para. 594, above). The breach of contract affected by section 96 does not include breach of a collective agreement but includes so much of any contract of employment as it implied or incorporated in that contract by reference to a collective agreement (for liabilities in connection with collective agreement, see Chapter 8).

Unlike the Trade Disputes Act 1906 which gave certain tortious **614**
immunities to "any person," the present section protects only a trade union (or employer's association), and those who acts on its behalf within the scope of their authority, from liability for unfair industrial practice. In the dockers' cases of 1972 it became apparent that neither unregistered unions, nor members of those unions, enjoyed any immunity under the section. Indeed the policy of the Act was to bestow upon unions a "policing" function over their own members; a function which unions were unwilling, as voluntary associations, to adopt. An amendment to the Bill which would have had the effect of freeing unions from liability unless they ratified the unofficial actions of their members failed. In the *Heatons* case (above), the union in question was held accountable for the actions of shop stewards notwithstanding that they had not authorised those actions and indeed had recommended their discontinuance in deference to desist orders from the Industrial Court. The position of shop stewards was examined for the first time in that case, the Court of Appeal holding the union free of liability for the acts of shop stewards in their role of representatives of their workmates and not in their role as agents or delegates of the union. The House of Lords, however, rejected the "dual role" of the shop stewards and held that they had acted within the scope of the implied authority given to them by the union thereby rendering the latter liable (the fines of £5,500 imposed on the union by the Industrial Court were re-instated by the House of Lords). It was this important finding as to union responsibility rather than individual responsibility which facilitated the release of the "five dockers" (see para. 629, below). All of the courts involved were, at least, unanimous that the committee of shop stewards who directed the various unfair industrial practices was not an "organisation of workers" because of its lack of regulative functions.

(2) *Industrial action in support of an unfair industrial practice.* **615**
Section 97 discourages supportive action of certain kinds in relation to action which is an unfair industrial practice. That section, with one exception, makes it an unfair industrial practice for any person, in contemplation or furtherance of an industrial dispute, to take or threaten to take certain steps with the purpose or principal purpose of furthering any action which has already been taken, either by him or another person, and which constitutes an unfair industrial

practice under the Act. The steps referred to are (a) the calling, organising, procuring or financing of a strike; (b) the organising, procuring or financing of any irregular industrial action short of a strike; and (c) the instituting, carrying on, organising, procuring or financing of a lock-out. The exception concerns a trade union, or employers' association, which takes, or threatens, steps in order to further action taken by one or more of its officials which constitutes an unfair industrial practice by virtue of section 96 (discussed above), and which is accordingly free of liability under the present section. The scope of the exception may be illustrated by reference to the shop steward who calls an immediate and unofficial strike thereby committing the unfair industrial practice contained in section 96. If his trade union ratifies his act and supports the strikers with strike pay, it does not incur liability under the present section although it is supporting an unfair industrial practice under section 96 committed by the shop steward. But the trade union would be liable if it commits (or fails to prevent) strike action which is in breach of a legally enforceable collective agreement because this is an unfair industrial practice outside section 96 (see section 36 of the Act).

616 (3) *Industrial action against extraneous parties.* Section 98 is based on the inarticulate assumption that third persons ought not to be involved in imbroglios which do not directly concern them. Under that section, it is an unfair industrial practice for any person in contemplation or furtherance of an industrial dispute to take or threaten to take any of the steps specified above (see (a), (b) or (c) in the preceding paragraph), if (a) he knows or has reasonable grounds for believing that another person has entered into a contract (not being a contract of employment) with a party to that dispute; (b) his purpose is knowingly to induce that other person to break that contract or to prevent him from performing it; and (c) that other person is an extraneous party. In the *Steer* case (para. 613, above), the threat to "black" at national level anyone who crossed the picket lines was held to constitute an unfair industrial practice in that those responsible had reasonable grounds for believing that other persons, customers or suppliers, had contracts with Midland (not being contracts of employment) and intended to induce the customers or suppliers (the extraneous parties) to break those contracts. The threats if carried out would have involved dockers in breaches of their contracts under the Dock Labour Scheme and thereby in irregular industrial action short of a strike (step (b) in para. 615, above). Unlike section 96, action to prevent performance of a contract is included.

A person is regarded as an extraneous party if he is not a party to the dispute and has not in contemplation or furtherance of that dispute taken action in material support of a party to it. Certain persons, broadly, associated employers, co-members of organisations, contributors to relief funds, and suppliers of goods and services are not, as such, regarded as parties to a dispute; the first of these puts a restriction on the secondary boycott against an associated company in the same group of companies.

(4) *Other unfair industrial practices.* The following unfair industrial **617**
practices involve separate issues discussed elsewhere in this book but may conveniently be set out here. All involve industrial action, or the threat thereof, in the form of the strike, irregular industrial action short of a strike and the lock-out, and certain actions connected therewith.

(i) Knowingly to induce or attempt to induce an employer not to perform his duties in connection with an agency shop agreement.

(ii) Knowingly to induce or attempt to induce a trade union or joint negotiating panel or other person to refrain from making an application for an agency shop agreement or for a "testing ballot" in connection with an existing agency shop agreement.

(iii) Knowingly to induce or attempt to induce an employer to enter into an agency shop agreement (other than one supported by ballot) after an application for such an agreement has been made, or to refrain from making an application for an agency shop agreement.

(iv) Knowingly to induce an employer or person acting on behalf of an employer to take any action *contra* section 5 (2) (trade union rights) or section 22 (1) (unfair dismissal). See para. 632, below, where the *Rookes* v. *Barnard* situation is discussed.

(v) Knowingly to induce an employer to enter, or comply with, a pre-entry closed shop agreement to the extent that the latter is, in whole or in part, void.

(vi) Knowingly to induce an employer to comply with a provision declared void by the Industrial Court as a "closed shop" on the application of a worker who has been refused employment.

(vii) Knowingly to induce an employer or an employers' association to join in making an application for an approved closed shop agreement under Part I of Schedule 1 to the Act.

Unfair industrial practices in connection with the sole bargaining agency and the collective agreement are discussed in Chapter 8.

Emergency procedures

618 The growth in this century of large-scale interdependent units of production together with improved transport and communications have resulted in a situation in which industrial action may now have secondary effects far exceeding that at the beginning of the century when the units of production were generally smaller and the tempo of production slower. An interruption of supplies through the docks, or a failure in the production of energy, can now precipitate a crisis of the first magnitude. One of the most intractable problems of labour law in this, and any other, country is how to reconcile the right of free men to withhold their labour with the interests of the community at large. Hitherto, governments have relied on the power conferred by the Emergency Powers Act 1920 which enable a state of emergency to be proclaimed when industrial action is likely to cause deprivation of the essentials of life.

619 Part VIII of the Industrial Relations Act 1971, which has some affinities with the American Taft-Hartley Act of 1947, makes provision for emergencies which is wider in terms than those in the 1920 Act in that it enables the Industrial Court to make a "cooling-off" order, not exceeding sixty days, on the application of the Secretary of State. The latter may apply to the Industrial Court for an order where it appears to him (a) that industrial action (*i.e.* a strike, irregular industrial action short of a strike, or lock-out) has begun or is likely to begin in contemplation or furtherance of an industrial dispute; (b) that such action has caused, or would cause, an interruption in the supply of goods or in the provision of services of such a nature, or on such a scale, as to be likely to be gravely injurious to the national economy, to imperil national security or to create a serious risk of public disorder, or to endanger the lives of a substantial number of persons or expose a substantial number of persons to serious risk of disease or personal injury; and (c) that in the circumstances it would be conducive to a settlement if the industrial action were discontinued or deferred. The Industrial Court may make the cooling-off order if it is satisfied on the evidence that there are sufficient grounds for believing that the condition specified in (b), above, is fulfilled.

620 Unlike the proposals of the Labour Government, as contained in the White Paper *In Place of Strife*, the Secretary of State cannot act on his own initiative, but must obtain an order from the Industrial Court. That court was satisfied that the necessary conditions for the making of an order were present in *Secretary of State for Employment* v. *Associated Society of Locomotive Engineers and Firemen* (1972), where a fourteen-day order (instead of the twenty-one-day

order suggested) was made. Whilst denying that it was just a "rubber stamp," the court in that case considered that it had "but a limited function" as regards conditions (a) and (c) (set out in the preceding paragraph), being content to see that the Minister has not misunderstood the law or otherwise misdirected himself. As regards condition (b), the court must not only be satisfied that in the Secretary of State's view the condition has been complied with, but must share that view.

The second feature of the "cooling-off" procedure lies in the 621
manner in which the order calling for temporary discontinuance of the industrial action is directed at those responsible for such action and not at those, such as strikers, who merely comply with directions given by their leaders. The order cannot compel individuals to return to, or to remain at, work, and cannot impose sanctions on any individual merely by reason of compliance with the wishes of his leaders. In the *ASLEF* case, above, the order was directed to the three railway unions and since these, like a corporation, can only act through individuals, the union's officers, servants and agents were also included. The order cannot include a person who has no responsibility for the industrial action except as a *trade union* official acting within the scope of his authority on behalf of the trade union. Those who act on behalf of unregistered organisations of workers enjoy no such immunity.

Part VIII of the Act also enables the Secretary of State to apply 622
to the Industrial Court for an order for a ballot where it appears to him (a) that industrial action has begun or is likely to begin in contemplation or furtherance of an industrial dispute; (b) that either condition (b) required for a cooling-off order is fulfilled (see para. 619, above), *or* the effects of the industrial action on a particular industry are, or are likely to be, such as to be seriously injurious to the livelihood of a substantial number of workers employed in that industry; and (c) that there are reasons for doubting whether the workers who are taking part, or are expected to take part, in the industrial action are, or would be, taking part in it in accordance with their wishes, and whether they have had an adequate opportunity of indicating their wishes in this respect. The Court of Appeal upheld the order for a ballot by the Industrial Court in *Secretary of State for Employment* v. *Associated Society of Locomotive Engineers and Firemen* (*No.* 2) (1972), notwithstanding the views of those who felt that a ballot would be supererogatory in the light of the degree of support which railwaymen seemed to be according to their unions in the matter of industrial action. It was enough that the Minister (who gave no reasons for doubting the attitude of railwaymen towards the action of their leaders) had in good faith taken a view of the law

and facts without misdirecting himself and without taking into account extraneous considerations.

Any ballot ordered by the order of the Industrial Court will be conducted by or under the Commission on Industrial Relations. As in the case of the cooling-off order, the order for a ballot is directed at those responsible for the industrial action, actual or impending, and pending the result of the ballot, will include provisions directing those responsible from taking further industrial action (which may involve the withdrawal of strike notices).

The Industrial Court and industrial tribunals

623 The 1971 Act establishes a new system of adjudication and investigation for industrial relations in which the Industrial Court and the tribunals have, for lawyers at least, an important place. The broad scheme of the Act is that the adjudicatory part of the new system should be handled by the Industrial Court (which would deal with the collective and, therefore, presumably, more important issues), and by the tribunals, which would deal with the individual issues from which, on questions of law, appeal would generally lie to the Industrial Court.

Industrial Court

624 The Industrial Court is a new statutory creation enjoying a status equivalent to that of the High Court, except that it differs from that court by having a limited jurisdiction (*e.g.* actions in tort are outside its jurisdiction), although that jurisdiction (unlike that of the High Court, or the Court of Session) is exerciseable throughout Great Britain. The court consists of a minority of nominated members, who are judges, and of appointed members who bring to it varying degrees of industrial expertise. The trade union "boycott" of the court under T.U.C. "instruction" has deprived the court of trade union experience which would otherwise have been available to it.

625 It also differs from the "ordinary" Courts in certain respects. From a substantive point of view, the court must pay regard to the four policy considerations on which the 1971 Act is based and can take into account the provisions of the Code of Practice, considerations which have led to the court to indicate that it will not necessarily follow common law "precedents" on matters now covered by the Act (*e.g.* the old interpretations of the term "trade dispute" in relation to the new term "industrial dispute"). It treats the decisions of the High Court as "persuasive," although like the High Court it can be set right by higher appellate courts. The procedure of the court is more informal than that of the ordinary courts and reflects, on occasions, an "inquisitorial" element contrasting with the "adversary" procedure employed by the latter courts. It also feels free to draw on the industrial experience of its non-legal members, sometimes, as has been indicated rather acidly, to the extent of supplying a want of evidence.

The jurisdiction of the Industrial Court which is relevant for present purposes is set out below, together with such remedial relief as it may grant, although it should be remembered that the court has diverse functions connected with matters such as agency shop agreements, approved closed shop agreements, procedure agreements, sole bargaining agencies, registration and emergency procedures, the main features of which have been mentioned in the appropriate contexts.

1. Complaints of unfair industrial practices taken against the **626**
complainant, other than complaints under section 5 (trade union rights), or section 22 (unfair dismissal). Where it considers it to be "just and equitable," the court may grant to the complainant one or more of the following remedies: (a) an order "determining the rights of the complainant and of the respondent in relation to the action specified in the complaint"; (b) an award of compensation to the complainant in respect of that action; and (c) an order directing the respondent to refrain from continuing to take that action, and to refrain from taking any other action of a like nature in relation to the complainant, or, where the action complained of consists of a threat or action carried out by means of a threat, a like order to restrain the same.

The amount of compensation which the court may award is such **627**
amount as it thinks just and equitable in all the circumstances, having regard to the loss sustained by the aggrieved party in consequence of the matters to which the complaint refers, in so far as that loss was attributable to action taken by or on behalf of the party in default. The amount may include expenses reasonably incurred by the aggrieved party, and the loss of any benefit which he might reasonably be expected to have had were it not for the action of the respondent, subject to an overriding duty on the part of the aggrieved party to mitigate his loss. Evocative of common law contributory negligence is the rule that the court, where it is just and equitable to do so, must reduce the assessment of loss to the extent to which the aggrieved party has caused or contributed to the matters to which the complaint relates. The rules for compensation, contained in section 116 of the Act, apply to complaints other than those discussed in this chapter, *e.g.* breach of a legally enforceable collective bargain or contravention of the guiding principles by organisations. One of the valuable privileges of registration (for those minded to avail themselves of it) is the limitation on the amount of compensation

which can be awarded against a trade union according to its size. These upper limits are—(a) for a trade union with less than 5,000 members—£5,000; (b) for one with less than 25,000 but 5,000 or more members—£25,000; (c) for one with less than 100,000 but 25,000 or more members—£100,000; and (d) for one with 100,000 or more members—£100,000.

628 An award of compensation is treated for the purposes of enforcement and devolution on death as if it were a judgment of the High Court or the county court (as the case may be), subject to the protection of non-militant funds, noted at para. 480, above. See Sched. 3, paras. 26–28, for enforcement of awards and order, including punishment for contempt. The latter requires the consent of an appointed member (see Sched. 3, para. 27 (2); interim orders may be made under r. 59 of the Industrial Court Rules 1971, S.I. 1971, No. 1777). 1972 saw unions fined for contempt of orders of the Industrial Court and individuals committed for the continuance of unfair industrial practices in defiance of Industrial Court orders (see *Midland Cold Storage* v. *Turner* (1972)). Some tension was discernible between the attitude of the Industrial Court and the Court of Appeal on the one hand, and between that of the Court of Appeal and the House of Lords on the other hand. Thus, in *Churchman* v. *Joint Shop Stewards' Committee* (1972), the Court of Appeal, thanks to the intervention of the Official Solicitor, was able to set aside orders for the committal of dockers which had been made by the Industrial Court at the suit of workers in a container depot, on the grounds of insufficiency of evidence and failure to give notice of the charges to those affected by the orders. On the other hand, the House of Lords re-instated the vicarious liability of an unregistered union for unfair industrial practices committed by its shop stewards in *Heatons Transport* (*St. Helens*) *Ltd.* v. *Transport and General Workers' Union* (1972), rejecting the "dual role" of the shop steward which had led the Court of Appeal to exculpate the union for certain actions of its shop stewards.

629 The House of Lords decision, whatever its theoretical attractions (and these have been doubted—see *Industrial Law Journal*, vol. 1, no. 4, p. 197), had the practical advantage of indicating that the proper course was to enforce awards and orders against *organisations* rather than *individuals*. Meanwhile, five dockers had been committed for contempt by the Industrial Court for refusing to discontinue the "blacking" of a container depot, the court holding that responsibility for unfair industrial practices rested with those who committed them and not necessarily with their union, as the Court of Appeal had found in the *Heatons* case. "This afternoon the situation is entirely changed," said Sir John Donaldson in *Midland Cold Storage Ltd.* v.

Turner (1972), when the Industrial Court, on the intervention of the Official Solicitor, released the dockers because their union was, in the light of the House of Lords decision in the *Heatons* case, "again responsible" for the "blacking." Despite the doubts concerning the relationship between the Industrial Court and government (emphatically rejected by Sir John Donaldson), the curiosity at the emergence of that hitherto obscure functionary, the Official Solicitor, and the novel notion of the "corporate," as opposed to the individual, responsibility of trade unionists, the public heaved a sigh of relief at the dramatic dénouement to the events of the summer of 1972.

2. Complaint by a trade union that an employer has not taken 630 requisite action to enter into or carry out an agency shop agreement, or that he has refused or failed to disclose to officials and other trade union representatives information for the purposes of collective bargaining. The court on such a complaint may make an order which (1) determines the rights of the parties, (2) directs the employer to carry out his duty, and (3) *quoad* failure to disclose information, authorises the presentation of a claim to the Industrial Arbitration Board.

3. Complaint by the Registrar, who has investigated an appli- 631 cation to him concerning an unfair industrial practice, arising from breach of either the guiding principles by an organisation registered under the Act, or its rules. The Industrial Court may grant one or more of the following remedies—(1) an order determinative of rights, (2) an award of compensation, and (3) a desist order.

4. Special provision as to certain complaints. Complaint of in- 632 dustrial action to induce an employer to take action *contra* section 5 (trade union rights) or section 22 (unfair dismissal) may be made to the Industrial Court *by the employer*. An employer who acts contrary to either section *himself* commits an unfair industrial practice which may be the subject of a complaint to the industrial tribunal on the part of the person who is unfairly dismissed, or whose trade union rights are infringed, and it will be no answer for the employer to say that he took the action in question for fear of industrial action. Thus, in a *Rookes* v. *Barnard* situation, where, for example, trade unionists bring pressure to bear upon an employer in order to secure the dismissal or other discriminatory treatment of one of the employer's workers, the latter may have a right to complain to the tribunal of the employer's action, whilst the employer may have a right to complain to the Industrial Court of the trade unionists' action. What is significant is that one cannot "square the circle," *i.e.* a latter-day Rookes cannot make a complaint of unfair industrial practice *against the trade unionists* (see para. 617 and, for joinder, para. 295, above). It will be recalled from the earlier part of this

chapter that the individual's rights in tort have been considerably diminished (see, for example, inducing breach of contract and intimidation, above).

633 Complaint of an unfair industrial practice involving industrial action against an extraneous party (see section 98, discussed at para. 616, above) may be made to the Industrial Court by either (a) the person who has been induced to break the contract, or who has been prevented from performing the contract—the "extraneous" party, or (b) the party to the industrial dispute with whom the contract was made.

Complaints in connection with collective bargaining and the breach of an enforceable collective agreement are described in Chapter 8.

The industrial tribunals

634 From their humble beginnings in 1964, the industrial tribunals have come to acquire a diversified jurisdiction over matters as disparate as training levies, particulars of employment, redundancy payments, selective employment payments (now abolished) and the definition of "dock work," to which will be added claims concerning equal pay (when the Equal Pay Act 1970 becomes effective) and, if the recommendation of the Robens Committee is accepted, industrial safety and health so far as improvement notices and prohibition notices are involved. The 1971 Act confirms their jurisdiction and adds to it in the following respects—

635 1. Determination of questions concerning conscientious objection to the payment of contributions to a trade union in an agency shop or approved closed shop, the charity to which such contributions should be payable, and the amount of the contributions.

636 2. Complaint of unfair industrial practices against an employer concerning:

(a) infringement of trade union rights (section 5—see paras 145 *et seq.*, above);

(b) unfair dismissal (section 22—see paras. 279 *et seq.*, above).

If conciliation has failed to produce a settlement, the tribunal may grant (a) an order determinative of the rights of the parties (for an example, see *Goad* v. *A.U.E.W.* (1972)); (b) an award of compensation (enforceable as a county court order and recoverable by way of execution or attachment of earnings if a county court so orders); and (c) a recommendation for reinstatement. Compensation and reinstatement are described at paras. 292, and 296, respectively.

637 3. Complaint against an organisation of breach of the guiding principles or breach of rules. The direct and indirect routes by which such a complaint may reach the tribunal are described at

paras. 488–489, above, but whichever route is used, the tribunal may make an order determinative of rights or award compensation (or both).

4. Complaint by a person employed in an undertaking against the employer who is owner of the undertaking that the latter has not fulfilled his duty with regard to disclosure of information. The tribunal can determine the rights of the parties on this matter but the jurisdiction to make an order directing the employer to issue a statement is reserved to the Industrial Court. Section 57, which confers the right to information, is not operative at the time of writing. **638**

The power given in section 113 to extend the jurisdiction of the industrial tribunals to include claims for damages for breach of the contract of employment, excluding personal injuries, has not so far been exercised. The exercise of that power will, by entrusting employment and industrial relations questions to the industrial tribunals and the Industrial Court, confirm that labour law has "arrived."

INDEX